House of Commons

Dismissal of the Reverend R.O'Keeffe from the office of Workhouse Chaplain and position of Manager of Callan National Schools : report, proceedings, minutes of evidence, appendix and index

House of Commons

Dismissal of the Reverend R.O'Keeffe from the office of Workhouse Chaplain and position of Manager of Callan National Schools : report, proceedings, minutes of evidence, appendix and index

ISBN/EAN: 9783741105272

Manufactured in Europe, USA, Canada, Australia, Japa

Cover: Foto ©ninafisch / pixelio.de

Manufactured and distributed by brebook publishing software (www.brebook.com)

House of Commons

Dismissal of the Reverend R.O'Keeffe from the office of Workhouse Chaplain and position of Manager of Callan National Schools : report, proceedings, minutes of evidence, appendix and index

REPORT

FROM THE

SELECT COMMITTEE

ON

CALLAN SCHOOLS;

TOGETHER WITH THE

PROCEEDINGS OF THE COMMITTEE,

MINUTES OF EVIDENCE,

AND APPENDIX.

Ordered, by The House of Commons, *to be Printed*,
18 *June* 1873.

Thursday, 15th May 1873.

Ordered, THAT a Select Committee be appointed to inquire into and report to the House the circumstances of the dismissal by the Commissioners of National Education in Ireland, of the Rev. Robert O'Keeffe from the office of Manager of the Callan Male, Female, and Infant National Schools, and the Newtown and Coolagh National Schools, by their Order, the 23rd day of April 1872, and of the removal of the said schools from the roll of National Schools by their Order, the 7th day of January 1873.

Thursday, 22nd May 1873.

Committee nominated of—

Mr. Secretary Cardwell.
Mr. Gathorne Hardy.
Mr. Whitbread.
Mr. Bourke.
The O'Conor Don.
Dr. Lyon Playfair.
Mr. Cross.

Ordered, THAT the Committee have power to send for Persons, Papers, and Records.

Ordered, THAT Three be the Quorum of the Committee.

Monday, 26th May 1873.

Ordered, THAT the Returns to the Orders of this House for the papers relating to the case of the Rev. Robert O'Keeffe be referred to the Select Committee on Callan Schools.

Wednesday, 18th June 1873.

Ordered, THAT the Committee have power to report the Minutes of Evidence taken before them to the House.

REPORT	p. iii
PROCEEDINGS OF THE COMMITTEE	p. iv
MINUTES OF EVIDENCE	p. 1
APPENDIX	p. 183

REPORT.

THE SELECT COMMITTEE appointed " to inquire into and report to the House the circumstances of the DISMISSAL by the Commissioners of National Education in *Ireland*, of the Rev. *Robert O'Keeffe* from the office of Manager of the Callan Male, Female, and Infant National Schools, and the Newtown and Coolagh National Schools, by their Order, the 23rd day of April 1872, and of the removal of the said Schools from the roll of National Schools by their Order, the 7th day of January 1873 ";——HAVE considered the matters to them referred, and have agreed to report the MINUTES of EVIDENCE taken before them to the House.

18 *June* 1873.

PROCEEDINGS OF THE COMMITTEE.

Friday, 23rd May 1873.

MEMBERS PRESENT:

Mr. Cardwell.
Mr. Gathorne Hardy.
Mr Bourke.
The O'Conor Don.

Mr. Whitbread.
Dr. Lyon Playfair.
Mr. Cross.

Mr. *Cardwell* was called to the Chair.

The Committee deliberated.

[Adjourned till Monday next, at Twelve o'clock.

Monday, 26th May 1873.

MEMBERS PRESENT:

Mr. CARDWELL in the Chair.

Mr. Gathorne Hardy.
Mr. Whitbread.
Mr. Cross.

Dr. Lyon Playfair.
The O'Conor Don.
Mr. Bourke.

Mr. *Patrick Joseph Keenan*, C.B., examined.

[Adjourned till Thursday, 5th June, at Twelve o'clock.

Thursday, 5th June 1873.

MEMBERS PRESENT:

Mr. CARDWELL in the Chair.

Mr. Cross.
Mr. Gathorne Hardy.
Dr. Lyon Playfair.

Mr. Bourke.
The O'Conor Don.
Mr. Whitbread.

Mr. *Patrick Joseph Keenan*, C.B., further examined.

Right Honourable *Mountifort Longfield*, LL.D., and Right Honourable Sir *Alexander Macdonnell*, were severally examined.

[Adjourned till Monday, 9th June, at Twelve o'clock.

Monday, 9th June 1873.

MEMBERS PRESENT:

Mr. CARDWELL in the Chair.

Mr. Cross.
The O'Conor Don.
Mr. Whitbread.

Mr. Gathorne Hardy.
Mr. Bourke.
Dr. Lyon Playfair.

Rev. *P. S. Henry*, D.D., examined.

Mr. *P. J. Keenan*, C.B., further examined.

Viscount *Monck* (attending by permission of the House of Lords) and Mr. *James Kelly* were severally examined.

[*Adjourned till Wednesday next, at Twelve o'clock.*

Wednesday, 11th June 1873.

MEMBERS PRESENT:

Mr. CARDWELL in the Chair.

Mr. Gathorne Hardy.
Dr. Lyon Playfair.
The O'Conor Don.

Mr. Cross.
Mr. Bourke.
Mr. Whitbread.

Mr. *William Homan Newell*, LL.D., Right Honourable Mr. Justice *Lawson*, and Rev. *C. L. Morell*, were severally examined.

[*Adjourned till To-morrow, at Twelve o'clock.*

Thursday, 12th June 1873.

MEMBERS PRESENT:

Mr. CARDWELL in the Chair.

Mr. Gathorne Hardy.
Mr. Whitbread.
Mr. Cross.

The O'Conor Don.
Dr. Lyon Playfair.
Mr. Bourke.

Mr. *W. H. Newell*, LL.D., further examined.

Right Honourable Mr. Justice *Morris*, Right Honourable Mr. Justice *Fitzgerald*, and Rev. *Robert O'Keeffe*, were severally examined.

Right Honourable Mr. Justice *Lawson* further examined.

[*Adjourned till Wednesday next, at Twelve o'clock.*

Wednesday, 18*th June* 1873.

MEMBERS PRESENT:

Mr. CARDWELL in the Chair.

Mr. Gathorne Hardy.
Mr. Cross.
The O'Conor Don.

The Committee deliberated.

Ordered, To Report the Minutes of Evidence to the House, together with an Appendix.
Ordered, To Report.

EXPENSES OF WITNESSES.

NAME OF WITNESS.	Profession or Condition.	From whence Summoned.	Number of Days absent from Home under Orders of Committee.	Allowance during Absence from Home.	Expenses of Journey to London and back.	TOTAL Expenses allowed to Witness.
				£. s. d.	£. s. d.	£. s. d.
Rev. C. L. Morell - -	Clergyman - -	Dungannon - -	5	5 5 -	6 - -	11 5 -
Right Hon. Mr. Justice Lawson.	- - -	Dublin - -	3	3 3 -	5 9 -	8 12 -
Mr. James Kelly - -	Secretary to Board of Education, Dublin.	- ditto - -	4	4 4 -	5 9 -	9 13 -
Mr. W. H. Newell, LL.D. -	- - -	- ditto - -	4	4 4 -	5 9 -	9 13 -
Right Hon. Mr. Justice Morris.	- - -	- ditto - -	4	4 4 -	5 9 -	9 13 -
Rev. Robert O'Keeffe -	- - -	Callan - - -	5	5 5 -	7 5 -	12 10 -
Mr. Patrick J. Keenan, C.B.	- - -	Dublin (twice) -	11	11 11 -	10 18 -	22 9 -
Rev. P. S. Henry D.D. -	- - -	- ditto - -	4	4 4 -	5 9 -	9 13 -
					TOTAL - - £	93 5 -

MINUTES OF EVIDENCE.

LIST OF WITNESSES.

Monday, 26th May 1873.

	PAGE
Mr. Patrick Joseph Keenan, C.B.	1

Thursday, 5th June 1873.

Mr. Patrick Joseph Keenan, C.B.	28
Right Hon. Mountifort Longfield, LL.D.	52
Right Hon. Sir Alexander Macdonnell	56

Monday, 9th June 1873.

Rev. Pooley Shuldham Henry, D.D.	58
Mr. Patrick Joseph Keenan, C.B.	71
Right Hon. Charles Viscount Monck	73
Mr. James Kelly	76

Wednesday, 11th June 1873.

Mr. William Homan Newell, LL.D.	83
Right Hon. Mr. Justice Lawson	84
Rev. Charles L. Morell	108

Thursday, 12th June 1873.

Mr. William Homan Newell, LL.D.	115
Right Hon. Mr. Justice Morris	117
Right Hon. Mr. Justice Fitzgerald	132
Right Hon. Mr. Justice Lawson	147
Rev. Robert O'Keeffe	148

MINUTES OF EVIDENCE.

Monday, 26th May 1873.

MEMBERS PRESENT:

Mr. Bourke.
Mr. Secretary Cardwell.
Mr. Cross.
Mr. Gathorne Hardy.

The O'Conor Don.
Dr. Lyon Playfair.
Mr. Whitbread.

THE RIGHT HONOURABLE EDWARD CARDWELL, IN THE CHAIR.

Mr. *Patrick Joseph Keenan*, C.B., called in; and Examined.

1. *Chairman.*] You are the Resident Commissioner?—Yes.
2. When were you appointed to that office?—In December 1871.
3. You have been connected with the Board for a much longer period have you not?—Yes.
4. When did you first become an inspector?—In May 1848.
5. When did you become head inspector?—In January 1855.
6. And then afterwards you became chief of inspectors, did you not?—Yes, in March 1859.
7. Have you brought with you the rules of the Board?—I have.
8. Will you be so good as to put them in?—(*The same were handed in,* vide Appendix.)
9. Will you be so good as to point out the section of the rules which relates to management?—It is Part 1, Section 6, and is as follows:—" The local government of the National Schools is vested in the local patrons thereof. The Commissioners recognise as the local patron the person who applies in the first instance to place the school in connection with the Board, unless it be otherwise specified in the application. If a school be under the local management of a school committee, such committee has all the rights of an individual patron. The patron has the right of nominating any fit person to act as his representative in the local management of the school, such representative to be designated the 'local manager.' The patron may at any time resume the direct management of the school, or appoint another local manager. This rule applies equally whether the patronship be vested in one or more individuals. When a school is vested in trustees, they have the right to nominate the local manager. When a school is vested in the Commissioners, the name of the patron or patrons is inserted in the lease. In the case of a vacancy in the patronship by death, the representative of a lay patron or the successor of a clerical patron is recognised by the Board

Mr.
P. J. Keenan, c.b.
26 May 1873.

Board (where no valid objection exists) as the person to succeed to the patronship of the school. If a patron wishes to resign the office, he has the power of nominating his successor, subject to the approval of the Board. In all cases the Commissioners reserve to themselves the power of determining whether the patron or the person nominated by him, either as his successor or as local manager, can be recognised by them as a fit person to exercise the trust. In all cases, whether the school be vested or non-vested, the patron when nominating a local manager ought to notify to the Commissioners whether or not the person so nominated is to exercise all the rights of patron during the period he acts as manager. When a school is under the control of a committee or of joint patrons, a 'local manager' should be appointed to correspond with the office, sign documents, &c., &c. The local patrons (or managers) of schools have the right of appointing the teachers, subject to the approval of the Board, as to character and general qualifications; the local patrons (or managers) have also the power of removing the teachers of their own authority. Patrons and managers are permitted to close their respective schools for a reasonable time during the year, subject to the interference of the Commissioners in cases of abuse; such periods of closing should be limited to six weeks in the year, including the recognised vacations. Managers of national schools are requested to notify all changes of teachers to the office, and to the inspectors of the respective districts."

10. When were those rules first drawn up and published?—They were first published in the year 1855 in the report of the Board for the year 1854. They were, however, drawn up, not in the form in which they now appear, but in various minutes recorded from time to time since the commencement of the operations of the Board.

11. Has there been any change since 1855?—None.

12. Then I understand you to say that they were first codified in 1855?—The rules as to management were.

13. And so far as they existed before, they existed in separate Minutes, and not in the form of a code?—Quite so.

14. Will you state a little more particularly what are the different classes of schools, in regard to their mode of management, which are dealt with in the section that has been read?—In reference to the question of management, the schools may be classified under four heads: vested schools, comprehending two classes, viz., those vested in the Board in its corporate capacity, and those vested in trustees; and non-vested schools, comprehending two classes also, viz., those under the control of committees and those under individual patrons.

15. What is the distinction in respect of the succession of managers?—In the case of schools vested in the Board in its corporate capacity, the name of the patron is inserted in the lease, and if the patron be a layman, his representative becomes the manager in the event of his death. If the name of the patron inserted in the lease be that of a clergyman, his clerical successor, *ex officio*, becomes manager.

16. By "clergyman," of course you mean a clergyman having the cure of souls within the parish?—Of course.

17. Is that rule applicable equally to all classes?—The rule which I have now referred to relates to schools vested in the Board in its corporate capacity. In the case of schools vested in trustees, the nomination of the manager is at all times at the command of the trustees, whether during the life of the manager, or when appointing a successor to him if dead.

18. Is that rule in print?—It is one of the rules which have been just read; "When a school is vested in trustees, they have the right to nominate the local manager." In the case of non-vested schools the succession, where no valid objection exists, proceeds in the case of a layman, to the legal representative, that is to say, to his executor; and in the case of a clergyman on his death, *ex officio*, to the clerical successor in the parish or congregation, as the case may be.

19. Is there any printed rule as to who is the manager in case of a disputed succession?—There is no printed rule; a case of disputed succession would necessarily be the subject of deliberation at the Board. The Commissioners would make their appointment consistently with their own rules.

20. That is to say, rules existing, not in the Code, but in the precedents of the office?—In both.

21. Executed

SELECT COMMITTEE ON CALLAN SCHOOLS. 3

21. Executed *cy-près*, as they say; that is, as nearly as possible?—Quite so.

22. Will you state the principal precedents with regard to disputed clerical succession?—I know only of one case of a disputed clerical succession, in addition to those referred to in the Parliamentary Papers on this subject.

23. First will you state, in the form of reference, all the cases, which begin, I think, with Mr. Keenan's case. What I mean by a disputed case is a case where a clergyman, being dealt with as having ceased to be a clergyman by the Board, disputes it and says that he has not?—The first case is that of the Rev. Dr. Keenan, which you will find at page 4 of Parliamentary Paper, No. 138, of 1873; the second is the case of the Rev. Mr. Wilson, at page 15. Before I proceed to the next case I must beg to remind you that the question you asked me was as to cases of disputed succession. In the case of Mr. O'Farrell, there was no disputed succession, and in that of the Rev. Mr. Sheridan there was a manifestation of feeling against his removal on the part of the committee. The only case of disputed succession not included in the Parliamentary Papers which I have been able to learn is that of the Rev. Mr Murray, who was parish priest, and had the management of the Kinceen, Creeves, Tourahowan, Ballyduam, and Tonore National Schools, county Mayo.

Mr.
P. J. Keenan, c.b.
26 May 1873.

24. Will you state the facts of that case?—The Rev. Mr. Murray left the country. He went, so far as I can learn from the documents, to Rome, but for what purpose does not appear. A Mr. Lynch then addressed the Board, and said that at the request of the Rev. Mr. Murray, he undertook the management of the schools *pro tempore*. That was in June 1845. After Mr Murray's departure, the Roman Catholic bishop of the diocese, the Right Rev. Dr. Feeny, appointed the Rev. Mr. Jordan as the administrator of the parish; and the Rev. Mr Jordan, thereupon, as administrator of the parish, wrote to the Board claiming the management of the schools. The order of the Board, which was made on the 31st December 1846, upon Mr. Jordan's letter, advancing his claim to the management of the schools, was "That the Roman Catholic bishop of that diocese be written to, explaining the circumstances of the case, and requesting him to state if the Rev. Mr. Murray has ceased to be parish priest, and if the Rev. Mr. Jordan has been appointed to succeed him as parish priest." On Saturday, when I found that I was to come over here at once for examination, I tried to obtain Dr. Feeny's letter in reply; but as Saturday was the Queen's birthday, and an office holiday, I was unable to obtain the document; the substance of it is, however, evidently in the following Minute: "that the Rev. Dr. Feeny be requested to state whether the Commissioners are to understand from his letter that the Rev. Mr. Jordan is the successor of the Rev. Mr. Murray as parish priest; and that he be informed of the practice of the Board as to the appointment of managers of National Schools." The following is the letter then addressed by order of the Board to the bishop: "Right Rev. Sir, having laid before the Commissioners of National Education, your letter of the 9th ultimo, we are directed to state that the general practice is, that if a National School has been under the management of a clergyman, on his removal his successor in the parish shall succeed to the management of the school. The Commissioners direct us to request you will have the goodness to state for their information, whether the Rev. Mr. Jordan has succeeded the Rev. Mr. Murray as priest of the parish in which the following National Schools are situated, viz., Kinceen, Creeves, Tourhaowan, Ballyduam, and Tonore. The Commissioners trust that the nature of the rule, as already explained, will be a sufficient excuse for troubling you with a second communication on the subject." Then on the 25th of February 1847, the Commissioners had Dr. Feeny's reply before them, which for the same reason I have not in my possession at this moment, informing the Board that the Rev. Mr. Jordan had been appointed administrator of the parish in which the National Schools (again named) are situated, in place of the Rev. Mr. Murray, who was formerly the patron of the schools. The order of the Board on that occasion was, "that the Rev Mr. Jordan be appointed successor of the Rev. Mr. Murray, as the manager of the above schools during the absence of the Rev. Mr. Murray, and that Mr. John Lynch be informed of this order."

25. *The O'Conor Don*.] Was Mr. John Lynch ever recognised as manager?—He was, *pro tempore*.

0.93.
A 2
26. Until

Mr.
P. J. Keenan, c.b.
26 May 1873.

26. Until the Board communicated that order to him?—Until the decision on the application of the Rev. Mr. Jordan to be accepted as manager.

27. And then he was removed from the managership?—Under that order which I have just now read.

28. Dr. *Lyon Playfair.*] Mr. Lynch was a layman?—He was.

29. *Chairman.*] What was the nature of the management in the case of each of these schools?—I have the report here containing the names of all the schools; and upon reference to this report, I could ascertain that, but it would take some little time. [They were all, I find, non-vested schools under an individual patron.]

30. Will you proceed with the history of the case?—The Rev. Mr. Jordan, it will be remembered, was appointed on the 25th of February 1847. On the 18th of January 1848 the Commissioners had under consideration two letters from the Rev. Mr. Murray wishing to assume the management of the schools. They also took into consideration the previous correspondence and proceedings in the case, and Ordered, "That the Right Rev. Dr. Feeny be written to for the purpose of ascertaining if the Rev. Mr. Murray has been re-instated in his former position as priest of the parish in which the Kinceen, Creevis, Ballyduame, Tourabowen, and Tonore National Schools are situated, and of which Mr. Murray was the recognised manager previous to his leaving the country." The bishop's reply to that last order was under the consideration of the Board on the 24th of February 1848. The Minute is, "Read letter, 543 T., from the Right Rev. Dr. Feeny, in reply to a question put to him by order of the Commissioners, acquainting them that the Rev. E. Murray is not parish priest of Kilfinan. Read, also, letters 6300 S., and 43 from the T., Rev. E Murray, claiming to be restored to the management of the National Schools in that parish. *Ordered*, that the substance of the Right Rev. Dr. Feeny's communication be ransmitted to the Rev. E. Murray, and that he be informed that the Commissioners cannot under the circumstances comply with his request." That is the only case of a disputed clerical succession, besides those published in the Parliamentary Papers, which I have been able to discover.

31. Can you tell us who the Commissioners were who were present on those occasions?—The Commissioners who were present on the 31st December 1846, when the case first came before the Board, were the Archbishop of Dublin (Dr. Whately), Archbishop Murray, the Provost, the Right Hon. Alexander Macdonnell, Robert Holmes, Esq., and J. R. Corballis, Esq.

32. Was the decision unanimous?—It was unanimous. The Commissioners who were present on the occasion of the second consideration of that case, on the 21st January 1847, were the Archbishop of Dublin, Archbishop Murray, the Provost, the Rev. Dr. Henry, J. R. Corballis, Esq., and the Right Hon. Alexander Macdonnell. Then the Commissioners who were present on the next occasion when the matter was under consideration, that is on the 25th February 1847, were Archbishop Murray, the Rev. Dr. Henry, the Marquis of Kildare, and the Right Hon. Alexander Macdonnell. On the next occasion. the 13th January 1848, the Commissioners present were the Archbishop of Dublin, Archbishop Murray, the Provost, the Marquis of Kildare, J. R. Corballis, Esq., and the Right Hon. Alexander Macdonnell. On the last occasion, the 24th of February 1848, the Commissioners present were Archbishop Murray, the Provost, the Rev. Dr. Henry (then President of the Queen's College, Belfast), the Right Hon. R. W. Groene, T. N. Redington, Esq. (afterwards Sir Thomas Redington), Robert Andrews, Esq., and the Right Hon. Alexander Macdonnell.

33. Were the decisions in every case unanimous?—In every case they were unanimous.

34. Then the decision of the Board, so far as it is not governed by their printed rules, I understand you to say, is governed by reference to these five precedents?—I should mention, in all candour, and in fairness towards those members of the Board who resisted the action of the majority, that when the case of the Rev. Mr. O'Keeffe was under consideration, the Rev. Mr. Murray's case to which I have now referred, was not submitted to the Board, because it was only quite recently that, on a most searching examination of the old documents, which are exceedingly numerous, and of the old minute books, which are imperfectly

fectly indexed, it was discovered. The other four cases were fully before the Board.

Mr.
P. J. Keenan, c.b.

26 May 1878.

35. The decisions of the Board, as I understand you, so far as they are not governed by the printed rules, are governed by the course of precedents?—Quite so.

36. So far as you knew, in dealing with the O'Keefe case, the other four precedents were the only ones; and so far as you know now, there are only five?—Quite so. That last case I submitted as a case of disputed succession, because the Rev. Mr. Murray on his return home applied to be restored to his position as manager, and the Board declined to accede to his application. But there were other cases of the dismissal of managers, whether clerical or lay, which from time to time occurred; as, for instance, in the year 1837, a Mr. Robert Gay, manager of the Attaghmore (County Tyrone) National School, vested in trustees, having stopped the salary which was transmitted to him for the teacher, was removed from the management, the Board ordering that they considered him no longer correspondent or manager of the school, and would appoint another; and on the appointment of another, the right of the trustees was of course respected.

37. Is that a lay or a clerical case?—A lay case.

38. Has it any bearing at all upon the subject of our inquiry?—I apprehend that the drift of your questions had reference to the power of the Board, or to its practice in dismissing managers generally, and hence I introduced that case. And there are, I have no doubt, many cases of the kind. Here is one of the year 1840. The school was the Ballinspittle National School, county Cork. The Commissioners' attention having been called to a letter, entitled "National Education," in the "Freeman's Journal;" and also to a letter addressed by the manager to Lord Morpeth: they "Ordered, that the superintendent of the district be directed to call upon the Rev. Mr. M'Swiney, and inform him that in consequence of the letters in question the Commissioners declined to hold any further correspondence with him."

39. Was Mr. M'Swiney the manager?—Yes. I do not know the nature of the communication to the "Freeman's Journal," nor that of the letter to Lord Morpeth.

40. Was Mr. M'Swiney dismissed?—As I interpret the last passage of the Minute, I understand him to have been dismissed when they declined to correspond any longer with him.

41. Mr. *Bourke.*] Was anybody appointed in his place?—I have not been able to look up the case; but as a matter of course some proper person must have been appointed. There were cases besides those which I have referred to where applications were made to the Board to remove managers, and where the Board declined, because, as they said, they saw no sufficient grounds to remove them; thus showing that the public had the impression, and the Board the conviction, that managers were removable. But going back again to the cases of absolute dismissal, I omitted to mention two other cases of dismissal of clerical managers which occurred. One was the case of a Rev. Mr. Malone, of Ballina (and it occurred in the year 1851), who gave the use of the schoolroom of Ballina for a political dinner. The order of the Board was, "That as the Rev. Mr. Malone admits that the school was used for the purpose stated, with his knowledge and consent, although he was at first opposed to such a measure, and that he was present at the demonstration, and was one of the secretaries of the committee who convened the meeting, his attention be called to the 3rd and 5th paragraphs of the 3rd section of the Rules of the Commissioners, being a fundamental regulation specially framed to prevent any meetings from being held in national schoolhouses which might be considered objectionable to any party; that be be informed that the Commissioners are clearly of opinion, from the published reports of what took place at the banquet in question, that it was a meeting of a political character, and consequently a marked violation of the rules of the Board, as above referred to; and that under these circumstances the Commissioners feel it to be their duty to decline corresponding with him in future as the manager of the Ballina National School; and further, the grant of salary to the master, &c., will be withdrawn on the 31st instant, unless in the meantime another manager be appointed." That order was made on the 19th of December 1851.

Mr.
P. J. Keenan, c.b.
16 May 1873.

42. *Mr. Gathorne Hardy.*] In whom was the appointment of the manager in that case?—If you will kindly allow me to read the remainder of the correspondence it will give you as much information on the case as at this moment is at my own command. That order was made, as I have said, on the 19th of December 1851. On the 13th of February 1852, the Board received an application for school requisites, signed by the Rev. Dominic Madden, as manager. The Board then ordered a reference "to letter of the 15th January 1852" (communicating the order which I have already read), "written to the Rev. Mr. Madden, enclosing copy of communication to Rev. P. Malone, in which he was informed that unless another manager be appointed the Commissioners must withdraw aid from the Ballina Male National School. As no manager or patron has since been notified to the Commissioners for their approval, they cannot, consistently with Order of 19th December 1851, comply with the requisition for books, and, therefore, return the money." A Post Office order for the full amount of money sent up was accordingly forwarded to the Rev. Mr. Madden on 16th of February 1852. Then, on the 17th February 1852, a letter was received from the Rev. Mr. Malone, stating that "He has been handed, by the Rev. Mr. Madden, a communication addressed to that gentleman in reference to the management of this school; that immediately on receipt of the Board's letter, in which he was informed that the Commissioners declined to correspond with him, he consented to resign the management to the Rev. D. Madden; that he thought the signature of that gentleman to the query sheet was sufficient notification of the fact; but he now wishes it to be understood that the Rev. Mr. Madden has taken his place as manager of the school." Then, on the 20th February 1852, the Board's Order on the foregoing communication was, " Quote substance of this letter, and state that appointment of Rev. D. Madden, as manager, is confirmed. Write to Rev. Mr. Madden, also, and state that books shall be sent."

43. In which of the three classes of schools was that?—The non-vested schools.

44. *Chairman.*] What do you consider the power of the Board to be, with regard to the dismissal of a manager?—I consider the power of the Board for the dismissal of a manager to be under Rule 9, Section 6. "In all cases the Commissioners reserve to themselves the power of determining whether the patron, or the person nominated by him, either as his successor or as local manager, can be recognised by them as a fit person to exercise the trust." Under that rule, fitness being an essential qualification to be submitted to, and acknowledged by the Board, if unfitness at any time be demonstrated, the Board manifestly reserve to themselves full power to dismiss, and, in the case of the Rev. Mr. Malone, of Ballina, it was unmistakeably because he was unfit to be a manager that he was dismissed, he having deliberately broken one of the rules of the Board in giving the use of the school-room for a political banquet.

45. There seems to be some doubt upon the part of the Committee, as to the extent to which you assert the right of dismissing the manager; I understand you to say that as soon as the Board is convinced that a man is unfit to be continued manager, they have the power to dismiss him?—Yes, that is so.

46. Mr. *Gathorne Hardy.*] They do not use the term "dismiss," but they "decline to continue correspondence"?—That is much the same thing.

47. Is the result of that, that a school is without connection with the Commissioners, until somebody else is put in?—As manager.

48. But you cannot remove him except in that way?—In the case of a school vested in trustees, the course, after the removal of the manager, would be, to apply to the trustees, and in the case of a school vested in the Board in its corporate capacity, to apply to the patron to nominate a successor; in the case of a non-vested school under an individual clerical manager, the invariable practice has been, if the outgoing clerical manager is dismissed, or resigns, or dies, to accept the clergyman taking his place as successor; or if the school be under a committee, to refer to its members for a nomination.

49. *Chairman.*] Suppose a clergyman not to be deposed, but to continue the clergyman, but in the judgment of the Board to have done as Mr. Malone did, to have broken one of the rules of the Board, do you, or do you not, take upon yourselves to dismiss him?—We d7

Mr.
P. J. Keenan, c.b.

16 May 1873.

50. *Mr. Cross.*] Under Rule 9, does not the word "recognised," refer to the first appointment?—As fitness is necessary upon the occasion of the first appointment, fitness is of course at all times necessary.

51. Does not the wording of the rule "can be recognised by them as a fit person," apply to the first appointment?—It applies to the first appointment, but the element of fitness being as I have said, an essential quality in the character of a manager at the time of his first appointment, it must be an element characteristic at all times of him in his connection with the management of the school.

52. *Chairman.*] You do not in any case put in a new manager?—Not in any case, except under the conditions I have stated. One other case of the dismissal of a clerical manager is contained in the following brief extract which I have made from the Minutes.

53. Are we still upon the Ballina case?—It is incidental to the Ballina case.

54. *Mr. Gathorne Hardy.*] I wish to get the Ballina case clear, and I want to ask you what position did the Rev. Mr. Madden occupy, whom you accepted in the place of Mr. Malone?—As far as I could gather (but I have no positive information on the point), he was one of the curates of Mr. Malone.

55. Mr. Malone remained in charge of the parish, did he not?—Mr. Malone remained in charge of the parish.

56. You refused to correspond with him, he nominated a curate, and you accepted the curate as manager in his place?—I can hardly say that the Board was influenced by his nomination; they simply looked for a successor to Mr. Malone, and announced that in case a successor were not in due time appointed, the salary of the teachership would be withdrawn. The first time that the name of the successor appeared before them was when the application was made for the books. It was clearly a disrespectful thing for a new clergyman who had undertaken the management to begin his communications with the Board by assuming that he had been actually appointed. The Board felt that they could not tolerate such a proceeding, and sent him back the money, and told him that they could not recognise him; but when they got a respectful communication from the Rev. Mr. Malone that the Rev. Mr. Madden had accepted the management, he having in his capacity, I presume, as parish priest, directed him to assume it, the Board at once recognised his appointment.

57. *Chairman.*] Does not it come to this, that there are two things necessary to a man's being manager; first, nomination by the local authority; and secondly, approval by the Board?—The first element is not one which is a necessity, because a clergyman, a parish priest, for instance, might on the removal or decease of his predecessor, or on his own establishment of a new school, propose himself, without anyone having nominated him to be the manager of the school.

58. But being so proposed, he must be approved by the Board before he can become the manager, must he not?—Yes.

59. And you would not recognise Mr. Madden until you had approved him?—Certainly not.

60. In the case of a school already in existence like that at Ballina, you having dismissed or discontinued your correspondence with the former manager, the nomination by somebody of the succeeding manager was necessary, was it not?—Yes, to show that the succeeding manager had some status in connection with the school or the parish.

61. The nomination was necessary?—Yes, in that case, to show that the succeeding manager was not an unauthorised person who came in and took possession of the school as its manager.

62. And being nominated, you approve of him?—Being nominated, and being a clergyman of the parish, we approved of him.

63. In the case of a disputed clerical succession, what would have been the course to be pursued?—As I understand your question it is, that if, for instance, after the Rev. Mr. Malone had been dismissed or any other manager had been removed to another parish or congregation, or had died, and that two or more clerical persons claimed the management, what would have been the course of the Board? The course of the Board, I take it, would have been (a case of the kind has not come to my knowledge personally) to consider all the circumstances of the case, to ascertain who the claimants for the management were, what were

Mr.
P. J. Keenan, C.B.
26 May 1873.

their status and pretensions, and whether they were proper persons to succeed to the management, and if the Board was satisfied upon all these heads, I have no doubt they would appoint the right man.

64. You wish to state another case, do you not?—I wish to state another case of the dismissal of a clergyman from the management. The extracts from the Minutes which I am about to read are very brief in form, but they will contain the substance of the case: "7th May 1872. Read reports of head inspector Molloy, and district inspector Nicholls, on charges affecting the character and position of Mr. John Broghan, teacher of Gort Male National School, also on the use of the Gort Female National School-room for a political meeting."

65. Mr. *Cross*.] Is that the teacher?—Mr. John Broghan is the teacher. "Letters from Mr. Nicholls are also submitted. Ordered, that the manager be informed of the report as to the banquet held in the Gort Female National Schoolhouse, by the supporters of Captain Nolan; that he be referred to the rules, and asked how he, as manager of a national school, actually sanctioned so gross a violation of the Commissioners' rules." And on the 14th of May 1872, "Mr. Justice Morris gives notice that he will, at the next meeting of the Board, on Tuesday the 28th instant, move that the Rev. T. Shannon, P.P., be dismissed from the management of the National Schools of which he is at present manager, for his defiant violation of the rules of the Board." Then upon the 28th May 1872: "Agreeably to notice given on the 14th instant, Mr. Justice Morris moves that the Rev. T. Shannon, P.P., be dismissed from the management of the national schools of which he is at present manager, for his defiant violation of the rules of the Board. The secretary reads letters from Mr. Nicholls, inspector of District 42, reporting the use of the Gort Vested Schoolhouse for the purposes of a political banquet given by the supporters of Captain Nolan, and afterwards for the purpose of an exhibition of ventriloquism. The letters addressed to the Rev. T. Shannon on the 9th and 15th instant, are also read, inviting him to offer any explanation in his power as to these violations of the rule. Ordered, that as the Rev. T. Shannon, P.P., has not replied to the two communications addressed to him on the 9th and 15th instant, he be again called on to say if he have any explanation to offer for the wilful violation of the rule of the Board referred to in those communications before the Commissioners proceed to consider the question of removing him from the office of manager of National Schools." Upon the 11th of June 1872 the Commissioners met to consider the case, but it is noted upon the Minutes that "The Commissioners take no action in reference to the motion of which Mr. Justice Morris gave notice on the 14th ult. for the Rev. Mr. Shannon's dismissal from the office of manager of National Schools, Mr. Justice Morris not being present." Then, upon the 18th June 1872, "The Commissioners consider the motion of which Mr. Justice Morris gave notice on the 14th May that the Rev. T. Shannon, P.P., be dismissed from the management of the National Schools of which he is at present manager, for his defiant violation of the rules of the Board, he having permitted the Gort Female National School to be used for a political banquet on the 1st January, and subsequently on the 9th May for an entertainment by a ventriloquist. Read letters of the 4th, 11th, and 20th May, from Mr. Nicholls, inspector of District 42; also, orders of the Board of the 7th and 28th May, calling on the Rev. Mr. Shannon to state if he has any explanation to offer for permitting the wilful violation of the rules of the Board on the occasions in question. The secretary having stated that no reply had been received from the Rev. Mr. Shannon: Ordered, that the Rev. T. Shannon not having given any reply to the several letters written by order of the Board, he removed from the office of manager of the National Schools of Gort, Male and Female, Kilmacduagh, Kiltartan, and Killomoran." Then, on the 25th June 1872, a letter from the Rev. T. Shannon, of Gort, to the following effect, was read: "1st. Complaining of the manner of conducting the late inquiry at Gort National School by the district inspector. 2. Stating that the dismissal of the teacher, John Broughan, will be considered an act of political partisanship on the part of the Board. 3. Stating that he always gave the use of the school-room for concerts, &c., and that he did not deem it contrary to the rules of the Board. 4. Stating that he did not advert till too late that the use of the school-room for a banquet was contrary to rules, and that

that had he done so, he would not have given it for the purpose; and,
5. Stating that he does not value the threat of removal from the management of National Schools. Ordered, that the Commissioners decline to alter the decision of the Board, dated 7th May 1872, withdrawing salary from J. Broughan, teacher of Gort National School; also that the Board's order of the 18th instant removing the Rev. Mr. Shannon from the office of manager of Gort Male and Female, Kilmacduagh, Kiltartan, and Killomoran, National Schools cannot be departed from." Then, upon the 27th August following, "The Commissioners take into consideration the question of appointing a correspondent to the National Schools in the parish of Gort, hitherto under the management of the Rev. T. Shannon, P.P., removed by order of the Board, dated 18th June 1872. Ordered, that the district inspector act as correspondent *pro tem.*, and sign the 'Quarterly Returns.'" Then, upon the 8th October 1872, "Read letter from the Very Rev. Dean Birmingham, the Protestant rector of the parish, on the subject of the management of Gort Male and Female (Vested) Schools. Read also letter from Mr. Molloy, head inspector, on the subject of the Rev. T. Shannon's removal from the management of the Gort and other National Schools, stating that the Rev. Mr. Shannon disavows all intention of discourtesy to the Commissioners; that he never wilfully intended to violate any of their rules, and asserts that he most certainly replied to the secretaries' letters, explaining as to the violation of rule, to which his attention was called. The head inspector further recommends a reconsideration of the case, with a view to the restoration of the Rev. Mr. Shannon to his former position as manager of Gort Male and Female, Kilmacduagh, Kiltartan, and Killomoran, National Schools. Ordered, that the head inspector be informed that the Commissioners decline to act on his recommendation. If the Rev. Mr. Shannon desires to resume the management of the National Schools in question, and should write a letter to the Commissioners, putting forward any explanation he may have to offer of his persistence in declining to reply to the letters addressed to him from this office, the Commissioners will be prepared to consider the question of his restoration. There is no record in this office of the receipt of any letter from the Rev. T. Shannon, in reply to any of the letters addressed to him regarding the violation of rule in the Gort Male and Female National Schools. And, from the reports of the district inspector, is evident that the Rev. Mr. Shannon was not concerned to conform to the rules of the Commissioners, with which he admitted he was conversant. Ordered, further, that no decision be made on Dean Birmingham's letter until the result of the foregoing communication to the head inspector be ascertained." Then upon the 12th November 1872, the following Minute is made: "Read letters from the Rev. T. Shannon, P.P. of Gort, inclosing a note from the Right Rev. Dr. McEvilly, Roman Catholic Bishop of Galway, containing recommendations, to which the Rev. Mr. Shannon subscribes, that he (Rev. Mr. Shannon) should apologise to the Commissioners for having violated their rules, and also make due reparation, by engaging to guard against such in future. Ordered, that as the Rev. Mr. Shannon has explained and apologised for his inattention to the orders of the Board, and for his allowing the rules of the Commissioners to be violated, has undertaken to discharge the duties of manager and correspondent, in accordance with the letter and spirit of the Board's rules in future, he be reinstated in his former position as manager of the following National Schools, from which he was removed; Gort male, Gort female, Kilmacduagh, Kiltarton, and Killomoran."

Mr.
P. J. Keenan, C.B.

26 May 1873.

66. *Chairman.*] Were those decisions unanimous?—They were unanimous.

67. *The O'Conor Don.*] Were those schools vested?—They were. [In the return from which I was quoting, all these schools were, by some clerical inadvertance, noted as vested. Hence my answer. But as my memory afterwards led me to think that Kiltarton and Killomoran were non-vested, I referred to the last annual report of the Board, and found that they are non-vested. The other three schools are vested.]

68. In whom?—In the Board; you might observe in the course of the Minutes, that the inspector was directed to act as correspondent *pro tempore* to enable an inquiry to be made with reference to the existence of the patrons, for the schools are very old, and if the old patrons still lived, to submit the case of the appointment of a successor to them.

0.93.   B   69. *Chairman.*]

Mr.
P. J. Kernan, c.b.
20 May 1873.

69. *Chairman.*] Then I understand that these cases show two things; first, that you have the power, and occasionally exercise it, of removing a manager, and, secondly, that the cases in which that power has been exercised are very rare?—The cases in which it has been exercised are very rare indeed.

70. *Mr. Cross.*] And you require an explanation from a man before you remove him?—In the case of the Rev. Mr. Shannon, we gave two or three opportunities of explaining the breach of rule.

71. *Mr. Gathorne Hardy.*] I see, with regard to non-vested schools, the words are that you "decline to hold correspondence," and in these vested schools you say the manager is "removed"?—I do not think that the difference was deliberate.

72. In the two former cases they both "decline to hold correspondence"?—In the drawing up of the latter Minute I do not think any difference between the words then employed and the words in the former orders was before the mind of the Board.

73. *Chairman.*] The effect of declining to hold correspondence is the same as removal, is it not?—Yes, it is.

74. *Mr. Gathorne Hardy.*] In the case of vested schools they must remain in connection with the Commissioners upon the terms in which they are founded?—They must.

75. With respect to the non-vested schools, they need not remain in connection with the Commissioners unless they choose?—Unless the legal owner of the house, or the manager chooses.

76. Therefore, in the case of non-vested schools, you have not the power to dismiss from the management of the schools, but only to dismiss from connection with the Board?—I take it that the latter, so far as the Board is concerned, is equivalent to the former.

77. Supposing the manager chooses to go on without asking for assistance, he goes on in the management of those schools, does he not?—Then the Board withdraws the grants.

78. But as regards the other schools there is a compulsion to remain in connection with the National Board, is there not?—Yes, as regard the schools.

79. Therefore in the one case you dismiss and force a new appointment, and in the other you withhold your supplies in case they do not agree to your terms?—That is a very expressive way of describing the action of the Board in such a case.

80. I am taking what you have given us evidence of?—Practically, anyone so addressed must understand that he is dismissed from the management.

81. *Chairman.*] The difference being in the control which the Board has over a school which is vested in itself or vested in trustees by the terms of its trust, and, upon the other hand, over a school which is not so vested; is that so?—It may have been in the minds of the Board at the time the orders which I first read were drawn up, that there was an appropriate expression for each class of case; but, in reading over the cases, I have come to the conclusion that they are all cases of dismissal from management.

82. *Mr. Whitbread.*] Do you know instances where having informed a manager that you ceased to correspond with him, which in your view is tantamount to dismissing him, the same man has gone on and kept the schools open without regard to the School Board?—We have the case of the Rev. Mr. O'Keeffe.

83. Have you no other case?—Yes, that of the Rev. Dr. Keenan, the first of the quoted precedents.

84. Have you no other case?—No other that I can remember.

85. *Chairman.*] Now are there any additional particulars regarding Mr. O'Keeffe's case, or any additional documents which you wish to lay before the Committee, in addition to those which are already before Parliament?—The whole of the correspondence between Mr. O'Keeffe and the Board from the time of the report of his suspension by Dr. Moran to the Board has already been published;

SELECT COMMITTEE ON CALLAN SCHOOLS. 11

lished; there is only one document antecedent to that period which I think the Committee might be interested in hearing, and that is the document upon which his original appointment was made to the non-vested schools in 1863.

Mr.
P. J. Keenan, c.b.
26 May 1873.

86. *Mr. Bourke.*] Was he connected with any schools in Callan before that appointment to the non-vested schools?—Mr. O'Keeffe's name in connection with the Callan Schools was first submitted to the Board in the letter which I am about to read to the Committee. This is the letter of the Rev. Edward Rowan, who was Mr. O'Keeffe's predecessor in the parish of Callan; so far as I can learn, he was the "Administrator," which practically means he had the charge of the parish: "Callan, 16th February 1863. Messrs. Cross and Kelly" [those were the secretaries], "Gentlemen, I send into the Commissioners of National Education my resignation of manager in the Callan, Newtown, and Coolagh National Schools, the Rev. Robert O'Keeffe having been appointed parish priest of those districts. Most respectfully, Edward Rowan." The order upon that was— "Note Rev. Robert O'Keeffe, manager of Coolagh and Newtown Schools, and inform the parties;" and the second part of the order was, "Call for nomination by committee in case of Callan National Schools, state the rule as to nomination of manager by committee, and they add that the Rev. E. Rowan was nominated by the committee."

87. *Dr. Lyon Playfair.*] You received afterwards the appointment of the Rev. Robert O'Keeffe, by the Callan school committee, dated 28th February 1863, did you not?—Yes.

88. Have you the original of that with you?—No; it having appeared in the Parliamentary Paper, I did not consider it necessary to bring it.

89. Is there not in the Parliamentary Paper an allegation that those signatures are forged?—Yes, there is a letter to that effect.

90. Could you show to the Committee, upon a subsequent occasion, the original of that appointment?—With pleasure; I shall write for it to-day.

91. *Chairman.*] Is that the nomination to which you have referred in your former answers to me?—Yes, it is.

92. *Mr. Gathorne Hardy.*] The Board, as I understand, accepted Mr. O'Keefe upon the letter of the "Administrator" as to two schools, and they required from that (it was in the hands of that committee) a further nomination?—They required a further nomination of the committee of the Callan male and female schools, because the rules of the Board required it. In the case of the Coolagh and Newtown non-vested schools, the Rev. Mr. Rowan having announced that the Rev. Robert O'Keeffe had been appointed as parish priest of those districts, the routine nomination was at once made in his favour in regard to those schools.

93. *Chairman.*] Will you put in the statistics showing the number of managers, clerical and lay, of each denomination, and the number of schools under each denomination?—I shall. The managers are classified under the heads clerical and lay. Clerical, Roman Catholic, 1,282; late Established Church, 179; Presbyterians, 322; other denominations of Christians, 46; making a total of 1,779 clerical managers. Lay managers, Roman Catholic, 188; late Established Church, 374; Presbyterians, 177; other religious denominations, 30; Officials (the Commissioners themselves, the Poor Law Guardians, &c.), 192; making a total of 961. Then the schools are classified under two heads, one clerical management, and the other lay management. Under Roman Catholic clerical management, 4,485; late Established Church, 284; Presbyterian, 605; other religious denominations, 67; making a total of 5,441. Then, under lay management, Roman Catholic schools, 315; late Established Church, 684; Presbyterian, 236; other religious denominations, 48; and Official, 258; making a total of 1,541.

[*The same was handed in, and is as follows:*]

0.93.   B 2

MANAGERS.

CLERICAL.					LAY.				
Late Established Church.	Roman Catholic.	Presbyterian.	Others.	TOTAL.	Late Established Church.	Roman Catholic.	Presbyterian.	Other Religious Denominations.	Official.	TOTAL.
179	1,239	322	40	1,779	374	188	177	30	192	961

SCHOOLS.

UNDER CLERICAL MANAGEMENT.					UNDER LAY MANAGEMENT.				
Late Established Church.	Roman Catholic.	Presbyterian.	Others.	TOTAL.	Late Established Church.	Roman Catholic.	Presbyterian.	Other Religious Denominations.	Official.	TOTAL.
284	4,485	605	67	5,441	684	315	256	43	258	1,541

N.B.—There are about 30 schools under joint management not accounted for in this Return.

30 April 1873.
J. C. Taylor.

94. Have you stated everything which you wish to state with regard to Mr. O'Keeffe's case?—I have no other documents having reference to the case to submit to the Committee.

95. Is there anything else that you wish to state relating to the facts of Mr. O'Keeffe's case which you think is not already before Parliament?—I think all the facts as contained in documents and communications with or from the Board, are already published.

96. The memorial of the 13 Commissioners, of whom you are one, refers to certain grave misstatements which have been made. Would you indicate to the Committee what you consider to be the nature of those misstatements?— I might briefly classify them under these heads: first, that the Commissioners were not authorised by the rules to remove the Rev. Mr. O'Keeffe. Secondly, that if the rules favoured the removal of any manager, they were strained in the Rev. Mr. O'Keeffe's case. Thirdly, that the precedents which were presented in the case failed to sustain the decision of the Board. And, fourthly, that the Commissioners were influenced by external pressure in arriving at their decision, especially by the influence of Cardinal Cullen and that of the bishop, the Right Rev. Dr. Moran, who communicated the suspension of Mr. O'Keeffe to the Board. Those appear to me to be the leading points which the Commissioners had in view when signing the memorial.

97. And in order to meet those statements, you wish, do you not, to state some additional facts with regard to Mr. O'Keeffe's case, and to explain anything which requires to be explained in regard to the four other cases?—I think that my examination by yourself, and the questions which the Committee were good enough

enough to propose to me, have elicited some important points in elucidation of rule and practice which bear upon the first heads of our case, and which it would be only tedious to refer back to now. The Commissioners who signed that document are perfectly satisfied that they adjudged the matter of Mr. O'Keeffe's removal, as they were bound to do by the unvarying practice of the Board, and by the unanimous understanding which prevailed amongst the oldest members, that the rule on which they pronounced their decision was that which had always been accepted and acted upon.

Mr.
P. J. Keenan, c.b.
16 May 1873.

98. Who are the oldest members of the Board?—The senior member of the Board is the Rev. Dr. Henry, whose letter on the subject has already appeared in a Parliamentary Paper; the next in seniority is the Marquess of Kildare, who takes the same view; the third in seniority is Mr. Gibson, who takes the same view; and the fourth in seniority is Judge Longfield, who, as the Parliamentary Papers show, strongly takes the same view.

99. Is it the intention of any of those gentlemen to offer themselves to the Committee?—Judge Longfield would have been most happy to have presented himself to-day, and it would have been a great relief and happiness to me if he had been able to do so, but he is at this moment suffering from severe illness, and confined to his bed. Dr. Henry, the senior member of the Board, is suffering also, and is very ill; but he hopes to be able to appear before the Committee after the Whitsuntide recess.

100. And Judge Longfield also?—Judge Longfield also entertains a confident hope that he may be able to appear before the Committee after the Whitsuntide recess. As regards the force of the precedents, the third point under which I classified those considerations, the Commissioners who signed the memorial entertain a firm conviction that the precedents were complete, and that they fully authorised their action; and as regards the last point, the external influence, especially that of Cardinal Cullen or Dr. Moran, the Roman Catholic Bishop of Ossory, I shall simply say, speaking for myself, that so far as Cardinal Cullen is concerned, I have never had a conversation with his Eminence upon this or any other subject in my life, or he with me, or any communication, direct or indirect, with him, and I will add that I have never heard it mentioned by any of the 13 members of the Board who signed that document that, directly or indirectly, the slightest communication in reference to the case was ever made to or received from the Cardinal. As regards Dr. Moran, as Roman Catholic Bishop of the diocese of Ossory, he frequently has business at the Education Office, and I have seen him there from time to time, but never have I or any other member of the Board been in the slightest degree influenced by him, nor has he ever made the slightest attempt to influence me in the discharge of my duty.

101. With regard to these four precedents and the facts of the several cases, do you wish to speak to the Committee about them, or do you leave it to the older Commissioners to speak upon the facts of those cases?—Whatever is the convenience of the Committee, I should be most happy to submit to.

102. Are there any facts which you propose to give evidence upon with regard to any one of those several precedents?—I should be very happy, if the Committee desired it, to proceed through the precedents under the various heads under which they might be classified, and as far as I might be able, to show their application to the case of Mr. O'Keeffe.

103. Will you have the goodness to do so; the first precedent is dated in the year 1845, is it not?—Yes; having regard to the discussions which have taken place, and the comments which have been made upon the proceedings of Mr. O'Keeffe's case from time to time since the matter became public, I thought it convenient, when I found that I was to appear before the Committee to-day, to classify under various heads the different features of the four precedents, and, if it be not too tedious to the Committee, I should be very glad to make a statement of them.

104. If the facts of any of those four cases are not already before Parliament, we shall be glad of any fresh documents which you think may remain to be supplied?—All the facts of the four cases, so far as the orders of the House of Commons tended to elicit them, have been already published in the Parliamentary Papers; but what I would propose to do, in answer to the question which you have put to me, would be to show how, and how far, the four cases run parallel as between

0.93. B 3 the

Mr.
P. J. Keenan, c.b.

26 May 1873.

the cases themselves and that of Mr. O'Keeffe. It would be only a new arrangement of facts.

105. *Mr. Gathorne Hardy.*] There is a long document in the name of Chief Baron Pigott; was that submitted to any of the Commissioners before its publication?—I should say all or most of the Commissioners got a copy privately after its presentation to the Board, but before its publication in a Parliamentary Paper.

106. Before it came out as a public document at all, did the other Commissioners, the 13 Commissioners, see it?—I cannot speak for the 13 Commissioners; I saw it, but not until after the Chief Baron sent it officially to the Board.

107. Was it submitted to you before it was a complete publication?—The proof only of the first sheet was shown to me by the Chief Baron, three days before the presentation of the letter in its entirety to the Board. The manuscript was never submitted to me.

108. *Chairman.*] It is substantially a statement of the 13 Commissioners, I suppose?—I cannot speak for anybody except myself; there is nothing in it which I dissent from.

109. You are quite ready to assent to it?—I am.

110. *Mr. Bourke.*] There was a memorial, as you are aware, from the majority of the Commissioners, asking that further inquiry should take place before a Parliamentary Committee; you have seen that memorial I suppose?—I signed it.

111. *Chairman.*] What was the date of the memorial?—I find that it is not dated; I signed it on the 5th of May.

112. *Mr. Bourke.*] Can you give the circumstances under which that was produced before the Board?—It was never produced before the Board; it was signed by some of the members in the Board-room, but never placed formally before the Board.

113. Did you sign it in the Board-room?—I did.

114. Who was it suggested by?—The first person who mentioned it to me as a proper and desirable thing was Judge Longfield.

115. Was that the day that you signed the memorial?—No, it was not then; it was on the occasion of a conversation which I had with him in reference to the then approaching debate in the House of Commons on Mr. Bouverie's motion. He said that he thought it would be exceedingly desirable, and only fair, especially to the senior members of the Board, who were the fathers, as it were, of these precedents, that the Board should be heard more minutely and more clearly than evidently the correspondence which had been published, was a presentation of the conduct and interests. That conversation was in Judge Longfield's house upon a Sunday.

116. Do you recollect whether in that conversation there was anything said about the Chief Baron's letter?—Not a word.

117. Was your conversation upon the basis of the Chief Baron's letter being known to you, or not known to you?—It was utterly irrespective of the Chief Baron's letter.

118. Was the Chief Baron's letter known to you at the time?—I rather think not. The Chief Baron's intention to write a letter was known to me a long time before that. I knew that he was at various times debating the question whether he ought to write a letter expressive of his own views.

119. Was it ever discussed by the Board whether Chief Baron Pigott's letter was a sufficient indication of their conduct or not?—The Chief Baron's letter was never read to the Board. Judge Lawson's letter, which preceded that, and Judge Longfield's, which preceded it again, were never read to the Board.

120. Do the Council think it indicates their views?—From conversations which I have had with some members of the Board, I am satisfied that they regard it with great satisfaction, but they do not put it forward as a complete answer on all the hearings of the case; nor would I. To-day I had an opportunity of drawing your attention to some important matters of rule and fact which were not touched upon in Chief Baron Pigott's letter at all.

121. *Chairman.*] Speaking for yourself as one of those who signed the document, do you adhere to the opinion that it was desirable that you should be heard

heard here in addition to the documents that are now before Parliament?—I respectfully do.

122. Will you now proceed to state the facts of the four precedents to which reference has been made?—The first head under which I would classify the analysis of these cases is, as to the form in which the suspension of the clergyman in each case was communicated to the Board. In the case of Dr. Keenan a communication was made through a letter of the Right Rev. Dr. Blake to Archbishop Murray, then a member of the Board.

123. Will you give the Committee the reference to the letter?—The letter is found in page 4 of Parliamentary Return, No. 138. In the case of Mr. Wilson, the document announcing the suspension, if the suspension were communicated in any document, is not forthcoming; search was made for it in the office, but no document on the subject could be found. Mr. Wilson himself, however, in his letter of the 23rd of June 1851, published at page 16 of the Return, says, " I am led to believe that during the period of my indisposition, when I was advised to remove to another neighbourhood, an application was made to the Commissioners to have my services dispensed with as manager of Glenvale School." The Commissioners themselves, in their Minute of the 26th of June 1851 (found also at page 16 of the same Return), say upon this point, that " having learned that he has been deposed from the ministry, they are under the painful necessity of declining to recognise him as manager of either the Glenvale or any other National School."

124. *The O'Conor Don.*] Just allow me to correct what I believe is a misprint in this letter of the 23rd of June; it states " about 10 or 12 years ago; " that should be "days," I presume?—It was a mistake of the printers. In the case of the Rev. Mr. O'Farrell, at page 17, the inspector, in his report, dated 10th July 1862, observes that " the manager of this school is under suspension from his bishop from all ecclesiastical duties." The Commissioners then referred to the bishop to ascertain whether that was the case. The answer of the bishop unfortunately cannot be found in the office; but clearly from the Minute of the 22nd of August which follows, that answer was in the affirmative. In the case of Mr. Sheridan, he was reported by the inspector in 1865 as " suspended from all sacerdotal functions in his parish"; that reference to Mr. Sheridan is to be found at page 19 of the same Return. In the case of the Rev. Mr. O'Keeffe, Dr. Moran, Roman Catholic Bishop of Ossory, announced in the letter of 22nd March 1872, " I regret it becomes my duty to inform you that the Rev. Robert O'Keeffe has been suspended from the exercise of all spiritual authority in the Catholic Church, and has also been suspended from the office which he held, of parish priest of Callan." That letter is found at page 17 of a Return, No. 244—1872.

125. *Chairman.*] You have now stated how the suspension was notified?—I have, and next I propose to state what was the action of the Board in each case, upon receiving intimation of the suspension. In the case of Dr. Keenan, the Board removed him (page 5 of the Return, No. 138) from the office of manager of the Magheral School, until judgment should have been pronounced by the proper authority on the appeal instituted by him against his suspension. In the case of Mr. Wilson the order was, that " the Commissioners, having learned that he has been deposed from the ministry, are under the painful necessity of declining to recognise him as the manager of either the Glenvale or any other National School." In the case of Mr. O'Farrell the action of the Board was " that, under the circumstances explained by the bishop, the Commissioners cannot recognise any longer the Rev. Mr. O'Farrell as manager of this school, and that the Right Rev. Dr. Kilduff be requested to state, for the information of the Commissioners, whether the Rev. Mr. Sheridan is the Rev. M. O'Farrell's clerical successor in the parish"; page 18 of Return No. 138. In the case of the Rev. Mr. Sheridan the order was, " That the Rev. P. Sheridan be informed that the Commissioners regret that they cannot continue to recognise him as manager, he being under ecclesiastical suspension." Then the order goes on to direct that the committees of the school should be made acquainted with the decision, and be informed of the Rev. Mr. Fulham's claims to become the manager, in the Rev. Mr. Sheridan's place. In the case of the Rev. Mr. O'Keeffe, the order of the Board, page 19 in the Parliamentary Return, No. 244, 1872, was, that " The certificate of the Roman Catholic Coadjutor Bishop of Ossory be received and acted on by the Board until the suspension therein mentioned shall have been removed, or declared invalid by a competent tribunal."

Mr.
P. J. Keenan, C.B.
26 May 1873.

126. What were the objections stated or entertained with reference to a suspended clergyman being a manager of a school?—The objections to suspended clergymen being managers may be classified under two heads: first, the secular, and, secondly, the religious aspect of the objections. In the case of Dr. Keenan, the bishop, in the Return, No. 138, page 4, speaks of Dr. Keenan as a "refractory clergyman, to whom I cannot conscientiously confide the care of the children." In the case of the Rev. Mr. Wilson the Board appeared to express their feeling with considerable emphasis, for they said that they declined to accept him as manager of Glenvale or any other National School; page 15 of the same Return. In the case of the Rev. Mr. O'Farrell and the Rev. Mr. Sheridan, the inspectors, from the fact that they felt it to be their duty to report the matter (one of them, Mr. Conwell, submitting the case whether or not a suspended clergyman should continue as manager of the schools) appear to regard suspended clergymen as unsuitable persons to whom to entrust the management of schools.

127. Upon the report of the suspension being received by the Board, was there any reference, in the first instance, before action was taken by the Board, made to the deposed clergyman?—Not in the case of Dr. Keenan, nor in that of the Rev. Mr. Wilson, nor in that of the Rev. Mr. O'Farrell, nor in Mr. Sheridan's case. The case of the Rev. Mr. O'Farrell was referred to the bishop first, with reference to the fact of the suspension, and next as to the succession in the incumbency of the parish. Following the precedents of those four cases, in the case of Mr. O'Keeffe there was no reference made to him.

128. The case of a suspension being reported to the bishop, were the grounds of suspension in any instance stated?—In no instance were they stated, neither in the case of Mr. Wilson, nor of Mr. O'Farrell, nor of Mr. Sheridan, nor of Mr. O'Keeffe. The only circumstance having reference to that point which occurred in the transactions, was in the case of Dr. Keenan, where the bishop observed, "I did not think it necessary to render an account to them," meaning the Commissioners, "of my reasons for suspending the Rev. John Keenan."

129. Did the Board in any instance demand to know the grounds of the suspension?—Never.

130. Did the Board express any unwillingness in any case to consider the grounds of suspension?—In the case of Mr. Wilson, page 16, the Board expressly ordered "That the Rev. Mr. Wilson be informed that it does not come within the province of the Commissioners to enter upon a discussion of the various matters relating to the sentence of deposition, which he admits to have been passed upon him, and further, that they see no grounds for altering their decision of the 26th of June, as already communicated to him."

131. Has the denial of the deposition, or of the validity of the deposition by the clergyman involved, been entertained by the Board?—They never entertained the denial of one or the other in their deliberations on such cases. In the case of Dr. Keenan, the only denial of the deposition which was before the Board, was that contained in the letter of Messrs. Kean and McArdle, two of the school trustees, in which they say, "Dr. Keenan is the parish priest, still in possession of the parish under the protection of an appeal, convicted of no crime, because he got no trial even in mockery." Mr. Wilson also denied the deposition in these words: "I am not deposed from the ministry, as it appears has been falsely represented to the Commissioners of Education. I took up credentials from the Magherafelt Presbytery, ample in their nature as to my status in the ministry, talents, and literary acquirements; I did so with the determination of connecting myself with another Church of the Reformation, and I have now all but concluded a negotiation with the ecclesiastical body to which I refer, to be taken under their care; my testimonials were not for a moment called in question, or considered inadequate. The original document I shall, with pleasure, submit to your inspection, if you wish it, confiding in your integrity as honourable gentlemen, that you will have it safely returned. I may here mention, that when the Magherafelt Presbytery found that I was about to join another body, they convened a meeting, and in the most preposterous manner, and contrary to all precedent and constitutional principle, did pass a sentence of deposition, just because I continued to preach the Gospel." In the case of Mr. O'Keeffe, there was no official denial addressed to the Board of his suspension, but it was well-known to the Board that he was contesting it. The only reference to that point made by Mr. O'Keeffe in any of his communications to the Board was made

when

when he signed himself " P. P. *Malgré vos dents,*" or " P. P., your suspension notwithstanding."

132. Then, as I understand you, the Board refused to entertain any question of that kind?—Invariably.

133. When it was known that an appeal or an action at law was instituted or threatened, did the Board stay proceedings?—No. In the case of Dr. Keenan, they pronounced their decision, removing him from the management, although it was known to the Board that he had instituted an appeal; and in their disposal of the case, they specifically point to the contingency of his restoration, in the event of the appeal being successful. Mr. Wilson, in his letter to the Board, refers to an action at law in this sentence : "This conduct I exposed through the medium of the public press, and intend shortly to submit it to the dispassionate consideration of a jury of my countrymen." However, the Commissioners, upon the consideration of that communication, declined to alter their decision in his case.

134. In the case of the dismissal of a deposed clergyman, what was the practice with reference to the appointment of a successor?—The appointment of the Rev. Mr. Macken as administrator in place of Dr. Keenan, was intimated by Dr. Blake in his letter to Archbishop Murray, and Mr. Macken was then appointed manager by the Board. In the case of Mr. Wilson, the document cannot be found in the office, in which the application for the appointment of a successor to Mr. Wilson is stated; but the fact that Dr. Templeton, the Presbyterian clergyman, who succeeded him in the Presbyterian congregation of the place, was appointed manager of the school, is on our books. In the case of Mr. O'Farrell, the Commissioners specially referred to the bishop, to ascertain who the clergyman was who was appointed in succession to Mr. O'Farrell, and upon learning that Mr. Sheridan was the clergyman, they appointed him. In the case of Mr. Sheridan, of Ratoath, the schools were under a committee. At first, the committee appeared to entertain a strong desire to continue Mr. Sheridan, the suspended clergyman, in the management; and in the Parliamentary Return, at page 21, the documents break off without showing whether the Rev. Mr. Fulham was appointed successor to Mr. Sheridan or not; that break off in the documents was consequent upon the terms of the Order of the House ; for the document appointing the Rev. Mr. Fulham, who was appointed subsequently, was not referred to in any of the Minutes having reference to the removal of Mr. Sheridan. The Order of Parliament was for " Copies of all Minutes of Proceedings, and of all letters and other documents referred to in such Minutes having relation to the removal from the office of manager of National Schools of the Rev. Dr. Keenan, the Rev. G. K. Wilson, the Rev. M. O'Farrell, and the Rev. P. Sheridan;" therefore, the document on which Mr. Fulham was nominated to the management did not appear in that Return.

135. Therefore there is a deficiency in the Return in that respect?—There is.

136. Which you now proceed to supply?—Yes. In the case of Mr. O'Keeffe, the Roman Catholic bishop announced that the Rev. Mr. Martin was the administrator of the parish of Callan, and as such, he was appointed to the schools which were non-vested. The Callan male and Callan female schools, which were under a committee, were reserved at the moment of the order, until the opinion of the committee of those schools could be obtained. The committee were referred to, and they nominated Mr. Martin, the new administrator, to the management of the schools.

137. Were there any appeals or remonstrances against the appointment of the new manager?—None, except in the cases of Dr. Keenan and Mr. Sheridan. In the case of Dr. Keenan the trustees, as I have already said, made a very earnest appeal against the removal of Dr. Keenan, and the appointment of Dr. Macken, and there were meetings, as the Parliamentary Return shows, of the subscribers to the school, and the friends of the Rev. Dr. Keenan and the teacher also remonstrating, but the Commissioners after considering those remonstrances declined to alter their decision. In the case of Mr. Sheridan, two of the three members of the committee were at first in favour of continuing Mr. Sheridan, but finally, they agreed to appoint the Rev. Mr. Fulham the administrator.

138. Is there any case in which any question arose of a difficulty between the manager and the Board being settled?—The case of the Rev. W. Shannon, of Gort, is one. The affairs of the Dr. Keenan's school were not settled until after Dr. Keenan's death, and after years of contention and ill-blood in the locality.

Mr. P. J. Keenan, C.B.

26 May 1873.

Mr.
P. J. Keenan, c.b.

26 May 1873.

During a long period of the contention, the Commissioners paid no salary to the teacher of the school.

139. The Board entirely ignored all such questions?—Entirely so.

140. Was the power of the new manager to transact the business ever frustrated by the dismissed manager?—In the case of Dr. Keenan it was for some years, and with considerable effect, as I have just stated in my last answer. In other cases there was no such resistance. In the case of Mr. O'Keeffe, the resistance as the last Parliamentary Paper shows, continues to the present time.

141. Has the Board ever communicated directly with the bishop with regard to the removal of a suspended priest?—Yes; in the case of Mr. O'Farrell special reference was made by the Board to Dr. Kilduff, the bishop; first, to elicit from him the fact of the suspension; and secondly, the fact as to the clerical succession to the Rev. Mr. O'Farrell. In their order, the Commissioners finally say, "Under the circumstances explained by the bishop" (thus showing that they had been in communication with him) "the Commissioners cannot recognise the Rev. Mr. O'Farrell any longer."

142. Does the fact of the suspended clergyman having himself founded the school, enter into the consideration of the Board?—No; if it was clear that he founded the school as clergyman of the parish or of the congregation. That was the case in Mr. Wilson's instance, for he was the original founder of the Glenvale School, and it was also the case of the Rev. Mr. O'Keeffe, who was the founder of the Infant School at Callan. In one case it was as minister of the congregation at Glenvale, and in the other case as priest of Callan.

143. Are there any other facts connected with any of these cases which you wish to lay before the Committee?—I think the Committee have nearly exhausted most of the leading points.

144. Are there any other regulations of any other public bodies to which you would wish to make any reference?—If it were not deemed irrelevant, I should like to refer to the rules of the Bequest Board, having reference to suspended clergymen, and also to the Statutes of the Queen's Colleges.

145. Mr. *Gathorne Hardy*.] They appear in the published Papers, I think, do they not?—They appear in the published Papers, but there is one point of analogy, as regards the reference, under certain circumstances, to the various Ecclesiastical authorities, between an important Minute of the Board and the regulations of the Bequest Board of Ireland, to which, perhaps, the Committee would permit me to draw their attention. In the Rules of the Bequest Board, it is provided that, "Whenever any reference "shall be made to the Roman Catholic Commissioners for the purpose "of ascertaining who is the person entitled to the benefit of any donation or "bequest which may be made to, or in trust for, the Roman Catholic priest of "any parish or congregation, it is to be understood that their duty will be merely "ministerial, and that it will be for them to act on the certificate of the Roman "Catholic Archbishop, or Bishop, or Vicar acting for the time being, instead of "the Roman Catholic Archbishop, or Bishop of the place, as to the person entitled "thereto, and to certify accordingly." And corresponding provision is made for the different churches which exist in Ireland in other regulations of the Bequest Board. Now, what appears to me to be an analogous regulation, was adopted by the Board in 1832. In Lord Stanley's letter, constituting the Board, it was laid down, "They, the Commissioners, will exercise the most entire control over all books to be used in the schools, whether in the combined literary or separate religious instruction; none to be employed in the first, except under the sanction of the Board, nor in the latter, but with the approbation of the members of the Board of the persuasion of those for whom they are intended." Accordingly, upon this instruction of Lord Stanley, the Commissioners made the following rule: "They will require to have the entire control over all books to be used in the schools, whether in the combined moral and literary or separate religious instruction. None to be employed on the former, except under the sanction of the Board, nor in the latter, but with the approbation of those members of the Board who are of the same religious persuasion with the children for whose use they are intended." That rule was modified by the Minute of the Board on the 10th of April 1832, to this effect, "It having been found that an objection involving religious principles has been made, particularly by Presbyterians, against vesting any

individual

individual with a control over books to be used in religious instruction by ministers of that communion; and that difficulties are likely to arise with respect to ministers of other denominations who are not represented on the Board as now constituted,—Resolved, that it be recommended to His Majesty's Government to permit the Board to alter Regulation IV., so as to stand as follows:— They will require to have the right of veto upon all books used in the schools for the combined moral and literary instruction. They will further require that all books used for religious instruction shall be used under the sanction of the minister recognised by the parents of the children for whose instruction they are employed; and that such minister shall obtain the consent, either of any one member of the Board, to whom he may choose to apply, or of the particular church to which he belongs, according to the rules of that church, namely, that an Episcopalian minister who does not choose to apply to any member of the Board, shall obtain and submit for the inspection of the Board the consent of his own diocesan; a Presbyterian minister, that of his own Presbytery; and a minister of any other denomination, the consent of whatever person or body of the denomination to which he belongs regards as possessing ecclesiastical authority." I should mention, although I am not able to explain when or under what circumstances the alteration took place, that the rule which I have just referred to stands now; "If any other books than the Holy Scriptures, or the standard books of the church to which the children using them belong, be employed in communicating religious instruction, the title of each is to be made known to the Commissioners whenever they deem it necessary."

Mr. P. J. Keenan, C.B.
26 May 1873.

146. Is there anything else that you wish to state to the Committee?—I do not know that there is anything else.

147. Mr. *Gathorne Hardy*.] I observe that in Dr. Keenan's case the heading is "National Schools vested in Trustees," that is in page 3 of the Return No. 138?—That is so.

148. The trustees of this school would naturally have the appointment of the manager?—They would, under the existing regulations.

149. Then how was it that in that case, upon the suspension of Dr. Keenan, the Commissioners took upon themselves, without any reference to the trustees, to appoint Mr. Macken to the management?—The point did not escape my attention, and the only manner in which I can account for it is that I see that the committee consisted of four persons then living, two of whom were in favour of Dr. Keenan, and two of whom were in favour of Mr. Macken.

150. But you will observe that the appointment of Mr. Macken was made before there was any communication with the trustees at all?—Unless some knowledge of the sort was in the possession of the members of the Board, I cannot account for the fact that they did not apply the ordinary rule of referring first to the trustees.

151. But I observe in the case of the Rev. Mr. Wilson that they do not substitute any one, but leave the question to the committee; there is no appointment made by the Commissioners in substitution of Mr. Wilson?—Yes, Dr. Templeton was appointed.

152. But there is no Minute or order of the Commissioners to that effect, is there?—There is no Minute upon the Minute book, and therefore the appointment of Dr. Templeton must have been made on some document which is not available.

153. By the committee of the school?—No; Mr. Wilson mentions in the postscript of his long letter, at page 16, "I beg further to direct your particular attention to the circumstance that the Glenvale school-house was built by private subscriptions, and has been kept in repair in the same way; there is no committee of management at present; the affairs of the school have for some time past been exclusively under my own control."

154. Then nothing appears with reference to the appointment of Dr. Templeton upon these Papers at all?—Nothing, except the fact that Mr. Wilson refers to Dr. Templeton as having claimed the management, and clearly understands that he has got it from the Board.

155. He understands that Dr. Templeton is his successor, but there is nothing in which he says that Dr. Templeton has got the schools; therefore, as far as what is before us here goes, there is nothing to show who succeeded Mr. Wilson in the management of the schools?—There is not upon the Parliamentary Paper; but I am in a position to inform you that it was the Rev. Dr. Templeton.

0.93. c 2 156. Do

Mr.
P. J. Keenan, c.a.

26 May 1873.

156. Do you know how long afterwards?—As well as I remember, Dr. Templeton was appointed actually before this Minute dismissing Mr. Wilson was passed.

157. *Chairman.*] Can you put in the date?—I cannot put in the date, because I cannot find the document, but I have a recollection to this effect; that Dr. Templeton wrote a letter to the Board stating, that he had become the successor of the Rev. Mr. Wilson, and that Mr. Wilson had left the place, and upon that letter as well as I can remember, from a consideration of the case a year ago, Dr. Templeton was appointed.

158. Mr. *Gathorne Hardy.*] Was Dr. Templeton appointed by the Commissioners?—By the Commissioners.

159. Under what circumstances; was it when the school was under a committee?—I cannot undertake to explain the circumstances of that non-reference to the committee, unless, probably, it had been ascertained at the time as stated by Mr. Wilson himself subsequently, that the committee had in the meantime become defunct. It constantly happens, that committees cease to operate, and that they are practically non-existent.

160. In the case of the Rev. Mr. Sheridan, he was suspended, and no one was put in his place by the order of the Commissioners at first?—Not at first; a reference was made to the committee.

161. Just so; there was a committee, and you ordered a reference to the committee?—Yes, that was so recently as 1865, when the details connected with such matters were carried out with greater precision than in the olden time; when sometimes rules of procedure were either for a moment overlooked in the action of the officer having to deal with the cases, or imperfect notings were made of the cases on the documents, or on the Minutes.

162. I see that the first order made by the Commissioners was the 21st January 1865. "Ordered, that the Rev. T. Sheridan be informed that they cannot recognise him further as manager"?—Yes, that is so.

163. Then the subsequent letters, which we find put in, seem to have been of an earlier date?—That is a mistake, as I understand, of the gentleman connected with the Parliamentary editing, for they are put in the inverse order all through this Return.

164. In January 1865, Mr. Sheridan's suspension was recognised by the Commissioners, but there appears to have been some inquiry respecting him previously, because I see by the letter of Mr. O'Reilly to Mr. Eugene A. Conwell, who was the inspector, that he applies to the inspector in November to delay the question, because it appears that the suspension had taken place, and Mr. O'Reilly says, "I find he has very sanguine hopes of a speedy restoration as an act of grace from the new bishop, and under the circumstances, am in favour of delaying any further proceedings with regard to changing his patronage for the present." You had had nothing previously before the Board, through your inspector or otherwise, up to the time at which the suspension was acknowledged?—In a letter of the inspector, dated the 5th November, he says, "In reply to your letters of 26th September and 18th October last, I beg to state that I requested the different members of the committee of the Rotoath National Schools to meet me there on the 26th ultimo." That action upon the part of the inspector must have reference to some instructions which he received some time previously to the period of the transaction, which is referred to by him in these Parliamentary Papers.

165-6. We have in this Paper no account of the period at which the suspension of Mr. Sheridan was communicated to the National Board; can you tell me at what period the suspension of Mr. Sheridan was communicated to the Board; must it not have been prior to the 26th of September 1864, because letters had been written by the secretaries of the Board of National Education to Mr. Conwell to find a substitute for Mr. Sheridan?—Certainly. It is evident that the letters written to Mr. Conwell had reference to communication with the committee.

167. It is quite clear that Mr. Sheridan was suspended at the time, because it says in the letter of Mr. Conwell, "Mr. Thunder was unable to attend, but Dr. O'Reilly and Mr. Eife attended, and said that, as personal friends of the Rev. P. Sheridan (who is suspended from all sacerdotal functions in the parish),"

therefore

SELECT COMMITTEE ON CALLAN SCHOOLS.

Mr.
P. J. Keenan, C.B
16 May 1873.

therefore it is quite clear that Mr. Sheridan had been suspended prior to the 26th September?—Yes.

168. And that it had been communicated to the Board?—Yes.

169. That it had been communicated to the Board, and yet that the Commissioners did not cease to recognise him as manager until January 1865?—Until the case was presented to them in its entirety with the letter of the inspector and its enclosures.

170. But in the case of Mr. O'Farrell you received from your inspector a notice that he was suspended, and then you immediately applied to the bishop to know the facts?—Yes, with regard to two points; first, whether it was the fact that he was suspended, and, secondly, who was his clerical successor.

171. But it is clear, that in the case of Mr. Sheridan, you did nothing of the sort, because the inspector reports to you that, practically, he was suspended before the 26th September 1864, and yet no step is taken by the Board until January 1865?—The step evidently is a step not taken by the Board, and, therefore, the subject of a Minute; but a step taken by the Executive in the office, in a communication addressed to Mr. Conwell to make the inquiries, which evidently elicited the communications which are in the Parliamentary Return; I can understand that any such communication addressed by the office to Mr. Conwell would not appear in the Parliamentary Return, inasmuch as it did not arise from, or was it mentioned in, a Minute; for, as I observed before, the whole of this Parliamentary Return has reference to Minutes, and correspondence hanging upon the Minutes.

172. Will you inform the Committee, upon inquiry, how early it was that the National Board of Education itself received the notice of Mr. Sheridan's suspension?—I shall.

173. There is no communication from the inspector to the bishop at all?—No.

174. Nor anything from the bishop with regard to the successor?—No.

175. In fact it appears from the letter of the 4th of November that negotiations were going on with a view to keeping Mr. Sheridan in his place on the part of some of the committee in the parish?— Yes, upon the part of two members of the committee.

176. Perhaps you will be able to explain to the Committee the difference of the action of the National Board with respect to Mr. Sheridan and with respect to Mr. O'Farrell?—I am hardly competent to indicate precisely what the views of the Commissioners were as distinguishing one case from the other, inasmuch as I was not at the time a member of the Board, and not present at their sittings; but if you would desire to hear what my opinion of the distinction between the respective courses of action was, I should be glad to give it.

177. I want you to give me certain dates: first, with respect to Mr. Sheridan; I want to know the date at which his suspension was notified to the National Board, and the earliest action that was taken by the Board afterwards?—Besides the dates I shall with pleasure obtain all the correspondence which passed in reference to this case of Mr. Sheridan, correspondence which could not properly have come under the terms of this Parliamentary Return.

178. We should be glad to see that?—I shall obtain that for the Committee upon their next meeting.

179. The two secretaries, I suppose, would be conversant with all these transactions, and the mode of working them?—Yes, they must be.

180. They conducted the whole correspondence?—Yes, they conducted the whole correspondence.

181-2. *The O'Conor Don.*] How long have they been the secretaries?—Mr. Kelly has been one of the secretaries for upwards of 30 years.

183. Dr. *Lyon Playfair.*] You are aware that there was a Royal Commission of Inquiry upon the whole of the Education in Ireland, which reported in 1870?—I am.

184. Are you aware that the Commission reported that there is no recognition of the managers *ex officio* by the Board, except they presume, in the case of workhouse schools?—If you are going to examine me upon the Report of the Royal Commission in its details, I should say that it is so long since I read it in detail, that I might be unacquainted with some of its recommendations.

185. I do

22   MINUTES OF EVIDENCE TAKEN BEFORE THE

Mr.
P. J. Keenan, c.b.
26 May 1873.

185. I do not want to go much into detail; are you aware that it was reported by the Royal Commission that there was no recognition of managers *ex officio* except in the case of workhouse schools?—It is so reported.

186. Are you aware that that was mainly in consequence of the evidence of Sir Alexander Macdonnell, which the Commissioners quote, and which was to that effect?—I should very much prefer that Sir Alexander Macdonnell, who is infinitely more capable of explaining a matter of that kind than I am, especially as the matter relates to his own evidence, should have an opportunity of answering that; I, however, can have no hesitation in answering, if necessary, the question.

187. Is it not the case that wherever there is a committee of a school or a patron of a school, whether vested or non-vested, the appointment of a manager rests in their hands?—I explained it so in the early part of my evidence.

188. Then in the official letter where the term "nominated by the Commissioners" occurs, is that consistent with Rule No. 9, which simply speaks of recognition and not of nomination; who is it that nominates to the position of manager?—Nomination, as I think I explained in answer to a question from the Right Honourable Chairman, is a term which applies to the case of schools vested in trustees, or vested in the Board in its corporate capacity, or to non-vested schools under committees.

189. It includes in fact all schools?—No; besides non-vested schools under a committee, there are thousands which are not under a committee, where the patron and manager are the same person, and it does not apply to those thousands.

190. Does the nomination of manager by a patron not apply as much to a vested school as to a non-vested school?—In the case of vested schools you must distinguish between schools vested in trustees, and schools vested in the Board in its corporate capacity. In schools vested in trustees the nomination, as I have already said, is in the hands of the trustees. In schools vested in the Board in its corporate capacity, the nomination vests in the patron whose name is inserted in the lease. But in the case of non-vested schools, the nomination comes from the committee where the school is under a committee; but, as I have said, thousands of schools are not under a committee.

191. But in none of those cases does the nomination come direct from the Commissioners; the Commissioners do not nominate directly, do they?—The Commissioners, in the instance of vested schools, reserve to themselves, in the event of the trustees in one set of schools or the patron in another neglecting their duties, the right to appoint trustees or patrons as the case may be, and in that case they have the right of nominating the persons, who have in turn the right of nominating managers under them.

192. But in all cases, nomination comes from the locality, does it not, and not from the Commissioners?—Except in this last case, the nomination of new trustees or patrons.

193. But you stated that you nominated the patron, while in reality the nomination comes locally?—The nomination of the manager always proceeds locally from the patron.

194. Is there power in your rules to do anything but recognise a manager, and not to appoint one?—"Recognition," and "appointment by the Board," are terms which from time to time have been used without concern or note. In some instances the word "recognition" is the word employed, and in others the word "appointment;" practically it comes to the same thing. If A. is nominated by the trustees to be the manager of a school, the Board sometimes "appoint" A. "Appoint" is a common word in use at the Board, and in the office. It might be that the Board simply "recognise" the nomination, in your interpretation of it.

195. I am not putting any interpretation upon it; I am anxious to ascertain the facts of the case; is it not the case that the principle upon which the Board act is to receive the local nomination; that the Board only reserves to itself the recognition of his fitness under Rule 9, but that the Board does not make the nomination at first?—The nomination is made, as I said, by the local authority, whether they are trustees, patron, or committee, in cases where there are trustees, patron, or committee, and the Board upon that nomination "recognise," or "appoint," whichever word they may use at the moment; but I should say, that in 99 cases out of 100 the word used is "appoint."

196. But

196. But the word in Rule No. 9 is "recognise"?—It is.

197. I think you stated that the Board reserved to itself the power of dismissing, in case of unfitness?—The Board have exercised such a power in several cases which I have quoted.

198. Would you consider entire neglect on the part of the manager in attending to his duties as a want of fitness?—Unfortunately the managers have not been very active in the discharge of their duties; and if neglect of duty were a cause of dismissal, we should long since have had to dismiss a very considerable number. Neglect of duty, however, has not been regarded as a cause of dismissal in the sense of that unfitness which would render it necessary on the part of the Board to dismiss the manager. But if the manager declined to do his duty to this extent, namely, to carry on all the necessary correspondence, to make the official returns, quarter after quarter, to the Board, and to give the statistics for the Commissioners' Annual Report to be presented to Parliament, then the Board, I apprehend, would naturally say that neglect like that would demonstrate such complete unfitness on his part as would warrant his dismissal, and as far as I am personally concerned, I certainly would advocate dismissal in such a case.

199. Is there a single case upon the records of the Board of a man who has ever been dismissed for neglect or want of attention to the management of the schools?—I quoted a case to-day, namely, the case of the Rev. Mr. Shannon, parish priest of Gort, whom we dismissed last year for neglecting to answer our communications; therefore if your question would cover such an instance of neglect as that, I answer "Yes;" because we dismissed Mr. Shannon last year on that ground.

200. At Question No. 40, before the Commissioners on Primary Education, Ireland, the question is put to Sir Alexander Macdonnell, "Have you ever dismissed managers for neglect or want of attention to the management of schools?" and his answer is, "No, not that I am aware of"?—Then I would make the same answer, except in the case of Father Shannon, which I have just referred to.

201. Might I refer you to page 20 of the Returns, with regard to the precedents, where you will find, "Ordered further, That the Rev. Mr. Fulham be informed that, as the schools are now vested, and under the directions of committees, it is necessary that he should be nominated by them, before the Commissioners can recognise him as manager;" that I suppose represents the action and opinion of the Board?—Certainly.

202. Was that action not altogether contradictory to the mode of dealing with the Rev. Mr. Keenan's case in the first precedent?—I have already answered that question to Mr. Gathorne Hardy.

203. Are you aware also that in that case the Board having received the remonstrances of the committee against the appointment of a successor to Mr. Keenan, consult the bishop as to what they should do. Referring to the bishop, they say, says: "We request you will favour them with your opinion as to the course which should be adopted?—You are quoting from a letter addressed not to the bishop but to the Right Honourable Anthony Richard Blake; he was a Commissioner at that time, absent from Dublin, in London, and the Board were anxious, as I understand from a study of the Minutes, and from a study of all the documents, to see that this case of Mr. Keenan, which is a precedent in all such cases, was well considered by all the members of the Board; and they adopted the unusual course of referring the papers to Mr. Blake, then in London, to have his opinion upon the question.

204. At page 13, in a letter of Mr. Adams', Mr. Adams, the chairman of the committee, asks you this, "May I be permitted to ask, respectfully, what right Dr. Blake has to have Mr. Macken, or any other man, appointed as manager of Magheral National School, in defiance not only of the Catholics, but also the Protestants and Presbyterians who support the school;" that refers, as I understand, to the committee, or to the meeting of subscribers; was any answer given to that letter by the Board?—The answer is to be found in the Return at the foot of page 14: Ordered, That the memorialists (and he was one of the memorialists) be informed that the Commissioners see no ground for altering their decision in this case."

205. But in that answer I do not see that the Commissioners state their grounds; they say, they "see no grounds"?—They say they "see no grounds for altering their decision."

206. But are you, as a Commissioner, of opinion that there was not excess of power

Mr.
P. J. Keenan, c.b.
26 May 1873.

Mr.
P. J. Keenan, C.B.
26 May 1873.

power in recognising the new manager when the committee had not nominated him, but refused to nominate him?—In answer to a question by Mr. Hardy, I expressed my strong desire that a question on that subject should be deferred until Sir Alexander Macdonnell should appear, as he is perfectly competent to explain the case.

207. Mr. *Gathorne Hardy*.] You cannot explain it?—I cannot explain it; I have, however, already given my opinion as to how it might have been brought about.

208. Dr. *Lyon Playfair*.] In the case you gave us to-day of the Rev. Mr. Murray, parish priest, did he not appoint a layman as his substitute as manager?—A layman, Mr. Lynch, notified to the Board, at the request of Mr. Murray, that he was prepared to undertake the duties, so that you may regard that of course as a nomination.

209. How long did Mr. Lynch act as manager?—A year and five months.

210. Was Mr. Lynch's nomination recognised by the Board, and did he act as manager with the knowledge of the Board?—Yes, his management of the school was accepted *pro tempore*, as I observed to-day, by the Board.

211. But you did not consider it was necessary to have *ex officio* a parish priest in that case in the management?—No; because the Rev. Mr. Murray continued to be regarded as the manager then abroad; Mr. Lynch, as his agent, simply transacting his affairs at home as *pro tempore* manager. But immediately that Mr. Jordan announced to the Board that he had become the administrator of the parish, and claimed the management, then the Board began to operate in the case, and to make inquiries of the bishop with reference to the facts.

212. But that is not the only case where a priest has appointed a layman to be his successor as manager of a school, is it?—I never knew of a case of a priest who appointed a layman as his successor in the management, the school being a parochial school: but I do know a case in which a priest permitted the landlord, who had founded a school, built it, and supported it, to take up its management. That case occurred in Carrick-on-Shannon: the landlord built a very fine house, and allowed the parish priest to become the manager. Subsequently the priest resigned his management of the school into the hands of the landlord. That arrangement has prevailed ever since, and we have refused to recognise anybody else but the landlord, or his representative, as manager.

213. Are there any cases within your knowledge in which the English or Presbyterian minister of a parish has appointed an English or Presbyterian layman as the manager?—I do not remember a case, but if you happen to know of any case, I might be able to recognise and explain it.

214. At page 18 of No. 138, it is stated that the Rev. Mr. O'Farrell had performed no ecclesiastical duties for several years past; during those several years was he recognised as manager?—He was.

215. Although he was performing no ecclesiastical duties?—The Board had no official intimation of the fact. Even if he had performed no ecclesiastical duties, that circumstance would not in the the slightest degree have influenced the Board. He might have had a staff of curates to carry on the work of the parish, and he might, therefore, not have been an active parochial clergyman, although he was parish priest.

216. In this case it was done in ignorance; you were not aware that he was not discharging the duties?—The Board was not aware.

217. Are there any cases in which the rector or priest of a parish, having removed to some other parish, still remains the manager of the schools in the parish which he has left?—I know a case; that of the Bishop of Derry, who was formerly rector of Camus-Juxta-Mourne; he was the manager of a parochial school in Strabane.

218. After he had left altogether?—When he was rector of Camus-Juxta-Mourne, Dr. Alexander became the manager of a school which had been parochial for upwards of a hundred years. Then he became Bishop of Derry, and his successor in the parish, the Rev. Mr. Wilson, as I collect from some statement which appears in the evidence of Mr. Matthews, the teacher, having had conscientious objections to the national system, Dr. Alexander, the Bishop of Derry, continued to be the manager of the school.

219. Although he was performing no ecclesiastical functions?—He was the bishop of the diocese. Since then, however, the curate of the parish, the Rev. Mr. Orr,

SELECT COMMITTEE ON CALLAN SCHOOLS. 25

if I remember rightly, became the manager, and upon Mr. Orr's removal from the parish as curate to some other district, the Rev. Mr. Wilson, who originally had conscientious difficulties about the case, undertook the management until a new curate could be appointed; I do not hold, however, that that is at all a case of a clergyman removed from a parish and continuing to be the manager of its schools. It is only 15 miles from Derry to Strabane, and half-an-hour by rail, and under the circumstances, the clergyman having a conscientious scruple about the case, it was a very natural and commendable thing that the bishop should retain the management.

220. But he was no longer rector?—He was no longer rector, but he was bishop of the parish. I should mention that another case strikes me at this moment, but it will not come under the category of a parochial school. It is the case of a convent school in Dublin which is managed by the Rev. Canon Keogh; he has been removed from Dublin, but continues to manage this convent school; he comes to town two or three times a week, is a very efficient manager, and still continues to be manager of this convent school. I can think of no other case of that sort at this moment.

221. At page 19, in the letter from the Board to the Right Rev. Dr. Kilduff, you speak of the bishop as having nominated the Rev. John Sheridan as manager; in that case had the bishop the right to appoint the manager; was he the patron of the school?—The word " nominated " may be open to a little exception there, but I take it that the term is derived from the Minute given at the upper part of the page, in which it is described that the bishop requested the Board of National Education, from the date of the communication, namely, the 16th of August, to " recognise the Rev. John Sheridan, of Drumana, county Leitrim, as manager of the Anraduff National School." The bishop's communication was in the form of a request that the Board might, from that particular date, recognise the Rev. Mr. Sheridan as manager, and in the quotation of that request by the secretaries, the word " nominated " perhaps is not quite the word that would have been most appropriate.

222. Do you happen to recollect who was the patron of the school?—It was a parochial school.

223. The patron was the previous priest?—The manager and patron both. In the case of non-vested schools of that class the patron and manager are one.

224. I suppose, practically, they mean much the same thing?—Practically, in a case of that kind, they mean nearly always the same thing.

225. In such a case you would not think the bishop had a right to nominate in the sense in which you understand the word " nomination "; you think the word was a mistake?—I think some other word might have been more appropriately used, as the bishop simply made a request that Mr. Sheridan might be nominated.

226. *Chairman.*] It is not used, as you consider, in a technical sense?—That is so.

227. Dr. *Lyon Playfair.*] Will you look at Rule No. 7, page 6; does not that rule apply solely to death, and not to resignation?—That rule, as so expressed, has reference to a vacancy in the patronage by death; but I read for you to-day, the order of the Board, and the letter to the Right Rev. Dr. Feeny, Roman Catholic bishop, in which the Board distinctly stated that in the case of a vacancy in the clerical management caused by the removal of a clergyman, the clerical successor was, according to the rule of the Board, accepted as the new manager.

228. But there is no such statement upon the face of your rules published for the information of Parliament and the public, is there?—There is no such rule stated in terms.

229. Is there a specific rule lately passed by the Board referred to in their letter?—No; that letter to Bishop Feeny is of very old date, January 1847; I may, however, remark that the practice of the Board, from the time of the announcement of this rule down to this moment, has been invariably this, that when there was a change in the clerical management, if the successor to the outgoing clergyman were not nominated by his predecessor and made application to the Board for the management, simply intimating that he was successor to So-and-so, who was removed to another district, the Board would accept him without hesitation. The procedure would be simply to say, that under the circumstances,

Mr.
P. J. *Keenan*, c.b.

26 May 1873.

stances, he was accepted, and to write to the outgoing person to say that So-and-so, a clergyman, was received in his room.

230. But there is no such thing upon the face of the rules, is there?—For instance, I recollect the case of a Methodist clergyman, the Rev. John Hughes, who in October 1869 wrote a letter to the Board, stating that his predecessor, the Rev. A. Armstrong, owing to the periodical changes in the arrangements of the Methodist clergymen, had been removed from Dungannon to another district, and that he had succeeded him in Dungannon, and begging to be recognised as manager of the Perry-street school connected with the Methodist congregation at Dungannon; he was at once accepted as such manager, a letter having been written at the same time to Mr. Armstrong, the outgoing clergyman, intimating what had been done.

231. Supposing Mr. O'Keeffe being alive, and not dead, had resigned his office under Rule 8, whereby if a patron wishes to resign the office he has the power of nominating his successor, would he, according to the rules of the Board, have been able to nominate the successor?—The Board, I think, would not permit him, supposing he nominated, for instance, some layman, to alienate schools which it was very well known to the Board had been practically founded long before he became parish priest, or his predecessor, or his predecessor's predecessor, became parish priest.

232. That would he upon the ground that he held it *ex officio*?—On the ground that he was in trust there as the manager of those schools *ex officio*, as parish priest; and I think if you observe the letter which I read to the Committee to-day, Mr. Rowan makes no nomination of Mr. O'Keeffe, but simply announces that he is resigning, as Mr. O'Keeffe is coming in as parish priest.

233. In the belief that he would be *ex officio* recognised at the Board?—Yes, in one set of schools there is absolutely a legal recognition. In the case of a school vested in the Board in its corporate capacity, the name of the patron is inserted in the lease, and if the name so inserted be that of a clergyman having charge of a parish or congregation, then the management attaches to every succeeding clergyman who is fit to act as manager.

234. Mr. *Bourke.*] With regard to the first of these precedents, namely, Mr. Keenan's, you observe that there is a letter from the Right Rev. Dr. Blake to Dr. Murray; that is the first letter, and the first sentence in that letter is, "In the month of February last I addressed a letter to the Commissioners of National Education:" where is that letter?—That letter is available; but not having been referred to in a Minute connected with the removal of Dr. Keenan, it did not come under the terms of this order; but that letter, if it is desirable, can be produced.

235. Was there any correspondence or information supplied to the Board with regard to Dr. Keenan's case before that letter of Dr. Blake's was read?—The order referred to, which was dated the 17th April 1845, and which was an order having reference to a reprimand administered to the teacher, of course shows that there must have been some communication about Mr. Keenan's school.

236. Were these disputes going on for long before this communication from Dr. Blake was made to the Board?—I cannot say what length of time they had been going on before.

237. Are the letters to the Board registered and kept?—Yes, they are.

238. Can you account for some of these letters being lost which I allude to?—The mass of letters which in the course of 40 years have been received at the office is something awful, and sometimes it is very difficult to get a document when it is required.

239. With regard to Dr. Keenan's case, you have said already that in a case of disputed succession the Board consider all the circumstances of the case?—They would consider all the circumstances of the case.

240. In Dr. Keenan's case did they consider other circumstances besides the circumstances of the suspension?—In Dr. Keenan's case the consideration appears to be entirely based upon the letter of Dr. Blake.

241. But you cannot tell whether they considered other circumstances as well?—I cannot tell, but I apprehend that they considered the simple fact of the suspension, as reported by Dr. Blake, and that simple fact only, when they decided on removing Dr. Keenan. They communicated with Dr. Blake upon the 12th of June.

242. Then

SELECT COMMITTEE ON CALLAN SCHOOLS. 27

Mr.
P. J. Kiernan, c.e.

26 May 1873.

242. Then with regard to the order of the 17th April 1845, which was mentioned incidentally, you do not think that had anything to say to the matter?—I think that it had reference more to the teacher, Mr. Grant, who had taken a strong view of his duty towards his former manager, Mr. Keenan, and advocated his cause; and, in fact, so far sustained him that he slept in the schoolhouse for a year or more in order to keep absolute possession of the school for him.

243. Now, one word with regard to the rule which the honourable Member for St. Andrew's University examined you upon with reference to the case of the death of a clergyman, and a successor being appointed; was that rule mentioned to the Board in the discussions which took place with regard to Mr. O'Keeffe?—It was commented upon and thrashed out with a great deal of criticism.

244. I suppose the argument was used of *expressio unius exclusio alterius*; was that argument used?—I should say so.

245. So that the point mentioned by the honourable Member for St. Andrew's University to you was taken at the Board?—It was.

246. Did the majority of the Board imagine that the rule with regard to death applied to the case of Mr. O'Keeffe?—The majority of the Board regarded the fact that there was a vacancy in the management of the schools at Callan, and that the rule applied just as if Mr. O'Keeffe had removed to another parish, or had died.

247. Then it was not only the practice, but, according to the majority of the Board, they acted upon that rule which applies to the case of death?—Yes, that is so.

248. Dr. *Lyon Playfair.*] Did the Board throw any doubt upon the authenticity of the nomination of Mr. O'Keeffe by the committee of 28th February 1863?—Never.

249. And is there any reason for the statement with reference to the nomination being a forgery?—The question was never before the Board that there was the slightest doubt with reference to the genuineness of those signatures to the appointment of Mr. O'Keeffe 10 years ago, and since then the matter has only become known to the Commissioners through the receipt of a communication alleging that those signatures are not genuine.

250. But my question is this, have the Board at the present time any doubt that the nomination was a genuine nomination?—The Board has never expressed any doubt upon the one hand, or any opinion upon the other hand, upon the case.

251. Did not 10 years elapse in which the local committee itself never expressed any such doubt?—From 1863.

Thursday, 5th June 1873.

MEMBERS PRESENT:

Mr. Bourke.
Mr. Secretary Cardwell.
Mr. Cross.
Mr. Gathorne Hardy.

The O'Conor Don.
Dr. Lyon Playfair.
Mr. Whitbread.

THE RIGHT HONOURABLE EDWARD CARDWELL, IN THE CHAIR.

Mr. *Patrick Joseph Keenan*, C.B., re-called; and further Examined.

252. *Chairman.*] FROM circumstances which were explained to the Committee, your examination on the former occasion was made without full preparation on your part, and there were some further particulars which you were to lay before us when we met again. Are you prepared to make any additions or explanations with regard to the evidence that you gave on the last occasion?—Yes. I was requested to supply the Committee with the original paper of the Committee of the Callan Schools, nominating Father O'Keeffe to the management. I produce that (*handing it in*). I was also asked whether the Chief Baron's letter was submitted to me before its publication in a complete form, and I answered that I thought it was submitted to me the day before its presentation to the Board. On considering the matter over, I, however, recollect that I only saw the first sheet of it before its presentation to the Board; that, in fact, I saw the remainder of the paper only after it had been presented to the Board by the Chief Baron. The manuscript was never submitted to me. I was also asked what the date of the memorial of the 13 Commissioners was, and I was unable on that occasion to specify it. It is not dated, I find; I myself signed it on the 5th of May; and it was sent from Dublin on the 6th. I was asked questions in reference to the appointment of a successor to Mr. Wilson, and I mentioned that the letter referring to his deposition and to the appointment of a successor could not be found. It has been found since, and I will put it in to-day. I was also asked to state the period of the notification of the suspension of Mr. Sheridan. I have the papers in the case with me, and shall have to refer to them in the course of my evidence to-day. I mentioned in one of my answers that the appointment of Mr. Fulham as successor to Mr. Sheridan was made, I thought, by the Committee. I was under that impression, as, indeed, were most of the people with whom I had conversed on the matter at the office before I left; but the whole of the documents have since, at my request, been obtained, and I find that the appointment was not made by the Committee; but I shall have to explain that by-and-by.

253. Is there anything additional to what you told us the other day, which has since become known to you, and which you wish to state now?—I mentioned, in the course of my examination on the former day, that the only precedents of the dismissal of clerical managers that had come to my knowledge, or that were known at the time, were the four given in the Parliamentary Paper. Sir Alexander Macdonnell and others, and I myself for a long time, were under the impression that there was another case; but it could not be discovered. It has, however,

however, been found, after much examination, among the old papers and minutes of the office; and, with your permission, I will now draw the attention of the Committee to it. This is a letter from the Rev. Dr. Henry, then Presbyterian clergyman at Armagh, and at the same time Commissioner of Education: "Armagh, 26th November 1842.—To the Secretaries of the National Board of Education. Gentlemen, I do not hesitate to say that Mr. Fisher ought to be removed from the managership of the Market Hill School. After a most painful investigation of five or six days by the Armagh Presbytery, Mr. Fisher was suspended *sine die* from the functions and benefits of the Christian ministry. That decision was confirmed, after an appeal, by the unanimous voice of the General Assembly. I hold, therefore, that it would be injurious to the interests of the Board of Education longer to retain as one of its patrons who is no longer permitted to exercise the functions of the ministry in Market Hill or elsewhere. Regarding the special matter in question, of the salary due, the mistress of the school passing through Mr. Fisher's hands, I have to state that, as he is in great pecuniary difficulties, this teacher and her husband have a strong objection to allow him to receive the money.—I am, gentlemen, your obedient servant, P. S. Henry. I forgot to mention that the congregation of Market Hill are about to elect a successor to Mr. Fisher, who will be the natural person to become manager in Mr. Fisher's place. In the meantime I would recommend Mr. Joseph McRee, of Market Hill, to be appointed *locum tenens*."

Mr. P. J. Keenan, C.B.

5 June 1873.

254. *Mr. Cross.*] Is there any record of any conversation or correspondence before that?—No, that is the first that has come to my knowledge. I have no doubt that it is the first. A great search was made for all the minutes connected with the case.

255. *Mr. Bourke.*] The question was before the Board in some shape or other before that, was it not?—No.

256. *Mr. Cross.*] You are only speaking from the books of the Board with regard to this case?—Yes.

257. You know nothing of the case personally?—No, nothing beyond the records of the office.

258. *Chairman.*] If you will proceed to state to the Committee what you know officially on the subject, we understand that Dr. Henry, who was a party to this proceeding, will be here very soon, and the rest of it we will hear from him. Will you state briefly what is officially recorded?—Dr. Henry's letter was submitted to the Board on the 22nd of December 1842. There were present on that occasion the Archbishop of Dublin, Archbishop Murray, the Right Hon. A. R. Blake, the Marquess of Kildare, the Provost, Mr. Greene, Mr. Holmes, Mr. Corballis, and Mr. Macdonnell. The order upon the letter of Dr. Henry was: "That Mr. Fisher be removed from the management of said school, and that he be informed be is so, in consequence of the decision of the General Assembly; and further, that the salary be paid through the Rev. P. S. Henry, and that he be requested to intimate to the persons connected with the school the necessity of appointing a fit person to act as manager." That order was communicated to the Rev. Mr. Fisher, and he replied as follows:—"To the Secretaries of the National Education Board.—Market Hill, 8th January 1843.—Gentlemen,—With all the contempt and scorn that a persecuted and innocent man can feel for gratuitous insult, I retransmit your letter to the place from whence it came. I know the man that has dictated this measure; and I know him only to despise his hollow heartedness and duplicity; and let me assure him, through you, that the day is not far distant when I shall have the dreadful means of restitution in my own hands. Since the days of the Inquisition there never was such systematic villany exercised towards any man, and after vainly endeavouring to establish a charge of immorality against me, and after admitting evidence that no court on earth would have sustained for one moment but the Assembly of Armagh, and after recording their conviction that the charge was not proved; when I had been entrapped into a resignation of my congregation, with the assurance of restoration in a little time; when they had me unsuspectingly in their power to accomplish their own wicked ends, they disannexed me from the congregation of Market Hill. Against their decision I appealed to the General Assembly, but that was not the place for a man of my politics and

0.93. D 3

Mr.
P. J. Keenan, C.B.

5 June 1873.

and general demeanour to get even-handed justice, and the sentence of the Presbytery was accordingly confirmed. The Commissioners have now audaciously re-echoed the same sentence without examining into the grounds of such a decision, and for this reason I now abandon for ever a course that I have advocated successfully for years, together when it was more than dangerous to do so. Besides, the schoolhouse is in my debt 64 *l*., owing to my devotedness to the principles of national education, and by this unjustifiable and insulting measure which you have adopted towards me, you have ruined a cause that was prospering beyond all calculation in such a place as Market Hill, and brought down upon yourselves the execration and contempt of all good and honourable men.—Yours, with every feeling of detestation, *John Fisher*." That answer was submitted to the Board on the 12th of January 1843, when there were present Archbishop Murray, the Provost, Mr. Blake, Mr. Corballis, the Marquess of Kildare, and Mr. Macdonnell, and the order made by the Board was, that no action was to be taken; the letter was marked "Up," and since that has never been acknowledged.

259. Is there any record of what became of the school afterwards?—As mentioned in the second part of the order of the Board, Dr. Henry was requested on the part of the Board to pay the salary of the teacher, and I find from the papers in the case that after some time the school was closed, and that in the course of a year Lord Gosford, who was the landlord, through his agent, attached seven or eight acres of land to it, converted it into an agricultural school, and was recognised by the Board as patron.

260. Do you know when it was closed?—The precise date I have not been able to ascertain, but from the correspondence, I gather that it was closed soon after the removal of Mr. Fisher, and re-opened, as I have said, under the auspices of Lord Gosford and his agent.

261. Are there any particulars that you wish to add to what you have stated with regard to the other cases?—As I shall have something to say to each of the four cases, perhaps you will be good enough to allow me to begin with the case of Dr. Keenan, which was the first I mentioned on the former day. The Committee will remember that in the Parliamentary Return, No. 138, of this year, in the letter of Dr. Blake, at page 4, to Archbishop Murray, reference is made to a letter written by him in the month of February, addressed to the Board; and I was asked a question in reference to that letter. I, therefore, requested that all the correspondence from the commencement of the case should be sent to me from the Education Office in Dublin, and I have it now before me. I shall not trespass upon the patience of the committee by reading the whole of this very voluminous correspondence; if necessary the whole of it may be inserted in the Minutes; but I shall just give an outline of its general nature. The correspondence commenced with a letter to the Board, from the Rev. Mr. Macken in January 1845, complaining that the teacher, Mr. Grant, had "acted as secretary at meetings, at which the most objectionable resolutions were passed, and expressions made in speeches afterwards published on the character of Dr. Blake and other clergymen;" and also complaining that he neglected his duty; that he was "wanting in his attendance during the regular school hours;" that the school was "closed one-half of the day, the children being dismissed frequently at 12 o'clock to enable him to attend" those meetings. That letter was referred to Dr. Keenan, then the recognised manager of the school; and Dr. Keenan, in reply, defended the teacher, denied the irregularities that were stated by Mr. Macken to have taken place, and thanked the Board for the promptness of their communication, and for giving him an opportunity "of making Mr. Grant's conduct appear in its true colours in despite of malevolent accusers." That letter was considered by the Board on the 31st of January 1845, and the decision, as communicated to the Rev. Mr. Macken, with regard to the charges against Mr. Grant, the teacher, was, that it did not appear that he had neglected his duties, or violated any rule of the Board. The Commissioners, however, directed the superintendent of the district to exercise a vigilant superintendence over the school. Mr. Macken was dissatisfied with that decision, and repeated his charges in a letter of the 3rd of February, in which he says, "If shutting the school-house on days on which it should be opened; if dismissing the children before the appointed hour; if non-attendance until comparatively late

SELECT COMMITTEE ON CALLAN SCHOOLS. 31

late hours in the day, be no violation of the rules of the Board, I shall trouble you no further." The inspector, as I mentioned, was directed to have a particular regard to the affairs of that school. He appointed a day to hold an inquiry. There was a miscarriage of that inquiry, as it had to be postponed to suit the convenience of Dr. Keenan; and in the meantime the letter of the bishop, dated the 22nd February 1845, referred to in the printed paper, was addressed to the Board. It is as follows: "To the Right Honourable and Honourable the Commissioners of National Education.—My Lords and Gentlemen,—A painful but imperative sense of duty obliges me to express to your Honourable Board my deliberate conviction that Mr. Grant, master of the Magheral School in this diocese (of Dromore), has rendered himself unfit for that situation. Without troubling your honourable Board with unnecessary details, I beg to assure you that neither by due attention to his proper business, nor by a pacific spirit, has he rendered himself useful to that parish; for he has been frequently absent from school during the hours for teaching; and he has made himself notorious by his violent and foolish speeches at public meetings, and by his scurrilous abuse of respectable Catholic clergymen. These few particulars I submit to your prudent consideration. I beg also to observe that as the Rev. J. Macken is now the approved Roman Catholic administrator of the spiritual or religious concerns of the Catholic population of Annaghlone and Drumballaroney parish, in which Magheral is situated, he, in my humble opinion, would be the fittest person to be the patron of the school.—I have the honour to be, with most profound respect, my Lords and Gentlemen, your obedient humble servant, *Michael Blake.*" The Board acknowledged that letter, informed Dr. Blake that the inspector had been directed to hold an investigation, and that the letter would be considered when the inspector's report should have been laid before the Commissioners. When the report of the inspector was received, the Commissioners ordered Mr. Robertson, who was at that time the senior of the Inspection Department of the Education Office in Dublin, to make further inquiry into all the circumstances of the case, to be assisted by the local superintendent, Dr. Lyons. Then there are various letters between the inspectors who were to investigate and the persons concerned (Mr. Macken, Dr. Keenan, and the teacher); and also letters from the Board to Mr. Macken. Then there was a petition presented by 424 persons, expressing their strong conviction that Mr. Grant was an efficient teacher, that the charges against him were unfounded, and praying the Board to consider his case favourably. All the papers were referred to the inspector. The routine in a case of the kind when investigation is pending, is to send every document relating to the case to the inspector who may have the carriage of it.

Mr.
P. J. Keenan, c.b.

5 June 1873.

262. Mr. *Bourke.*] What was the date of the petition?—The 24th March 1845.

263. *The O'Conor Don.*] This petition, and the correspondence that you have alluded to, was with reference to the master's conduct, was it not?—The gravamen of the correspondence is entirely in relation to the master; and the Board, in its dealing with the case so far, as you may perceive, refers entirely to the question of the master's conduct. Then, as I was observing, the inspector made his report, which is a somewhat long one, but the following decision of the Board will represent the view taken of the case. "The Commissioners of Education have had before them Mr. Robertson's report of his investigation into the charges preferred against Mr. Grant, teacher of Magheral National School, County Down, and also the several documents transmitted to them in reference to the case. The Commissioners are of opinion that, although the charges affecting Mr. Grant, as a schoolmaster, have not been proved, he has nevertheless been guilty of great indiscretion in having taken a part in any local disputes, as such conduct is calculated to impede his usefulness as the teacher of a national school. In consequence, however, of Mr. Grant's general efficiency hitherto, the Commissioners do not deem it necessary in the present instance to inflict a more severe punishment than a reprimand; but they require that Mr. Grant will in future abstain from all controversy, and that he will not do anything either in or out of school which may have a tendency to injure the school committed to his charge, or which may interfere with the proper discharge of his duties as a schoolmaster. The above order has been communicated to the Rev. J. S. Keenan, the manager of Magheral National School."

0.93. D 4 That

Mr.
P. J. Keenan, C.B.
5 June 1873.

That letter was addressed to the Rev. Mr. Macken, who was practically the complainant in the case. The date of it is the 19th of April 1845. In the course of that correspondence, as the Committee will have observed, Dr. Blake, in his letter to the Board of 22nd February mentioned that the Rev. J. Macken was then the approved Roman Catholic administrator of the spiritual and religious concerns of the parish of Annaghlone and Dromballyroney, and that in his humble opinion he was the fittest person to be the patron of the school. Mr. Macken himself incidentally, in one of his letters, referred to the fact that Dr. Keenan was a suspended priest; but the Commissioners, in the consideration of the whole of this correspondence, referred simply to the original question of complaint, the conduct of Mr. Grant. The next part of the correspondence begins with the letters published in the Parliamentary Paper, with the exception of one letter, the acknowledgment of the letter of Dr. Blake, of the 8th of May, intimating to him that it will be brought before the Board at the first meeting at which a full attendance of the members of the Board can be secured. Then came the proceedings, as published in the Parliamentary Return. The Committee will remember that the Board ordered the removal of the Rev. Dr. Keenan, and the appointment of the Rev. Mr. Macken, the administrator, in his place. I was asked many questions upon the subject of that appointment of the Rev. Mr. Macken, especially in relation to the fact that no reference had been made to the trustees of the school for a nomination. From the time of the last Minute published in the Parliamentary Papers, having reference to the year 1845, it appears that nothing occured until the 5th October 1847; and I think it proper to mention to the Committee what occurred upon and after that date. The two trustees, Andrew Kean and Patrick M'Ardle, address the Board on the 5th October 1847, and inform them that they have lately heard of the demise of Mr. John Clarke, who was one of the trustees to the Magheral School. Then they go on to say that after mature consideration they have the pleasure of nominating a Mr. Daniel M'Mullen as their colleague in the trust; and they also express their conviction that Mr. Macken never could be an efficient patron of the school, and propose that the new trustees should appoint a neutral party, a gentleman in every way qualified, a Dr. M'Court, of Rathfriland.

264. *Mr. Gathorne Hardy.*] Was that gentleman a clergyman?—No, he was a medical doctor. That was 5th October 1847. That communication from the trustees was referred by the Board to one of its legal members, Mr. Corballis, and Mr. Corballis having returned the papers, the case was considered, and the Board expressed their readiness to approve of the appointment of Mr. M'Mullen as the third trustee. There appears to have been in the case of Magheral, not only a committee of trustees, but an ordinary committee, evidently having reference to parochial affairs in connection with the finances, and so on, of the school; for Mr. Adams, as chairman of that ordinary committee, upon learning the decision of the Board, conveyed the thanks of the committee to the Board for having sanctioned the appointment of Mr. M'Mullen as trustee in place of Mr. Clarke, and expressed the opinion that the appointment of Dr. McCourt, as manager, should be approved by the Board. The Board, upon the consideration of that letter, ordered, "That the appointment of Dr. McCourt as manager of the Magheral School be approved, it appearing that all the trustees concur in the propriety of such appointment." The Committee may remember that on the former occasion, although I was unable to explain why reference was not made to the trustees when Mr. Macken was appointed, I expressed the opinion that possibly it was because it was known to the Board that they were not at the time unanimous; and the appointment of the new manager is the last stage in that case that I think it is of any importance or interest to refer to.

265. *Chairman.*] Did Mr. Macken take any steps upon these proceedings?—Mr. Macken at first expressed his disapprobation of the proceeding, but ultimately fell in with it, and approved. I should mention that Mr. Grant, the teacher, continued to keep forcible possession of the school up to this period; and that there was a memorial from the new manager to the Board, to take into favourable consideration the case of Mr. Grant, and to award him the arrears of salary. The Board, however, declined to award him any salary beyond October 1845.

266. When did Dr. Keenan cease to be manager?—In June 1845.

267. And Mr. Grant received his salary up to October 1845, as I understand you?

you?—Yes; the case was at that time finally settled, as regards the remonstrances of the trustees and subscribers, and friends of the school.

Mr. P. J. *Keenan*, c.b.

5 June 1873.

268. Is that all that you wish to say about the case of Dr. Keenan?—Perhaps I should add, that the Board wrote to the new trustees to say that if they did not cause the removal of Mr. Grant from the occupation of the school, legal proceedings would be instituted on the part of the Board; that after a short time Mr. Grant did vacate the school; and that the Board, taking a merciful view of his case, pronounced him eligible for an appointment in some other national school. He did obtain an appointment in an other national school, and continued to hold it until very recently.

269. Is that all that you wish to say with reference to the case of Dr. Keenan? —Yes.

270. *Mr. Cross.*] Judging from the Report of the Inspector, which I hold in my hand, Dr. Keenan seems to have given assistance to the inspector?—Yes; he was quite well disposed to facilitate the inquiry in every sense.

271. The inspector seems to have laid to Dr. Keenan's charge that he had obliged the schoolmaster to be absent from the school, and that he had done so for the purpose of inducing the schoolmaster to make speeches on behalf of Dr. Keenan himself?—That was Mr. Robertson's opinion, I remember.

272. *Chairman.*] Do you wish to add anything with reference to the next case; the case of Mr. Wilson?—Yes. I was asked on the former occasion a question with reference to the document in which the suspension of the Rev. Mr. Wilson was communicated to the Board. That document could not be found, although as the whole strength of the office had been since engaged in working up all the documents and papers in these cases. A document in which the suspension of Mr. Wilson is communicated has, however, been sent to me; it is a letter from the Rev. Dr. Templeton, who was the successor of Mr. Wilson in the management of the school, and is dated the 25th of May 1851.

273. That letter reports from Dr. Templeton the suspension of Mr. Wilson?— Yes. It was upon that letter of the Rev. Dr. Templeton that his nomination to the management of the school was made. The order nominating him to the management was simply in these words: "Note, writer correspondent for Glenvale National School, in room of the Rev. G. K. Wilson, as he has left the country." The Roman Catholic clergyman of the place, the Rev. Mr. Doherty, simultaneously with Dr. Templeton, made a claim for the management; but he was at once informed that the Rev. Mr. Templeton had been appointed in the place of the Rev. Mr. Wilson, whom he had succeeded in the district.

274. Did anybody else apply for the position of manager?—No other person but the Rev. Mr. Templeton and the Rev. Mr. Doherty, who had no claim.

275. *Mr. Gathorne Hardy.*] Is that all the correspondence in the Templeton case?—All about Mr. Templeton himself.

276. I see that this school was under a committee; is there any allusion to the committee?—Not a word of reference in Mr. Templeton's letter. In Mr. Wilson's letter, if you remember, there is a reference to it in which he says it has ceased.

277. But the Board nominated Mr. Templeton upon his own application without any reference to the committee, is that so?—Yes.

278. *Chairman.*] Is that all that you wish to say upon Mr. Wilson's case?— One letter from the Rev. Mr. Wilson, the letter in which he expresses his indignation at his removal, is already published in the Parliamentary Papers. There is a letter referred to in the Parliamentary Papers, about which a question was put to me on the last occasion; it is the letter commencing, "About 10 or 12 years ago" as a misprint for "10 or 12 days ago." The letter referred to as having been written "10 or 12 days ago," I have now before me. It is dated the 11th of June 1851, and it is simply an intimation on Mr. Wilson's part, that he has had it in contemplation for some time past to have two additional schools established in the district, and he then goes on to make inquiries in reference to the rules as regards building grants.

279. Dr. *Lyon Playfair.*] Have you any explanation in the additional correspondence

0.93. E

Mr.
P. J. Keenan, C.B.

5 June 1873.

spondence of that unusual formula of dismissal that the Board will not recognise him as manager of "either the Glenvale or any other national school"?—Nothing to explain it in point of reference specifically in the correspondence; but I myself have formed an opinion since I have read the whole of the papers why that unusual addendum was made. It was the opinion of the Board at the time, probably, that there were reasons for it.

280. *The O'Conor Don.*] And if he had applied for the establishing of other national schools, would not that be a reason for putting it in?—Possibly; that may have also been before the mind of the Board on that occasion.

281. *Chairman.*] That is all you wish to add about Mr. Wilson's case?—Yes.

282. Do you wish to add anything with reference to Mr. O'Farrell's case?—Yes. The first point that I wish to add to the facts which I have already stated in reference to Mr. O'Farrell's case is, that one of the two letters of the bishop referred to at page 18 of Parliamentary Paper, No. 138, as lost, has been found; it is the first letter referred to, and it is dated the 26th August 1862. The letter is: "Gentlemen, I am in receipt of your letter, 25th August 1862, in which you ask me to state, for the information of the Commissioners of National Education, if the Rev. John Sheridan, whom I have nominated as manager of the Annaduff Male and Female National Schools, is now the priest of the parish, in place of the Rev. Mr. O'Farrell. In reply, I beg to say that the Rev. John Sheridan is at present the sole officiating priest in the parish in which the school at Annaduff is built.—I remain, Gentlemen, your very obedient servant, *John Kilduff*." The other letter has not been found; and I may assure the Committee that every effort has been made by every person in connection with the Education Office to find all the correspondence and documents and papers in connection with all these cases. I have now, in reference to this case of Mr. O'Farrell, to draw attention to the order of the Board when the Rev. Mr. O'Farrell was removed, and the clerical successor, the Rev. John Sheridan, was appointed. The words of the order were, "That the Rev. John Sheridan be appointed manager of this school, in the place of the Rev. Mr. O'Farrell." That school was the Annaduff School; and it evidently was not before the Board, and, indeed, the fact only came to my own knowledge within the last few days, that the Rev. Mr. O'Farrell was also manager of another school, called the Lisduff School. It happened that the Annaduff School was in one school district, the head-quarters of which were at Longford, and that the Lisduff School was in another school district, the head-quarters of which were at Boyle, county Roscommon; and the order of the Board, therefore, the fact of Mr. O'Farrell having the management of the Lisduff School not having been submitted to their consideration, referred only to the case of the Annaduff school; but Mr. Sheridan, on the 6th September 1862, the order having been made on the 29th August previous, addressed the Board in the following terms: "Gentlemen, I beg to inform you that the above-named national school (Lisduff) is situate in the parish of Annaduff, of which I am the officiating priest. I therefore claim to be appointed local manager of the above-named school, in place of the Rev. Mr. O'Farrell, for the same reason as I was appointed to the local management of the Annaduff School, and of which appointment I have received due notification. I presume that the Right Rev. Dr. Kilduff, Roman Catholic Bishop, was not aware that the management of the Lisduff schools was also in the Rev. Mr. O'Farrell's hands; otherwise, he would have applied for my appointment in the latter instance as well as in the former." That letter was brought before the Board on the 19th of September, and on inquiry it was ascertained that the Lisduff School was one of a very limited class of schools in Ireland, a class of schools secured by bond; that is to say, by surety in a bond to be kept open for the purposes of national education, at all times.

283. Can you state the number of such schools?—Less than 100; between 90 and 100.

284. Will you state the nature of the bond?—It is a bond on the part of a surety or sureties engaging to keep the school open for the reception of children of all religious persuasions, and for the observance of the rules of the Board.

285. Dr. *Lyon Playfair.*] Still non-vested?—They are classified under the vested

SELECT COMMITTEE ON CALLAN SCHOOLS. 35

Mr.
P. J. Keenan, c.b.

5 June 1873.

vested in consequence of the obligation imposed upon the surety corresponding to that imposed upon the trustees in case of a school vested in trustees. The Board, on considering that letter from Mr. Sheridan, ordered, " That the Rev. Mr. Sheridan be informed of the rule as to the appointment of the manager in the case of schools secured by bond; and that before he can be appointed manager of Lisduff National School as desired, it will be requisite for Mr. Keppel" (that is, the honourable Colonel Keppel who was at that time Lord Albemarle) " to signify to the office that the arrangement meets with his approval." A letter was accordingly written to Mr. Sheridan containing the substance of that order, that is, that he should obtain the nomination of Mr. Keppel, or as it ought to have been stated, Lord Albemarle. That letter, from the office, was dated the 29th September 1862. It devolved then upon Mr. Sheridan to obtain from Lord Albemarle that nomination. No communication, however, was therefore received from Mr. Sheridan. No notice appears to have been taken in the office of the neglect of Mr. Sheridan in procuring the nomination until the receipt of a letter from Mr. Sheridan, so far on as the 7th of April 1865, again applying for the management, and apparently utterly oblivious of the instruction that he had received in September 1862 from the Board as to the necessity of obtaining a nomination from Lord Albemarle. He was then reminded of the letter of 1862, and told that the nomination of Lord Albemarle was a necessary condition of his appointment; and accordingly on the 24th May Lord Albemarle writes to the Commissioners of National Education: " Gentlemen, I beg to nominate the Rev. John Sheridan, Drumsna, County Leitrim, to the managership of the Lisduff National School."

286. *Chairman.*] Is that all that you wish to state about the case of Mr. O'Farrell? – Yes.

287. Do you wish to state anything further about the case of Mr. Sheridan? —Yes.

288. Mr. *Cross.*] Did you know that Mr. O'Farrell was insane?—I never heard any such imputation on him, and there is no such statement in the office, nor in any of the returns connected with the case to show that. Passing now to the case of the Rev. Mr. Sheridan, of Ratoath, I was asked as to the nature of the correspondence which preceded the letter of Mr. Conwell, given at page 20 of the Parliamentary Return, No. 138, especially having reference to the letters of 26th of September and 18th of October, to which Mr. Conwell's letter purported to be a reply. I have since the last occasion of my appearance before this Committee got all the papers in this case, and I find that it began as far back as the 28th January 1863, in a letter of the Rev. Mr. Fulham. Mr. Fulham's letter was as follows: " Gentlemen,—I beg leave to inform you that I was appointed, and am, for more than the last year, the administrator of the united parishes of Ratoath and Ashbourne, in the county of Meath. The Rev. Mr. Sheridan, whose successor I am, is a suspended priest. He still, however, continues the manager of the two schools under the National Board of Education, and, naturally, though not reasonably, declines to resign in my favour. Under these circumstances I apply to the Board, and inform it that I am ready to undertake the care of their schools if I be appointed their manager. —I am, Gentlemen, yours very truly, *John Fulham*, Administrator." That letter was not brought before the Board, but on the 19th of February 1863, the secretaries replied to it as follows: " In reply to your letter of the 28th ultimo, respecting the managership of the above-named national schools (Ratoath and Ashbourne), we are to inform you that the schools of Ratoath and Ashbourne are under local committees, and that it is the privilege of these committees to nominate a manager for the respective schools. We must, therefore, request you will procure letters from the committees nominating you, and on the receipt of such communications we shall be happy to note your name on the office books as manager.—We are, Reverend Sir, *Maurice Cross, James Kelly*, Secretaries." That letter was addressed to the Rev. Mr. Fulham, and he never replied to it. The matter then appears to have lain in abeyance in the office, evidently through some oversight on the part of the person having the custody of that letter which I read from the Rev. Mr. Fulham, until the 26th September 1864, when a letter was addressed by the secretaries to Mr. Conwell, the inspector. This letter is one of the two referred to in Mr. Conwell's letter of the 5th of November, published in the Parliamentary Return at page 20, and it is as follows:

0.93. B 2

Mr.
P. J. Keenan, c.b.
5 June 1873.

follows: "Sir,—The Rev. J. Fulham informed us in a letter dated the 28th of January 1863, that he was appointed administrator of the united parishes of Rotoath and Ashbourne in succession to the Rev. Mr. Sheridan suspended. He further stated that Mr. Sheridan declined to resign the management of these schools in his favour. As we find on reference to the books of this office that when these schools were taken into connection they were under a committee, we have to request you will state whether it still exists, and if so, that you will inform us of whom it is composed." Mr. Conwell replied, that the committee did exist, and that it was composed of the following persons: Mr. Michael Thunder, Dr. O'Reilly, Mr. Eife, and the Rev. P. Sheridan, the manager of the school. Mr. Conwell adds, "Mr. Thunder has not attended any of the meetings since the suspension of the Rev. P. Sheridan." I again observe that the matter was not yet brought before the Board; the routine of the office, as I suppose, was still proceeding; and on the 18th of October 1864, the secretaries wrote to Mr. Conwell: "With reference to your letter of the 11th inst., in relation to the application made by the Rev. J. Fulham to be recognised as the manager of the Rotoath Male and Female National Schools, county Meath, we are to request that you will cause the committee you name to write to this office, nominating a manager in the room of the Rev. P. Sheridan, if they consider such a step necessary. We are, Sir, your obedient servants, *James Kelly, William McCreedy,* Secretaries." On the 5th of November Mr. Conwell replied, as you will find at page 29 of the Parliamentary Return, enclosing the letters of Mr. Thunder, Mr. Eife, and Dr. O'Reilly; and then for the first time, and the only time, as far as I can gather, the case was brought before the Board on the 27th of January 1865; and upon that occasion, having taken into consideration Mr. Conwell's letter, and of course his instructions, and that remarkable expression in the secretaries' letter, "if they consider such a step necessary," the Board ordered the removal of Mr. Sheridan, and further ordered, "That Mr. Fulham be informed that as the schools are non-vested and under the direction of committees, it is necessary that he should be nominated by them before the Commissioners can recognise him as manager." As regards the subsequent proceedings of the case, I have to repeat what I took the liberty, through the indulgence of the Committee, of saying at the commencement of my examination to-day, that on the last occasion I fell into a mistake as regards the nomination of a successor; I was under the impression that the nomination was made by the committee; I find, however, from a perusal of the correspondence which I have been able to obtain since, that such was not the fact; I regret having for the moment led the Committee into error on that point.

289. *Chairman.*] What did take place?—What took place was this, that the Board communicated their order dismissing Mr. Sheridan, and announcing that it would be necessary for Mr. Fulham to obtain the nomination of the committee to Mr. Conwell, the inspector, and requested him to convey their decision to the committee of the Rotoath and Ashbourne National Schools, "and to acquaint them of the claims of the Rev. J. Fulham, as the administrator of the parish, to the management of the schools." There is a letter referred to in the books of the office, but which unfortunately cannot be obtained, from Mr. Thunder, I suppose having reference to his view of the case in favour of the appointment of Mr. Fulham; but as the letter itself cannot be found, it is only the office index to it that can be referred to, and that index simply runs, "Management of Rotoath and Ashbourne National Schools. Encloses note of Mr. Thunder regarding." It was in January 1865 that the Rev. Mr. Sheridan was removed, and that Mr. Fulham got the intimation that on the nomination of the committee he would be appointed manager. Nothing appears to have been done by Mr. Fulham; the committee does not appear to have made any nomination, and on the 2nd of June following the teacher of the school writes to the inspector in these terms: "Sir,—There is every danger that the few subscribers still attached to these schools may fall off in a short time. There is no secretary to communicate with them, no treasurer to receive their contributions, and no manager to look after the welfare of the institution. The rooms are sadly in want of repairs. I have expended a large sum for the last 10 years on works that could not be dispensed with. It is now time for others to take an interest in the matter.—Your obedient servant, *Thomas Gillie.*" That letter was enclosed by Mr. Conwell, the inspector, to the secretaries,

with

with the following letter: "I append a letter just received from the teacher of the above schools, pointing out the loss and inconvenience of the want of a recognised manager. I may add that the coadjutor bishop, Right Rev. Dr. Nulty, is anxious that Rev. John Fulham should be recognised instead of Rev. P. Sheridan." The case then presented itself at the office, as a case where the school was without a manager, where the salary of the teacher could not be paid, and where the teacher himself was complaining of the falling-off condition of the school; and on that letter of Mr. Conwell, a noting was made, "Note, Rev. John Fulham, manager, and inform him and inspector." That was on the 23rd of June 1865. Now, in a case of that kind, where a committee fails to discharge its duty, or where trustees fail to discharge their duty, or where the patron of a school vested in the Board fails to discharge his duty, frequently an appointment like that is made by the executive as a provisional appointment, subject, of course, to rectification by the committee, trustees, or patron, as the case might be. However, since that time, the 3rd of June 1865, no reclamation has ever been received from the committee of that school, so that it is to be assumed that they were satisfied with the arrangement.

Mr. P. J. Keenan, c.b.

5 June 1873.

290. And has Mr. Fulham continued to be manager?—He has, and is now manager. In the case of the Ashbourne School, Mr. Fulham reported to the Board that there was "no committee in existence," and upon that statement he was accepted as the manager of that school.

291. Is that all that you wish to say on Mr. Sheridan's case?—Yes.

292. Is there anything else that you wish to add to your former evidence?— I am not aware of anything else.

293. Mr. *Gathorne Hardy*.] How comes it that the notes of the Board in this case of Mr. Sheridan's are not in the Parliamentary Paper before us?—Because the Parliamentary Return, if you refer to the title of it, did not embrace them, and it was a great misfortune that it did not. The Return was for, "Copies of all Minutes of Proceedings, and of all Letters and other Documents referred to in such Minutes, having relation to the Removal from the Office of Manager of National Schools of the Rev. Dr. Keenan," and the other clergymen named; "Of the Names of the Commissioners present at each Meeting of the Board, at which the Decisions referred to in the said Minutes were arrived at; with Lists of the Votes on every said Minute on which the Board divided; and Statement whether the Teachers in each case acknowledged the Authority of the newly recognised Manager, and received the Board's Salaries through him." Now, the only occasion on which there was any Minute in the whole proceedings of Mr. Sheridan's case is, that Minute of the 27th of January 1865, and the only letters referred to in the Minute are those which are given, in the Parliamentary Return, Mr. Conwell's letter and the enclosures. Hence the other letters could not legitimately form part of that Return.

294. Then it appears, as a matter of fact, that from January 1863 to January 1865, a suspended priest remained in the management of the schools referred to? —That is so.

295. And that the secretaries of the National Board received their information with respect to the suspension as early as January 1863?—Yes.

296. In the case of the school which Dr. Keenan held, it was afterwards transferred to a layman as manager?—A layman was subsequently appointed by the trustees, it being at all times competent for the trustees, in the case of a vested school, to appoint whomsoever they like, lay or cleric, as a fit person.

297. In those cases where there is an appointment by the trustees the manager would not hold *ex officio*, would he?—Certainly not.

298. On what ground, then, would it be that Dr. Keenan, if he were not an *ex officio* manager, would he necessarily succeeded, in the view of the Commissioners, by Mr. Macken, the administrator of the parish?—I take it that the Board, when they were removing Dr. Keenan, and considering the question of the appointment of his successor, acting for the best in the interests of the school, thought it their duty to nominate Mr. Macken.

299. But that would be on the ground, would it not, that he was a clerical successor; whereas the school was not necessarily held by a clergyman?—That he was the clerical successor, in the estimation of Dr. Blake, the bishop, and in the apprehension of the Board there was no doubt; but it was not *qua* priest and as clerical successor that he could have a status in a vested school. The words of the letter to Dr. Keenan removing him are these: "The Commissioners have,

Mr.
P. J. Keenan, c.b.

5 June 1873.

have, after mature consideration, resolved upon transferring from you to the Rev. Mr. Macken the management of the Magheral School (to which they appointed you as manager, in 1834, on the ground of your being administrator of the parish) until judgment shall have been pronounced by the proper authority on your appeal."

300. Then, in fact, Dr. Keenan had been appointed; that is, he had been recognised by the Board on the appointment of the trustees or the committee?— I really am not aware precisely how it was that Dr. Keenan, except from the statement contained in the letter, removing him, was appointed in 1834.

301. May I not assume, from these subsequent cases in which the Board referred to the committee for their nomination, that such would be the case in the ordinary course?—Very likely it was so, but I cannot say positively that it was.

302. Now, suppose a clerical manager, who was appointed by a committee not as the priest of a chapel, but in his capacity generally as a resident in the place, then, in such a case, would the suspension of such a clergyman by his ecclesiastical authority be a ground for his being deprived of the management?
—As I understand your question, it supposes a clergyman to be the manager, but not a clergyman having the cure of souls. I think that no such case has ever occurred; within my knowledge, certainly not; and if it did occur, I myself (but this is my own individual opinion only, and must be taken simply for what it is worth) would not regard the rule which banned a suspended clergyman as applying in all its strictness to such a case.

303. Suppose that a clergyman of any denomination holds one school, for instance, as attached to his cure, and that he is manager of some other schools which are not attached to his cure, to which he is appointed by committees irrespective of his position as a clergyman, would his suspension by his ecclesiastical authorities, in the view of the Commissioners, deprive him not only of the one which he held in respect of his cure, but of all of those others which he held irrespectively of that position?—Most certainly; because in that case the clergyman is in the position of the pastor of the people, and the objection that is entertained to the employment of a suspended clergyman as manager of a national school in the parish or district in which he had been officiating would, of course, equally apply to him.

304. Then a clergyman so deprived, even supposing that he were to obtain a decision in an ordinary court of law that his suspension had been invalid, would not receive restitution to his place, as manager of the school, from the Board, unless it was acknowledged by his ecclesiastical superiors?—A case of the kind has never yet come before the Board.

305. May I call your attention to a passage in a letter of the Rev. Dr. Henry's at page 19 of the Parliamentary Return, No. 244; it is the second paragraph in that letter, and I want to know whether that in your view is the rule of the Board: "Mr. O'Keeffe may have appealed to legal tribunals, but that does not alter our position as Commissioners, for it is clear that no legal decision, or any issue that would be sustained in a court of justice, could reinstate him as parish priest contrary to ecclesiastical jurisdiction"?· That proposition, so far as I know, has never been discussed at the Board, and I do not think it is likely that it ever has been. Dr. Henry himself will have the honour of attending the Committee on Monday next, and perhaps he may be able to give more information on the point than is at present possessed by me.

306. *Chairman.*] The object of the question is not to ask you Dr. Henry's opinion, but to ask you whether that particular opinion is embodied in any rule or any transaction of the Board?—No.

307. Mr. *Gathorne Hardy.*] Then may I ask you a question in reference to page 20 of the same Return; you will see that the words which are used in the notice from the secretaries to Mr. O'Keeffe, of his suspension are, "until the suspension referred to shall have been removed or declared invalid by a competent authority"?— Those words followed very much the precedent of Dr. Keenan.

308. You were a party to this decision?—I was.

309. Will you be good enough to tell me what the Board meant by "a competent authority"?— The Board did not, at the moment of drawing up that resolution, define what the competent authority or tribunal might be.

310. Did

SELECT COMMITTEE ON CALLAN SCHOOLS. 39

Mr.
P. J. Keenan, c.b.

5 June 1873.

310. Did they mean a legal authority or an ecclesiastical authority?—The question was never discussed as to the interpretation of those words.

311. Mr. *Whitbread.*] Had those words any definite meaning at all?—They had; but no official interpretation has ever yet been put upon them by the Board in any Minute or in any communication addressed by the Board to any person.

312. Mr. *Gathorne Hardy.*] In the case of Dr. Keenan, in page 5 in Parliamentary Paper, No. 138, can you tell me what "appeal" is referred to in the letter of the secretaries of the Board, where it says, "That the Rev. Mr. Macken has been duly appointed administrator of the parish until the appeal which you have instituted against your suspension shall have been decided;" have you any record what that appeal was, for I do not myself find any trace of it?—In one of the letters of Dr. Keenan there is a reference to an appeal, and that appeal, I take it, is undoubtedly to an ecclesiastical tribunal.

313. I do not find the letter to which it refers; will it be in the correspondence which you have produced to-day what the appeal was?—Yes, I think that a passage in that correspondence will indicate that the appeal was to an ecclesiastical tribunal or authority.

314. Then, in that case, I observe that the secretaries intimate that a decision upon an appeal of that sort would be binding upon the Board?—That it would be an expression of a removal of the suspension, and a declaration of the eligibility of the clergyman again to serve as manager.

315. Dr. *Lyon Playfair.*] I think you gave us some instances where managers were dismissed for wilful violation of the rules of the Board in your evidence on the last occasion?—I did.

316. Were all those cases of dismissal which you gave us, for direct violation of specific rules?—The case of Mr. Malone, of Ballina, is the first that strikes me, and in that case Mr. Malone was dismissed because he gave the use of his school-room for a political banquet; a proceeding which was contrary to an express and declared rule. The next case that strikes me which I referred to, was that of the Rev. Mr. Shannon, parish priest of Gort, who was charged with giving the use of his school-room also for the purposes of a political banquet; but he was removed because he declined to answer the letters of the Board addressed to him for explanation upon the matter. There is no specific rule in our code that if a manager declined to answer the Commissioners' letter within a given time, he will be dismissed; but it was clearly a case in which the Board felt that it was utterly impracticable to carry on business with a gentleman who refused to correspond regularly and respectfully with them.

317. But on the 28th of May 1872, did not Mr. Justice Morris move the Rev. J. Shannon's dismissal "for his defiant violation of the Rules of the Board"?—That notice of motion of Mr. Justice Morris had reference to the breach of a specific rule by the Rev. Mr. Shannon, that specific rule being that the school-room is not to be used for any political purposes.

318. And in those cases of dismissal a parish priest was dismissed, although he held the position *ex officio* as a parish priest?—In the case of the Rev. Mr. Shannon, the case that has just been referred to, he held his position as manager under the nomination of the trustees in three of the cases, Kilmacduagh, Gort male and Gort female. In the cases of the other two schools he held his position as parish priest; how nominated to that position, or how he obtained it, I am not at this moment able to say.

319. But the successor in those dismission cases was not a parish priest; in the dismission cases which you gave us, where a parish priest was dismissed, his successor was not then holding the office of a parish priest when succeeding him, was he?—In the case of Mr. Madden, of Ballina, the successor, although a clergyman, was not a parish priest. In the case of Gort there was an interval, during which no manager was appointed, and ultimately Mr. Sheridan was restored to his position as manager.

320. If the manager held his position *ex officio* as parish priest, how could you dismiss a manager holding an *ex officio* position?—I think that you are attaching to the words "*ex officio*" a much stronger force than I intended to apply to them; for your question appears to me to indicate the interpretation of *ex officio* as applied to the management of schools would be, that a manager was irremoveable; but I have all along endeavoured to convey to the

0.93.   E 4   Committee

Mr.
P. J. Keenan, C.B.

5 June 1873.

Committee not only my own opinion, but the practice of the Board; that the Board felt themselves at all times at perfect liberty to remove a manager for sufficient cause; therefore that extreme interpretation of the words "*ex officio*" cannot be applied in my opinion.

321. You rather intend the meaning of *ex officio* to be a clerical manager, I suppose?—I rather intend the meaning of *ex officio* to be simply this, that if A., being a manager, is the parish priest of a certain place, and he is removed to some other place, or dies, and B. steps in as his successor in the parish, B. stepping in as his successor, has a claim from his position as priest to be manager.

322. A general claim?—A general claim.

323. Not an *ex officio* claim?—Not in the sense in which *ex officio* would imply, that he would have an absolute right to the position and he utterly irremovable.

324. I think you have given us an instance to-day where a parish priest was substituted by a medical man, where the committee desired it?—In the case of the Magheral School, that was a school under trustees.

325. Let us go now to the case of Mr. O'Keeffe. Was his dismissal from the male and female Callan schools on account of any direct violation of the rules of the Board?—It was simply because he was a suspended priest, and because it was understood at the Board from the oldest times (I gave an instance to-day which happened in 1842), that a suspended priest was not a proper person to be the manager of a school.

326. Of any school whatever?—Of any school over which he was appointed when a priest, having the cure of souls in the parish.

327. But the male and female Callan school was a school of a very old date, was it not?—Of very old date.

328. And could the committee of the school, if it had wished, have appointed Robert O'Keeffe, whether he was a parish priest or not, as the manager?—They could have appointed anybody they chose.

329. Under what circumstances do you consider that that school necessarily was deprived of Mr. O'Keeffe's services, if the committee could have nominated whom they liked?—Because, as think I observed in substance, a few minutes ago, the Rev. Mr. O'Keeffe was the pastor having the charge of the souls of the Roman Catholic population of the parish of Callan, and in the face of the people of Callan he was, according to the certificate of his bishop, a suspended priest, and therefore, in the opinion of the Board, ineligible for the office of manager in his parish.

330. Even in a school which was managed by a committee, and which was not necessarily a clerical school?—Yes.

331. That is the view of the Board, is it?—The action of the Board demonstrates it, for he was removed from those schools, as from the others.

332. Then, in addition to your general rule of dismissing managers for direct violation of rules, you also would dismiss from a school managed by a committee, any manager if the bishop tells you that he is suspended, or if the Presbytery tell you that he is suspended?—Yes; in the case of a school managed by a committee, and the clergyman having to deal with the school being a clergyman having the cure of souls in the parish or district, whether in connection with the Presbyterian General Assembly, or the Roman Catholic, or any other church.

333. And supposing that the next day the committee were to nominate Robert O'Keeffe as manager of such a school independently altogether of his position as a clergyman, would your rules not permit such a nomination as a proper and legal nomination?—The question of the fitness of the person nominated by the committee is at all times considered; if such a person as that were nominated by the committee, the question of fitness would at once direct inquiry as to the subject of his suspension; and I think that if it appeared to the Board that the person so nominated was a priest suspended, still living in the parish of which he had been the pastor, the Board would not accept him as manager.

334. Even supposing that he had not been suspended for any immorality or for any crime, but from some mere ecclesiastical censure?—Into the cause of the suspension the Board has never yet made inquiry, and, as I think I observed on the last occasion, the Board, in Mr. Wilson's case, deliberately refused to entertain the question of the cause of the suspension.

335. Then I understand that your term "fitness" in such a case as that simply means that you would consider that a local committee had not the power to appoint any person who had come under ecclesiastical censure, and who was suspended?—What I mean by my answer as regards fitness, I may say briefly

briefly is this: if the person proposed be a clergyman and he is put forward at a moment when he is in a degraded position, the Board would naturally say, "Such a person as that is not the person to command the confidence of the people, and therefore he is unfit for the moment to act as manager of the school."

Mr.
P. J. Keenan, c.b.

6 June 1873.

336. In the case of Dr. Keenan, where the Committee were persistent and declined to take your recommendation of the administrator of the parish, you ultimately gave way and allowed the Committee to nominate a layman?—At the time that the Board refused to listen to the appeal of certain members of the Committee, the Board I think observed that the Committee was divided in opinion, but when the Board assented to the recommendation of the Committee the Committee were unanimous in their view, and I perceive a very great distinction in the position of the case having regard to the unanimity in the one case and the known want of unanimity in the other.

337. *Chairman.*] If the appointment of any particular manager, whether clergyman or layman, would be a cause of discord in the parish, would that operate with the Commissioners in considering his fitness? Decidedly.

338. Dr. *Lyon Playfair.*] You consider that under the general term "fitness"? —A person whose presence in a National School is an emblem of strife or discord, we should, I think, consider to be anything but a suitable person to be the manager of schools.

339. In all those cases of clerical managers who were suspended, is it not the case that with one exception the inquiry was a very long and protracted one before the Board finally decided in the matter?—The best way to answer your question, I suppose, is to recapitulate the cases. In the case of Dr. Keenan the question of his suspension was proposed to them as a matter for special consideration in Dr. Blake's letter of the 8th of May. The previous correspondence, although from it could be gathered the fact that Dr. Keenan had been suspended, had special reference to charges against Mr. Grant the teacher, and the Board in the first instance dealt with that portion of the previous correspondence only. The interval that elapsed up to the final determination of the case was from the 8th of May to the 5th of June, the date of the removal of the manager.

340. As a matter of fact, did not the whole correspondence with reference to Dr. Keenan's case, commence on the 2nd February 1845, and terminate in 1847? —The first part of the correspondence, as I have already more than once observed, had special reference to the charges brought against Mr. Grant. Incidentally, the bishop and the complainant, Mr. Macken, referred to the position that Dr. Keenan occupied. For the moment, Dr. Blake, however, did not specifically say, until he said it in his letter of the 8th of May, that the Rev. Mr. Keenan was a suspended clergyman.

341. But did he not say on the 8th of May 1845, "I did not think it necessary to render an account of my reasons for suspending the Rev. John Keenan"? —Yes.

342. And from then up to 1847 the correspondence continued upon this case?—So far as the Rev. Dr. Keenan is concerned, his removal under the order of the 5th of June 1845 was final.

343. When was the first application for the removal of the Rev. John Keenan? —It was contained in Mr. Macken's letter, dated the 12th January 1845, but only as an incidental matter. That letter particularly conveyed a complaint against the teacher, Mr. Grant; and the complaint was again referred to in the letter of the bishop; that is the letter of the 22nd of February, in which he said, "I beg also to observe that as the Rev. J. Macken is now the approved Roman Catholic administrator of the spiritual or religious concerns of the Catholic population of Anaghlone and Drumballaroney parish, in which Magheral is situated, he, in my humble opinion, would be the fittest person to be the patron of the school." But that was incidental to the declaration of what he said, a painful but imperative sense of duty compelled him to express, namely, his deliberate conviction that Mr. Grant was not a suitable person to be the teacher of the school.

344. And as a matter of fact, Dr. Keenan remained as manager of the school for a considerable time?—He remained as manager of the school until the 5th June.

345. Till then, so far as you were concerned; and for sometime afterwards, so far as you were not concerned?—Subsequently he exercised very considerable influence over the affairs of the school, without having any official status in it.

0.93.   F   The

Mr.
P. J. Keenan, C.B.
5 June 1873.

The second case is that of Mr. Wilson. The interval in Mr. Wilson's case was only about a month. In the case of Mr. O'Farrell, it was from the 10th of July 1862 to the 22nd of August of the same year. And in the case of Mr. Sheridan, it was longer than would appear from the documents in the Parliamentary Paper, for it began in January 1863, and terminated, as stated in the Parliamentary Paper, on the 27th of January 1865. I explained, however, that in the case of the Rev. Mr. Sheridan, the matter came before the Board only on one occasion, and that was the 27th of January 1865. The long interval that preceded the communication of the suspension by the Rev. Mr. Fulham, and the proceedings of the 27th of January 1865, was partly, I am quite certain, owing to some oversight on the part of the person having charge of Mr. Fulham's letter in the office.

346. In Mr. O'Keeffe's case the action of dismissal was tolerably rapid after you received information of his suspension, was it not?—I think the letter of the inspector was dated the 29th of November 1871, and we dismissed Mr. O'Keeffe on the 23rd of April 1872. The matter, however, was not brought under the consideration of the Board until the 9th of April.

347. I want to draw your attention to a passage which I find here in the Report of the Royal Commission upon primary education in Ireland, and which is contained in a letter from the prelates of Ireland to the Home Secretary, of date 14th of January 1866; it is signed by Cardinal Cullen and the Irish prelates. "The pastoral authority of the clergyman is ignored, and he himself may be excluded from every non-vested school; the manager of the non-vested school, may have any religious instruction he pleases, or none at all." Would you consider from that, that the Roman Catholic prelates understand that any priest can be appointed *ex officio* in a school, because he is parish priest?—I think I tried to explain to-day before, that that expression "*ex officio*" seems to be taken in your question in a much wider sense than I intended it.

348. You do not understand "*ex officio*" in the true technical sense?—No, certainly not; and in regard to the passage that you have just quoted, it is perfectly true that in the case of non-vested schools the clergy have not, unless they are managers, the right to rule the school and to take part in its proceedings, or to interfere with the religious instruction of the pupils.

349. But here the prelates say, that the pastoral authority of the clergyman is ignored; they do not understand that the parish priest *ex officio*, and as priest, will become manager of a non-vested school?—Undoubtedly a parish priest has control and influence only in those schools over which he has been formally recognised by the Board as manager.

350. *The O'Conor Don.*] I will ask you some questions on what Dr. Playfair has just been asking you about, with respect to the dates at which the notification of suspension was made and acted upon by the Board. Now with respect to Dr. Blake's first letter of the 22nd of February, is there one single word in it about Dr. Keenan?—No, there is no reference to him by name.

351. There is therefore no formal statement made to the Board, that Dr. Keenan was suspended?—None in that letter; at the same time, no one can read the letter without seeing that it is implied.

352. Although, therefore, the removal of Dr. Keenan from ecclesiastical jurisdiction in that parish might be implied from the statement that Mr. Macken was the authorised administrator, it appears that the Board in that case considered that there was no formal statement made to them that Dr. Keenan was suspended, but that the letter dealt chiefly with complaints against the teacher, and they consequently ordered inquiry into that?—As I was not a member of the Board at the time, I of course cannot tell what passed at the Board, or what were the views of the Commissioners engaged upon the case; but judging from the documents which I have had under consideration, I am convinced that in the whole of that early correspondence, the Board had reference simply to the complaint against Mr. Grant.

353. And the first distinct statement made to the Board in which it is stated by the Bishop, that Dr. Keenan is suspended, was brought before the meeting of the Board on the 22nd of May, not on the 8th of May, as would be implied by the question of Dr. Lyon Playfair?—The 22nd of May was the first date on which it was brought before the Board.

354. The subject of Dr. Keenan's suspension was brought formally before the Board for the first time on the 22nd of May?—Yes.

355. And

SELECT COMMITTEE ON CALLAN SCHOOLS. 43

Mr.
P. J. Kernan, c.b.

5 June 1873.

355. And his removal from the managership of the school was on the 5th of June?—It was by the Board's order of the 5th of June.

356. Was any explanation asked of him when the communication of his suspension was made to the Board?—None.

357. Was no reference made to him?—None.

358. He was not informed that the Board were about to remove him?—Certainly not.

359. Now, with regard to Mr. Wilson's case, you have already stated that the time there was very short?—Yes.

360. No reference was made to him?—None whatever.

361. And no explanation was asked?—No.

362. Now, with respect to Mr. Farrell, the first communication made to the Board by Dr. Kilduff as to the suspension of Mr. O'Farrell was of what date?—The first communication from the Bishop was dated the 16th of August 1862.

363. And Mr. O'Farrell was removed from the managership on the 22nd of August?—Yes.

364. Without any reference being made to him, or an explanation being asked?—None whatever was made or asked.

365. With respect to the case of Mr. Sheridan, are the Committee distinctly to understand that that case was never brought before the Board in its corporate capacity until the 27th of January 1865?—Not until that day.

366. The proceedings up to that time were proceedings of the secretaries, and what you call the office?—Yes, the routine.

367. Mr. *Gathorne Hardy*.] But I understood you to say that the case ought to have been brought before the Board sooner?—I do not like to offer an opinion upon the procedure at a period that I myself had nothing to say to.

368. *The O'Conor Don*.] It appears by these Papers that on the 27th January, the first occasion on which this case was brought before the Board, the Board were informed that the majority of the committee of management were in favour of the continuance of the suspended priest as manager of the school?—They were by the Inspector, Mr. Conwell.

369. In spite of that fact, and although they knew that the committee of management were in favour of his continuance, they immediately ordered his removal?—They did.

370. And in the case that you quoted to-day with regard to Mr. Fisher, immediately that the announcement was made to the Board that he was a suspended clergyman, he also was removed?—He was.

371. And no application was made to him in the first instance, and no notice was taken of his complaints when they were afterwards made?—None.

372. I suppose in quoting these precedents which have been alluded to, the Committee are not to understand that you mean to imply that they are in all the details similar either to each other or to the O'Keeffe case?—Certainly not.

373. They have been referred to as showing that in certain important points relating to clerical management, there seems to have been uniformity of practice?—Yes.

374. Am I right in assuming that they are quoted as showing uniformity of practice with respect to clerical managers in the following points?—First, that on an official formal statement by the recognised ecclesiastical authority of any church or religious body that a clerical manager was suspended by them, that manager was at once suspended from his position of management of a school?—That he was removed is my statement.

375. With as little delay as was consistent with the necessities of the case?—So far as the Board appear to me to be concerned, it was done at once, that is, as soon as they had an opportunity of deliberating upon the case.

376. In the second place, that he was removed without any communication being addressed to him before removal?—Invariably so.

377. And without any explanation being asked of him?—Invariably.

378. And that in all the cases of non-vested schools without school committees, the clerical successor was appointed to succeed him?—Yes.

379. And I suppose that these cases are referred to also as showing that clerical succession was recognised in cases of suspension as well as in cases of death, and removal as mentioned in the rules?—Yes.

380. I want to ask you some questions with reference to this *ex officio* management.

Mr. P. J. Keenan, C.B.
5 June 1873.

management. When you state that there are such persons as *ex officio* clerical managers, you do not mean that every parish priest of a parish has, *ex officio*, the right to be manager of the school in that parish?—I have endeavoured to explain to Dr. Lyon Playfair that no such opinion has ever entered my mind.

381. What you mean to convey is that there are certain managers of schools in Ireland, who have been appointed the managers because they were the parish priests, and so far *ex officio*, appointed on account of their office?—On account of their office in succession to some predecessor in the same office.

382. And so far as that is concerned, that there are such persons as *ex officio* clerical managers?—So far, under the limits of that answer which I have just given.

383. You do not mean to convey that there are *ex officio* clerical managers of schools in the same way as there are *ex officio* members of the Poor Law Board?—Certainly not, because every magistrate, in virtue of his office, is a member of a poor law board; but being a clergyman you are not a manager, simply because you are a clergyman.

384. Was not the co-operation of the clergy of all denominations always sought for from the commencement of the establishment of a system of national education in Ireland?—It was always courted, and always appreciated.

385. And are not a considerable number of the schools, to all intents and purposes, parochial schools?—The Royal Commission observed upon that point, I remember, that a very considerable proportion of the non-vested schools of the country are in reality as much secured for the purposes of public education as are the schools which are vested in trustees, or in the Board in its corporate capacity. The proportion is, I think, 52 per cent. of the non-vested schools, which may be regarded as parochial, that is, as being part of the parochial or ecclesiastical arrangements.

386. And has it not been the practice of the Board with respect to these parochial schools to recognise the clergyman for the time being as the manager?—Yes, if he is the successor of a clergyman who had the management of the schools. If the clergyman himself is the applicant he is recognised as being a fit and suitable person as an applicant, but not because he is a clergyman; and when he dies or is removed, and the school is absolutely and undoubtedly a parochial school, his successor will step in and take the place.

387. *Chairman.*] Supposing him to be fit?—The question of fitness is never omitted from the consideration of the Board.

388. *The O'Conor Don.*] And even if the applicant, the founder of the school, happens to come under ecclesiastical censure, he is removed from the school, and his clerical successor appointed?—Yes. In the case of Mr. Wilson, the school was founded by Mr. Wilson himself, but Dr. Templeton, his clerical successor, obtained the management.

389. Now, coming to Father O'Keeffe's case, was not Father O'Keeffe the clerical manager of the two schools which are not under a committee?—Yes; of Coolagh and Newtown.

390. He became the manager of them immediately on his coming to the parish, and without any formal application on his part to be manager?—The only document which I have seen on the subject (and I believe no other document exists) is, that which I quoted on the last occasion; it was a statement by the Reverend Mr. Rowan his predecessor, that he resigned, as Mr. O'Keeffe had come to the place as parish priest.

391. With respect to two schools, Callan male and female, which are under the committee, have not the successive priests of the parish been always nominated as managers of those schools?—I apprehend that such was the case; but not always because of the nomination of the committee. When the school became connected with the Board first, the Reverend Mr. Mullens was the parish priest; he was the applicant on the part of the committee, and was accepted therefore as manager; his successor was the Reverend Mr. Salmon, who obtained the management of the school by an oversight in the office, without any nomination from the committee, and continued down to the time of his death to enjoy the position; but as a matter of course he must have had the approbation of the committee, for they never remonstrated with the Board against his appointment or continuance as manager. Then in the case

of

Mr.
P. J. Keenan, c.b.

5 June 1873.

of Mr. Rowan the nomination was made by the committee, and of course again, as you are aware, in the case of Mr. O'Keeffe it was so.

392. As a matter of fact, these schools from the first time that they were attached to the National Board were under the management of the successive parish priests of Callan?—That is so.

393. And the nomination of Mr. O'Keeffe to the management was obtained by him in his capacity as parish priest?—Certainly. "We request you will have the goodness to appoint the Reverend Robert O'Keeffe, p.p., Manager of the Male and Female Schools, at Callan, County Kilkenny." Those are the words of the Callan School committee.

394. Has not the whole contention of Mr. O'Keeffe, first and last, been, that he is parish priest of Callan still?—He maintains to this day that he is.

395. And he complains of having been removed from this managership, and from his other position, he being still the parish priest?—No formal complaint has ever been received by the Board from Mr. O'Keeffe as to his removal, and the only expression of his disapprobation of the conduct of the Board in removing him, is that contained in those letters where he signs himself "Robert O'Keeffe, p.p., *malgré vos dents*," Robert O'Keeffe, p.p., "Notwithstanding your suspension."

396. Regarding him in the light of a clerical manager, was not the action of the Board quite in accordance with their invariable rule with respect to clerical managers under suspension?—That is the decided opinion of the Board.

397. I think you have stated already, that the Board could not recognise a suspended clerical manager, even if the committee nominated him for the management of a school?—Supposing the school to be in the parish of which he had previously been the recognised clergyman in full enjoyment of his position as such, I think they would not recognise him.

398. And that is proved in the case of Dr. Keenan, and also in the case of Mr. Sheridan, where the committees supported the suspended clergymen?—Yes.

399. Now it has been said, as you are aware, that the Board acted in obedience to Cardinal Cullen in this matter; had the Board any communication whatever with Cardinal Cullen?—The Board had no communication, direct or indirect, not only on that, but on any other occasion with Cardinal Cullen.

400. The action of the Board was upon the certificate of the bishop of the diocese?—Entirely so.

401. If the Board had acted upon the proposal of Judge Morris to refer to Mr. O'Keeffe for an explanation, would they not have adopted an unusual proceeding, quite opposed to the precedents?—It would have been quite new in the procedure of the Board.

402. And was not the desire of the majority of the Board a *bonâ fide* desire to act impartially, and in accordance with what they believed was the rule as laid down by precedents?—Quite so.

403. After the removal of Mr. O'Keeffe from the management of the schools, were they conducted in accordance with the rules of the Board?—No, they were not. Our inspector was refused admission to the Callan Schools, and the recognised manager was also refused admission.

404. The subsequent action of the Board therefore in striking these schools off the roll became a necessity?—Certainly; the Commissioners had no control over them; they had no quarterly returns of the attendance of the pupils; they had no annual statistics to present to Parliament in connection with them; they had no evidence that any of their rules were observed, inasmuch as their inspector had not the *entrée* to the schools; and, according to the invariable practice of the Board, when the rules of the Board cannot be or are not carried out, the schools are struck off. In every annual Report to Parliament there is a list of the schools which have been struck off during the year, with the causes stated; showing that the Board are from time to time striking schools off for various causes, all causes having relation to a breach of rule, or to a want of conformity with the rules of the Board.

405. Now, with respect to the infant school at Callan, you are aware that was in a different position from the other four schools, Mr. O'Keeffe having been the applicant regarding that infant school?—Yes.

406. Was not a portion of that school situated in the very building of the schools under the committee?—It was.

407. And,

Mr.
J. Kernan, c.s.
5 June 1873.

407. And, although Mr. O'Keeffe was the founder and applicant, in regard to that school, was it possible to separate it from the previously existing schools in respect to managership?—No, it was impossible.

408. Was it not clearly a school established by him in his capacity as parish priest and manager of the other schools?—In his original application he subscribed himself "Robert O'Keeffe, P.P.," and it was understood that he made the application in his position as parish priest.

409. Under any circumstances, could you have recognised two district forms of management of these schools, the National Female School and the Infant School; that is to say, one manager for one school, and another manager for the other school?—Well, it would be quite possible for anybody else to have been the manager of that Infant School.

410. Without trenching upon the rights of the committee, would it be possible?—Of course, I assume that it would be with the entire concurrence of the committee.

411. But without the concurrence of the committee, you could not have appointed a distinct manager to the Infant School?—The committee could at any time have exercised its right to remove whoever might be the person occupying that portion of the Infant School which was part of the premises under their own control.

412. You were asked on the last day a question with respect to the Camus-Juxta-Mourne School; Dr. Alexander, after he became Bishop of Derry, was continued as the manager of that school; and, as I understand that case, the successor to Dr. Alexander had a conscientious objection to become the manager of the school?—At first.

413. And I suppose the proceeding was to appoint Dr. Alexander as bishop manager of the school?—No; Dr. Alexander had, before the appointment of the Reverend Mr. Wilson to the rectorship of the parish of Camus-Juxta-Mourne, been the rector himself; when he became bishop, he continued to act as manager of the school, inasmuch as his successor, the Reverend Mr. Wilson had, it would appear some conscientious scruple about attaching himself to the national system; but in the course of time the bishop permitted a curate, the Reverend Mr. Orr, to undertake the management; and, as I observed on the former occasion, the Reverend Mr. Wilson is now acting as manager.

414. So that, in that case, as soon as the clerical successor in the parish was willing to undertake the management, it was handed over to him?—Yes. I have this morning got the letter containing the resignation of the bishop, dated 14th October 1871: "Gentlemen,—I hereby resign the office of Patron or Superintendent of the Parochial National School, Strabane, Co. Tyrone.—Yours respectfully, *William Derry*." And then upon that resignation, although there is no nomination, you observe, of a successor in it, the Rev. Mr. Wilson was noted as patron, and Mr. Orr continued as correspondent.

415. So that, practically, that case shows the recognition of clerical succession as much as any other?—I think so.

416. With respect to the removal of clerical managers for breach of rules, in such cases you have asked for an explanation before you removed the manager, have you not?—Yes, as far as my knowledge goes, invariably. In the case of Mr. Shannon, his removal was ordered because, after we had referred to him for explanation, he failed to reply to our communication.

417. In fact you feel bound, before removing him for a breach of your own rules, to state the case against him, in the first instance, and to ask him for an explanation?—We have always felt ourselves so bound, and have acted upon that.

418. Because that was a subject upon which you could enter, and examine the validity of his answer?—Yes.

419. You do not know a single instance in which, in the case of a suspension, an application was made to the person reported as suspended for an explanation?—In no single instance has there ever been an application of that sort made.

420. *Chairman*.] The practice has been to take the certificate of the ecclesiastical superior?—To take the certificate of the ecclesiastical superior as definite.

421. Mr. *Cross*.] You view it in this way, that when you have the certificate of the ecclesiastical superior, the function of the National Board becomes purely ministerial?—Purely ministerial.

422. Upon

Mr.
P. J. Keenan, c.b.

5 June 1873.

422. Upon this purely ministerial removal, of course the Board has to be called into action before the person suspended can be removed?—Of course.

423. But upon the purely ministerial removal by the Board, we will assume that the successor is nominated by the same person upon whose certificate the party suspended has been removed from his position as manager; do you then inquire into his fitness?—Certainly.

424. You do not take the certificate of the ecclesiastical superior with reference to the fitness upon appointment as sufficient?—The certificate of an ecclesiastical superior upon the appointment of a clergyman to be the manager of a school would very naturally be treated with such respect as to be regarded as most influential in determining the case.

425. But do you take the nomination of the successor by the ecclesiastical superior as of such weight as to make the function of the Board also ministerial in making the appointment?—No

426. In the case of Mr. O'Farrell, if you look at page 18, Letter No. 4, you will see that in the middle paragraph it is stated that "the Rev. Mr. O'Farrell has performed no ecclesiastical duties for several years past"?—Yes, I observe that.

427. Do you know whether there was any communication made to the Board during these several years past with reference to Mr. O'Farrell not having performed any ecclesiastical duties?—I am not aware; I have not seen any statement that would lead me to think so.

428. Have you made any search in the records of the National Board to see whether any complaint had been made with regard to Mr. O'Farrell during those years?—No such particular inquiry has been directed in reference to Mr. O'Farrell, but I did direct immediately after the examination which I underwent upon the last occasion, an examination into all the documents relating to these four cases preceding and subsequent to the removal of the late manager, and no document containing any such complaint as that which you refer to is amongst the papers sent to me.

429. But it is stated that Mr. O'Farrell has performed no ecclesiastical duties for several years past. Can you say whether that was in consequence of suspension by his ecclesiastical superior or not?—I cannot.

430. Could you not have further search made to ascertain whether it was not known to the Board many years before this, that Mr. O'Farrell had been suspended from his ecclesiastical functions?—I will have that search made.

431. And I should like to direct your attention in making those inquiries to this; could you endeavour to find out whether some complaint had not been made; I think about the year 1855 or 1857 in regard to the female school which led to this intimation being given?—I will make inquiries about that.

432. Could you furnish the Committee with any correspondence which had taken place relating to these Annaduff Schools previously to the correspondence which led to Mr. O'Farrell's removal?—With pleasure.

433. Do you know when he was appointed?—No.

434. Now with regard to the nomination of clerical successors, are you aware that somewhere about the year 1857 there was some complaint made with reference to the action of the Inspectors relative to the appointment of clerical successors?—I should be speaking from recollection.

435. Would you be good enough to furnish the Committee with certain circulars issued by the National Board, dated 16th March and 27th of July 1857, upon the subject of clerical succession?—I shall.

436. Do you know whether there has been any alteration in the practice of the National Board with regard to taking down the votes upon the questions which are brought before them?—I do not know that; I can only speak from my own experience.

437. At the present time are the names taken down when there is a division?—At the present time the form, so far as I have observed it, since I first had the honour of a seat at the Board, is that the secretary reads out the names of the Commissioners present in the order of their seniority, and each Commissioner answers affirmatively or negatively, as the case may be, and the names of those voted *pro* or *con.* are recorded in the Minutes.

438. Has that always been so?—I can only answer for the practice during the time I have been a member of the Board; I could tell you, as a matter

Mr.
P. J. Keenan, c.b.

5 June 1873.

of fact from my perusal of the Minutes, that such and such divisions took place; but whether they have all been taken in a certain manner, I could not say.

439. Will you make inquiries whether the practice was changed about the year 1852, and whether previously to that time the divisions were noted?—Judge Longfield, who has been a Commissioner since 1853, and who possesses complete mastery of the procedure of the Board, tells me that the divisions were not in the olden time registered as they now are, and that when a member of the Board dissented from the views of the majority, he requested his dissent to be recorded upon the Minutes.

440. If he liked?—If he liked; and I myself can add from a perusal of the Minutes that dissents are to be met with from time to time.

441. With regard to that memorial which has been presented to this Committee, was that memorial ever brought forward befor the Board?—Never.

442. It was never put upon the agenda paper?—That memorial never was.

443. Was not that memorial brought before the Board, and the consideration of it adjourned?—A proposal was made by one of the Commissioners, Dr. Henry, who will have the honour of appearing before the Committee, at a meeting of the Board, that a resolution in the general sense of the memorial should be adopted by the Board.

444. At what date was that?—Upon the 6th of May; but immediately that it was observed that he was out of order in making such a proposal without having given previous notice of it, he simply gave notice of his motion for the following Monday, and in the meantime the House of Commons had determined upon appointing this Committee and of course it became unnecessary to pursue that resolution.

445. This matter about the resolution was to have been discussed the week after the 6th?—Dr. Henry's motion was to have been discussed upon the 12th.

446. But in the meantime this motion had been made in the House of Commons, and then this notice of motion of Dr. Henry was dropped?—It was.

447. When were the signatures put to this memorial?—As I mentioned to-day, I signed it upon the 5th, and the other signatures were either before or after me.

448. Was it signed by the other Commissioners?—It was signed by 13 of the Commissioners.

449. Mr. *Bourke*.] Will you just take the paper of precedents in your hand and look at page 3; at the head of the page you will find the words " vested in trustees;" there was a committee there as well, was there not?—A committee, the constitution of which I explained to-day, more indeed from conjecture than from positive knowledge. It was, I think, a committee in aid of the trustees, having reference to the finances and general working of the school, but not a committee recognised by the Board in the technical sense of the word.

450. Was it a committee in the same sense as the word " committee " is used in the other cases?—No, the trustees were the only persons extra to the manager himself recognised by the Board; that committee was an entirely extra official one.

451. Was the committee in Dr. Keenan's case different from other committees?—Entirely.

452. They had different legal rights?—They had no rights as far as the Board was concerned; the Board recognised the trustees only.

453. Did they recognise the committee as well?—No; no official power was given to the committee.

454. Now with reference to the next point, " Non-vested under a committee;" that is a correct description of the schools in Mr. Wilson's case, is it not?—Yes, that is so.

455. Whom do the schools belong to?—Mr. Wilson himself was the original founder of the schools.

456. They were vested in the manager, in fact?—They were part of the property of the congregation of which he was the minister, he himself being the representative of the congregation as minister.

457. Now take the next one, Mr. O'Farrell's case; is it a correct description

to

SELECT COMMITTEE ON CALLAN SCHOOLS. 49

Mr.
P. J. Keenan, c.b.

5 June 1873.

to say non-vested; was there no committee there?—There was no committee there.

458. In the case of Mr. Sheridan, I think it is incorrect to say that there was no committee?—It says, "Ratoath non-vested, under a committee;" that is right, as it is stated there.

459. It is stated also "non-vested, no committee;" is that correct?—That is correct, according to the statement of Mr. Fulham as regards the Ashbourne school; previously it had been understood at the office that there was no committee, but Mr. Fulham announced that the committee had ceased to exist.

460. It is now correct to say that there is no committee?—It is now correct.

461. Now with regard to the action of the Poor Law Commissioners upon Mr. O'Keeffe's case, was the action of the Poor Law Commissioners ever mentioned at the National Board?—I rather think it was referred to in an incidental way during the discussion of Mr. O'Keeffe's case.

462. Are any of the members of the National Board also members of the Poor Law Commission?—No.

463. Do you recollect whether the action which had been taken by the Poor Law Commissioners was alluded to at all before the Board?—I think only in an incidental way, but certainly the action of the Poor Law Commissioners in the case had no influence whatever upon the Board in the determination of the issue.

464. But it was mentioned?—I cannot say positively, but I rather think it was; I think some member of the Board did in a passing way make some allusion to it, and I also think that some other member, when that passing allusion was made, objected to the introduction of any reference to the action of the Poor Law Commissioners.

465. In Dr. Keenan's case there was no doubt at all with reference to the legality of the suspension, was there?—I can offer no opinion upon that point.

466. There was no doubt mentioned at the Board?—In no cases has any doubt been expressed with reference to the validity of the suspension, as to its operating in an ecclesiastical sense.

467. To make it legal it must be valid, must it not?—The legal recognition of these suspensions is a question which may be for some other tribunal.

468. Was not the validity or the legality of the suspension of Mr. O'Keeffe specifically and pointedly brought before the notice of the Board?—Some of the members of the Board pointedly referred to it.

469. Was it not a matter of discussion for a long time at the Board?—Certainly not; the majority of the Board never entered into the question of its validity; they simply dealt with the suspension as certified by the bishop.

470. But with reference to the validity of the suspension, was it as a fact mentioned at the Board?—By some members of the Board it was urged as an important point.

471. Did you read Mr. Justice Lawson's letter?—I did.

472. Do you not recollect that he says in that letter that the pleadings in the case of O'Keeffe *versus* Cullen, were mentioned and brought before the Board?—One of the members of the Board drew from his pocket a large paper, and read in the course of his argument against the views of the majority of the Board, a few extracts, which I suppose were the pleadings.

473. And therefore the question of the legality of the suspension of Mr. O'Keeffe was brought prominently before the Board?—I must simply repeat what I have already stated, namely, that this question of the suspension of Mr. O'Keeffe as the subject of litigation in a court of law, was mentioned by some members of the Board.

474. Was any reference to any fact of that kind, as far as you know, ever brought before the notice of the Board in the other precedents which you have mentioned?—I cannot say, as I have had no experience upon the Board, I am happy to say, in other cases.

475. Could you say whether you have been able to find in any proceeding which you have looked at, whether a question of that kind was ever raised at the Board, when a case of suspension was before the Board?—I have never seen any reference to such a question in any of the Minutes on the cases, even in the

Mr.
P. J. Keenan, c.s.

6 June 1873.

case of Mr. O'Keeffe, and I should add there is no record of the speeches of individual members.

476. You recollect conversations about the case of Mr. O'Keeffe?—I recollect various conversations.

477. So far as you have been a member of the Board, do you recollect any case in which a question of the kind has been brought forward?—The case of Mr. O'Keeffe is the only one which has been brought forward since my connection with the Board as a Commissioner.

478. Have you any reason to believe that there has been in any of the cases which you have mentioned as precedents, any discussion with reference to the legality of a suspension?—I cannot form any opinion upon that matter; I have no knowledge whatever upon the point.

479. What is your opinion upon the point?—I have no objection to give my opinion. In the case of Mr. Wilson; I see that Mr. Wilson threatened legal proceedings; I daresay that, very likely, was debated at the Board, and in the face of that the Board decided to remove him.

480. You say the Board generally acknowledge the ecclesiastical superiors of the various clergy?—Yes, in the case of suspension.

481. In the case of the suspension of a Presbyterian minister, who does the Board recognise as his ecclesiastical superior?—I am really not quite competent to pronounce an opinion; I have had no experience of a Presbyterian case. In the first case, namely, that of Mr. Fisher, which I brought under the notice of the Committee to-day, the Rev. Dr. Henry attested as to what happened at the Presbytery at Armagh; and also what happened at the General Assembly at Belfast.

482. But Mr. Wilson's case never did come before the General Assembly?—I cannot say. As I said to-day, a letter of the Rev. Mr. Templeton has been found, in which the deposition of Mr. Wilson is referred to, but my opinion is that there might have been some other document which has not been found, which contains a representation of the fact that Mr. Wilson had been suspended by the Magherafelt Presbytery.

483. Mr. *Whitbread.*] I want just to clear up one of these rules relating to the management of national schools, which seems to me to involve a little confusion; it is Rule 4: "The patron has the right of nominating any fit person to act as his representative in the local management of the school, such representative to be designated the 'local manager;' the patron may at any time resume the direct management of the school, or appoint another local manager;" what is the meaning of the word "appoint"?—That is to say, remove the manager be had previously appointed, and appoint a new one.

484. Had he any power of appointing a new one?—"Nomination" would be the more appropriate word.

485. But we have got already into some confusion by using these two words as if they meant the same thing; as I understand, the committee having the same power as the patron, the only authority that the patron or committee have in relation to the manager is to nominate a person for the approval of the Board? —Quite so: "nominate" would be a better word to employ in that rule.

486. "Nomination" is the word which conveys the sense I have just ascribed to it, but the word "appointed" has no reference at all to the power of the patron?—It would certainly be an improvement in that rule, if, instead of the word "appoint," "nominate" were substituted.

487. Then upon that other point of *ex officio* succession, am I right in interpreting the rules and the practice of the Board to be this, simply that where A. being a parish priest of a parish is removed to another parish, having been the manager of schools in the first parish, B. his successor, is recognised by the Board as the local manager unless there is some reason against him?—Yes, if the new clergyman, B., the successor, applies for the management, unless there is something against him the Board would at once accept him. At the same time, if the preceding clergyman were in some other parish, a communication would be made to him, to intimate that an application had been made by the Board, and that he had been recognised as his successor.

488. That is the whole extent to which there is any *ex officio* succession?— Practically, that is the full extent of it.

489. *Chairman.*] What I understand you to say is, that for the appointment
· of

of manager two things are necessary, nomination by the local authority, and recognition by the Board?—Exactly.

490. That where a clergyman, having the cure of souls in a parish, has been the manager of the schools there, you would be prepared to recognise the succession unless there be some reason to the contrary?—Quite so.

491. And that in cases where a clergyman has been deposed, it has been the practice of the Board to accept the certificate of his ecclesiastical superior, as a proof of the fact of deposition?—Quite so.

492. Mr. *Gathorne Hardy*.] As the only proof of the deposition?—As proof conclusive; the certificate being genuine.

493. In all cases do you obtain that before removing a person?—In the case of Father O'Keeffe we obtained it.

494. No doubt; but I think you will find that in one case you did not?—In one case we did not.

495. *Chairman*.] Where the fact is known to you, you proceed upon it?—Quite so.

496. But the proper proof in case of a dispute is the certificate of the ecclesiastical superior?—Quite so.

497. In the case of a Presbyterian, or any other clergyman, as well as of a Roman Catholic?—Yes.

498. What I understand you to say is, that where the occupant ceases to be manager, the Board have appointed a temporary manager until the local authority shall nominate a manager?—Quite so; whenever there are trustees or a committee in existence, or a patron, and the Board deem it necessary for the interests of the school to appoint a manager, as in that case of Ratoath, without having previously received a nomination from the committee, trustees, or patrons, such an appointment is regarded by the Board as provisional, and at any time liable to rectification by the committee, trustees, or patron, as the case might be.

499. Mr. *Bourke*.] Supposing that a clergyman is suspended, and the committee wish to appoint a layman, in that case what would the Board do; would they recognise the ecclesiastical superior with reference to the succession?—The nomination of the committee, whether of a layman or of an ecclesiastic, would be accepted by the Board.

500. Then it would follow that an ecclesiastical successor is not always appointed by the body as the person in succession to the person who has been suspended?—In all the cases of suspension it has happened that clerical persons were appointed in succession to the deposed clergyman.

501. Dr. *Lyon Playfair*.] Would you just look at page 6, Rule 12, "The local patrons (or managers) of schools have the right of appointing the teachers;" in that place the word "appointing" means the appointment of the teacher, not merely the nomination, but the appointment?—It is subject to the approval of the Board, and perhaps in that case again the word "appointment" is too strong a word, for in every case the appointment is subject to the approval of the Board with reference to competency and character, and so on.

502. In the rule above that the word "appointed" occurs. "When a school is under the control of a committee, or of joint patrons, a 'local manager' should be appointed, to correspond with the office, sign documents, &c., &c.;" are "appointment" and "nomination" equivalent terms?—So far as local parties are concerned, when the word "appoint" is used, "nominate" would be the more appropriate word; but "appointment" and "nomination" are used locally, and even by the Board itself sometimes, without much or any discrimination.

503. But is it not the case that these rules, which have been the rules since 1855, had been modified over and over again with great care before 1855?—Judge Longfield will be the most eminent authority to speak to those rules.

504. *Chairman*.] Could you give the Committee the number of removals of managers which you could quote; I think they are very few?—Very few indeed. Since 1865 there have been only the cases of Mr. Shannon, of Gort, and Father O'Keeffe, of Callan, both occurring in 1872.

The Right Honourable *Mountifort Longfield*, LL.D., called in; and Examined.

Right Hon.
M. Longfield, LL.D.

5 June 1873.

505. *Chairman.*] You are one of the oldest members of the Board of Education, are you not?—There are three before me, the Marquess of Kildare, Dr. Henry, and Mr. Gibson, and I am the fourth. I have been about 20 years a member.

506. When did you become a member?—In the summer of 1853.

507. You have heard, and are acquainted with, the principal part of the evidence of Dr. Keenan?—The chief part I have listened to to-day, and I have read part of it.

508. Has the Board ever recognised a suspended clergyman as the patron of a school?—No, I think it has not.

509. What has been the conduct of the Board upon such occasions?—They have, when it came officially before them, removed the clergyman, sometimes more expeditiously, sometimes less, pretty much depending upon the activity of the persons who were bringing the question forward.

510. By the persons who were bringing the question forward, do you mean the local people, or whom?—Whoever made the complaint.

511. Has the course of the Board been uniform? — I think it has been uniform in substance, but in details often varying according to chance, pretty much.

512. What jurisdiction has the Board over the patronage? — None whatever; it does not claim any except to decline to correspond with an improper patron; the Board is merely a civil corporation, and has no jurisdiction over anybody.

513. Has the conduct of the Board been guided by printed rules relating to management?—They have not contradicted those printed rules, but in point of fact the printed rules relating to management were taken from the practice of the Board which existed before them. The rules relating to management were, I believe, first made in the autumn of 1853.

514. Soon after you joined the Board?—Almost immediately; there had been some disputes in 1852. Previously to 1852 everything had gone on very smoothly with the Board, who were generally unanimous. In 1852, disputes arose, which led to the secession of Archbishop Whately and two other members of the Board. In the autumn of 1853, we found it necessary to revise the rules and to have them clearly printed, inasmuch as disputes had arisen as to the meaning of some of them.

515. What action does the Board take if a committee of management insists upon maintaining a suspended priest as patron?—The only action they can take is to withdraw the salary and cease to correspond with the patron.

516. Then in that case the school would be stopped, and the children would lose their education by the action of the committee?—Unless the scholars themselves would pay the schoolmaster, or unless the parents would pay him, the State acting through the Board would not pay him; it is the only mode in which the Board can enforce its rules by saying we will not pay if the rules are not observed.

517. Is the power of the Board to remove or appoint patrons different in the three kinds of schools? — In three kinds of schools, namely, those vested in Commissioners, those vested in trustees, and non-vested schools, they have no power of removing or appointing the patron; they treat them all alike. I heard Mr. Keenan state it as if there was a difference in the case of bonded schools. As I understand, a school with a bond is merely a vested school, in which the title is not very good, and we confirm it by a bond, and as we spend money in building the schoolhouse we require some security.

518. Then, for your purpose, it is a vested school? — It is a vested school in every case.

519. Do you think it right to act without notice in such a case?—I think no mischief is done by acting without notice in such a case, because, although we verbally dismiss the patron, it is really only giving him notice that we will not correspond with him in future, therefore he has ample time if there is any mistake made to set us right.

520. Having

SELECT COMMITTEE ON CALLAN SCHOOLS. 53

Right Hon.
M. Longfield, LL.D.

5 June 1873.

520. Having heard Mr. Keenan's evidence, do you wish to state anything further?—There is some difference between us, with reference to an *ex officio* patron. I do not think a clergyman is in any case an *ex officio* patron; he is the patron for the same reason that any one else is a patron, because he is named in the deed, or because he is the person who has the power of nomination. I may give a portion of land, and erect a schoolhouse upon it, and vest it in trustees, and direct that the churchwarden shall be a trustee; but I would not call him an *ex officio* patron; it is only because he is named in the deed.

521. And when a clergyman has been a patron of a school, and is suspended, you remove him from the school immediately upon receiving notice of the suspension?—That is our practice; there might be delays from the Board not meeting, or from delays in the office, but that is the rule.

522. You cease to communicate with him?—We cease to communicate with him, and withhold the salary after a reasonable time, unless the school is put under a proper patron.

523. And appeal to the local authority to appoint a proper successor?—They appeal to the local authority to appoint a proper successor, the difference being that where a clergyman is appointed we generally make no inquiries about him, and will not listen to any argument; the mere fact of his being a clergyman in a recognised church is sufficient ground for believing him to be a fair and proper man; and when we speak of inquiring into the fitness of a man, it merely means that we take his fitness for granted, unless there is some objection made.

524. When a clergyman is nominated, *primâ facie* you consider him fit?—We consider him fit.

525. But if a specific objection were made against him, what would you do?—We should inquire into it, to see if it was a proper case for continuing him.

526. Mr. *Gathorne Hardy*.] I see the terms which you use are not quite in accordance with your statement, because you do not speak of corresponding, but you say the Commissioners "feel themselves obliged, in accordance with their uniform practice, to remove you from the office of manager of the following National schools: Callan male, Callan female, Callan Infant, Newtown, and Coolagh;" so that you give notice that you absolutely remove him?—I think that is not a happy form of expression, but the meaning is very clear.

527. Then you go on to say, "Until the suspension referred to shall have been removed or declared invalid by a competent authority;" what do you consider a sufficient declaration of its invalidity?—If the bishop certified to us that the suspension had been removed, we should consider that sufficient.

528. Would a legal decision affect that in any way?—I can hardly imagine a legal decision *in rem* upon the question, because the ecclesiastical laws of Rome are not recognised as laws of the land.

529. Take the case of the Church of England?—In the case of the Church of England we should see the records, and now, as the Church of Ireland is not established, I think we should have to take the certificate of the bishop.

530. Then the only competent authority, in your opinion, is the ecclesiastical superior?—I think we must go by that, because we cannot go into the general rules of all the churches in Ireland. All we can do is to take the statement of the man who, by the rule of the church, is the ecclesiastical superior.

531. You mean that the expression is tautologous whether the suspension is removed or declared invalid, because it would mean the same thing?—Yes; I think it means the same thing, certainly. I may add that there is a possibility of a difference of meaning; the suspension being removed might mean that it was a good suspension, and had ceased by his submission, but whether it was invalid, I do not know.

532. The cases which have occurred since 1853 have been all since you were connected with the Board?—All the cases which have occurred since 1853.

533. When the secretaries receive notice from anyone of a suspension, is it their duty to lay it before the Board upon the earliest opportunity?—It is, I think.

534. We find, in one case here, that a period of two years elapsed before the case came before the Board; can you at all account for that?—I cannot; there was some delay in the case of Magheral. I can only account for it so far as this, that

Right Hon.
M. Longfield, LL.D.

5 June 1873.

that there were serious charges made against the schoolmaster, and the secretary, while attending to the charges against the schoolmaster, which were very important, neglected the important fact of the suspension of the clergyman.

535. Dr. *Lyon Playfair*.] What has the manager to do in relation to the National Board?—He appoints and dismisses the teacher; he dictates the time for religious instruction in case it is a vested school, and in case it is a non-vested school he is the arbiter of the point whether there is to be any religious instruction at all or not, and at what times; and he corresponds at all times with the Board, and, according to the Order of the Treasury, he receives the money for the payment of the teacher instead of its being sent direct to the schoolmaster.

536. Has the Board anything to do with the manager in his clerical capacity?—Nothing whatever in his clerical capacity.

537. It is purely as the secular manager that the Board corresponds with him?—Purely as the secular manager.

538. When the committee of a school has appointed legally a manager, do you think that the Board has sufficient justification, from the mere fact of his suspension as a clergyman, in suspending him from the appointment which he has received?—I think so, because I concurred in doing it. I consider that the suspended clergyman of a parish is not a fit and proper person, while the suspension lasts, to be the manager of a school, having entered into the position of manager upon the strength of holding that position.

539. But, supposing a layman had been appointed as manager of the Callan School, would you not have considered that it was necessary that he should commit a very heavy crime before you dismissed him as manager; would it be a light offence for which a layman would be dismissed from the management of a school?—I should be very much indisposed to dismiss the manager of a school for any light offence, unless it were an offence in contravention of our rules, in which case we should dismiss him.

540. In case of neglect of duty you would be very chary in dismissing the manager?—I do not think we have ever dismissed a manager for neglect of duty.

541. You would consider ecclesiastical suspension, apart from any unfitness to manage the school, quite a sufficient ground for dismissing the clergyman?—We do think so. We think that to retain a man who was appointed as clergyman, and to have that man using the influence which his position as clergyman gave him to hold the school, in defiance of the Church, would give rise to much discord.

542. Supposing the parents of the children and the committee of the district wished him to be retained?—I think still it would be improper; it would be an influence which he had gained by being a clergyman, and it should be a long time before he should be permitted to recover possession of it again.

543. But did he get it, or did he claim it as a clergyman. You state that there is no *ex officio* appointment. If the committee nominate the Rev. Robert O'Keeffe, does he cease to be the Rev. Robert O'Keeffe, although he is suspended?—No; suspension does not deprive him of orders, but we assume that when there has been a clergyman appointed, that was the reason why he was nominated or appointed manager of the school.

544. Is he capable of making the quarterly return?—Perfectly.

545. Is he capable of judging of the fitness of a teacher?—Perfectly.

546. Is he capable of doing all the duties of the school, even though he is under suspension?—He is capable of doing them all, but I do not think it is likely he will do them to the satisfaction of the Board which appointed him as the representative of the Church.

547. But he is not a representative of the Church; he is appointed by the committee of the Male and Female Callan Schools, not necessarily *ex officio* as parish priest?—But I understand that whenever a man is appointed who is the parish priest, that is really the reason why he is so appointed; we know that the parish priest is nobody except as parish priest. Nobody would have selected the Rev. Robert O'Keeffe except as parish priest.

548. Do you consider that a clergyman should be under greater disabilities than a layman in the manner in which he is dismissed from the secular management

ment of a secular school?—Certainly. I consider he must take the disadvantages and the advantages. I feel quite certain that if he had been a layman he would never have been manager of the school.

Right Hon.
M. Longfield, LL.D.

5 June 1873.

549. Can you give any evidence of that?—We have a knowledge of the country; and when we see that such an enormous number of the managers are parish priests, we know that that cannot be a mere coincidence.

550. But take a case where the committee insist upon retaining a suspended priest as the manager; what was the opinion of the Board in such a case, seeing that the committee continued to nominate him as manager; why did not the National Board in such a case attend to the wishes of the committee?—They thought the proper course was not to permit the suspended priest of the parish to hold a status which would, in their opinion, be disastrous to the cause of united education in Ireland generally.

551. When a layman manages the secular part of a school well you retain him, but if a clergyman manages the secular part of a school well, but is suspended, you dismiss him?—If he is suspended we dismiss him, and dismiss him with as little delay as need be.

552. *The O'Conor Don.*] Whatever your opinion may be as to the abstract question of the dismissal of a suspended manager, the practice of the Board has been upon all occasions to dismiss?—I approve of the practice; but even if I did not approve of it, I would favour it; for the practice being known has prevented the ecclesiastical authorities taking steps to protect themselves, which they would not have taken but for our practice; they could easily have appointed the bishop as patron, and the parish priest as manager, and then the bishop would only have to hold up his finger and he would go out. The rule might be altered, but in any case I would feel it my duty to act upon that rule in Mr. O'Keeffe's case.

553. Had the Board acted as Mr. Justice Morris suggested, and asked for an explanation, they would have acted contrary to all precedent?—I think they would have acted contrary to all precedent, but we should have had no objection to inform the Rev. Mr. O'Keeffe of our intention, if it had been put in that way.

554. But you objected to going to him for an explanation?—Yes, as that would have led to a statement of the causes of his removal; a question which we were not called upon to go into. For instance, if he stated that he believed in more than two sacraments, I as a Protestant, should not be a proper person to go into a question of that kind; but I myself, and the Lord Chief Baron, and several more would have voted in favour of the notice.

555. *Mr. Cross.*] You are one of those who signed this memorial, I believe?—I am.

556. I see this memorial states: "Having regard to grave mis-statements of facts;" would you be kind enough to state what mis-statements of facts you allude to?—It was stated that we acted under the influence or under the mandates of Cardinal Cullen; it was stated that we acted contrary to our precedents; it was stated that the precedents were totally different in material facts from the particular case that was brought before us.

557. I have not made myself clear; you are aware that certain papers were laid before Parliament; do you mean any mis-statement of facts in those papers?—Of course there was no mis-statement of facts in those papers, because the papers were true, as they were merely records of the Board's acts.

558. There was no statement of motives in those papers?—The papers stated no motives at all.

559. What are the additional facts that you would wish Parliament should have before it?—We wish that you should have the facts of all those cases in which we removed a clergyman; that we removed him without any doubt or hesitation, and that we were not influenced in any way by Cardinal Cullen, or by ecclesiastical authority whatever.

560. But a return was ordered for all facts connected with those cases; what facts do you wish to be brought forward which could not be brought forward in these papers?—These papers were limited. Mr. Keenan explained to-day the circumstances relating to one of those papers, which he produced, because they did not come within the Parliamentary Order. When we get a Parliamentary Order, we always look at it very carefully to see that we do not incur displeasure by giving too much or too little.

561. Mr.

Right Hon.
M. Longfield, LL.D.

5 June 1873.

561. *Mr. Bourke.*] You stated that one reason why the Board adopted the practice of recognising the authority of the bishop in suspending clergymen, would be that you would otherwise introduce discord into the parish of a suspended clergyman?—Yes, and through Ireland.

562. Would the Board take into their consideration the fact, that by recognising the successor to a suspended priest they would introduce discord into the parish?—No, I do not think they would.

563. So that whether the appointment of a successor to a suspended priest produced discord in a parish or not, they would not have taken that into consideration at all?—I think not, and for the obvious reason that it is not calculated to produce discord by nature, and although its accidentally producing discord might be very probable, that would not lead us to alter our conduct.

564. But if it did come under the notice of the Board, would that alter your decision?—Certainly not; it is what is likely to produce discord that we consider.

565. Do you know any case in which the legality of the suspension of a clergyman was brought prominently before the notice of the Board before they acted upon the certificate of suspension?—I am under the impression that it was done to some extent in Mr. Wilson's case and in Dr. Keenan's case; in Dr. Keenan's case he appealed, and I believe he succeeded in his appeal; in Mr. Wilson's case he denied that he was in fact suspended, as he stated that he had still his congregation, and everything of that kind; but it is not likely that it was brought prominently before the Board, for the simple reason that we should think it immaterial, and take no notice of it.

566. *Chairman.*] What you look at is the fact that he is or is not, according to the rules of his communion, the clergyman of that parish?—Yes, we accept the ecclesiastical jurisdiction or power of taking the clergyman off. In the case of the Presbyterians, we take the certificate of the moderator just as we should take the certificate of the secretary of a club, that a man was a member of it or not.

567. What you have to ascertain is the fact?—Yes, without going into great litigation, which might be incurred by going into the proceedings of every voluntary church.

568. *The O'Conor Don.*] You were a member of the Board at the time the case of the Rev. Mr. Sheridan was brought forward, were you not?—I was.

569. Do you remember that case?—I do not remember that case. I read the papers connected with it; but upon looking at the names of those present, I do not perceive that I was present.

570. Are you aware that that case was never brought before the Board before the date mentioned in this paper, the 27th of January 1865?—I cannot state that of my own knowledge.

The Right Honourable Sir *Alexander Macdonnell*, called in; and Examined.

Right Hon. Sir
A. Macdonnell.

571. *Chairman.*] You were the resident Commissioner from the year 1839, I think, till 1871?—I was.

572. You are aware of the evidence which has been given by Mr. Keenan and Judge Longfield?—In a general way, I am.

573. Do you generally concur in that evidence?—As far as I know.

574. Are there any observations which you wish to make with regard to the *ex officio* appointments of clergymen having the cure of souls in the parish?—I think that under the National Board there is no description of persons in Ireland who have anything like an *ex officio* right; there are certainly many schools in which the manager, being either a Protestant or a Roman Catholic clergyman, has succeeded, generally speaking, in the management of the school by his succession in the management of the parish or congregation; in a certain sense, some people would consider that an *ex officio* appointment, but I do not; I think there is no, strictly speaking, *ex officio* appointment made by the Board.

575. Do you agree with what Judge Longfield said upon that subject?—I do.

576. The

576. *The O'Conor Don.*] During your long experience as Commissioner of Education, have you ever known the Board to yield to the pressure of the Catholic clergy?—I am very happy to have that question asked me. I was Commissioner of Education for 32 years, and I can say with the greatest deliberation that upon no one occasion did I ever know a single change made by the National Board, or an improvement introduced, under Catholic dictation or pressure. I have lamented, over and over again, that our improvements did not take place sooner, improvements which were calculated to satisfy the Roman Catholic interests; but I never recollect a single instance in which we were induced by Catholic dictation or pressure to do anything which our consciences did not think necessary or just.

577. Have you upon the other hand yielded to pressure from the Protestant clergy?—I could not say that; there has been nothing which you could call pressure upon the Protestant side; there are strong feelings upon both sides, but certainly the Board was not influenced by either in a way to do harm.

578. Mr. *Bourke.*] With regard to the improvements which you have alluded to, do you know what they are?—I could mention some of them; I think it a great improvement that whereas at the commencement of the Board there were only two Roman Catholics out of a Board of seven to represent the interests and feelings of four-fifths of the people, under Mr. Cardwell's Government that was altered, and an equality of numbers was created between the Roman Catholic and the Protestant Commissioners; I think that a great improvement.

579. *Chairman.*] Do you consider what has been done in the case which we are called upon to investigate, conformable to the precedents of what has occurred during your time?—Decidedly so.

Right Hon. Sir
A. Macdonnell.

5 June 1873.

Monday, 9th June 1873.

MEMBERS PRESENT:

Mr. Bourke.
Mr. Secretary Cardwell.
Mr. Cross.
Mr. Gathorne Hardy.

The O'Conor Don.
Dr. Lyon Playfair.
Mr. Whitbread.

THE RIGHT HONOURABLE EDWARD CARDWELL, IN THE CHAIR.

The Reverend *Pooley Shuldham Henry*, D.D., called in; and Examined.

Rev.
P. S. Henry, D.D.

9 June 1873.

580. *Chairman.*] You are the President of the Queen's College at Belfast?—I am.

581. What other office do you hold under Government?—I am still Commissioner of National Education, and a member of the senate of the Queen's University. Formerly I was agent of the Synod of Ulster, and a Commissioner of Charitable Bequests afterwards, both of which I resigned.

582. When did you become a Commissioner of National Education?—In the year 1838.

583. Were you the first Presbyterian Commissioner?—No; Dr. Carlisle was the first. He was appointed in conjunction with Archbishop Whately and Archbishop Murray, each representing a Church, and the three representing the three leading Churches of the country. At that time I may state to you a very bad feeling existed between the General Assembly, or the Synod of Ulster, as it was called at that time, and the Board of National Education; very protracted negociations had taken place, and they failed, and Dr. Carlisle retired from a variety of circumstances, which, I suppose, I need not now go into. I was immediately appointed upon his retirement to take his place, and I have, what I cherish very much, the original autograph letter of Lord Morpeth, asking me, in fact (for I had never thought of the office, and never applied for it), to accept it at the time, and to accept it on the ground of my possessing the confidence of the Presbyterian body. That was in the year 1838. I was, therefore, appointed clerical representative of the Synod of Ulster at that time.

584. It appears from the Return before us, that although, on the first occasion of the discussion in Mr. O'Keeffe's case, you were present at the Board, you did not by recording your vote express your opinion on the matter?—The reason was that I was then suffering under a very severe attack of illness, which confined me to bed for a fortnight afterwards. I left the room during the discussion, very much to my own regret, to return to Belfast before the division took place. A few days afterwards the programme of the business of the 23rd of April reached me whilst in bed. I had often, when unable to attend the meetings of the Board, been in the habit of expressing my opinion in writing through the secretaries, on any important matters noted in the programme; and I wrote then a letter, which is in evidence before you; but as I have an addition to make

to

SELECT COMMITTEE ON CALLAN SCHOOLS. 59

to that letter, which was sent in, and which, through mistake, was not forwarded, I should be very much obliged if you would allow me to read it, adding the part which has not appeared in evidence, because I hold it to be of importance. The letter to which I refer is given in Captain Archdale's Return at page 18, and is in these terms, " I believe the Commissioners have no course left them but to recognise Mr. Martin as manager of the schools now under the management of the Rev. R. O Keeffe, whose ecclesiastical suspension is notified to the Board by the Roman Catholic coadjutor, Bishop of Ossory, and also by the inspector, Mr. Harkin. The uniform practice of the Board has been to recognise in the case of any deposed clergyman, as his successor in the office of manager of schools, the clergyman who may have been ecclesiastically appointed in his place to exercise spiritual functions. The Commissioners having before them official notification on these points in the present case, are, in my opinion, bound to accede to the request of Mr. Martin, unless they are prepared to involve themselves in investigations (*ultra vires*) of the reasons, grounds, justice or injustice, of ecclesiastical censures. Mr. O'Keeffe may have appealed to legal tribunals, but that does not alter our position as Commissioners, for it is clear that no legal decision, or any issue that would be sustained in a court of justice, could reinstate him as parish priest, contrary to ecclesiastical jurisdiction. The simple fact of the notification of deposition by the moderators of the General Assembly, or of its synods, has always been held by the governmental and legal authorities, as deprivation of official standing. I enclose a section from a chapter of the Statutes of the Queen's Colleges, which contains a general principle applicable to this case." This is the point to which I wish especially to draw your attention, and that of the Committee. I sent it forward, having cut it out in print, to the Board of Education, but somehow in the office it fell aside. I hold in my hand the charter of the Queen's College, and in that charter, chapter 16, " Of the Residences of Students and the Deans of Residences." I find it stated in one of the paragraphs that the Queen is charged with the appointment of Deans of Residences in the Queen's College "for the better maintenance of moral and religious discipline in the licensed boarding-house;" "such clergymen or ministers as we shall from time to time, by warrant under our sign manual, appoint Deans of Residences, shall have the moral care and spiritual charge of the students of their respective creeds residing in the licensed boarding-houses." Therefore, the Queen appoints the Deans of Residences. I, myself, receive from Her Majesty all the warrants appointing such in Belfast College. "No clergyman or minister shall be competent to assume or continue to hold the office of Dean of Residences unless approved of by the Bishop, moderators, or constituted authority of his church or religious denomination." That I sent forward with the letter which appears in the Parliamentary Paper.

585. Now, in writing that letter, had you before you the various precedents that influenced the Board?—At the time I wrote this letter, which I have read, I had not a record or document of the past proceedings of the Board before me, but the principle involved in the question and all the former decisions of the Board were so indelibly impressed on my memory, that I never framed a memorandum with more ease or less embarrassment. The special analogous cases I was not at the moment able to recall, but I had no more doubt than I had of my own existence that the unbroken, and up to that time the unquestioned, practice of the Board was, that when any Bishop, moderator, or ecclesiastical authority certified to the Commissioners the deposition of any clergyman under their peculiar control, that clergyman having been, in virtue of his office, the recognised clerical manager of national schools in his parish or connected with his congregation, the Commissioners withdrew from him his managerial powers, and as a rule of practice, recognised as his successor in the office of manager, the clergyman ecclesiastically appointed as his successor, to exercise spiritual functions.

586. How did this suspension of Mr. O'Keeffe come to your knowledge?—The Roman Catholic coadjutor, Bishop of Ossory, and also Mr. Harkin, the inspector, had notified to the Board the ecclesiastical suspension of Mr. O'Keeffe, and Mr. Martin, you will find, administrator of the parish of Callan, had asked the Commissioners to recognise him as manager of the national schools in the parish. Though Mr. Harkin had used the name of Cardinal Cullen in his letter of the 29th of November 1871, to the Board, and had referred to the decree

Rev.
P. S. *Henry*, D.D.
9 June 1873.

Rev.
P. S. Henry, D.D.
9 June 1873.

decree of suspension by his Eminence, I can, as one, assure the Committee that the name of the Cardinal or his decree had no influence upon me, one way or the other, in writing my memorandum. I thought merely of the common basis of the recognition of the independent and internal discipline that we had all recognised.

587. The Presbyterian Church joined the National system in the year 1840, did it not?— It was at the close of 1839.

588. Did you take any part in the negotiations that preceded and accompanied that?—I was called upon to take a very prominent part on that occasion. I told you before that the Synod and the Board of Education were on very bad terms. A misunderstanding had existed regarding the application of the rules. When I accepted office I had some doubt about yielding to the requests of Lord Carlisle, because I was rather running in the face of the decisions of my own body. However, I still saw common ground enough to induce me to accept office, and about a year after that Dr. Cooke wrote me a private letter, asking me to interpose to have arrangements adopted between the two parties. I immediately wrote to the Board, and to Lord Ebrington, then Lord Lieutenant. A deputation was sent up from the Synod of Ulster, and after several interviews it was resolved to send in an application on the part of the Synod, in what we still call the Correen case; and that has existed hitherto, as, in fact, the basis of the agreement between the Board and the Synod, which led immediately to a great influx of Presbyterian ministers joining the Board. You will see from looking at the Report, that the year after this a great increase took place, and I find this reference to it in the 6th Report of the Commissioners of National Education at the 145th page, "We had, at the close of the last year, 136 applications undisposed of, and having received several since, we have altogether 205 now before us, of which 62 are from ministers of the Synod of Ulster. The whole of these 62 appear consequent on a grant which we have made to the Rev. Robert Stewart, D.D." (that was the model case), "a member of that body, and to which, therefore, as it was attended by peculiar circumstances, we think it necessary particularly to advert. Your Excellence received a deputation from the School Directory of the Synod, on the 24th of January last, when such members of the Board as were able to attend, were present at your desire." You will observe that it was a church which was making application by a particular case, presented in order to effect a junction between that church and the National Board, and through me as negociating the whole of the arrangements. I need not, I suppose, go into the grounds of that agreement.

589. Now, did anything take place at that time about the recognition of deposed clergymen?— There was no rule. If it had been proposed as part of the arrangement between the Synod and the Board, or the Government, that their certificate should not be received as stating the ground of deposition of a minister, I am quite certain that my Church, the General Assembly, would never have accepted aid from the Board. It would have been a direct interference, I think, with their discipline and internal government.

590. Do I rightly understand you to say that it would have prevented the junction of the Presbyterian Church at that time?—I am quite sure that if it had been put forward as a positive proposition it would have prevented it. I cannot conceive of the case; and I think it is quite right to state that the Presbyterian Church has always stood strongly out for the recognition of the status of their own ministers.

591. Now, will you have the goodness to state, summarily, the objections entertained by you to the recognition of a suspended clergyman as the manager of a national school?—In the first place he would be among the children as giving religious instruction, and I do not think that a suspended clergyman is in a position to give religious instruction (and he is the person to impart that instruction) to the children under his care. Let us suppose that in this case we had, for the first time, departed from our settled practice, and had declined to act upon the certificate of the Roman Catholic coadjutor, Bishop of Ossory; let us suppose we had continued to recognise Mr. O'Keeffe as manager, and violated the common principles of our agreement as churches, he being suspended at the time, I believe that the Roman Catholic Church would have been entitled then to charge the Board with a line of procedure injurious to authority and subversive of discipline if he had continued in that post. I entertain, therefore, a settled conviction,

viction, which no combination of circumstances can ever alter, that the Board acted wisely, justly, consistently, and in good faith, when they passed this Order on the 22nd of April: "That the certificate of the Roman Catholic Bishop of Ossory be received and acted on by the Board until the suspension therein mentioned shall have been removed or declared invalid by a competent tribunal."

Rev. P. S. Henry, D.D.

9 June 1873.

592. You were a party to nearly all the decisions in the cases which have been quoted as precedents, were you not?—I was present at them all but one, I think.

593. As the oldest member of the Board, could you give the Committee any information as to the early deliberations of the Board in the treatment of deposed clergymen, which is not contained in the Parliamentary Papers?—I have no hesitation in saying, that at that time I had the honour of being very often consulted by both Archbishop Whately and Archbishop Murray whenever any case of an ecclesiastical nature occurred. I remember most distinctly that both those very eminent and wise men agreed with myself in saying, that a deposed clergyman ought in no case to be continued as manager of a school; and that principle guided them and me, and guided other Commissioners, whose names are before you (amongst other Presbyterian Commissioners, Dr. Hall, a very eminent man, and Mr. Gibson), without any division to the same result. I had a private conversation two or three times with Dr. Whately and Dr. Murray, and Dr. Whately said, "We can never involve ourselves in the meshes of the law in a case of this kind, because it would be destructive to our harmony within, and to peace without." As far as I remember, those were his words.

594. Mr. *Bourke*.] What case was that in?—Generally, running through the whole of the negociations.

595. But when were the expressions that you allude to used?—I remember distinctly their being used at the fireside, in the board room.

596. *Chairman*.] Had that remark reference to any one of the precedents?—It had reference to the whole that took place afterwards.

597. Was it with reference to any one of the early cases that it was made?—It is a long time since, but I think it was in reference to Dr. Keenan's case.

598. Mr. *Gathorne Hardy*.] I see that in your letter you speak of "the notification of deposition by the moderators of the General Assembly, or of its Synods." The moderators in that case would be speaking as the organs of the tribunals that had acted in the case, would they not?—They certify the deposition of the clergyman, as the bishop does.

599. But the moderator in your case would be acting, would he not, as the organ of a Synod, and not personally?—We recognise him as we would a bishop at the Board of Education.

600. I quite understand that, but I want to get at his particular position in reference to a case. Take a case for instance, that is in the precedents, the case of Dr. Wilson; by whom had Dr. Wilson been tried?—I have a record from the Synod here; a gentleman, who acted at that time as the clerk of the Synod, gives me this information, he takes it from the minutes of the Assembly: In 1850 the Presbytery of Magherafelt reported (that was to the General Assembly at a meeting of the General Assembly), "That on the 29th of October they withdrew the credentials of Mr. Gilbert Kirke Wilson, and degraded him from the office of the holy ministry." That minute was received, and acted upon by the General Assembly.

601. Did Mr. Wilson appeal to the Assembly from that?—He threatened to appeal, and the threat was included in his letter to us; but we did not enter into that at all.

602. I am speaking now not of what passed at the Board, but in the General Assembly; at the time that they confirmed the degradation, was there any appeal to them on the part of Mr. Wilson?—I am not aware of that; I have no record.

603. The moderator then, in certifying the fact to the Board of Education, would certify that there was a deposition by the Presbytery, confirmed by the General Assembly, and that in fact there was an absolute cessation of the proceedings?—Yes.

Rev.
P. S. Henry, D.D.
9 June 1873.

604. *Chairman.*] What exactly did the moderator certify to the Board; what we want to know is what the certificate was upon which the Board acted; have you got the certificate that was made to the Board?—No, I cannot tell what it was.

605. (To Mr. *Keenan.*) Are you able to produce the certificate upon which the Board acted in the case of Mr. Wilson?—I mentioned on a former occasion that the only document which is at present available is a letter from the Rev. Mr. Templeton, the successor of Mr. Wilson, and that I conjectured that some other document must have been presented to the Board; but that at present it cannot be found.

606. Mr. *Gathorne Hardy.*] Your impression is that there must have been some prior document?—I am convinced, from a study of the papers, that, antecedent to Mr. Templeton's letter, or at the same time, there must have been some other document, which cannot now be found.

607. (To Dr. *Henry.*) I suppose that the case of Mr. Wilson is the only Presbyterian case that there is?—There is a very important one which I discovered last week, and I have only got the documents since.

608. You mean the one that Mr. Keenan notified to us the other day, in his evidence, namely, the case of Mr. Fisher?—Yes; I was mixed up myself very much in that case. I have a distinct remembrance of the man's degradation; but I had ceased in the long lapse of years, to remember that he was trustee of the Market Hill School; and perhaps you will allow me to read my own letter at the time to the Commissioners of Education.

609. In that case I observe that you were the informant of the Board?—I think I was moderator of the Armagh Presbytery that year; but I was, at any rate, a Commissioner of Education. I was a friend of Lord Gosford, and be asked me to interpose, and I wrote the letter in question to the Board.

610. That is the letter which is already in Mr. Keenan's evidence, is it not?—Yes; but I want to refer to one or two points in it. I think it embodies general principles applicable to this case: "Armagh, 26th November 1842.—To the Secretaries of the Board of National Education.—Gentlemen, I do not hesitate to say that Mr. Fisher ought to be removed from the managership of the Market Hill School. After a most painful investigation, of five or six days, by the Armagh Presbytery (at which I was present), Mr. Fisher was suspended *sine die* from the functions and benefits of the Christian ministry. That decision was confirmed, after an appeal, by the unanimous voice of the General Assembly. I hold therefore" (I drew your attention and that of the Committee to this), "that it would be injurious to the interests of the Board of Education longer to retain as one of its patrons, one who is no longer permitted to exercise the functions of the ministry in Market Hill or elsewhere. Regarding the special matter in question, of the salary due to the mistress of the school, passing through Mr. Fisher's hands, I have to state that as he is in great pecuniary difficulties, this teacher and her husband have a strong objection to allow him to receive the money." "I forgot to mention that the congregation of Market Hill is about to elect a successor to Mr. Fisher" (to his church that is), "who will be the natural person to become manager in Mr. Fisher's place. In the meantime I would recommend Mr. Joseph McKee, of Market Hill, to be appointed *locum tenens.*" I find on this extract, from the proceedings of the Board on receiving that letter, "22nd December 1842.—Present: the Archbishop of Dublin, Archbishop Murray, the Right Honourable A. R. Blake, the Marquess of Kildare, the Provost, Mr. Greene, Mr. Holmes, Mr. Corballis, and Mr. Macdonnell. Read letter from Rev. P. S. Henry, giving reasons for removal of Rev. Mr. Fisher from the management of Market Hill National School. Ordered, that Mr. Fisher be removed from the management of the said school, and that he be informed that he is so in consequence of the decision of the General Assembly; and further, that the salary be paid through the Rev. P. S. Henry, and that he be requested to intimate to the persons connected with the school the necessity of appointing a fit person to act as manager." Then, again, on the 12th of January 1843, "Present: Archbishop Murray, the Provost, Right Honourable A. R. Blake, J. R. Corballis, Esq., Marquess of Kildare, and A. Macdonnell, Esq. Read, letter from Rev. J. Fisher, protesting against his removal, by order of the Commissioners, from the management of the Market Hill National School, County Armagh." No action was taken on this protest, and I have in my hand the letter of Mr. Fisher, concluding in a very odd way.

611. Now,

SELECT COMMITTEE ON CALLAN SCHOOLS. 63

611. Now I see you state in your letter to which you first referred, written to the Board in April 1872, "That the uniform practice of the Board has been to recognise, in the case of any deposed clergyman as his successor in the office of manager of schools, the clergyman who may have been ecclesiastically appointed in his place to exercise spiritual functions"?—Yes; I believe it has been the uniform practice.

612. Now, in the last case of those precedents, I find that the Board referred to the committee, and did not recognise the successor?—I suppose the school was under a committee; that was a distinction in that case.

613. In any case, then, where a school is under a committee, you would not necessarily recognise a successor?—I do not know that. They refer to the committee, because the committee there stands in place of the patron.

614. Now, in that case which you have referred to of Market Hill, can you tell me at what period the suspension of that gentleman, Mr. Fisher, took place by the Armagh Presbytery?—The General Assembly holds its meetings in the summer, and, I suppose, it must have been two or three months before that letter, which has been read, was written.

615. But he was suspended originally by the Presbytery of Armagh?—He was degraded by it, which the Synod confirmed.

616. Upon his degradation by the Synod of Armagh, was any representation made to the Board of that degradation?—I cannot tell that; I have no means of knowing it.

617. If there had been a representation, what would the result have been?—If there had been a representation, he would at once have been certified to the Board as a degraded clergyman.

618. Notwithstanding his appeal to the General Assembly?—I think so; I myself read the Minutes to the Assembly, and the Assembly at once recognised him as degraded; but what action was afterwards taken by the body I cannot tell.

619. But, as a matter of fact, the degradation of Mr. Fisher was not notified to the Board to take action upon until its confirmation by the General Assembly?—I cannot tell that.

620. Your letter seems to imply that, because it is dated the 26th of November 1842, and you say that the decision had been confirmed after an appeal by the unanimous voice of the General Assembly?—I may have been looking back to the Minutes. You know I take it that the Board took that from me.

621. They accepted your statement that he had been degraded, you mean?—Yes.

622. I understand that; but what I want to get from you is, that though he was degraded originally by the Presbytery of Armagh, no action was taken by the Board of Education until that degradation was confirmed by the General Assembly?—I do not think that they took any action until they received my letter on the subject.

623. You were Moderator of the Presbytery of Armagh at that time?—I think I was; at any rate, I was a Commissioner of Education.

624. And you took no action, as a Commissioner of National Education, until after the confirmation of that degradation by the General Assembly?—I merely refer to the fact; I cannot tell the motive.

625. I want not your motive, but your action?—I cannot remember my action. I remembered the fact of his being degraded; but I had no recollection of the case until that letter was put into my hands.

626. But as a matter of fact, Mr. Fisher, having been tried by the Presbytery before the General Assembly met in the summer, it was not until the 26th of November that he was removed by your Board?—I merely state that the General Assembly usually meet in the summer; they have sometimes met after for special cases; and I cannot tell with certainty when they met in that year.

627. I find that in the case of Dr. Keenan it is stated that he had appealed, and I presume that means to the spiritual authorities; but it does not appear that there was any appeal to any legal tribunal; why, in that case, was the suspension acted upon immediately, and not in the case of Mr. Fisher?—Because in the one case it was notified to the Board; in the other it may not have been. The school, I must say, at Market Hill, after I assumed its management, was in a very bad state. There is a report from an inspector to the effect that it was

Rev. P. S. Henry, D.D.
9 June 1873.

Rev.
P. S. Henry, D.D.
9 June 1873.

was all shattered, and it had been in a very bad state; and I think I wrote a letter to Lord Gosford on the subject. At that time Mr. Fisher was out of the country.

628. But he was still recognised as manager by the Board, was he not?—I am quite sure that in the one case, Dr. Keenan's, it was notified to the Board directly; but I cannot say as to the other.

629. I see that Mr. Fisher was removed by an order of the Board on the 22nd of December; therefore, I presume, up to that time he was recognised as manager by the Board?—It is impossible for me, in the multitude of cases, to remember one in particular.

630. But would there be any occasion to remove a man from the management of a school if he were not the manager of it?—He may or may not have been.

631. You have alluded to Mr. Fisher's letter, and from that it appears that he was not abroad?—You are taking it, that I stated as a fact that he was abroad; but I did not mean to state that as a fact. I think it very likely that he kept calling at the school for a time. I know that he annoyed Lord Gosford, and Lord Gosford afterwards spoke to me, and I said that I would write a letter about it.

632. And in the end Lord Gosford became the manager of the school, did he not?—I believe he did, because it was reorganised and became an agricultural school.

633. Therefore in that case, what you have stated to be the uniform practice was not followed?—I think it is not an exceptional case; it is a peculiar case.

634. As a matter of fact in that case, the successor of Mr. Fisher in the ministry did not succeed to this school?—He did not ask it; I remember who he was, and if he had applied for it, I am certain he would have got it.

635. I see that in that letter you use the expression of "removing a manager" from the school; do you agree with Judge Longfield, that the Board of Education has no power to remove a manager from a school?—Well, you know that we have the power to withhold their salaries and supplies, and then it is practical removal. If my salary was withheld from me as president of Queen's College, I think it would be practical removal.

636. I see that in the memorial, which you addressed in this case, praying for a full inquiry as one of the Commissioners, you speak of it as a "dismissal from position of manager;" you say, "the circumstances which induced and have followed his dismissal from the position of manager of five National schools at Callan"?—The withdrawal of his ecclesiastical recognition.

637. I need hardly ask you this question, but I wish to have it on the notes; I understand you to say in your letter, that no legal decision would have any influence on the Board unless it was reorganised by the ecclesiastical superior? —I do not know. It would depend upon the case very much. I think a dead lock might be caused.

638. You say, "It is clear that no legal decision or any issue that would be sustained in a court of justice could reinstate him as parish priest contrary to ecclesiastical jurisdiction"?—Not in our eyes; not as we deal with churches.

639. You mean that you would take no notice of a legal decision unless it was recognised by the ecclesiastical authority?—We would not, unless forced by pains and penalties, take notice of it.

640. And that would extend not only to schools, which if not held *ex officio*, he held in his clerical capacity, but also to schools to which he was appointed by a committee?—In that case we would consult the committee very likely.

641. If he were a suspended clergyman, you would remove him from all the schools, as I understand you?—Yes, if he were a suspended clergyman we should.

642. But if the committee refuse to remove a person whom they have the appointment of, what then?—I should hold him, if the ecclesiastical authority continued his suspension, as, in my mind, an unfit person.

643. In your view you would dismiss or remove him by withdrawing the supplies?—We should at once.

644. Now, supposing that in the case of a lay manager you received a notification,

SELECT COMMITTEE ON CALLAN SCHOOLS. 65

cation, say from the bishop of the diocese, that he was under an excommunication and unfit to give religious instruction, or to superintend the religious instruction in the school, would you take any notice of such a proceeding as that?—I think the general character of the man would have weight with us, even though it were a lay manager.

645. In that case, then, you would enter into the grounds of the excommunication?—No; but if it were certified to us by competent authority that he was so-and-so, we have dismissed many managers on grounds of bad character.

646. I want to know whether you would enter into the grounds of his excommunication in that case?—That case has never occurred to us of a layman being notified to the Board as under excommunication.

647. Have you ever had any case that you remember before the Board of Education in which the Board were called upon to take steps to have a schoolmaster dismissed on the ground of ecclesiastical censure?—I cannot remember such a case.

648. Have you ever called upon managers to dismiss a particular schoolmaster?—It is impossible for me to enter into those matters of detail.

649. Dr. *Lyon Playfair*.] From your long experience at the Board perhaps you will recollect the time when it was first the practice of the Board to appoint clerical managers of one particular denomination, without reference to the others, as manager of a school?—I think I recollect it.

650. Can you tell me the date when the practice began of appointing a clerical manager of a single denomination the manager of a school?—It gradually crept in. It had existed previously to the union of the Synod of Ulster with the Board, and then the number of those cases was largely increased.

651. Was it the original intention, in Lord Stanley's letter, that there should be such appointments?—There was an option given, I think, for a union of the different churches to apply.

652. Perhaps I may save you the trouble of reading Lord Stanley's letter; I think it was to this effect: "The Board will probably look with peculiar favour upon applications proceeding either from: first, the Protestant and Roman Catholic clergy of the parish; second, one of the clergymen and a certain number of parishioners professing the opposite creed; or, third, parishioners of both denominations"?—Yes, that was previous to my appointment, considerably. That has been very much departed from. The trial was made upon that basis, and it had not succeeded; very few Presbyterians had joined the Board up to the period of the junction of the Synod of Ulster.

653. I think you had not the term "manager" till 1838?—It was introduced in the year 1838.

654. And after that the non-vested schools were treated very much as *quasi*-denominational schools, were they not?—There was a good conscience clause, you know. The Synod of Ulster stipulated that they should have their own religious instruction, of course given by their own ministers; but there was this provision, that no child was required to be present at the religious instruction given contrary to the wishes of the parent. There was a strong conscience clause, as strong as you have in the Scotch Bill.

655. What did you exactly mean when you stated to-day that unless you had dismissed Mr. O'Keeffe, the Roman Catholic Church would have considered it subversive of discipline; subversive of whose discipline?—Of their own, and of ours too.

656. Have you anything to do, as a National Board, with whether the Roman Catholic Church consider anything connected with you as subversive of their discipline?—If our enactments interfered with their discipline with respect to the schools, I think they would have a fair right to object.

657. But do you recognise their schools as the schools of the Roman Catholic Church?—Well, our whole system goes very much upon that. Our returns are denominational returns of Presbyterians, Roman Catholics, &c.; and I may state for my own body, that they always call them their own schools.

658. What I want to know is this: if the manager of a school is performing his secular duties as connected with your Board, have you anything to do in the National Board as to what is done external to his duties as a manager of a school;

Rev.
P. S. Henry, D.D.

9 June 1873.

0.93.   I

school; have you anything to do with his relations to the church to which he belongs?—Not in that particular case; but if a man is a minister, a clergyman under his church, that is a different question.

659. You consider it is desirable then that you should have to do with his relations to his church?—Yes.

660. You said that you could not keep a suspended clergyman as manager of a school, because he is the person to impart religious instruction to the children under his care. In which of your rules is it provided that a clergyman shall give the religious instruction?—The parents originally you know had the right, but it has fallen, I think, into the hands of the clergy naturally to give the religious instruction.

661. But my question is, in which of your rules is it provided that the clergyman shall give religious instruction, and not the teacher?—There is no rule preventing him.

662. But is there any rule enjoining him to do it?—No; but it is a matter of practice into which they have naturally fallen.

663. But if there is no rule that the clergyman shall give the religious instruction, why is his suspension, as a clergyman, a sufficient reason for his dismissal from the school?—Because in the case of almost every priest and Presbyterian minister, who is manager of a school, the clergyman is the person who gives religious instruction; and I suppose, indeed I am certain, that the Board knew that Mr. O'Keeffe was placed over the children as their spiritual adviser.

664. The patron, as patron, or the manager, has no right to give religious instruction in a school, has he?—No right; but as I said before, in the case of a clergyman, he is the natural person, because he generally has applied to be the manager, and then he is the person who gives religious instruction.

665. Is that so generally, that a clerical manager does give religious instruction, or does he not allow the teacher to give it?—He may depute the duty to the teacher, but I believe, in most cases, they weekly examine children themselves. That was my own practice; my teacher gave religious instruction from 2 to 3 o'clock; and I examined the children myself once a week, and very often more, when I was patron of a school.

666. What did you mean by your expression that the dismissal of Mr. O'Keeffe was necessary for "independent internal discipline." How did it increase the independence of the Board?—It is the discipline of the church that I allude to; I think it would produce a very bad effect in the country if that discipline were subverted.

667. Then you spoke of the independence of the church when you said that the dismissal of Mr. O'Keeffe was necessary for independence?—I said that it was necessary to enable a church to sustain its discipline. That if our acts should interfere with that they would have a right to complain.

668. I want to know what you meant when you said it was necessary for independent and internal discipline. Was it the independent and internal discipline of the school?—The school, and the parish, and the neighbourhood. I think it would have a very bad effect upon any church if that discipline were subverted.

669. And that, therefore, the dismissal of any suspended clergyman increases independence?—No, but I think that the retaining of him would decrease the harmony and the peace of the parish.

670. *The O'Conor Don.*] In respect to the last point but one on which Dr. Lyon Playfair has been asking you questions, is it not the fact that the managers of non-vested schools have the decision as to who is to give religious instruction to the children?—In the non-vested school that is the case.

671. And, therefore, if the manager were a clergyman, he having the decision in his own hands as to the person who should give religious instruction, he can appoint himself to give it?—He would either give it himself or appoint a teacher; or both.

672. And he being a suspended clergyman, you do not think it desirable he should have the power of giving the religious instruction himself, or of determining who is to give it?—Certainly not.

673. Which

673. Which power belongs to him as manager?—That power belongs to him as manager.

674. The Committee do not wish to go into the rules and proceedings of the Presbyterian Church in detail, but with reference to the particular case of Mr. Fisher, I would ask you, was Mr. Fisher a suspended Presbyterian clergyman before he appealed to the General Assembly?—He must have appealed, or else the case would not have been considered, and I have the recollection that he did appeal. He was first found guilty by the Presbytery, and then in the Presbyterian Church there is an appeal from a Presbytery to either a Synod or the General Assembly: sometimes to the Synod, but the final appeal is to the General Assembly.

675. But, unless the clergyman appeals, does the case come before the General Assembly at all?—Not at all. It is noted in the Minutes, and passes; it does not come otherwise before them than in the report of the Presbytery.

676. With reference to Mr. Fisher's case, so far as the Minutes of the Board can be taken as recording the fact, his case does not appear to have ever been before the Board until after his suspension had been ratified by the General Assembly?—I am certain that it was not from the tenour of my letter. There is one thing which I beg to refer to, with the permission of the Committee. I said that Mr. Fisher had left the country. I only got the letter yesterday to look at, and I see that I applied that he should not be paid. That proves that he had not left the country, so that I was under a mistake on that point.

677. With respect to Mr. Wilson's case, is it not the fact that before the Board removed him from the management of the Glenvale School, they had a letter from him in which he stated that he was not deposed from the ministry, and that it was a false representation to state that it was so?—I think there is a letter in which he admits that he was degraded, and it is embodied in a Minute of the Board afterwards.

678. Does he not say, "I am not deposed from the ministry"?—"I am not deposed from the ministry, as it appears has been falsely represented to the Commissioners of Education." That is a very common thing.

679. Does he not further on in the same letter say that he intends shortly to appeal to a jury of his countrymen?—He does.

680. And with that letter before them, the Board decided to remove him from the management of the schools?—They did.

681. Mr. *Whitbread*.] Does he not go on to say that he continues regularly to officiate in his own meeting-house?—He does, but not under that body; he had joined another body.

682. And does he not further on still dispute that Mr. Templeton was his successor?—I suppose he disputed everything.

683. And he further states, does he not, that the school was built by private subscription, and then The O'Conor Don's question comes in?—Yes.

684. *The O'Conor Don*.] And in spite of all this, the Commissioners having all these statements before they removed him?—Yes.

685. Mr. *Whitbread*.] They not only removed him, but declined to enter upon a discussion of the various matters relating to his deposition?—Yes.

686. *The O'Conor Don*.] And did they not decline to recognise him as the manager of either Glenvale or any other national school?—Yes.

687. With regard to Dr. Keenan's case, I suppose you are not aware of what the appeal that he referred to was?—No, not at all.

688. You are not aware whether it might not have been an appeal to Dr. Murray, who was one of the Board?—It might have been.

689. You have already stated that you took a very active part in bringing about the junction of the Presbyterian body with the national system of education?—Yes.

690. And also that if any formal rule had been made known to the Presbyterian body at that time, to the effect that a suspended clergyman of their persuasion might be continued in the management of their schools, you think they would not have joined?—They would certainly have remonstrated very strongly, and endeavoured to get that rule removed; but I am sure that if the Commissioners had continued to act upon that rule, they would not have joined; at least, that is my impression.

691. It

Rev.
P. S. Henry, D.D.
9 June 1873.

691. It is your impression that the Presbyterian body joined the national system upon the understanding that the contrary was the rule and practice of the Board?—The Presbyterian body knew it perfectly, and never questioned it.

692. If it were desirable to alter that rule in any way, would it not be only fair to the Presbyterian and other religious bodies in Ireland, before the alteration should be made, that notice should be given to all the managers of the schools in the country?—Certainly.

693. And it would be a breach of faith to the managers to alter it in a particular instance, like Father O'Keeffe's, without notice?—Yes.

694. I believe that from the commencement you have been one of the most uncompromising adherents of the system of non-sectarian secular education?—I have; but I have been always a friend to the connection of religious instruction with the secular, and the basis of our Board of Education is this, united secular and separate religious instruction.

695. And was there not a great desire from the very commencement of the establishment of national education in Ireland to get the co-operation of the different religious bodies, the clergy of all denominations?—There was a great effort made, in fact the first efforts of Dr. Carlisle and the Archbishop of Dublin were upon that foundation, but they did not succeed; and I am quite certain that in Ireland, in very few neighbourhoods, could you succeed in having three ministers of different denominations to co-operate in carrying on a school; I believe it would be utterly futile.

696. But has not the adhesion of the clergy of all denominations to the national system of education been very general?—Very general of late. Since the Correen case, when the non-vested system was introduced.

697. And all previous attempts to establish a national system of education in Ireland had failed to obtain that assistance from the clergy?—They did not co-operate at all; and they do now.

698. Do you think that that co-operation could ever have been obtained if the practice of the Board had not been what it was with regard to suspended clergymen?—My impression is that it would have been extremely limited, and that the opposition which exists now on the part of some of the ecclesiastical authorities would have been infinitely stronger than it is; I am quite sure of that. I believe that the priesthood generally in the country are favourable to the national mode of education on its present foundation.

699. And I presume we may take it that the majority of the Commissioners with whom you acted with regard to the case of Father O'Keeffe, acted in a *bona fide* endeavour to carry out what they believe to be the uniform practice of the Board?—Certainly, every one of us; there is not the slightest doubt about it.

700. You stated at the commencement of your examination to-day, that you were not present when the vote took place on the first occasion with regard to Father O'Keeffe's case?—No, I was ill.

701. I presume we may take it, that if you had been present you would have voted with the majority?—I certainly would have voted as I have done all through; I have never hesitated.

702. Mr. *Bourke*.] With regard to Dr. Keenan's case, it is hardly fair to ask you, have you got a vivid recollection of it all?—No, I do not remember much about it; I remember the result.

703. You do not recollect whether the Board were unanimous on that question or not?—They were perfectly unanimous I believe, and there was no difference of opinion.

704. Was there any record kept at that time of any divisions that took place at the Board?—They say that some record was lost at that time; I saw a note to that effect, but I am quite sure that there was no difference of opinion on any of those cases of precedent.

705. When was the practice first introduced of recording the names in the divisions that took place at the Board?—Subsequently to that; I cannot tell exactly when.

706. It was long subsequently to that, was it not?—I believe it was.

707. Do you recollect in Dr. Keenan's case, how long Dr. Keenan was retained by the Board after it became known to the Board that he had been suspended?
—I cannot

SELECT COMMITTEE ON CALLAN SCHOOLS. 69

—I cannot enter into the details of the dates now. My own impression is, that his dismissal, or whatever it was, took place soon after. There was a great deal of disturbance in the neighbourhood at the time; he had a number of adherents and there were a number on the other side; but we never entered into that; we had no opportunity or machinery for doing so.

Rev. P. S. *Henry*, D.D.
9 June 1873.

708. Do you recollect Mr. Wilson's case sufficiently well, to state positively, that the action of the Board with regard to him was taken entirely and solely because he had been suspended by the Presbytery?—Not the slightest doubt of it.

709. There were no other reasons for the action of the Board?—The school was very badly conducted, I believe, at that time.

710. There was no other reason, you think?—I do not think that any other reason was taken into account but the deposition. I am certain there was not any other.

711. With regard to that case, was there an application from Mr. Doherty to be made manager?—I think he was parish priest?—I cannot recollect that.

712. And you do not recollect whether, in fact, Mr. Templeton was or was not appointed as his successor as manager of the school?—I think he was.

713. But you are not sure?—No.

714. With regard to other persons, has it ever come before the Board that there were certain clergymen who were suspended and remained managers of schools?—I never knew an instance.

715. Do you recollect a gentleman who was very well known in Ireland called Father Daly?—The Galway man you allude to, I suppose. I remember him.

716. Was he suspended?—I cannot enter into the circumstances of the case. I know that he was a very popular man, and had a great following, but I cannot recollect whether he was suspended or not.

717. Do you know whether he was the manager of a school under the National Board?—I have no recollection.

718. You do not recollect that he was manager of several schools under the National Board?—He may have been. My recollection was of the good dinners that he gave and got.

719. That was not incompatible with his remaining manager of national schools?—Not at all.

720. *The O'Conor Don.*] With regard to that last question about Father Daly, whether Father Daly was suspended or not, was his suspension ever brought before the Board?—I cannot remember it.

721. Do you believe that suspended clergymen have ever been continued in the management of schools after their cases were formally brought before the Board?—Never. I do not believe it could be so; I am perfectly certain that we are unanimous on that, and uniform in our practice.

722. If there had been any difference of opinion with reference to these cases referred to in this Parliamentary Paper, you would have remembered that difference of opinion, would you not?—Perfectly. We were all of one mind all through the whole of those cases. I mean that the senior Commissioners were, and there are four of them remaining still, I believe, who remembered the uniformity, and who were guided by the past precedents in deciding this case.

723. *Mr. Cross.*] Do you know, as a fact, whether Mr. O'Farrell was insane? —I do not know. There was a report that he was; but I merely heard it as a report.

724. Do you happen to know when it was that Mr. O'Farrell was first suspended?—No.

725. *Chairman.*] Is there anything further that you wish to say?—Yes; considering the matter in my own mind, from time to time, this was my view: The Rev. Mr. O'Keeffe succeeded a priest in all his schools, except the Callan Infant School, which Mr. O'Keeffe added to the Male and Female National Schools. Having succeeded a priest as manager, he became that *ex officio*, and when he no longer held that office he no longer had that right. He was suspended from office by his ecclesiastical superior, who had a right to exercise jurisdiction, and the Commissioners have always recognised that jurisdiction. They have always

Rev.
P. S. Henry, D.D.
9 Jan. 1873.

always held that a priest, who must be a nominee of the bishop, is a fit person to be patron of the national schools in his own parish; and that a priest who has been suspended or degraded is unfit. The fitness in the one case, and the unfitness in the other, are both determined by the act of the ecclesiastical superior. The nomination and his suspension depend on the bishop, and his certificate of his act has ever been held by the Board as conclusive evidence in either case. A clerical patron has charge of providing religious instruction for the children attending his schools of the same religious denomination; but if he be deprived of the cure of souls in the parish by the authority of his church, he is certainly unfit to be entrusted with the charge of religious teaching. The precedents acted on by the Board all proceed on these broad and long-established grounds. The Commissioners have no power to institute any judicial inquiry as to the validity in any particular case of the exercise of ecclesiastical jurisdiction. No religious body would allow the Commissioners to usurp any authority in the matters of church discipline and authority. It is necessary that the Commissioners, under every change of administration in the Government or of the executive for the time being, should have the confidence of all religious bodies, who must not interfere with their jurisdiction as long as religious instruction is allowed to be given in the school at the time specified in the time table. The system of combined secular and separate religious instruction implies that the latter element shall be always under the surveillance of religious authority, having the approval of the parents or guardians of the children. The confidence of the parents in a suspended or degraded clergyman cannot be assumed, whilst as public functionaries the Commissioners are bound, I think, by the most weighty considerations to avoid in all their decisions the appearance of fostering insubordination, contumacy, or rebellion in any of the churches represented at a mixed Board for common objects. Besides, it is to be assumed by the Commissioners that, if the spiritual authority of the parents' child withdraws a clergyman from his functions, the latter is unfit to exercise them, and cannot, as a rule, be approved by the parents as a fit and proper person to watch over the religious education of the children.

726. Those you give as your opinions?—Those are my opinions.

727. But not anybody else's?—I speak for myself, not for others.

728. Dr. *Lyon Playfair*.] You give those as your opinions as a Commissioner?—Yes.

729. Do you disagree then with Judge Longfield and Sir Alexander Macdonnell in their view that there are no *ex officio* appointments recognised by the Board?—The rule of practice is that the clerical successors become successors in the schools also.

730. But you have used the term *ex officio*. Is it your opinion, as a member of the Board, that *ex officio* appointments are recognised by the Board?—I will give you an instance if you will permit me; a minister lately died in my church having 12 schools under him; his successor will apply to us to be admitted, and we shall admit him at once, as his successor.

731. Are you aware that Judge Longfield and Sir Alexander Macdonnell both said that the Board recognised no clerical successor *ex officio*?—They mean necessarily. As a rule the clerical successors are recognised.

732. That is not the meaning of your term *ex officio*, then?—The meaning is, that as a general rule, it is the case.

733. In the ninth rule as to "The Management of National Schools," it is said that, in all cases the Commissioners reserve to themselves the power of determining whether the patron is a fit and proper person to exercise the trust. Is that compatible with your statement just now, that the fitness and unfitness are both determined by the action of the ecclesiastical superior?—If nothing to the contrary is produced against the man, the authority of his ecclesiastical superior would be taken.

734. My question is this, do the Board renounce their own right of determining fitness, and pass it over to the ecclesiastical superior?—Not absolutely.

735. Relatively?—Well, I would say, as the rule and practice, it is so.

736. *Chairman.*] Judge Longfield is asked, "When a clergyman is nominated *primâ facie*, you consider him fit?" and the answer is, "We consider him fit." Then he is asked, "But if a specific objection were made against him, what would

would you do?" and he answers, "We should inquire into it, to see if it was a proper case for continuing him." Do you agree with that?—I entirely agree with that.

Rev.
P. S. Henry, D.D.

9 June 1873.

737. Mr. *Whitbread.*] Fitness, according to your view as guaranteed by the ecclesiastical authority, only holds good till some objection is raised against it?—Yes.

738. *The O'Conor Don.*] You do not mean to say that the Commissioners relinquish their right of deciding upon his fitness, but that they take the statement of the ecclesiastical authority into consideration, and act upon that?—Yes.

739. In themselves determining whether he is fit or not?—Yes; but if any evidence were laid before us that a manager, recommended by whom he might, was an unfit person, I am quite certain we should not appoint him.

740. And you would consider a suspended clergyman to be an unfit person to be the manager of any school?—Certainly.

741. Mr. *Gathorne Hardy.*] Do you give that opinion upon any facts as the action of the Board, or as your own opinion only?—It arises from a number of circumstances; they have always acted upon it.

742. That is what I want to know; has there been any case where the ecclesiastical superior has declared a man to be fit, and you have declared him to be unfit?—I cannot remember a case.

743. Mr. *Cross.*] Do you agree with the answer to Question 423 given by Mr. Keenan; he is asked, "But upon the purely ministerial removal by the Board, we will assume that the successor is nominated by the same person upon whose certificate the party suspended has been removed from his position as manager; do you then inquire into his fitness?" and he answers, "Certainly"?—We inquire into his fitness.

Mr. *Patrick Joseph Keenan*, C.B., re-called; and further Examined.

Mr.
P. J. Keenan, C.B.

744. Mr. *Cross.*] You undertook to put in two circulars, and to produce some correspondence; do you produce the correspondence relating to the Annaduff School?—Yes (*producing it*). With regard to the circulars, one is dated the 6th of March 1867, and is issued by the order of the Board. The other is dated 27th of July 1857, and was not submitted to the Board, or issued under its authority; it is an office circular.

745. *Chairman.*] Will you explain what you mean by that?—In the routine of the administration from time to time, circulars are issued on business matters to the inspectors, sometimes relating to the details of their work, sometimes to the explanations that are required on various points of interest, and sometimes to expositions of rules or practices of the Board.

746. I suppose they have the authority of the resident Commissioner?—This circular is of so old a date, that I did not think it necessary to ask Sir Alexander Macdonnell whether he remembered it.

747. Who would issue that circular to which you refer?—It was issued by the secretaries. I have not the slightest recollection of it, or of its origin, and the secretaries are utterly ignorant of its origin also. The first Circular is this: " Sir,- We are to inform you that the Commissioners of National Education have decided that, in the cases of change of managers of national schools by death, transfer to some other locality, or from any other cause, the parties recommended to succeed, if laymen, will be considered as only acting *pro tem.* until such time as the opinion of the inspector, to whom the matter in each case will be referred, shall have been obtained as to their eligibility.—We are, Sir, your obedient servants, *Maurice Cross, James Kelly,* Secretaries." That circular was issued by an order made by the Board on the 13th February 1857, the circular itself being dated 6th March 1857. The second Circular, that dated the 27th of July 1857, is as follows: " Sir,—We find that when vacancies occur, from time to time, in the management of non-vested national schools by the removal from the locality of clergymen who had previously acted in that capacity,

Mr.
P. J. Keenan, C.B.
9 June 1873.

capacity, it is the practice of many of the Inspectors to return as managers, in their reports, the names of the clerical successors of such clergymen, without any authority from this office for so doing. We have to remind you that this practice is irregular, and gives rise to much inconvenience; for although in the great majority of instances the late manager's successor in the clerical capacity succeeds likewise to the management of the school, yet such does not follow as a matter of course, inasmuch as the out-going manager, where the school is not under a committee, has the right of nominating as his successor whoever he thinks proper, subject to the approval of the Commissioners. It is only when the vacancy is caused by the death of the late manager, and where school is not under a committee, that his clerical successor is recognised to have a *de facto* right to the management of the school. We are, therefore, to request that in future you will be good enough to attend to the following regulations on this subject: 1. In case the vacancy arises from the decease of the late manager, and school not under a committee, you will state so in your report and insert the name of his clerical successor. 2. In the event of the vacancy being caused by the late manager's removal, and school without a committee, you are to communicate with him on the subject of nominating his successor, and forward his reply, with your report, accompanied by your own opinion as to the fitness of the person whom he nominates. If necessary, you will be permitted to detain your report for a few days, awaiting his reply, but in this case you will be careful to state on your journals the cause of such delay. 3. Where a school non-vested is under a committee, the appointment of the local manager or correspondent in every case rests with them. It is desirable that you should not recognise any person as manager of a National school until you shall have received notice from this office that his appointment has received the sanction of the Commissioners.— We are, Sir, your obedient servants, *Maurice Cross* and *James Kelly*, Secretaries." That evidently was intended by the secretaries as an exposition of the rule upon the subject at the moment as it was understood by whoever framed that circular.

748. And carries with it in the eyes of those who received it the authority of the Board, I suppose?—Well, as an instruction from the office, it had of course on the inspectors as much incumbency as if it had originated practically with the Board.

749. *The O'Conor Don.*] But, as a matter of fact, it never was before the Board?—No, never; I have caused inquiry to be made in reference to that.

750. *Chairman.*] But do you mean to throw any doubt upon those being known to the Board at the time as the instructions under which the inspectors were acting?—The circular clearly was never before the Board, and never placed on its Minutes; but I do not mean to impute the slightest doubt as to the genuineness of it as an official document emanating from the office.

751. Has it ever been cancelled?—Not that I am aware of.

752. It has been in operation, therefore, ever since?—I can hardly speak to that, inasmuch as I myself was utterly ignorant of the existence of it.

753. Is it part of the instructions of the inspectors?—It would naturally remain in force if some subsequent circular altering the conditions laid down in it had not been issued.

754. So far as you know, there has been no circular altering the conditions, has there?—No.

755. So far, therefore, as you, the Resident Commissioner, know, it is part of the instructions of the inspectors at this hour?—It is practically part of the instructions that an inspector has for his guidance, as derived from the records of the circulars and instructions of the office.

756. And if any inspector failed to act upon it, he would be violating his duty?—He would.

757. *Mr. Whitbread.*] How does an inspector get his instructions when he is appointed?—There was a code of instructions drawn up, I think, about the year 1855, for inspectors, and published in the annual report, I think, of the same year, which was intended as a general code of instructions for the inspectors. Then, they receive in detail, instructions from time to time upon various points connected with their duties, and are bound to keep upon a file all such instructions emanating from the office.

758. But, supposing that an inspector were appointed to-day, how would he become

become acquainted with that circular?—If an inspector be appointed to-day he is brought to the office, and the person who is charged with the Inspection Department is commissioned to acquaint him with the various details of his duty, and to give him an opportunity of reading all the circulars that have ever been issued from the office on points connected with the inspection of schools.

Mr. P. J. Keenan, c.b.

9 June 1873.

759. *The O'Conor Don.*] You were an inspector for some time yourself, were you not?—I was.

760. You were so at the time that the circular was issued, I suppose?—Yes.

761. Do you remember having received it?—I entirely forget it; but I can account for that forgetfulness, as at the time I was engaged upon a special duty.

762. *Mr. Bourke.*] Have you looked into the Minutes of the Board as to whether there are any Minutes with respect to that circular?—I sent instructions on Thursday evening (after I was requested by the Committee to produce the circulars) to the secretaries to send me the circulars, and also the original document or authority upon which each circular was based. In reference to the first circular which I have read, I was informed that it was issued by the Board's order of the 13th of February. In reference to the second, I was informed that no trace could be found in the office as to its origin, that it is not on the Minutes, and that the substance of it is not to be found on any document to be met with. The third point that I was requested to obtain information upon, had reference to the practice of obtaining votes at the Board. I find that the first expression of dissent on the part of a member to an order of the Board, was made on Thursday, the 24th of December 1846.

763. *Mr. Cross.*] But the names at that time were not taken down, were they?—The names of all who were present were taken down, as, for instance, in the case before me, they were all taken down; the names were, the Archbishop of Dublin, the Provost, Archbishop Murray. the Marquis of Kildare, Robert Holmes, Esq., J. R. Corballis, Esq., and the Right Hon. Alexander Macdonnell. And then, when the order is set forth in full, there is appended, "Robert Holmes, Esq., expressed his dissent to the above order."

764. But on a division the names were not taken down as they are in a Committee-room here till a much later period, were they?—In effect I should think it meant much the same; but in the way of regular voting the first instance I see occurred on the 17th of June 1853. Then I find various divisions, those voting for the question being given in one column, and those against it in another.

765. And since that time that has been the practice of the Board?—Since that time it has been the ordinary practice of the Board.

The Right Honourable *Charles* Viscount *Monck* (attending by special permission of the House of Lords); Examined.

766-7. *Chairman.*] How long have you been a Commissioner?—I was appointed, I think, in the end of 1871 or the beginning of 1872.

Right Hon. Viscount *Monck.*

768. Had you any previous acquaintance with the working of the system of National Education in Ireland?—Yes; I have been manager of schools for, I suppose, 25 years.

769. You are acquainted with the rules of the system and with the practice?—Yes.

770. What do you consider to be the right of appointing a manager, and deciding whether a patron or his appointee shall be manager?—I think that that knowledge is to be obtained from the rules, which seem to me to be perfectly explicit on the subject. The rules reserve to the Board absolutely in all cases the right of saying whether a patron or his appointee is a fit person to exercise the trust; and therefore it appears to me that those rules absolutely exclude the notion of *ex officio* right to apointment.

771. With regard to clergymen who have been suspended, and the succession to their vacancy, what do you consider to be the rule of the Board upon that subject?—In order to explain my view on that subject, I must state what I conceive to be one of the great objects of appointing managers of schools at all.

0.93. K Everyone

Right Hon.
Viscount *Monck*.
———
9 June 1873.

Everyone who has taken any part in popular instruction knows that one of the great difficulties that we have to contend with is securing the regular attendance of children at the schools, and I think that one of the first qualities we should look for in a manager is the possession of that kind of moral influence in the district surrounding the schools which will enable him to obtain the attendance of the children.

772. We are asking you what you do, not what should be the practice?—When I say "should," I think that we do that. It is to be collected from the rules; at least, that is my view as a Commissioner. Now, I do not know any person who would so completely fulfil those conditions as the recognised pastor of any communion within the district. His recognition by the people gives him that moral influence with them which we desire to appropriate for our purposes. But if he gets into a dispute with his ecclesiastical superiors on the one hand, or with any large portion of his flock on the other, I think he loses necessarily the qualities to which I have adverted, and loses that moral influence with the people. It is inconceivable, I think, that a clergyman could be suspended by his ecclesiastical superiors in a parish, without creating two parties in that parish, and with one of those parties he would lose the moral influence which we conceive to be necessary, or which I, at least, conceive to be necessary, for the proper discharge of his duty as manager of the schools. I may mention that there is evidence, that in the case which the Committee is investigating, that has occurred in Callan parish; because Mr. O'Keeffe, in his evidence the other day in the trial which took place in Dublin, stated that since his suspension his income, as parish priest, had considerably fallen off, in consequence of missionary fathers having been sent down there. Now, that could only occur by a considerable portion of his flock availing themselves of the ministrations of their missionary fathers; and that would be an indication that there is even in that parish a considerable party opposed to Father O'Keeffe.

773. You consider that the appointment is not made *ex officio*, but on the ground of fitness?—Yes.

774. As a *primâ facie* evidence of fitness, open to the judgment of the Commissioners upon any case stated to the contrary?—Certainly; I think his existence, as a recognised clergyman in charge of the parish, is *primâ facie* evidence of his fitness; but like all *primâ facie* cases, is liable to be upset by investigation or evidence.

775. Is the case of his being suspended proof of unfitness?—*Primâ facie*, I think it is.

776. Dr. *Lyon Playfair*.] Is the chief reason of your appointment of clerical managers the motive of obtaining regular attendance at the school?—I only spoke my own opinion; it is with me.

777. Do you know as a fact, to guide the precedents of the Board, that there is a larger attendance in schools with clerical managers than with lay managers?—I cannot speak to that fact as a Commissioner, but from my own knowledge of the country, I should say that there was.

778. Are you aware that throughout the whole of Ireland there is the extraordinary amount of 54 per cent. of truancy in the Irish schools?—I know that it is very large.

779. And that in England it is only 20 per cent.?—I was not aware of the figures.

780. Then that primary object has not been attained by the appointment of clerical managers, has it?—It is very hard to answer that question, because it might have been much worse if there had not been clerical managers.

781. *The O'Conor Don*.] You are aware of course that in England, for a long time, there has been payment of teachers by results?—Yes.

782. And that in Ireland, until this last year, there has been no such system?—No; and I may mention, as this question has been raised, that within my own experience the attendance in the schools with which I am personally acquainted, has increased largely since the system of payment by results has been introduced.

783. Mr. *Cross*.] You said that suspension you would take as *primâ facie* proof of unfitness for the position of manager of a school?—As *primâ facie* proof of the loss of the influence for which the man was originally appointed.

784. But

SELECT COMMITTEE ON CALLAN SCHOOLS.

Right Hon.
Viscount Monck.

9 June 1873.

784. But capable of being rebutted by other evidence?—Yes.
785. And therefore by the evidence of the man who had been removed, among other evidence?—Yes.
786. Then in accordance with your view, in order to find out whether that *primâ facie* evidence could be rebutted, it would be desirable to call the person who had been dismissed, as well as others, to rebut that *primâ facie* evidence?—I do not think that the Commissioners could do that; they have not the machinery for the purpose; and I think we should act on the *primâ facie* case in each instance.
787. If it is a *primâ facie* case it must be capable of being rebutted; and then you must hear the evidence on the other side, must you not?—I did not say that we should enter into the evidence on each case; we have not the means of doing that. I used the words "*primâ facie* evidence" more with reference to the fitness than to the unfitness. We take the fact of a man's holding a particular position as *primâ facie* evidence of his fitness for the management of schools, and we appoint him, unless there is some evidence to the contrary. But when it comes to a question of his losing the influence in respect of which we appointed him, I do not think it is conceivable that he could be fit; because I think that it is impossible to conceive a case in which the deprivation of a clergyman by his ecclesiastical superiors would not deprive him of his influence with a considerable portion of his people.
788. Then do you agree with Mr. Keenan, that the office of the Board in that case is simply ministerial, or do you think that it is merely *primâ facie* proof of unfitness?—I admit that there is a difficulty in answering that question. When I came to the conclusion in my own mind, that the position in which a man has been placed has deprived him of the qualities in respect of which he has been appointed, I should remove him. Perhaps I was wrong in using the words "*primâ facie*" in respect to that class of cases.

789. Mr. *Bourke.*] Would the Board, as far as you know their practice, take into consideration in appointing a clerical successor to a suspended clergyman, whether the appointment of that successor would have the effect or not of removing the discord likely to arise in the parish, to which you have alluded, in consequence of the first clergyman having been suspended; would they take into consideration the fact that the appointment of the successor might continue the discord or might increase the discord in the parish in case he was appointed?—I think the rule of the Board, or rather as there is no rule on the subject, the practice has been, when a clergyman has been suspended to appoint his successor; *primâ facie* we assume that the successor, as we did about the original manager, is a fit person. But as in this instance, when it is shown that he is not, the schools are removed from connection with the Board. In this case, a successor to Mr. O'Keeffe was appointed, but we found that it would not work, and we have struck off the schools altogether. I think there is a little misuse of terms in talking of "removing" people from the management of schools. What we really do is to remove ourselves from connection with them. In 99 cases out of 100 we have no power to remove the manager; the schools are his own property.
790. You cease to correspond with him?—We cease to correspond; that is the only thing that we can do.

791. Mr. *Whitbread.*] It would be quite possible, would it not, for the Committee of that school to remove Mr. Martin, and to suggest to the Board another manager?—Of course it would.

792. *Chairman.*] You consider the practice to have been uniform in the case of a suspended clergyman, that he has never been continued in the management of a school which he obtained as a clergyman?—Well, I have been so very short a time a Commissioner, that I was dependent upon others for a statement of the practice of the Board; but before I came to a conclusion on this case, I heard all the precedents that we could get together, and it seemed to me, that the practice was perfectly uniform.

0.93.

Mr. *James Kelly*, called in ; and Examined.

793. *Chairman.*] You are one of the Joint Secretaries of the Board?—I am.

794. How long have you been so?—Since the year 1841.

795. Then you have been secretary during the whole time that the precedents referred to in this evidence have taken place?—Yes.

796. Are you cognisant of the evidence that has been given before the Committee?—No.

797. Mr. *Gathorne Hardy.*] You were secretary during the periods of all these precedents, you say?—Yes.

798. When you as secretary receive intimation of the suspension of any clerical manager, do you communicate it forthwith to the Board, or do you take any step before such communication?—I may say that although I was joint secretary during that time, yet nearly all the business of the Board was transacted at that time by my colleague, Mr. Cross. The practice was to bring the cases of suspension before the Board at once.

799. Can you tell me, in the case of the Rev. Mr. Sheridan, which is given on page 19 of the Report moved for by Mr. Pim, No. 138, at what period the secretaries of the Board became cognisant of the suspension of Mr. Sheridan; it does not appear on the printed documents, but we have had from Mr. Keenan a statement that shows us that a letter was written announcing the suspension of Mr. Sheridan as early as January 1863; is that so?—Yes.

800. And that the secretaries replied to that on the 19th of February 1863?—Yes.

801. Now can you tell me how soon the suspension of Mr. Sheridan was communicated by the secretaries to the Board of Education?—On the 27th of January 1865.

802. After receiving that intimation in January 1863, can you tell me whether the secretaries took any step to obtain information about Mr. Sheridan?—I find that there was a letter written stating the rule of the Board in such cases, " And that, as the schools in question are under committees, it is their privilege to appoint managers." This is in reply to a letter from the Rev. Mr. Fulham, communicating the fact that he was administrator of the parish, and that Mr. Sheridan, whose successor he was, was a suspended priest. There was a letter written stating that it was their privilege to appoint a manager; and requested him to procure letters from them appointing him, and that on receipt of such letters we would be happy to enter his name as manager. It was not communicated to the Board, I observe.

803. Mr. *Bourke.*] Who is that signed by?—The Rev. Mr. Fulham it was who wrote to us.

804. Mr. *Gathorne Hardy.*] But the secretaries' letter, I presume, was signed by Mr. Cross and yourself?—Yes.

805. Then, as I understand that letter, you, the secretaries, without communicating with the Board at all, supposed that Mr. Sheridan was absolutely removed by his suspension?—If I might offer an opinion, I find I noted this letter myself, and it strikes me that it occurred to me that as soon as the appointment by the committee took place, and we received a letter from them announcing the successor, then the matter would not require any further investigation.

806. From what documents did you derive the rule that you say was stated in that letter?—In this case the school was non-vested and under a committee. In such a case the committee, according to the rules of the Board, have the power of appointing a successor.

807. But that is assuming that there is a vacancy, is it not?—I would suppose that the committee would have the power of removing a manager.

808. That is what I want to understand; that you wanted to leave upon the committee the duty of removing the manager who was suspended?—The explanation may be possibly that I did not advert to the fact, that he gave notice that Mr. Sheridan was a suspended priest when noting that letter.

809. *Chairman.*] Have you a copy of the letter that you wrote to Mr. Fulham?—No, I have not a copy of it; but it is stated in answer to Question 288.

810. Mr.

810. Mr. *Gathorne Hardy*.] Your letter was written to Mr. Fulham referring him to the committee for his appointment?—Yes.
811. You never communicated with the committee directly?—No.
812. Nor did you make the Board acquainted with the information that you had received, that Mr. Sheridan was a suspended priest?—No.
813. May I ask what reason you had for keeping that from the Board so long as two years, if you had any reason?—The letter passed away from me into the corresponding department, and possibly it never occurred to me afterwards to look it up and bring it before the Board.
814. Have you had any other case of a similar kind, where you have had noted to you the suspension of a priest which never has come before the Board at all?—I do not recollect any.
815. Can you say, with confidence, that there never have been any during the time that you have been secretary?—I cannot recollect a case occurring.
816. Have you referred, in looking for precedents, only to those cases where the Board have acted, or have you looked also for cases where you had received as secretaries a notification of the suspension?—Well, the instruction was to look for all such cases amongst the records.
817. What cases; cases where the Board had acted?—No; cases where we had notice of a suspension.
818. In general, I suppose, the notice would come to you as secretaries?—Yes.
819. Then, do I rightly understand you to say, that in the case of Mr. Sheridan it appears to have been a case of neglect from the latter getting into the correspondence office, and no further notice being taken of it?—Well, I should say so.
820. How often are the schools inspected in Ireland?—The rule is to inspect them three times a year.
821. Would the inspectors duty be to ascertain whether the manager was a suspended priest or not?—If it came under his notice he would be bound to report it.
821*. Did the inspector bring to the notice of the Board the suspension of Mr. Sheridan?—The inspector, in his reports of the 13th February and 30th September 1863, and 10th February and 17th May 1864, the only reports received from him between the dates referred to on the Natoath National School, returns the Rev. P. Sheridan as manager. The fact of the Rev. P. Sheridan having been suspended, was brought to the inspector's notice by the secretaries' letter of the 26th September 1864.

Mr. J. Kelly.
9 June 1873.

822. Dr. *Lyon Playfair*.] I suppose that in the case of Mr. Fulham, who was claiming the managership of these schools, it would hardly be possible for the inspector to go into the parish without ascertaining that Mr. Sheridan was a suspended priest; would not that be so?—I suppose so. He would be very likely to hear it.
823. Mr. Fulham at that time was acting as administrator of the parish, was he not? He was; so he states.
824. And I suppose that during the whole of that two years, Mr. Sheridan was the person who was corresponded with as manager of the school?—Yes, I think so.
825. It must be so, must it not; you would not pay the money through anybody who was not the recognised manager?—No.
826. Have you the reports of the inspector of that district during that two years?—I have not got them here.
827. But you could find them?—Yes.
828. Perhaps you will be good enough to put on the notes of your evidence, whether or not the inspector in the course of those two years brought to the notice of the Board the suspension of Mr. Sheridan?—Yes.
829. Can you tell me whether there have been any cases of schoolmasters dismissed in your time on account of ecclesiastical censure?—I do not recollect any case of the kind.
830. Can you tell me also, whether in the practice of the Board, a case has ever occurred to your knowledge, of a lay manager being dismissed by the Board, or his removal called for, on account of any ecclesiastical censure?—No.

0.93.   K 3   831. Can

Mr. *J. Kelly.*
9 June 1873.

831. Can you speak with certainty on that subject; may I take it that to the best of your recollection there is no such case?—There is no such case within my recollection.

832. In all cases of dismissal of a manager, except in the cases which have been before us, do the Board enter into an inquiry as to the charges which are made against a manager; we have been told here that in the case of a clerical manager being suspended, the fact of suspension is taken from his ecclesiastical superiors without inquiry; in any other cases of charges against a manager, do the Board inquire into the truth of those charges?—There is a case in which an inspector stated to the Board that a manager was unfit, and the Board decided that as he had been manager of a school previously, and no objection had been made to him, they must decline to remove him.

833. Did they go into the charge that the inspector made as to the grounds of his unfitness?—Well, I think the statement was, that he was not qualified to act as the manager.

834. Was that a first appointment, or after he had been acting as manager?—It was on his appointment to a school for the first time.

835. Was that the case of a committee's appointment?—No; it was a case where there was a non-vested school, and where there was no committee.

836. Was he named by his predecessor, or did he propose himself?—It was a case in which he applied to place the school under the Board.

837. He had a school which he applied to place under the Board, and the inspector said that he was not fit to be manager; is that what you mean?—Yes.

838. That is hardly one of the cases that I was asking about; but in cases where a manager is acting as manager of a school, and some charge is made against him as to his unfitness for the place, would the Board generally make inquiry through their inspector otherwise as to those charges?—I do not recollect a case of the kind coming before the Board.

839. Do you recollect any cases of dismissal of managers by the Board except these which are upon the precedents?—There have been very numerous removals of managers caused by death.

840. But I was speaking of removal for misconduct?—I do not recollect any others.

841. Then, in fact, as far as you know, the only cases of removal by the Board are these four or five clerical cases which have been recorded in the precedents before us?—I should say it is very much confined to those.

842. With respect to schoolmasters, if you have a complaint, there is an inquiry in those cases, is there not always?—Yes, always.

843. *The O'Conor Don.*] Does that last answer apply to non-vested schools?—Yes.

844. Has not the manager of a non-vested school absolute power to dismiss a schoolmaster without any application to the Board?—Yes; but in case he did not dismiss him, and the inspector reported anything unfavourable to the teacher, then an inquiry would take place.

845. Mr. *Gathorne Hardy.*] Of course a manager may dismiss his schoolmaster, and, I presume, without coming to the Board at all; but where it comes before the Board the Board, through their inspector or otherwise, make an inquiry?—Yes.

846. Then you have no other evidence to give us as to the cases of suspension than those which we have already on our record?—No.

847. Nor are you able to add any facts as to the cases as reported there?—No.

848. *The O'Conor Don.*] With respect to this case of Mr. Fulham and Mr. Sheridan, is it not the fact, that although Mr. Fulham applied to be nominated in place of Mr. Sheridan on the 19th of February 1863, and you wrote back to him the letter, stating that if he were nominated by the committee his name would be entered as manager, he took no notice of that letter, and made no renewed application to the Board before the 26th of September 1864?—I see that that is so, as the papers have been furnished to me.

849. So that Mr. Fulham himself apparently left the matter in abeyance for this very long period of time?—Yes.

850. And

SELECT COMMITTEE ON CALLAN SCHOOLS.

Mr. J. Kelly.
9 June 1873.

850. And you account for the fact of its not being brought before the Board by the fact that probably the letter was put aside and forgotten?—Yes.

851. And no renewed application being received from Mr. Fulham till September 1864, it was not brought again to the notice of the secretaries?—No.

852. Now, with respect to the ordinary practice of the Board, is there any programme of the proceedings of the Board furnished to the Commissioners before the day on which they are called to attend?—There is an abstract of the previous day's proceedings furnished, and there is also a statement or programme of the papers to be submitted to the Board at the next meeting.

853. So that the members of the Board are aware of what is going to take place at the following meeting?—Yes.

854. Could you procure the abstracts submitted to the Board upon the days on which all these four precedents were taken into consideration which are before Parliament?—I rather think that some of them occurred. Mr. Keenan's case certainly occurred before it was the practice to send abstracts to the Commissioners.

855. When was that practice first introduced?—I cannot say. I think it was on the motion of the Rev. Dr. Henry, the last witness; and I cannot exactly say when it was introduced.

856. Could you procure for us the abstracts furnished in as many of these cases as there were abstracts furnished to each of the Commissioners?—The programmes were first issued about 1854, and the abstracts in November 1861; and as the proceedings in the Magheral and Glenvale cases took place prior to 1854, programmes or abstracts were not sent to the Commissioners. Mr. Newell will bring over all the programmes and abstracts which could be found in relation to the Annaduff, Natonth, and Ashbourne cases.

857. *Mr. Bourke.*] Were you present during all the discussions that took place in Mr. O'Keeffe's case?—Only on one occasion.

858. Which was that?—On the 25th March 1873.

859. Was your colleague present at all the others?—Yes.

860. You cannot recollect, then, whether something which I was going to draw your attention to took place in 1871 with regard to Mr. O'Keeffe?—I think the O'Keeffe case commenced in 1872.

861. But you cannot recollect anything about it in 1871?—No.

862. I will just draw your attention to Mr. Sheridan's case. Have you got the document which appointed Mr. Fulham the manager of the school?—On the 18th day of February 1865 there was an order made: "That the Rev. Mr. Fulham be recognised as manager of the Ratoath Schools." That was signed by the then Resident Commissioner.

863. Have you got the document of June 1865 which recognised him as manager?—I have not got the letter; I understood that it was sent over.

864. *Mr. Bourke* (to *Mr. Keenan*).] By whom was that letter written?—It was signed by Sir Alexander Macdonell, the then Resident Commissioner.

865. (To the *Witness*.) I want to know whether that appointment of Mr. Fulham depended solely and entirely upon the signature of Sir Alexander Macdonell?—It did.

866. There is nothing to show that it was the action of the Board beyond that?—Certainly not.

867. Do you remember any cases of suspended clergymen who have been continued or allowed to remain as managers of national schools?—In the Annaduff case the manager was also manager of Lisduff School, and after he had been removed as manager of the Annaduff School, be continued as manager of the Lisduff School. That may be accounted for in this way, that the first intimation of his being under suspension (it was the Rev. Mr. O'Farrell), only referred to the one school, the Annaduff School, and it was not inquired into whether he was manager of any other schools.

868. But it was known to the Board that he was suspended at that time?—Yes, it was known to the Board; he had been removed then from the management of the Annaduff School.

869. Do you recollect any other cases which came before the Board, or to the knowledge of the Board, in which suspended clergymen were managers of national

Mr. J. Kelly.
9 June 1873.

national schools, and were allowed to continue managers of national schools?—I do not recollect any case.

870. Do you know who Father Daly, of Galway, is?—Yes.

871. Do you know whether he was suspended or not?—I may have heard it, but I never knew it officially.

872. *Chairman.*] Do you know it at all?—Well, I have heard it by report, but not further.

873. Mr. *Bourke.*] I suppose you have only heard that the others have been suspended; you have not seen the documents which absolutely suspended them? —No.

874. Mr. *Whitbread.*] But the other cases have been brought officially to your notice, have they not?—Not by the documents conveying the suspension, but by letters stating that they were suspended. In the case of the Rev. Mr. Daly there was no official document stating that he was.

875. Mr. *Bourke.*] But you knew that at the time when you heard he was suspended he was manager of national schools under the Board?—At the time of his reported suspension he was manager of national schools. I cannot say that I heard of his suspension at that time; I may have heard of it subsequently.

876. Have you got any letters of Mr. O'Keeffe's, of 1871, before these letters which are in the Papers before the Committee?—I am sure there are such letters from him, but I have not got them here.

877. Do you recollect any letter from Mr. O'Keeffe, dated in 1871, in which he informed the Commissioners that he had been suspended for the fifth time? I do recollect such a letter. I know in some letter in the Return here it is referred to. Perhaps I am confusing the dates. I have no recollection of the particular date, but I know in some letter of his he stated that there were several suspensions.

878. You do not know whether or not that letter is in the correspondence which is now before the Committee?—I do not.

879. Do you know any reason why that letter is not before the Committee?— I am not quite certain that there was such a letter received in 1871; but I know that there was a letter from him, although I do not know the date of it.

880. (To Mr. *Keenan*). Do you recollect the letter that the Witness alludes to?—I do not.

881. Is that in this correspondence which has been laid before us?—If it was in the year 1871 it cannot be in that correspondence; because the first Return ordered by the House of Commons is, Return, Number 244, and the Order is, "Copies of any Correspondence which has taken place between the Poor Law Commissioners of Ireland, Cardinal Cullen, and others, relative to the Dismisal of the Rev. Robert O'Keeffe, P.P. of Callan, from the Office of Workhouse Chaplain. Of the Order of the Board for his Dismissal. Of any Correspondence which has taken place between the Board of National Education in Ireland, Cardinal Cullen, and others, relative to the Removal of the Rev. Robert O'Keeffe from the position of Manager of the National Schools. Of the Order of the Board for his Removal. Of the Minutes of the Proceedings of the Board of National Education at the Meeting held on Tuesday the 23rd of April" (that is 1872), "as far as relates to the Rev. Robert O'Keeffe, and of the Names of the Commissioners who voted for and against the Proposal of Mr. Justice Morris, to the effect that Notice should be given to Mr. O'Keeffe of the Demand for his Dismissal." Then the second Return, Mr. Bouverie's, is for, "Copies of all Minutes of Proceedings, and of all Correspondence of the Board of National Education in Ireland, relating to the Schools at Callan, or to the Rev. Robert O'Keeffe, since the 7th day of May last." Then Lord Hartington's Return continues the correspondence up to this time. So that the commencement of the correspondence, as ordered by Parliament, is the 23rd of April 1872.

882. Allow me to call your attention to Lord Hartington's Return, "Copies of all Minutes of Proceedings and of all Correspondence of the Board of National Education in Ireland relating to the Schools at Callan or to the Rev. Robert O'Keeffe"?—"And of the Names of the Commissioners Voting for or against any Motion in the said Board on such Subjects (in continuation of Parliamentary Paper No. 85)." No. 85 is Mr. Bouverie's.

883. The

SELECT COMMITTEE ON CALLAN SCHOOLS.

Mr. J. Kelly.
9 June 1873.

883. The correspondence then, so far as we know anything about it, does not go further back than 1872?—Than the 23rd of April 1872.
884. Then are there any other letters on the subject before the 23rd of April 1872?—Multitudes.

885. (To the *Witness*.) Can you tell the Committee when it was that the Board first heard of Mr. O'Keeffe's suspension?—It was first communicated by the inspector, Mr. Harkin, in November 1871.
886. Do you recollect whether that notification was prior to the notification made by Mr. O'Keeffe himself, that he had been five or six times suspended?—I do not recollect the date of that letter that I have in my mind, in which he notified that he had been suspended several times.
887. Would the notification by a clergyman himself that he had been suspended be considered official notification by the Board?—I cannot say what the Board might consider it.

888. *Chairman.*] Will you have the goodness to make search for, and let the Committee have, the first official intimation of Mr. O'Keeffe's suspension, and state whether or not it was brought before the Board?—The first official intimation of Mr. O'Keeffe's suspension was the letter of Mr. Harkin, Inspector of National Schools, dated 29th November 1871; that letter, together with the letter from the Right Rev. Mr. Moran, dated 22nd March 1872, and the letter from the Rev. W. Martin, were brought before the Board on 23rd April 1872, the letters from the Rev. W. Martin and Right Rev. P. F. Moran having been before the Board on 9th April. (*See* Parliamentary Paper, 244, 1872, pp. 16, 17, 18). The letter from the Rev. R. O'Keeffe to the Department, dated 18th January 1871, will be produced by Mr. Newell.

889. *Mr. Bourke.*] And also any communication upon the subject of his suspension made by Mr. O'Keeffe?—Yes.
890. I think that you have said that you were present at the Board during the discussion on Mr. O'Keeffe's case on only one occasion?—Yes.
891. Do you recollect whether any of these precedents that we have been speaking about were mentioned to the Board on that occasion?—No; there was no discussion on that point on that occasion. That was the 23rd of March 1873, when he applied to place one of the schools from which he had been removed under the Board again, and there was no discussion then as to his suspension. The Board decline to make an order on the matter until the application was regularly before them.
892. Do you recollect Mr. Sheridan's case yourself?—No.

893. *Mr. Whitbread.*] I suppose letters arrive at the office occasionally, complaining of the unfitness of managers, do they not?—I do not think that there are many cases of the kind.
894. What is the practice of the Board in regard to them when they do arise?—The Board in such a case, I conceive, would direct the inspector to inquire into the case.
895. But there has been no case brought before the notice of the Board from an outsider, complaining of mismanagement or misconduct by a clerical school manager, which has been substantiated to such a degree as to enable the Board to cease to hold correspondence with him?—I do not recollect such a case.

896. *Mr. Bourke.*] With regard to the reports that are made by inspectors, supposing an inspector reports that an ecclesiastic has been suspended, is that reckoned official notice by the Board?—Yes; the Board have considered that sufficient notice.
897. Do you know then whether any inspector ever reported to the Board that Father Daly had been suspended?—I do not recollect that that was ever officially communicated.

898. *The O'Conor Don.*] With respect to Father Daly, do you know, as a fact, that he was suspended at all?—I do not.

899. *Mr. Whitbread.*] In Father Daly's case, if you knew of his suspension, was there any official application to appoint a manager in succession to him?—I do not believe that the thing was ever officially communicated.

0.93.
L
900. There

Mr. *J. Kelly.*
9 June 1873.

900. There was no application to appoint a successor, or any official communication on the subject?—No, I think not.

901. Mr. *Gathorne Hardy.*] But when you receive a notification from the inspector, has it been the practice of the Board to refer to the ecclesiastical superiors?—There have been cases of that kind.

902. Is not that so in all the cases, except one, that the ecclesiastical superior is referred to?—In the case of Dr. Kilduff he was referred to.

903. In all those cases except the case of Mr. Sheridan, was it not so?—I think, in the case of the Magheral School, that is the case of the Rev. Mr. Keenan, the bishop communicated himself in the first instance, and there was no application from the Board.

SELECT COMMITTEE ON CALLAN SCHOOLS.

Wednesday, 11th June 1873.

MEMBERS PRESENT:

Mr. Bourke.
Mr. Secretary Cardwell.
Mr. Cross.
Mr. Gathorne Hardy.

The O'Conor Don.
Dr. Lyon Playfair.
Mr. Whitbread.

THE RIGHT HONOURABLE EDWARD CARDWELL, IN THE CHAIR.

Mr. *William Homan Newell*, LL D., called in; and Examined.

904. *Chairman.*] You are the other Secretary of the Board of Education, Mr. Kelly having been already examined?—Yes.

905. Do you produce the papers which Mr. Kelly was asked for at the last sitting of the Committee?—Some of them.

906. Will you have the goodness to put in those which you have?—Yes (*putting in the same*).

907. And what are those which you have not?—Those which I have not are the programmes that were asked for in the cases of Magheral and Glenvale. There were no programmes issued at the dates of those cases.

908. Are these, which you call programmes, what are sometimes called agenda, a notice sent to each Commissioner of what is proposed to be considered at the next meeting?—Yes, they are similar to the agenda, and also an abstract of the proceedings of the previous Board day, a summary of which is sent out to each Commissioner.

909. *The O'Conor Don.*] Were there no programmes issued before 1862?—There were no programmes until after September 1854.

910. *Mr. Bourke.*] I asked your colleague whether he recollected any letter before the letters that are alluded to in this Parliamentary Paper which begins with 1872, with regard to Mr. O'Keeffe?—I recollect such letters.

911. Have you that correspondence?—I have all the correspondence with me, but I have not brought all of it here.

912. Do you recollect when the correspondence with regard to Mr. O'Keeffe began?—We have had correspondence with Mr. O'Keeffe since 1862 in connexion with schools at Callan.

913. What I wanted to get was any papers relating to the suspension of Mr. O'Keeffe?—I have the first two papers that I could trace relating to the suspension (*handing them to the honourable Member*).

914. Do you recollect any paper which contains a statement of Mr. O'Keeffe, saying that he had been five or six times suspended?—It is in one of those which I have handed in to you. The first of those letters is as follows:—"Callan, January 18th, 1871.—The Secretaries, Education Office, Dublin.—Gentlemen, I wrote you on yesterday, and no doubt when we quarrel (*quod Deus avertat*), you can at least, with some propriety of language, request me to cease forwarding

Mr. *W. H. Newell*, LL.D.

11 June 1873.

Mr. *W. H. Newell,*
LL.D.

11 June 1873.

to you lengthened statements of my views; but as we live in an age of 'suspension,' I must ask you, Has my infant school, too, been put on your suspended list? With a little aid from your district inspector, I was suspended a fifth time on the 11th instant by the Lord Bishop of Ossory, and for no other reason, that I can make out, either from the documents themselves or otherwise, but that I have not submitted in perfect silence to have my Callan Male School denounced to four congregations as a godless institution. The school itself was publicly suspended by your inspector on the 14th ultimo, and the sentence was confirmed by you on the 10th instant. Episcopal suspensions may sometimes be a mere *brutum fulmen*, but I can tell you that yours are no joke. I need scarcely say to you that I have no reason in the wide world to think that my infant school has been put on your list, but when receipts are three weeks in your hands without acknowledgment, and when we are commemorating the Slaughter of the Innocents, there are grounds, at least, to fear that even the infants may be in danger. It is true that another receipt was in your hands for three months before you said you suspended its payment; but then the three months to come are in the future time, and I must tell you that I am no prophet. We say in logic, '*Ab actu ad posse valet consecutio.*' *Verbum sap.*—I remain, Gentlemen, yours respectfully, R. O'Keeffe, P.P."

915. *Chairman.*] You having read the letter of the 18th of January, I will ask you whether you have the answer that was sent from the Board to that letter of the 18th of January?—I think it is likely that I have amongst the papers that are at my hotel. It appears that it was dated the 24th of January.

916. Have you any docket that will show what the purport of the letter of the 24th was?—Unless I have the letter itself, I have no docket.

917. Will you read the other letter which you have handed in?—That is dated January the 26th 1871, "Gentlemen, I have your letter of the 24th instant (396 and 634, '71). You say you do not furnish copies of inspectors' reports; yet you have full confidence in the man who takes it upon himself to furnish such a report to an adversary of mine. If this be your notion of impartiality, I must tell you that it is very far from being mine; and though I lately deprecated a quarrel with you, I envy your enemies, the very people that have quarrelled with me; because, unfortunately for myself I am in friendship with you. I was suspended twice by Dr. Walsh, of Kilkenny, and then I was invited to a trial. Your inspector suspended my school before the public on the 14th December, and you confirmed the sentence on the 11th instant. After the two suspensions, like Mr. Harkin's new friend, the man that had him denounced from his pulpit as an enemy of the Cross of Christ, you, too, think it only fair to me to give culprits a trial. Most other people would think that the trial ought to be first, and the suspension last; but the Bishop of Ossory is a great hand at putting the car before the horse; and it seems other people, too, can tackle the animal according to the improved method. But really, gentlemen, has it ever occurred to you to think that what is sport to you may be death to an unfortunate teacher who has done good honest work (making all due allowance for the effects of inanition), every day for the last seven months without receiving a penny for it from the people who amuse themselves with playing at thunderbolt?—I am, Gentlemen, yours respectfully, R. O Keeffe, P.P."

918. *The O'Conor Don.*] Are those the only letters that you have brought over?—No; I have brought over all Mr. O'Keeffe's letters; I think those are the only letters with the word "suspended" in them.

919. You have not brought over any document showing the action of the Board on the receipt of those letters?—As I said before, I am not sure that I may not have them at my hotel.

The Right Honourable Mr. Justice *Lawson*, called in; and Examined.

Rt. Hon. Mr.
Justice *Lawson*.

920. Mr. *Gathorne Hardy.*] I BELIEVE you were appointed Commissioner in 1861?—Yes.

921. And you had been friendly to the Irish system previously?—Yes; I was always

SELECT COMMITTEE ON CALLAN SCHOOLS. 85

always a friend of mixed education. Mr. Cardwell, I think, was Chief Secretary when I was appointed.

Rt. Hon. Mr. Justice Lawson.

11 June 1873.

922. Have you since that time attended pretty regularly?—Yes: I have attended the meetings of the Board since as regularly as my other avocations would allow.

923. And have you made yourself, as far as you could, acquainted with the rules and practice of the Board?—Yes.

924. Now, have you ever understood there to be a rule either in express terms or implied, from any other rule of the Board, that a clergyman who is a manager should, upon his suspension, be removed from his office of manager?—No; I never understood or heard that there was any such rule. There is no such rule in writing. The only rule that bears upon the subject is the rule in Section 6, No. 7, at page 6 of the book of the rules, which provides, "In the case of a vacancy in the patronship by death, the representative of a lay patron, or the successor of a clerical patron, is recognised by the Board (where no valid objection exists), as the person to succeed to the patronship of the school." Now, that rule provides only for the case of death, not for the case of disputed successions; and even in the case of death, it carefully reserves a discretion to the Board as to whether the successor of the clerical patron is to be the person to succeed to the patronship of the school.

925. Now, do you agree with Judge Longfield, that there is no such thing as an *ex officio* manager?—There is no *ex officio* manager ever recognised by the Board. I may mention that this is so stated by Sir Alexander Macdonnell in his evidence before the Primary Commission, Vol 3, page 3, quoted in Parliamentary Paper, No. 85, page 38; and I have always known the Board to act upon that principle.

926. The principle of the system of Irish education would in all probability have prevented it, would it not?—Yes; from its nature it forbids the idea of an *ex officio* clerical manager, because the schools are open to the children of all communions, and they are emphatically national schools and undenominational.

927. Are there any schools that may be called specially parochial schools?—There are no such things known as parochial schools, or district schools, and no clergymen of any denomination can claim to be a manager *ex officio*, of any school according to my reading of the rules and according to my knowledge of the practice of the Board.

928. How does that affect your view of the question, whether there is any rule of the Board as to suspension being the ground for removal?—Why, if an office does not carry with it the right to the managership, it would evidently be absurd to have a rule that the loss of the office should entail the loss of the managership. Our rules must all receive the sanction of the Lord Lieutenant, and I can scarcely imagine any Lord Lieutenant sanctioning an express rule that the suspension of a clergyman should forfeit his title to the managership, especially if there were added to it, as must be in this O'Keeffe case, "without notice to the person affected and without inquiry;" for that is the result of what has taken place according to my view in this particular case.

929. Then what view do you take as to the Board's duty with respect to the removal of a manager and the recognition of a successor?—My view is that the question of either the appointment or the removal of a manager is one of great importance and of expediency, to be determined in each case by the circumstances of the case; and the paramount consideration ought to be what the interests of education in the district require.

930. Now I have asked you about the rule; has it ever come to your knowledge, that there was a uniform practice of dismissal of a manager in a case of suspension?—I never heard of any practice to dismiss a manager in case of suspension without inquiry, and without considering whether it was a thing which, under the special circumstances of the case, ought or ought not to be done.

931. You have no doubt had your attention directed to the precedents which have been laid before the Committee and the House?—Yes.

932. I think two of those were during the time that you have been at the Board?—One of them, I think Mr. Sheridan's, the last in number, is the only one at which it is stated on the minutes that I attended. I may mention that I

0.93.　　　　　　　　　　L 3　　　　　　　　　　have

Rt. Hon. Mr.
Justice *Lawson.*

11 June 1873.

have no recollection of that particular case, or of any decision with reference to it; but it appears even upon the minutes in that case that there is a letter from our inspector stating that this Mr. Sheridan admitted that he was suspended, and hoped to be shortly restored, as an act of grace, by the bishop; therefore, so far from disputing his suspension, he acknowledged it to be a very proper suspension, and hoped to be restored.

933. And I observe, also, that in one of the letters, the letter from the district inspector, he puts the question, "I submit the point to the Commissioners whether or not a suspended clergyman should continue as manager of the schools?" Would that tend to confirm your view that there was no absolute rule on the subject?—Of course it does. If there were an absolute rule our inspectors and secretaries would at once have acted upon it, and have brought every case of suspension immediately under the notice of the Board, in order that the rule should be carried out. That is the clearest proof, in my mind, that no such rule or practice was understood to exist.

934. I do not understand you to say that the suspension or degradation of a clergyman is not a matter which ought to be carefully considered by the Board?—On the contrary, I think that the suspension or degradation of a clergyman is a most grave matter to be taken into consideration in determining whether you are to remove him as a manager or not; and further than that, in some cases it would be conclusive in my mind. For instance, if a clergyman were suspended for any crime, drunkenness, immorality, or any conduct bringing him into evil repute, I would, of course, consider that the interests of education would be injured by continuing, as the manager of a school, a man who had fallen into public disrepute of that kind.

935. Then the grounds in some of those cases of suspension would be with you conclusive, if they were of such a character as you have described?—Certainly. On the other hand, I could conceive a great many cases of suspension in which I should be very sorry to consider the suspension any ground for removing a clergyman from a school. For instance, in the present Irish Church, supposing (as is very likely to happen) that a clergyman were suspended by the new ecclesiastical judges or tribunals for preaching doctrines that they did not like, suppose it was for preaching ritualistic doctrines or otherwise, but that he did not lose thereby the confidence of his congregation, I should be very sorry to think that that suspension would afford even a *prima facie* ground for removing him from a school. Every case must depend upon its own circumstances.

936. What I understand you to object to is, to its being supposed that suspension, *ipso facto*, brings to a conclusion the office of manager of a school?—Yes. I admit that it forms a *prima facie* ground for inquiry, and that in some cases, to my mind, would be conclusive as to the propriety of removing him as manager. I would also wish to state that, with respect to those instances of removal of a suspended clergyman which have been given, they do not at all prove the existence of any such alleged rule, that suspension, *ipso facto*, determines the managership; for in all these cases the removal may have been a most proper one under all the circumstances of the case. And I would further mention that all the circumstances of the case do not appear at all upon the documents connected with it, because the practice of the Board always has been to receive the statement of any Commissioner at the Board, who knew the facts of the case, especially of the Resident Commissioner, Mr. Macdonnell, a gentleman for whom we had the greatest respect; we always asked him his opinion on the matter, and he was almost always in possession of more information on the matter than any other Commissioner; and if he reported to us that he knew that the man's suspension was of such a character that it would be injurious to the cause of education to allow him to continue in the managership, the Board would, as a matter of course, endorse that opinion, and immediately remove him.

937. Now I observe that in the case of Mr. Sheridan, the Secretaries seem to have known of the suspension for two years before the Board took cognisance of it?—Yes, and that shows that they were not aware of any such alleged practice as this; otherwise in the discharge of their duty they would at once have communicated the matter to the Board, in order to have the rule of the removal of the manager immediately carried out.

938. Can

938. Can you tell me whether in any instances that have come to your knowledge suspended clergymen have continued in the management of their schools? — I only know that by hearsay. There was a very well known gentleman, Father Peter Daly, whose suspension created perhaps nearly as much public attention as that of Mr. O'Keeffe has done, and every one knew that he was suspended; but I never heard that he was removed from the managership of the schools which he possessed. And with respect to Mr. O'Keeffe himself, I heard a letter read to-day informing the Board of his previous suspensions; and Mr. Harkin's letter, which is in the Parliamentary Paper, of the 29th of November 1871, apprises the Board that he had been suspended by Cardinal Cullen. That letter led to no action on the part of the Board, and would not have led to any action until Dr. Moran, the Bishop of Ossory, wrote his letter of the 22nd of March, four months afterwards, calling for the removal of Mr. O'Keeffe. All those circumstances lead me to believe that my impression of the practice of the Board is accurate. And indeed to suppose that there could be a practice establishing a rule, which rule, if it were written in express terms, I can hardly conceive receiving the sanction of any Government, I think is rather a strong thing to contend for.

939. Do you think it is an important thing to know whether a suspended clergyman has been cited, and has obtained a fair hearing before the tribunal which has suspended him? — Yes; I think so. I pay every respect to the decision of a tribunal taking cognisance of a matter which falls within its own province; and if I were asked to consider a suspension as one of the grounds for removing a clergyman, I should require to be satisfied that the clergyman was cited before his proper ecclesiastical superior to answer a charge which *prima facie* would justify his suspension, and that he was heard and condemned; and I have no hesitation in saying, that if all that appeared I would treat the suspension as valid, and would decline to consider whether on the merits the decision was one sustained by the evidence or not. All I would ask is, to show that the man received notice that there was a charge made against him which would justify his suspension, and that he was heard; and then I would not allow the case to be re-agitated, but I would treat that suspension as a valid one; and then I would consider whether, under all the circumstances, and having regard to the grounds of that suspension, and the position that be filled in the parish, and the interests of education, he ought to be removed; and then I would act accordingly.

940. That is to say, that if you found that a clergyman had been tried, say for immorality, before his ecclesiastical superiors, and upon evidence satisfactory to them they had concluded that he was guilty, you would never enter into the inquiry whether they had come rightly or wrongly to that conclusion? — Certainly not; in that I follow the analogy of our courts of law. We regard a foreign judgment if it appears that proper proceedings have been taken; but I may also say that our courts decline to consider a foreign judgment as valid, if it appears that the defendant never was served with process in the action; that is so contrary to the rules of natural justice that the courts will not even allow an action to be maintained upon that judgment.

941. Unless you take some course of that sort, does not any other rule place at the absolute disposal of the ecclesiastical superior all the managerships that are held by clergymen? — Yes, it would make the Board the mere registrars of the edicts of the bishops or superiors.

942. That is to say, a statement by an ecclesiastical superior that he had suspended a clergyman, if conclusive would have that effect? — Yes.

943. You say that the paramount consideration with you, as I understand, would be the effects upon education in the locality? — Yes.

944. Do you consider that that question was gone into at all in the case of Mr. O'Keeffe? — No; I do not consider that it was gone into at all; the majority of the Board appear to have acted upon the *quasi* judgment of Dr. Moran, stating that he was suspended.

945. Were the circumstances that you have stated as necessary to what you think should be a suspension, acting upon the minds of the Commissioners present in the O'Keeffe case? — No; in my opinion, every one of the circumstances which I have enumerated was absent in the O'Keeffe case, and was known to the Board to be absent. In the first place, Cardinal Cullen, whose suspension of Mr. O'Keeffe, Mr. Harkin communicated to us by his letter of the 29th of November

Rt. Hon. Mr.
Justice Lawson.

11 June 1873.

November 1871, was not the ecclesiastical superior of Mr. O'Keeffe; he was Archbishop of Dublin; Mr. O'Keeffe was a clergyman in the diocese of Ossory, and therefore, *prima facie*, Cardinal Cullen had no jurisdiction whatever as an ecclesiastical superior over Mr. O'Keeffe. Then again, the only offence laid to Mr. O'Keeffe's charge, as stated before the Board, and as appearing in this Parliamentary paper, was that he had brought an action against a brother ecclesiastic. Now, I stated that I should expect a man, before he was removed from a school, to be charged with an offence which, *prima facie*, would justify his suspension or degradation; and I must say, that for myself, as a British judge, I could not, at least without hearing it discussed, assume at once that the resorting to one of Her Majesty's Courts for the redress of a civil inquiry was a circumstance which would either justify suspension according to the laws of any church, as interpreted by the law of the land, or which would justify us in acting upon that as a ground for removing him from the managership.

946. Did it come before the Board that there was a question being tried as to the validity of this so-called suspension?—Yes; I remember very well that Mr. Justice Morris read the pleadings in the action which was was then pending, of O'Keeffe against Cardinal Cullen, and read out the issue which was knit between the parties, and which was then for trial, namely, the one side alleging that he was legally suspended, and the other side denying that he was legally suspended. Now the attention of the Board was called to this, and it appears to me, and it appeared to me then, that when a suit was pending between the parties for the purpose of determining the legality of the very suspension, it was rather a strong measure to ask the Board to act upon that as a matter concluded.

947. Did it appear before the Board that Mr. O'Keeffe was *de facto* in possession of the schools?—Yes; it was admitted that Mr. O'Keeffe was in possession of the schools, carrying them on as before, and he remained in possession of his chapel, and in possession of his schools, acting as parish priest; and it appears from the report of our inspectors, that the parents of the pupils, and the teachers, and the pupils themselves, all adhered to Mr. O'Keeffe, and that the schools were carried on without any interruption whatever, just as before.

948. Did you take into consideration your position as a judge as well as a commissioner in viewing this case?—Certainly; I felt the moment that my attention was called to that action pending, that I might be called upon as a judge to give my opinion upon that very matter, whether this gentleman was legally suspended or not, and that I could not conscientiously vote for treating him as suspended when I knew that I might myself be called upon to give a judicial opinion upon that very matter.

949. Now, in the decision of the Commissioners the terms "a competent tribunal" are used. Do you put any interpretation upon those words as meaning a spiritual or a legal tribunal?—Really at first, when those words were used, I understood them to include a competent legal tribunal; but I find that that is not the case in the opinion, at all events, of some of the members of the Board, for I observe that the Chief Baron, in his letter which has been published, says that even if the action were decided in Mr. O'Keeffe's favour, he would not be restored to his status as parish priest of Callan. The words "until the suspension is removed or declared invalid by a competent tribunal" are certainly ambiguous. I should suppose that some of the Commissioners like myself, at least those who would not question the power of the Court of Queen's Bench to decide upon the point, must have considered that those words would include a competent legal tribunal; but it appears that others, for instance Dr. Henry, as I find, consider that the phrase only means an ecclesiastical tribunal.

950. In your judgment would it be the duty of a public board to give effect to a legal decision on the question of suspension?—I think, of course, it would. The law of the church must be interpreted and expounded by the law of the land, according to all our authorities, and it is the duty of every one to give effect to a decision of the law of the land. If the law of the land decides that Mr. O'Keeffe is not legally suspended as parish priest, I think every good subject is bound to act upon the supposition that he is not.

951. Otherwise, as you have said before, the bishop would be perfectly absolute in the matter?—The bishop would be absolute in the matter.

952. Whether he had grounds for continuing the suspension or not?—Yes.

953. So far as that is to say as the board is concerned?—Yes, of course, if the true

true meaning of the reservation in the order of the 23rd of April is that he is not to be removed from his managership until the suspension is removed by a competent ecclesiastical tribunal, the practical result of that is that he remains removed as manager unless the Pope reverses the suspension pronounced by Cardinal Cullen.

Rt. Hon. Mr. Justice *Lawson.*

11 June 1873.

954. Then do I rightly understand you that while there is a pending litigation on a subject of this sort you think it advisable that the Board should not interfere in the dispute?—Certainly; if there is a *bona fide* litigation, I think the Board ought not to interfere in the dispute. For instance, if a clergyman is suspended by an ecclesiastical tribunal, and there is the right of appeal from that, I should not alter his status while that appeal is pending if it is a *bona fide* appeal. In like manner, if a man goes to law and brings an action for the purpose of *bona fide* trying whether he fills that office or not, according to our old maxim, *pendente lite nihil innovetur*. I think matters ought to be allowed to remain in *statu quo* until the decision of that action. I can imagine a case in which the interests of education would justify the removal of a manager, and in which the Board would be prepared to remove him, no matter what became of that action; but that is a matter to be very gravely considered in each case.

955. I am only speaking of the imperative effects of the suspension. You would not enter into an inquiry into other circumstances?—I should not enter into an inquiry whether the judge had arrived at a sound conclusion upon the merits. The only thing that I should inquire would be whether there were grounds for giving the judgment. The grounds for giving the judgment are, first, that the man was cited; secondly, that he was cited before his proper ecclesiastical superior; and thirdly, that he was cited for an offence which I could recognise as an offence that would justify his degradation or suspension.

956. How does the result which has happened with respect to the Callan Schools confirm you in the opinion that you have expressed?—I think that the result of what has taken place has been, so far as the interests of education are concerned, very injurious in this Callan case. The result was to throw everything in the schools into confusion, and ultimately to lead to a complete withdrawal, the striking off of all the schools from the roll. That was a result, I think, greatly to be deprecated, and I struggled as much as I could against it.

957. In fact, the teachers and the children have suffered on account of the proceeding?—The teachers and the children have suffered on account of the contumacy or supposed contumacy of Mr. O'Keeffe to his ecclesiastical superiors.

958. Now it appears that the inspectors spoke favourable of his schools, as to the mode of their conduct?—Yes. After these schools were struck off the rolls, Mr. O'Keeffe applied again to have them placed in connection with the Board; and it was referred to the inspector, and the inspector reported that if it was an ordinary application it should be granted as a matter of course; and according to the practice of the Board, there was a magistrate, Mr. Gregory, referred to on the occasion, and he reported that the interests of education required that the school should be kept up; but still it was considered, as it would appear, that that disqualification of being a suspended priest still attached to Mr. O'Keeffe, and rendered him, in the opinion of the majority of the Board, ineligible to be or to become a manager of schools.

959. That is in cases where his position as a priest was not the ground of his being manager of the school, but his election by a committee?—Yes, after be was suspended as a priest and we were informed of that, he then applied as a person in possession of the schools to get aid for them, and it was considered that the old disqualification still attached to him, and that he could not get aid.

960. Might not that operate very injuriously; supposing a clergyman to change his religion, for instance, he might then be precluded from setting up a school in connection with the Board, because of his suspension under other circumstances? —Certainly; and I have no hesitation in saying that I would not consider the fact of a clergyman changing his religion any ground for removing him from the schools, if the schools were carried on as before, and if the scholars attended them; having reference to the fact that our schools are undenominational, I would not consider that any ground for removing him.

961. Of course, where there is a committee they would act as they thought proper in that respect?—Yes.

0.93.

M

962. Now,

962. Now, you wrote a letter to the secretaries on this subject, did you not?—I did.

963. There has been some comment made upon that letter by Bishop Moran?—Yes, I may mention, that I wrote that letter because, finding that Dr. Longfield, a member of the majority of the Board, had written a letter justifying his action in the case, I thought myself, as a member of the minority, at all events, as well entitled to put on record the course which I took personally in the matter; and I did so with a view to show that my motive in the case was to protect, as far as I could, the education of the children.

964. As I asked you before, Bishop Moran commented upon that statement, as to the effect upon education, and he referred to a school called the Callan Lodge School, did he not?—Yes. I stated in that letter of mine that the effect of the action of the Board was to put Callan under an educational interdict, so far as the Board were concerned. Dr. Moran contradicts that, and he states that the Callan Lodge School which he represents as an existing school, afforded ample means of education for the children of Callan. It now appears from the papers that that school has been made a convent school; and therefore the only schools now in operation in Callan, so far as I am aware, are the Christian Brothers' Schools, in opposition to which Mr. O'Keeffe originally set up the National schools, and a convent school; and I need not say that a convent school, although it is in connection with the Board, is not a school at which children of other denominations are, in point of fact, very likely to attend.

965. Now, may I ask you, with respect to the proceedings of the Board in appointing a successor, do you consider that the Board has the power to appoint a successor?—Not in cases, of course, where they have a committee: in strictness, they have no power to appoint a successor.

966. In what way is it that they recognise an appointment by a bishop of a successor, where there is a committee?—Of course, if the manager dies and there is a vacancy, they consider whom to appoint then, and if the clerical successor is a proper man, they appoint him.

967. Now I think, in Dr. Keenan's case, for instance, which is one of the cases brought forward as a precedent, the Board appointed Mr. Macken?—That was quite illegal; because there was a committee, and there were trustees, and in that case the nomination must be made by the trustees; and you will find that that distinction was acted upon by the Board in this O'Keeffe case; for they asked the committee to nominate a new manager of the school of which they were the trustees; but they themselves recognised immediately the Rev. Mr. Martin, the administrator of the parish, as the manager of the schools in respect of which a committee had not been appointed.

968. And he has not been able to obtain the possession of the schools, has he?—He never could obtain possession of the schools; in fact, Mr. O'Keeffe held possession of the schools, and of the parish, and Mr. Martin could not enforce his rights, if he had any.

969. In the memorial, which was signed by 13 members of the National Education Board, there is a statement that there have been "grave misstatements of facts," and "error and misrepresentation." Now, is there, in your opinion, anything of that sort in connection with the circumstances which came before the public on authentic documents?—When I found that statement, that there were grave misrepresentations of facts, of course, I having been the only person who published a letter on the subject, naturally thought that perhaps that might apply to something stated in my letter. I have read that letter over very carefully, and I cannot find that any fact in it has ever been at all contradicted; and on looking to the evidence of Mr. Keenan and Dr. Longfield, which has been given here, I find that the misrepresentations of fact which they mentioned are, first, the statement that they did not act according to precedent. I said nothing about that; that is not a misrepresentation of fact. Another thing they say is, that their motives were misrepresented, and that it was stated that they acted in subserviency to Cardinal Cullen. I beg to say that I did not impute any motives to any one; I only stated the facts, and everyone can draw his own inference from them; and, in justification of myself, I may observe that I find that the Chief Baron, in his letter, thinks that I imputed that to him; but I really and conscientiously believe that the Chief Baron's motive is exactly what he stated, namely, that he did not wish to offend, or had a fear of offending,

Rt. Hon. Mr.
Justice Lawson.

11 June 1873.

ing, the Roman Catholic bishops and priests if he acted in any other way. I am quite sure that was the reason why he acted so.

969*. And that leading to the withdrawal of schools from connection with the Board?—Yes. I may mention myself, from my experience of the Board, that that is a threat which has been continually held out to the Board. In our discussions people have said, "If you do so and so the result will be that all the Catholic schools will be withdrawn from the Board." I must confess, for myself, that I never entertained those apprehensions.

970. And has the result in general confirmed your view that they are not very formidable threats?—I think so.

970*. Is there any other matter that you would wish to add to the evidence, that you have given?—I do not think there is; of course I have only stated the matters that came under my own cognisance.

971. Dr. *Lyon Playfair*.] Are you aware who are the legal owners of the five non-vested schools?—I do not know.

971*. You do not know whether the parish priest as parish priest is the legal owner?—I do not.

972. But I think you distinctly stated in your evidence, that in the case of a school vested in a committee, you do not think that the mere fact of the suspension of the clergyman, if he has not committed any immorality or done anything that would render him an unfit manager, should be a cause of his dismissal?—I certainly should say not.

973. And that is your opinion as a Commissioner?—That is my opinion as a Commissioner. I think it furnishes a *prima facie* case for inquiry, but the moment you say that it is only a *prima facie* case, it follows that there must be notice to the man affected, and that there must be an inquiry.

974. And supposing it is found that he is properly able to superintend the secular part of the instruction, do you think that the Board should continue him as manager?—I think so.

975. *The O'Conor Don*.] With respect, in the first place, to the last answer that you gave to Mr. Hardy, you spoke of threats being held out to the Board on certain occasions, that if certain action were taken, the Roman Catholic schools would be withdrawn; would you state what those cases were?—Yes; when a motion was brought forward in the Board to improve the position of teachers, that is, to render them no longer liable to dismissal, unless they got a certain notice, three months' notice, it was discussed at the Board, and Sir Alexander Macdonnell, who was then the Resident Commissioner, stated expressly, that if that motion were carried, the result would be, in his opinion, the withdrawal of the Roman Catholic schools from the Board.

976. But that was an expression of opinion from Sir Alexander Macdonnell?—Quite so.

977. I understood you to say, in answer to Mr. Hardy, that some threat of the withdrawal of those schools was held out by some parties in Ireland?—I never meant that; but it was stated at the Board as a consequence, and stated on many occasions by the Commissioners, that if so and so is done, the schools will be withdrawn.

978. All you meant to imply then by the answer was, that on certain occasions some of the Commissioners have expressed their opinion, that if certain things were done, certain results would follow?—Yes.

979. But there has been no threat issued to the Board by any parties?—No; I did not mean to convey that.

980. Now, I understand you to hold very distinctly, that there are no such appointments as *ex officio* appointments of any sort or description to the office of manager of a school?—Yes, I hold that opinion.

981. And that no clergyman, I presume, has any right to be appointed to the management of any school?—I think so. I think there is a circular of the Board to that effect.

982. And that, although clergymen are in a great many cases appointed managers, that is not on account of any right attaching to their office of clergymen?—I think if a clergyman is the manager of a school, and he dies or leaves the parish, the natural person to be appointed manager of the school is the successor in the parish; but the printed rule, which I have read already, expressly says, "if no valid objection exists," showing that the Board always reserve to themselves

0.93. M 2

themselves the discretion of considering whether the successor in the clerical office ought to be the successor in the managership of the school.

983. In short, the Board reserve to themselves complete discretion as to the continuance or discontinuance of managership of the school, whether he be a clerical manager or a layman?—Yes.

984. Now, with respect to the effect of the removal of a manager in non-vested schools, has the Board, in reality, any power of removing the manager of a non-vested school?—No; the only power that they have, is to say, "We will not recognise you as manager, or correspond with you."

985. So that, in fact, the expression, "dismissal and removal of a manager" of a non-vested school, is an inaccurate expression?—It is practically the same thing.

986. What really takes place is that the Board refuse to correspond with the manager, and to pay the salaries of the teachers through the manager?—Yes.

987. You have referred to the fact that you wrote a letter to the Board of Education?—Yes.

988. Have you a copy of that letter before you?—Yes.

989. Will you look at page 54 of that Parliamentary Return, No. 85, in which your letter appears. I see you state in the 6th paragraph of that letter, on page 54, that you expressed your surprise that at a meeting of the Board, "to a large extent composed of privy councillors, and persons holding a judicial position, it could be seriously proposed to condemn a person unheard, and to proceed to deprive him of a civil right without giving him notice of any such intention." What is the civil right that they proceeded to deprive him of?—Managership of the schools.

990. But I understood you to say that he had no right to the managership of the schools?—He was in possession and enjoyment of the office of manager.

991. But I understood you to answer me a moment ago that he had no right whatsoever to that management?—He had no right to get it, unless the Board appointed him to it; but they did appoint him; and my argument was that he should not be deprived of that right without their hearing him.

992. As he had no right in the first instance, do you mean that the mere fact of appointment by the Board created a civil right which had no existence before?—Decidedly; if a person is in possession of an estate, although he had no original right to it, you cannot put him out of it without hearing him.

993. But as I understood you to state in a former answer, the Board had perfect and absolute control in removing managers if they thought proper?—Certainly, upon proper grounds; but they had no right, according to natural justice, to remove a man from being manager without giving him an opportunity of showing why he should not be removed; that is my view.

994. Do you think that by the fact of being nominated manager, a civil right to continue in that office became vested in him?—Certainly.

995. Although the discontinuance from that office simply amounted to the Board declining to correspond with him?—You know that, practically, it amounted to cutting off the sinews of war, which is the great point, stopping the supplies.

996. In regard to this letter of yours which we have now before us, I presume you intended it as a narrative of the proceedings that took place in the Board, as well as a justification of the course which you thought it your duty to follow?—I did not mean it at all to be a complete narrative of all that took place at the Board. If I had it would have extended to great length; I meant it to be a justification of the course which I myself took in the matter.

997. I presume that the letter is, to a great extent, a narrative of the proceedings of the Board?—Yes.

998. And I presume you mean it to be a fair and impartial narrative of those proceedings?—Certainly.

999. Not an *ex parte* statement?—Certainly.

1000. Looking at it in that light, I would refer you to paragraph 4 of that letter on page 54; you say there that "Mr. Justice Morris moved, as an amendment to the motion for Mr. O'Keeffe's instant removal, that notice be given to Mr. O'Keeffe of the proceedings;" was that the whole of Mr. Justice Morris's amendment?—No; because at page 19 of Paper 244, I find this: "Proposed as an amendment by Mr. Justice Morris, and seconded by Mr. Waldron, that, 'Before any action should be taken on the letter of the Reverend Mr. Martin to the Board, or on the letter of Dr. Moran, Coadjutor Bishop of Ossory, to the

Resident

Resident Commissioner, the Reverend Mr. O'Keeffe got the opportunity of knowing the nature of the application made, and of offering an explanation."

Rt. Hon. Mr. Justice Lawson.

11 June 1873.

1001. So that there is an addition to that motion which you do not mention in your letter, namely, the words, " of offering an explanation"?—Yes.

1002. Do you not consider that a very important addition to the motion?—I do not consider it any important addition. I assume that, if a man gets notice, it is that he may offer an explanation. There is no use in giving him notice if he is not to take any notice of it. The meaning of giving him notice is to give him an opportunity of explaining what is charged against him.

1003. As a fact, was not the discussion in the Board upon that occasion rather as to giving Father O'Keeffe an opportunity of explaining, than as to giving him notice of the proceedings?—No, the discussion was principally as to giving him notice of the proceedings. The Chief Baron, I think, proposed that he should get notice of the proceedings, accompanied with an intimation that he was not to offer any explanation. No one supported that view of the case; but I contended strongly that, as a matter of common justice, he should get notice of what we were going to do, and be at liberty to offer an explanation if he thought proper.

1004. Then the real discussion between you representing the minority, and the Chief Baron as one of the majority, was not with respect to giving Father O'Keeffe notice, but it was as to asking him for an explanation?—No, clearly not; it was as to giving him notice.

1005. Does it not appear from your previous answer that the Chief Baron agreed with you as to the propriety of giving notice to Father O'Keeffe, and only differed as to the advisability of asking for an explanation from him?—No, he objected to giving him notice unless that notice was accompanied with an intimation that he was not to be at liberty to say a word.

1006. When you say that " he was not to be at liberty to say a word," do you mean that he was not to be at liberty to enter into discussion or explanation of the grounds of suspension?—Any explanation at all.

1007. Does not that bear out what I suggested to you before, that the real difference of opinion between the minority and the majority was, as to the advisability of submitting the question as to whether an explanation should be asked of Father O'Keeffe or not?—No I cannot agree with you at all. My contention was, that according to the principles of natural justice, as I stated in that letter, it never was heard of, that a person could be condemned without giving him notice of the charge that was brought against him.

1008. And giving him an opportunity of explaining it?—As incident to that notice, giving him an opportunity of explaining it.

1009. Was not that the point on which you and the majority differed?—No; we differed as to whether he was to have notice or not.

1010. The Chief Baron in his own letter states, that he was quite ready to give notice to Father O'Keeffe of the intention of the Board in his regard, but he states in his letter that he did object to allowing Father O'Keeffe to offer any explanation with respect to his suspension?—And I stated, and now state again, that no person at the Board seconded that proposition of the Chief Baron's. It fell to the ground, and the issue knit was whether the man was to have notice or not to have notice.

1011. Have you seen Judge Longfield's evidence?—Yes, I have seen it.

1012. Did you see that in that evidence Judge Longfield expressed his willingness also to give Father O'Keeffe notice, but his objection to having any explanation asked from him?—I do not recollect that having occurred at the Board; but of course if Dr. Longfield says so, it did.

1013. I will read to you Judge Longfield's answers to questions on that point. He was asked the question, " Had the Board acted as Mr. Justice Morris suggested, and asked for an explanation, they would have acted contrary to all precedent?" and he replies, " I think they would have acted contrary to all precedent, but we should have had no objection to inform the Rev. Mr. O'Keeffe of our intention if it had been put in that way. Q. But you objected to going to him for an explanation?—Yes, as that would have led to a statement of the causes of his removal, a question which we were not called upon to go into. For instance, if he stated that he believed in more than two sacraments, I,

Rt. Hon. Mr.
Justice Lawson.

11 June 1873.

as a Protestant, should not be a proper person to go into a question of that kind; but I myself, and the Lord Chief Baron, and several more, would have voted in favour of the notice"?—I can only say that my recollection is entirely different from that. And now I beg to say, with respect to that answer, "that they would have been acting contrary to precedent in doing that," there is no precedent, except this case, of a Commissioner moving that a man should get notice, and of that motion being rejected by the Board.

1014. Might not that statement cut both ways, and show that up to that time the unanimous opinion of the Board was so strong in favour of acting at once upon the certificate of the bishop, that no member of the Board ever thought it necessary to bring forward a proposal to give notice to the clergyman?—I do not think so.

1015. As a matter of fact, were not clergymen removed without any notice being given to them after being suspended?—I dare say.

1016. Are you not aware of the fact?—I am not aware of it personally, myself. The only case that I ever was present at was that case of Mr. Sheridan's.

1017. But have you not read the Parliamentary Papers?—Yes, I have. It would appear, as far as those Parliamentary Returns furnish information, that they did proceed without notice; but as I said before, there was no case in which a member of the Board proposed as an act of common justice that a man should get notice, and that motion was rejected by the rest of the Board.

1018. Apparently, then, up to the time when Mr. O'Keeffe's case was brought forward, no member of the Board has thought it necessary to propose that notice should be given to a man before he was removed when there was a certificate brought before the Board that he was a suspended clergyman?—Then, according to my notion, I think that any member of the Board failed in his duty, unless there was a case known to the Commissioners of immorality, or something of that kind, who, if there was really a dispute as to the legality of a suspension, would vote for removing a man without giving him notice.

1019. Were you a member of the Board in this case of Father Sheridan's?—Yes.

1020. And no notice was given to him, was there?—Father Sheridan, in that letter, admits that he was suspended, and hopes to be restored, as an act of grace, by the bishop.

1021. Is that in a letter from Father Sheridan to the Board?—No; it is stated in the letter from Mr. Conwell, I think.

1022. Is there any letter from Mr. Sheridan to the Board stating that fact?—Not that I am aware of. In a letter of the 4th of November 1864, Mr. O'Reilly, writing to Mr. Conwell, says, "Having had some communication with Father Sheridan on the subject of the national school, I find he has very sanguine hopes of a speedy restoration as an act of grace from the new bishop." That was the letter that I referred to as showing that Mr. Sheridan, so far from disputing the suspension, acknowledged it, and hoped to be restored as an act of grace from the bishop.

1023. That letter was written on the 4th of November 1864?—Yes.

1024. And the case came before the Board on the 27th of January 1865, did it not?—Yes.

1025. And when it came before the Board, then it appears by the papers that you were present?—Yes.

1026. And you did not think it necessary to refer to this Rev. Mr. Sheridan to know whether he still continued under suspension?—I have mentioned already that I have no recollection of that case whatever; and, moreover, according to the practice of the Board, if you came in at any time during the meeting, you would be taken down as attending at the meeting, whether you were there when that particular matter was discussed or not.

1027. But had you not information furnished to you before you attended the Board that day, that this question was to come on?—I suppose there was a programme furnished.

1028. It is the usual practice of the Board, is it not, to have programmes furnished, upon which are stated the cases that are to come on?—Yes; but I can only say that if I had been there, as I suppose I may have been when this was discussed, and if I had had a letter from the inspector of this kind, stating that

SELECT COMMITTEE ON CALLAN SCHOOLS. 95

that Father Sheridan had "sanguine hopes of a speedy restoration," I would have considered that an admission from him that he was properly suspended.

Rt. Hon. Mr. Justice Lawson.

11 June 1873.

1029. But what was the date of that letter, I must ask you again?—4th of November 1864.

1030. And the date of the meeting when the case came before the Board was what?—27th of January 1865.

1031. And you would consider a letter from the District Inspector some months before, sufficient justification for removing a clergyman who had at that time sanguine hopes of a speedy restoration, without ever communicating with him?—I would, if all the other circumstances of the case were such as in my opinion to justify his removal. I have already stated that I would never remove a man without considering all the circumstances of the case; and I take for granted that the Resident Commissioner, when that came before us on the 27th of January 1865, according to his custom, explained the nature of the case and gave us his opinion, on which we acted, that it was a proper case to remove this gentleman.

1032. But are you aware that the opinion of the late Resident Commissioner, Sir Alexander Macdonnell, is, that it is a sufficient case to remove a manager if he be certified as having been suspended?—I differ from him entirely in that.

1033. You are aware that that is his opinion?—Yes.

1034. You were satisfied to accept his opinion in the cases before you without any inquiry?—We were always satisfied to take the opinion of Mr. Macdonnell, who knew so much more about the case than we did, and if he stated why the man was suspended we should take that from him.

1035. Do you undertake to state that Sir Alexander Macdonnell stated that on that particular occasion?—Indeed I do not.

1036. At all events, you having had furnished to you in the programme an intimation that the case of a suspended priest was to come before the Board, with the view of his removal from the management of schools expressly upon the ground of his being suspended, did not think it worth your while to make any particular inquiries about the circumstances of the case at the Board?—The answer which I have already given is, that I do not recollect any of the circumstances of the case, is an answer to that question. I repeat, that the production of that letter I have referred to would have been sufficient to satisfy me that the man did not dispute either the fact or the validity of his suspension.

1037. Father O'Keeffe, I presume, did not dispute the fact of his suspension?—Decidedly he disputed the fact of his suspension by a person who had power to suspend him. He did not dispute that he was suspended by Cardinal Cullen; but he stated that Cardinal Cullen was not his proper ecclesiastical superior, and that he had no jurisdiction to suspend him.

1038. He did not dispute the fact that by an authority in his church he had been suspended?—He could not dispute that a suspension had been issued and read out in his church. But a suspension made by a stranger is no suspension at all.

1039. Did you, in 1865, in the same year when you did not consider it necessary to take any particular notice with respect to the removal of Mr. Sheridan, think it necessary to write specially to the Board with respect to the case of a proposed alteration in the rules on religious instruction in convent schools?—I wrote some letter to the Board about a proposed change in a convent school in Wexford; I think that is what you refer to. I considered that to be a concession which the Board ought not to make. It was something, as far as I recollect, about being at liberty to give religious instruction in a different way from what it was usually given before. I have not seen the letter lately, but that is my recollection of it.

1040. You consider that the removal of a clergyman, according to your letter of the 30th of January 1873, without applying to him for an explanation of the grounds of his removal, is not only contrary to British law, but even to natural justice?—I do, distinctly.

1041. And although you had a programme submitted to you in 1865, stating that a case of this sort was to be brought before the Board, you did not think it necessary to take any steps whatsoever regarding that case?—That is an observation which requires no answer by me, I think.

1042. Is that the fact, I ask?—That has been answered already. It is a fact that I did not.

0.93.   M 4   1043. I understand

Rt. Hon. Mr.
Justice *Lawson*.

11 June 1873.

1043. I understand you to believe that the action of the Board with regard to Father O'Keeffe was, to a certain extent, a decision as to the legality of his suspension. I will ask you plainly, was it, or was it not, a decision as to the legality of his suspension?—Distinctly, it was acting upon the suspension as a valid suspension.

1044. And it was, therefore, an expression of opinion on the part of the Board that he was validly suspended?—That is my opinion. I could not have voted for it, conscientiously, because I considered that it would involve me in the position of expressing the opinion that he was validly suspended; whereas I might have, judicially, to consider that question afterwards.

1045. Supposing that instead of its being, as we are told by the majority it was, the practice of the Board, it had been the practice and rule of the Board that a clergyman who was certified as having been suspended should be removed from the management of a school, would you have considered that the action of the Board upon such a rule would be an expression of opinion as to the legality or illegality or validity of a suspension?— No; if the Board were bound by a written rule to act on a suspension, that would not be an expression of opinion at all; it would be only registering something which another man did.

1046. If the majority of the Board held the opinion that the practice of the Board was so uniform as to practically amount to a rule, holding that opinion, would they have expressed any judgment upon the validity or invalidity of the suspension by removing the suspended person?— I can only answer for myself. I do not for a moment say that they thought they were doing so. I can only say that my own feeling was, that I could not vote for that without feeling that I compromised myself; but any other man may entertain different opinions. I do not impute anything of that kind to any member of the Board.

1047. You do not impute to any member of the Board, that he acted in such a way as to impair his impartiality as a judge afterwards?— I certainly do not make any such imputation, but I think it was a mistake at the same time for a judge to put himself in that position that anyone could say that he had done so. But everyone must judge of his own actions in that respect. I blame no man.

1048. You are aware that this rule with regard to acting on the certificate of the ecclesiastical superior is the rule with regard to the allocation of funds under the Charitable Donations and Bequests Act?—Yes. There is, however, a great deal of misapprehension about that. It has no application to this case whatever. There, if a gift is made to a person as the clergyman of a parish, it cannot be given to any other person; that is an *ex-officio* gift, and he must show, before he is entitled to get it, that he is the clergyman of the parish; but as I have already stated, there is no *ex-officio* managership with us; that makes all the distinction.

1049. But supposing that he be the clergyman of the parish, and that he be in receipt, we will say, of a sum of money annually that has been bequeathed to the clergyman of the parish, and supposing a certificate be sent in to the Board of Charitable Bequests by the bishop or ecclesiastical superior that he has been suspended, what would be the action of the Charitable Bequests Board upon that?—If it were disputed it would be no justification whatever to the Charitable Board if they made a wrong payment. Supposing a bishop turned out to be wrong, if he represented a man to be the rector of the parish that was not, it would be no justification at all to the Charitable Board. That rule is not a rule for disputed cases at all, but a rule for ordinary cases; and if there were a litigation brought under the notice of the Charitable Board between two persons, each claiming to be the rector of a parish, they would not be justified in parting with the fund until that litigation had been determined, and they could not accept the certificate of the bishop as conclusive on that question.

1050. But they could accept, and would be bound to accept, the certificate of the bishop, so far as refusing to pay it to the gentleman suspended went, would they not?—Yes; if there was a dispute about it, they would hold their hands till it was legally settled.

1051. Suppose the bishop certified that the clergyman was suspended, would they not be bound, to act upon that certificate, so far as refusing any longer to pay the amount to the suspended priest?— I think they would be quite justified in refusing to pay it when there was a question who was

SELECT COMMITTEE ON CALLAN SCHOOLS.   97

was the right man to receive it. But if the bishop certified, such a man is suspended or another man has succeeded him; if there was a dispute they would not be justified in taking his certificate as conclusive. If he turned out to be wrong, they would be guilty of a breach of trust if they acted upon his certificate.

Rt. Hon. Mr. Justice Lawson.

11 June 1873.

1051. Further down in your letter you stated this: "On my return, after the vacation, to the meetings of the Board in October, I found everything relating to these schools in confusion, and the Board involved in a litigation not very creditable to it, with respect to the salaries of the teachers." With regard to that, I should like to ask you, assuming that Father O'Keeffe was properly removed, what was there discreditable in the action of the Board in refusing to pay these salaries, which resulted in this litigation?—I think, when a man does work he is entitled to be paid for it, and these men did work, and they were entitled to be paid for it; and the only offence they committed was that they would not receive the money at the hands of Mr. Martin.

1052. You think, then, as a general rule, that if the teachers in any school do the work, no matter whether they recognise the manager recognised by the Board or not, they ought to be paid?—I do not say that as a general rule; but I think every one will acknowledge that a man who does work ought to be paid for it.

1053. No matter whether he does it in accordance with the rules on which the grant is made or not?—He did it in this case in accordance with the rules on which the grant was made; but the only offence was that he would not receive the salary through the hands of Mr. Martin.

1054. But is not that one of the necessary rules for all grants, that they should pass through the hands of the manager?—It is.

1055. And the refusal of the Board (assuming now that Father O'Keeffe was properly removed), which involved them in litigation, was a refusal to pay salaries in cases where the rules of the Board were not carried out?—The reason why they were involved in litigation was because they did a thing which they had no power to do, namely, to appoint Mr. Martin manager of schools over which he had no control.

1056. You say that the teachers in this case had done everything that would otherwise have entitled them to the payment of their salaries?—Some of the teachers, that is those who we thought ought to be paid; two of them, I think, did their work.

1057. If you look at page 55 I think you will see some reference to that: "Mr. Justice O'Brien, upon the facts appearing before him, suggested that the same course ought to be taken with respect to Miss Keogh, a female teacher, who had earned her salary, and had been guilty of no offence except that of refusing to acknowledge the authority of the Reverend Mr. Martin; she had been offered her salary if she would accept it through Mr. Martin, but she refused, so that the condition of the schools as appearing in a public court was that the Board seemed to offer to the teachers their salary in order to induce them to acknowledge a manager who had really no control over the schools, and withheld them as a punishment for their contumacy in not doing so, thus appearing to starve them into submission to ecclesiastical authority." Now, first of all with respect to that, when had she been offered her salary?—I cannot tell.

1058. Are you quite certain that she had been offered her salary by the Board, before Judge O'Brien's decision, upon any terms?—The orders were sent down, according to the usual practice, to Mr. Martin for the salaries of the teachers, and if the teachers had signed their receipts and given them to Mr. Martin they would have been paid; that is what I mean.

1059. You do not mean then, as I should have imagined you meant, from this sentence, that the money had been actually offered to this teacher as a bribe for adopting a certain course?—No, I did not mean any such thing. I meant that she would have got her salary, and knew that she would have got it if she would sign a receipt for it as received through the hands of Mr. Martin; and she refused to do that.

1060. And you represent that as if it showed that the Board were endeavouring to "starve" the teachers into submission to ecclesiastical authority?—I think it had that appearance: If you acknowledge the Rev. Mr. Martin as your manager, I will pay you, and if not, I will not.

1061. Is not that a condition with respect to every school at present under

0.93.   N   clerical

clerical management? —The rule in every school is that the teacher must be paid through the manager.

1062. And if the manager be an ecclesiastic, the offer made to the teacher is, "You will be paid if you will acknowledge So-and-so as the manager"?— Yes.

1063. So that that course of the Board, which in this particular instance you represent as an endeavour to starve them into submission to ecclesiastical authority, is what takes place in every school in Ireland?—I did not say "an endeavour" but "thus appearing to starve them into submission to ecclesiastical authority."

1064. As something like an attempt to starve them into submission to ecclesiastical authority; yet that is a course of proceeding which takes place in every case of schools under clerical management in Ireland?—There is no starving in the case when there is no question as to who the manager is.

1065. But if a teacher refused to admit the authority of the manager, that rule would be enforced in reference to that teacher, would it not?—Yes, of course.

1066. It is a necessary rule that the teacher should submit himself or herself to that ecclesiastical authority, so far as that goes?—Yes, but it had a very unpleasant appearance in my mind in this case. The teachers did everything entitling them to be paid, and their only offence was that they wished to receive the salary through the clergyman whom they recognised as manager, and that they refused to receive it through a person whom the Board had no legal right to appoint as manager.

1067. I thought you said that the Board had a right to recognise anyone whom they thought proper, as the manager of a non-vested school?—They have a right to remove a manager; but they have no right, against the will of a manager in possession of the schools, to appoint another manager over him; as shown by what happened in this case; because the only way in which they could carry out their view was by striking the schools off the roll.

1068. With respect to the schools under a committee, the committee appointed the Rev. Mr. Martin as manager?—Yes.

1069. So that, so far as those schools are concerned, the Board had a right to recognise him as manager, had they not? - Yes.

1070. Was not the teacher of one of those schools Miss Keogh?—She was a teacher in one of the schools; but in which of them I do not know.

1071. You do not know whether it was in a school that was under the committee?—I do not.

1072. Do you know in what school the other was?—I do not.

1073. But if they were in a school that was under the committee, the action of the Board would have been quite proper in their regard, would it not?—I do not think that the action of the Board was proper at all.

1074. You do not think that the action of the Board in recognising the person nominated by the committee as manager was right?—I do not think their action was right in removing Mr. O'Keeffe, without giving him notice that they were going to remove him; and the rest all followed from that; therefore, I cannot say that anything was right. But assuming that they were right in removing Mr. O'Keeffe, and were right in appointing the other man, then they were right in everything else that they did.

1075. Assuming that they were right in removing Father O'Keeffe, so far as the schools under the committee were concerned, they were right in recognising Mr. Martin as manager?—Yes.

1076. And there was nothing discreditable in their refusing to pay salaries to teachers who refused to recognise that manager, was there?—They acted under the general rule in this respect, no doubt. I pointed out this as a serious inconvenience, resulting from what I thought was a very improvident order.

1077. If you look a little lower down in your letter referring to your motion, you say, at page 55, "As a corollary, therefore, to the decision in Miss Keogh's, I moved, 'That, pending the decision by a competent tribunal as to Mr. O'Keeffe's suspension,' adopting the language of the 23rd April, the salaries of the other teachers should be paid through the head inspector, and that the Treasury should be asked to sanction this mode of payment while the dispute was pending?— Yes.

1078. And you state that your motion was "defeated upon this occasion by an

SELECT COMMITTEE ON CALLAN SCHOOLS. 99

an amendment, declaring that such a payment would be a misapplication of the public funds"?—Yes.

Rt. Hon. Mr. Justice Lawson.

11 June 1873.

1079. But here again you do not give the terms of the amendment in your letter?—I was not going to write it again in the letter. The things had all appeared on record. I could not make them any better or worse

1080. Did you think it fair, in a statement which you intended to be, so far as the narrative of facts was concerned, a fair and impartial, and not an *ex parte* statement, to show your own motion *in extenso*, and to leave out the words of the amendment?—I thought it was perfectly fair and impartial; and I think that anyone reading it will think the same.

1081. *Chairman.*] I understand that the purpose of your letter was to explain and justify the course which you individually had taken?—Yes; I did not mean to give a complete history of the Callan schools, if I had done that, my letter would have surpassed even the dimensions of the Chief Baron's letter. I wished to show the motives of my own action, and to show that my sincere desire was to protect the interests of the children who I thought were suffering from the withdrawal of education from them.

1082. *The O'Conor Don.*] In carrying out that view, you had to state what were the motions proposed to the Board, and your action regarding them?—Yes

1083. And you thought that it was not wanting in impartiality to omit the full terms of the motion which you opposed, and to state simply the motion which you made yourself?—I have always understood that, when you refer to a document, it is quite sufficient to refer to it without setting it out. Every member of the Board knew that document, and therefore there is nothing to justify you in supposing that there was any concealment on my part.

1084. But, although the full terms of the resolution might be known to the Board, I presume you anticipated at least that this letter might become public property and be circulated far outside?—I did not anticipate anything of the kind. When I found that another Commissioner had put his views on record, I thought I would do the same.

1085. *Chairman.*] Your object was not to state both sides impartially, but to state your own side, and to do it in a fair manner?—Yes; I intended it as a justification of what I did in the case. I wanted to show honestly what my motives were, and I think I conveyed them in language of studied moderation. I am excusing myself now for not having stated *in extenso*, in this case, documents that were as well known to the persons to whom they were written, namely, the secretaries and the Commissioners, as to myself.

1086. *The O'Conor Don.*] But you perceive that in this paragraph which I am alluding to, you represented that your motion was defeated "by an amendment declaring that such a payment" (a payment which you in the preceding sentence had explained) "would be a misapplication of the public funds"?—Yes.

1087. Now, referring to that amendment, I find that it was in the following words: "That, as it appears the teachers have refused to recognise the Rev. Mr. Martin as manager, or to receive their salaries, or to furnish the quarterly returns of attendance of pupils through his hands, that the Rev. Mr. Martin has been denied by the teachers of the Callan National Schools the right to visit the schools, which the Board's rules secure to every member of the public; and as it further appears that the head inspector, through the intervention of the late manager, Rev. R. O'Keeffe, was refused access to the school records, and that the district inspector whilst in the discharge of his duty was by the said late manager, Rev. Mr. O'Keeffe, prevented from inspecting, and forcibly expelled from the schools, and as, in consequence, the head and district inspectors and the manager are unable to give information to the Board as to the names and qualifications of the teachers, the sufficiency of the attendance of the pupils, the quality of the instruction, or the observance of any of the rules of the national system, it would be contrary to precedent, and an unwarrantable application of the public money, to accede to Mr. Justice Lawson's motion." That is the amendment. Does not that amendment set forth reasons for refusing to accede to your proposal which seem somewhat inconsistent with your explanation of your proposal, namely, "I fully explained that my intention was that the head inspector should satisfy himself

0.93. N 2 self

Rt. Hon. Mr.
Justice Lawson.
11 June 1873.

self that the teachers had done their duty, and that the schools had been properly conducted," and so on. Does not that amendment appear to be inconsistent with your explanation of your motion?—It contains a great many recitals which I did not think it at all necessary to introduce.

1088. But does it not contain a great many recitals of grounds for refusing the grant in which you would concur?—I think that everything that is stated in those recitals already appears on my letter, namely, the refusal of the teachers to acknowledge the authority of Mr. Martin, and to receive the salaries through him, and so on; I think all that appears sufficiently on my letter already.

1089. Does it not appear that none of the rules of the Board were carried out at all in these schools according to the terms of that amendment?—There is a recital to that effect; I consider that when I refer to the amendment, I refer to the amendment as it was. If I had said that I was defeated by an amendment of such a date, I consider that it would have been quite enough. I put in the operative part of the amendment, as a man generally, when referring to a document, leaves out the recitals and states only the operative part. I state the operative part after all these long recitals, declaring that that payment would be a misapplication of the public funds.

1090. *Chairman.*] You considered that this was a sufficient reference on your part to the terms of an amendment, which was too long to be set forth in that place?—Yes, certainly.

1091. *Mr. Gathorne Hardy.*] And that letter was for the use of the Board itself, which had all the documents?—Yes, and was addressed to the Secretaries, and it lay in that office and would have lain there *ad infinitum*, only that some one moved for it to appear in the Parliamentary Papers.

1092. *The O'Conor Don*] You have before referred to the fact of the educational interdict, which you stated was placed on the children of Callan by this action of the Board; and I presume from your letter, as well as from what you have stated to-day, that you consider that, quite irrespective of Father O'Keeffe's conduct, or of any action of the Board in his regard, it was very undesirable that the children should be punished for an act with which they had nothing to do?—I do.

1093. Does not that take place in every case where managers are removed from the management of a school on account of some personal misconduct?—The innocent often suffer for the guilty, I suppose; but I always try to prevent that taking place.

1094. But in every case where a manager is removed from a school in consequence of some act of his own, is it your idea that the locality is placed under an educational interdict?—No, I do not say so; but here it was perfectly clear that if the interests of education in the district had been consulted, things would have been left as they were, because they were going on rightly, and as before; and the Board would just have waited until the decision of this litigation, and would not have mixed themselves up in a quarrel with which they had nothing to do; and if they had done that the interests of education in the parish would not have been sacrificed as I think they have been by what has been done.

1095. When you say that the Board have mixed themselves up in a quarrel with which they had nothing to do, are you not aware that the majority of the Board are of opinion that they have not mixed themselves up with such a quarrel at all?—Yes; I am only stating it from my own point of view; I say at the end of my letter, "It has all arisen from the Commissioners mixing themselves up in a quarrel with which they had nothing to do: as long as the schools were managed in accordance with the rules of the Board, the Commissioners should not have interfered. This is the position for which I have in vain contended, while ready to entertain any complaint to be made against Mr. O'Keeffe with respect to the actual management of the schools." That is the position for which I struggled throughout.

1096. But is that really the position that you struggled for throughout, considering that the first amendment that was proposed was not one to the effect, that so long as Mr. O'Keeffe conducted his schools in accordance with the rules of the Board, he should be continued in the management, but one to the effect of asking him for an explanation of his suspension? - What I anticipate would have occurred, if he had received notice that he was

going

going to be removed in consequence of this suspension, is this: I suppose he would have come forward and said, "The schools are managed as before; I am *de facto* parish priest, and I deny the legality of this suspension, because I was suspended by a person who had no jurisdiction over me and for an offence which is not a breach of any law human or Divine, namely, going to law with another man," and if he had said that, I think the Board would have said, "We had better leave things as they are."

Rt. Hon. Mr. Justice *Lawson*.
11 June 1873.

1097. But I understand that your view with respect to management of schools under ecclesiastics is, that so long as the school is conducted in accordance with the rules of the Board, they have no business to go beyond that, or to make any inquiries as to the relations between this ecclesiastic and his superiors? —If the ecclesiastic has been guilty of immorality, or any crime that makes him an unfit person to be manager of schools, I say of course remove him; but I have already put the case of a clergyman of my own church being suspended for preaching what was supposed to be heretical doctrine, and I said that I would not consider that the slightest ground for removing him from the management of the schools.

1098. But you would consider it sufficient ground for suspending him from the particular church to which he belonged, would you not?—Assuming that it was so, still it would not be sufficient ground for me to act upon that suspension, or to pay the slightest attention to it, because it might be a suspension in respect of a matter which did not touch the moral character of the man, or his position as a person engaged in the work of education.

1099. Then the mere fact of a clergyman being suspended, in your mind, would not be sufficient reason for removing him from the position of manager without inquiring into the grounds of the suspension?—As I said before, I would inquire into all the circumstances of the case. And that is the point of the case. If there is no absolute rule that a suspended man, *ipso facto*, ceases to be manager, then an inquiry into all the circumstances of the case is necessary.

1100. Did you think it necessary in the case of Father Sheridan to inquire into all the circumstances of the case?—I have answered that question already.

1101. You answered it before by stating that he admitted his suspension; but now I understand you to say that, whether a clergyman admits his suspension or not, the Board are bound to inquire into the grounds of that suspension; and if it be not what they consider a proper ground for suspension, the Board should take no notice of it?—I have no doubt that, in Mr. Sheridan's case, the Board were satisfied that the reasons for which he was suspended rendered him an unfit person to be a manager of schools.

1102. *Chairman.*] Do you consider that when the clergyman disputes the validity of the suspension, the Commissioners should ascertain the ground on which that suspension has proceeded?—I do.

1103. And if they found it was only on ecclesiastical grounds, should they permit him to continue manager?—They should permit him to continue manager unless the suspension was on such grounds as would interfere with his usefulness in an educational point of view.

1104. *The O'Conor Don.*] Then, supposing a clergyman admitted the fact of his suspension, but disputed the advisability of removing him from the management of a school, you would consider it necessary to inquire into the facts of the case?—I would consider it necessary that the Board should satisfy themselves whether it was advisable to remove him or not.

1105. But in this case of Mr. Sheridan, are you aware that Mr. Sheridan declined to relinquish the management of the schools?—I have already stated that I have no recollection whatever about Mr. Sheridan's case; that my mind is a blank on the subject. I have no recollection whatever of it, and my only information about it is derived from those Parliamentary Papers that are printed, and, from my knowledge of the practice of the Board at that time, that a great many matters were stated at the Board and formed the foundation of the decision at which the Board arrived, which do not appear from any written document at all; and the inference which I draw from that case of Mr. Sheridan is this, that the Board were satisfied that this gentleman was suspended according to his own admission that he was suspended, and on grounds which rendered it inexpedient that he should continue to be the manager of the school.

Rt. Hon. Mr.
Justice Lawson.
11 June 1873.

1106. Are you aware that all the older members of the Board hold it to be a sufficient ground for removing a manager, that he is certified as having been suspended?—I am aware that some of the members who have come here have stated that. I beg to say, however, that I am not a young member of the Board; I believe I am the fifth oldest member of it; I have been a member of it since 1861.

1107. Can you quote any instance in which the Board continued to recognise a suspended clergyman after the ecclesiastical authority certified to the Board that he was so suspended?—I cannot.

1108. Can you quote any instance in which a reference was made to an alleged suspended clergyman for an explanation?—I have not examined the records of the Board, and do not know anything of them. I am not aware of any instance. This Return before you has been presented to Parliament, and I am not aware what other instances there are.

1109. Are you able to give the Committee any evidence as to the condition of the Callan Schools before this suspension of Mr. O'Keeffe?—None whatever; I never saw them in my life.

1110. I mean from information furnished to you as a Commissioner at the Board?—No.

1111. Are you aware that before this, in the year 1871, the schools not being properly conducted in accordance with the rules of the Board were struck off the roll?—I have heard that, and I have always stated that I was perfectly ready to entertain any application to remove Mr. O'Keeffe, on any alleged ground that he had misconducted himself in the management of the schools.

1112. Mr. *Cross*.] One question about the Ratoath case, Mr. Sheridan's case; we have had it in evidence that that began as early as January 1863; were you aware of that?—So I see it is stated.

1113. And that the letter, No. 145, referred to at the bottom of page 19, in Parliamentary Paper, No. 138, practically, was written in consequence of instructions to the inspector which had been given in 1864 by the secretaries?—Yes.

1114. So that all that matter would have been called to the attention of the inspector for some time before he made the report, and the matter, in fact, had been progressing with the knowledge of Mr. Sheridan all that time?—Yes.

1115. I understand you to say that in all these cases which are called precedents, the general circumstances of each case would be made known to the Board by the Resident Commissioner?—Certainly.

1116. And that facts, therefore, would be in their knowledge which would not appear upon any documentary evidence which now remains in the records of the Board?—Certainly.

1117. And that those facts stated by the Resident Commissioner, according to the practice of the Board, would have weight with the Board in coming to their decision upon that case?—Would have most material weight. I scarcely ever knew in my experience any instance in which the Board did not act on Mr. Macdonnell's opinion as to what was expedient to be done in a particular case; we had that confidence in him.

1118. And they acted on the facts of the case as he stated them?—Yes.

1119. And therefore no present officer of the Board could, from merely looking into the records of the office and bringing them before us, lay before us what was laid before the Board when each particular case was decided?—Certainly not.

1120. Mr. *Gathorne Hardy*.] Would the Resident Commissioner have always the inspectors' Reports of the different districts before him before he came to the Board?—Always; he would be quite posted up in them all, and would know the whole history; the Board know very little of the details of what is brought before them, and therefore they always used to turn to the Resident Commissioner, in whom they had the greatest confidence, and ask his opinion in the matter; and I scarcely ever knew them to depart from that.

1121. *Chairman*.] All the traditions and proceedings of the Board would be present to the mind of Sir Alexander Macdonnell as familiarly, I suppose, as anything could be?—Yes.

1122. *The O'Conor Don*.] And all those reports to which you have alluded are

SELECT COMMITTEE ON CALLAN SCHOOLS.

Rt. Hon. Mr. Justice *Lawson*.

11 June 1873.

are kept and preserved in the records of the office, are they not?—Everything, I suppose is kept; it ought to be.

1123. And they can be referred to at any time?—I suppose so.

1124. Mr. *Cross*.] But any facts stated at the time by the Resident Commissioner to the Board would also have weight?—Yes.

1125. In the case of Mr. O'Farrell, do you know whether he was insane?—I do not know that; I have heard it.

1126. Supposing it had been stated to the Board by the Resident Commissioner that Mr. O'Farrell was insane, that would have had weight with them in their judgment?—Yes; or if it had been stated that he had left the parish, or was suspended for drunkenness, or anything of the sort, that would have been conclusive of the case.

1127. I want to call your attention to one answer of Sir Alexander Macdonnell's, given in answer to a question put by The O'Conor Don, Question 676: "During your long experience as Commissioner of Education, have you ever known the Board to yield to the pressure of the Catholic clergy?" The answer: "I am very happy to have that question asked me. I was Commissioner of Education for 32 years, and I can say, with the greatest deliberation, that upon no one occasion did I ever know a single change made by the National Board, or an improvement introduced, under Catholic dictation or pressure. I have lamented over and over again that our improvements did not take place sooner, improvements which were calculated to satisfy the Roman Catholic Interests; but I never recollect a single instance in which we were induced by Catholic dictation or pressure to do anything which our conscience did not think necessary or just." Do you agree with that answer?—I am perfectly sure that Mr. Macdonnell would not do anything under any pressure which his conscience did not think necessary or just, and I do not mean to say that there was any Catholic dictation or pressure *ab extra*. All I meant to convey to the Committee was this, that the Board were often influenced in their deliberation by the reason that if they did not take a particular course, the Catholic bishops or clergy would withdraw their schools from the Board; that influenced the action of the Board. I do not mean to say that there was any threat or dictation, or anything of that sort.

1128. During your experience as Commissioner, has the Board yielded to pressure from the Roman Catholic clergy?—I think I have mentioned one or two matters already that I thought were concessions granted under the apprehension that if they were not granted, schools might be withdrawn; things of that kind took place.

1129. Mr. *Bourke*.] With reference to Mr. Sheridan's case, do you recollect all the circumstances of the case from reading the documents?—I have read the very meagre papers connected with them; but I do not remember a single circumstance connected with it.

1130. Do you think that under all the circumstances of that case, the admission on the part of Mr. Sheridan that he was suspended, was not only an admission of the fact that he was suspended, but also an admission that that suspension took place under such circumstances as made it impossible that he could remain manager of the schools?—I think that was an element in the case; but it must be taken in connection with all the other circumstances of the case. If a man admitted that he was suspended for what has been called here an ecclesiastical offence, breach of discipline, or something of that sort, even although he admitted that, I would not consider it any reason for removing him at all, unless it was a suspension for a cause which interfered with his usefulness as a man managing a school.

1131. Mr. *Whitbread*.] I understood you to say sometime ago, in answer to a question of Mr. Hardy's, that you had to consider your position as judge, as well as your position as a Commissioner, and I think I gather your opinion clearly, that it was more compromising to your position as a judge, to accept the certificate of the Bishop of Ossory as the suspension of Mr. O'Keeffe, than it would have been to have examined Mr. O'Keeffe himself to have gone into the whole circumstances of the case with him, and then to have decided the question, whether the charge was one upon which he could properly be suspended or not?—I have not said that. If Mr. O'Keeffe had made an explanation, and had stated that his case was under litigation,

0.93. N 4

Rt. Hon. Mr. Justice Lawson.

11 June 1873.

litigation, and was the subject of a pending suit, I would still have felt my position as a judge to be such that I ought not to give any opinion which of the parties in that litigation were right, but I would have said, "Let matters remain as they are; I will not decide either in favour of one or the other." That is what I should have done.

1132. Then does that answer go to this extent, that so long as Mr. O'Keeffe could have kept his case before any court, you would not have thought the suspension sufficiently clear to act upon it?—Yes; as long as there was a *bona fide* litigation pending as to the validity of the suspension, I would have considered that, as a judge, I ought to respect that litigation, and not have voted as if the suspension were valid, which a competent tribunal was about to decide to be valid or to be invalid.

1133. But you went further, I think, in another direction, in answer to questions, and said that you considered that the Commissioners ought to ascertain whether the charge was one which would justify the suspension?— Yes. Suppose what was laid to his charge was that he did not obey the commands of his bishop in a matter which the bishop had no right to order him to do; I would not consider that to justify suspension.

1134. Mr. *Bourke.*] I understood part of your objection, with reference to your position as judge, was, that you yourself might be a member of the "competent tribunal" that might hereafter decide on the validity of the suspension?—Certainly.

1135. Mr. *Whitbread.*] And you felt that accepting a certificate endorsed that certificate of suspension?—Yes, for the purposes for which we were going to use it, for the purpose of displacing the man from the position which he then held.

1136. In answer to the questions asked you a short time ago by, I think, The O'Conor Don, you said that if the paramount interests of education alone had been kept in view, things would have been allowed to go on as they were, because they were going on well. Had you in your memory at that time the report of the chief of inspection upon the Callan School, dated January 1873?— Yes.

1137. What had been the condition for the two years previously, according to that report of the Callan Boys' School; had it been conducted according to the rules of the Commissioners?—There were violations of the rules as reported by the inspector, but the schools were going on, and the children were attending them and receiving education. I do not mean to say that Mr. O'Keeffe was faultless as a manager; I think he was the reverse; and if he had been impeached on that ground, I would have been prepared to consider it. But all I say is, that the effect of what the Board have done is to suspend the schools altogether, and that the effect of allowing them to go on would be that they would have been carried on, and the children would have been receiving education.

1138. But if the schools were not being conducted according to the rules of the Board, that is one of those circumstances which you would take into consideration when you were dealing with his case, is it not?—Yes.

1139. I understood your position and that of the minority to be, that the certificate of suspension was not, *ipso facto*, sufficient, but that all the circumstances of the case should be considered?—Quite so.

1140. And in dealing with this case you must have taken into consideration this report of the chief of inspection?—No; it was not taken into consideration, because the action of the Board, by the order of the 23rd of April, was based exclusively upon the supposed legal ground that the man was a suspended clergyman, and not upon his having misconducted himself in any way in the management of the schools. And in like manner the refusal of the Board, according to the motion of Lord Monck, to take the schools again into connection, as you will find, was based upon this, that he was a suspended clergyman, that that suspension had never been removed or declared invalid by any competent tribunal, and that, therefore, he was actually disqualified from being manager of the schools.

1141. But it was hardly justified, was it, by the report of the inspector, when you said that the schools were going on well?— I did not mean that they were going

going on well in the sense of perfectly; I would withdraw that expression. They were going on as they did before, which was indifferently, perhaps.

1142. I will call your attention to an answer given by Judge Longfield, at Question 552; the question is put by The O'Conor Don: "Whatever your opinion may be as to the dismissal of a suspended manager, the practice of the Board has been upon all occasions to dismiss;" the answer is, "I approve of the practice; but even if I did not approve of it, I would favour it; for the practice being known has prevented the ecclesiastical authorities taking steps to protect themselves, which they would have taken but for our practice; they could easily have appointed the bishop as patron, and the parish priest as manager, and then the bishop would only have to hold up his finger, and he would go out." Now do you concur in that opinion, that the ecclesiastical authorities had the power to have taken those steps if they had chosen to do so, and had not relied upon the understanding which the majority of the Board believed to have existed? — I think that if the Commissioners had acted upon the suggestion made there, to appoint the bishop of the diocese as patron of all the schools and the parish priests as managers, they would not have been carrying out the Trust confided to them by Parliament; they would then have been making the schools strictly ecclesiastical schools, and every manager removeable at the option of the bishop, without any reference to them; which in my opinion would not be in conformity with the rules of the Board, or the mode in which they ought to administer the funds.

1143. But who brings these schools to the Board; does the Board appoint the patron of the schools, or does the patron bring the school to the Board?—The patron brings the school to the Board; he says "I have a school here which is conducted, and I am ready to obey the rules, and I ask you to give me aid;" and then they send their inspector down, and he reports whether it is a proper school and whether it ought to be taken into connection. And I may state that Judge Longfield, at the close of that printed letter of his, says (it is at page 34 of Parliamentary Paper, No. 85), "If Mr. O'Keeffe should hereafter apply to become manager or patron of any school in his private character, it would be necessary for the Board to inquire into all the circumstances of the case, and into his conduct since his suspension, in order that the Board might decide whether a compliance with his application would promote the cause of national education." Now I entirely agree in that position, but then it is at right angles with what the Board did when Mr. O'Keeffe made his application to have the schools taken into connection again; because so far from considering whether a compliance with his application would promote the cause of National Education, they decided that he was disqualified from being received as manager.

1144. If the bishop brought the school in the first instance to the Commissioners, would he not, according to Rule 2, be recognised as patron of it?—Yes.

1145. And he might appoint, under your own rules, his manager?—Yes.

1146. Then it would not be acting in opposition to the rules of the Board at the present time, if the bishops had brought the schools in the first instance to the Board, and they had appointed the priests as managers?—Of course not; if the bishop was in possession of the school, and applied to place it in connection with the Board, he might have appointed his manager. All I say is, that appointing the bishop wholesale to be patron of all the schools in the diocese, *ex officio*, would not be, in my judgment, a fulfilment of the trust of the Board.

1147. But from your answer, I cannot make out how the Board would have avoided doing that if the ecclesiastics had chosen to take that course, acting under their own rules; not doing it, I mean, wholesale, but doing it in every individual case?—But still, the parish priest so appointed by the bishop would not be *ex officio* manager; he would be a manager, because he was named by the patron.

1148. But he would be removable by his ecclesiastical superior, not only when he was suspended, but at any moment that that ecclesiastical authority chose to remove him; acting upon your own rules, would he not?—That appears to be so.

1149. Rule 4 says this: "The patron has the right of nominating any fit person to act as his representative, to be designated the 'local manager.' The patron may, at any time, resume the direct management of the school, or appoint another local manager;" and the question which I now put to you is this:

Rt. Hon. Mr. Justice *Lawson.*

11 June 1873.

Rt. Hon. Mr.
Justice Lawson.

11 June 1873.

if the ecclesiastics had, in the first instance, not relying upon the Board's consideration of their decrees of suspension, taken this course of having the bishops made the patrons, and the parish priest the manager, would not the schools then have been far more under ecclesiastical authority and jurisdiction than they are now, or could become now, under the present state of things?—I cannot answer that question.

1150. *Chairman.*] If such a state of things had occurred would you have considered it a state of things which required to be met by some new regulations of the Board?—It is very hard to answer what I would do in a particular state of things that I have never considered before. I cannot tell. In reference to one matter that Mr. Whitbread referred to, I think that we are bound to give all proper weight to decrees of suspension, and I give the same weight to them as I would to the judgment of any other Court. I have already explained that if it were seen that the principles of law were properly applied to it, and if the man were cited for a proper offence before a proper tribunal, I never would think of questioning the justice of that decision, and that is, I think, the fullest extent to which any reasonable person ought to expect that weight would be given to such a decision.

1151. Mr. *Bourke.*] I see that in Rule 3 it is provided, "If a school be under the local management of a school committee, such committee has all the rights of an individual patron;" so that, with regard to all schools under a committee, it would be impossible then for any bishop to exercise the rights of a patron?—Yes.

1152. Mr. *Gathorne Hardy.*] I understood you to say (I am sorry to revert to that subject) that, in regard to the case of Mr. Sheridan, you have no recollection whatever of it?—No, I have none.

1153. Is it the fact that one man may be recorded as having been present at the Board on a particular day without having been present at a particular transaction brought before the Board on that day?—Certainly.

1154. And the fact of your having been named as present merely shows that some time during the day you appeared there?—Certainly.

1155. I understand your objection to acting in this question upon the suspension to be that you should act upon the suspension absolutely without any inquiry of any description whatever, except as to the fact of the suspension?—Yes.

1156. Your view is that the patrons or managers are appointed on their own merits under that rule to which you refer?—Yes.

1157. And you object to the word of any third person being taken without any question of merit being inquired into at all?—Yes.

1158. When the question was put to you about a suspension for change of opinions or heretical opinions, I understood you to answer that you would not act upon the suspension *per se* without further inquiry?—Certainly; suppose that a man was suspended for heretical opinions, and the consequence was that all the children left the school, I would act upon that suspension.

1159. And in the case of removal from the place in the same way?—Yes.

1160. But you think that you are not bound to act upon the mere statement of suspension which may be from a person who has no jurisdiction, and upon grounds which it may be wrong to acknowledge?—Yes.

1161. With respect to the report of the inspector referred to by the honourable Member for Bedford, dated in January of the present year, that is a report entirely subsequent to the action of the Board, which was in April 1872?—Yes.

1162. Therefore that was not at all before the Board when they acted in 1872?—No; and in 1872, at that meeting in April, there was no question of the general conduct of Mr. O'Keeffe. The question was, "There is Bishop Moran's letter, and there is nothing to do but to act upon it."

1163. I am reminded that the report of Mr. Sheridan, the inspector in 1873, puts together a variety of reports of former years; but those reports were not before you in 1872 except in their scattered condition, and I understood you that unless that is brought before you by the Resident Commissioner, you do not look yourselves into the inspectors' reports?—No, certainly not.

1164. Mr. *Whitbread.*] But the Resident Commissioner can hardly have forgotten

SELECT COMMITTEE ON CALLAN SCHOOLS.   107

gotten that the Board had very recently struck at least one of these schools off the rolls?—I think they restored it again; did they not?

Rt. Hon. Mr. Justice *Lawson.*

11 June 1873.

1165. That the Callan Schools be retained on the rolls for further trial?—Yes.

1166. Mr. *Gathorne Hardy.*] But in April 1872, no question was before the Board, but the question whether you should adopt the suspension *per se* or not?—That was the only question, and I always invited any motion on the subject. I challenged the members, and said, "If he is an unfit manager, bring forward a motion to remove him, and make out that, and I should be very happy to vote for it."

1167. I should like to ask you this question: supposing that there had been a question of a trust connected with the priest of Callan, or with the manager of the Callan Schools, would the courts have recognised the *de facto* manager or priest; would they have taken the one who was, during the appeal, appointed as administrator, or would they have refused to act at all?—They would have refused to act at all, as long as the matter was in litigation.

1168. That would be the case in a court of justice?—Of course it would be the case in a court of justice; and as I said before, when a man has a status as a parish priest, it is of great importance to preserve it; and we know from the evidence of Dr. Doyle, that the parish priests have a tenure in their office during good behaviour, and are not removable at pleasure, but only for some canonical offence. I think when a man is in possession, holding an office of that kind, succeeds in holding it, and challenges by an action the person who says that he is not in it, and has removed him from it, any public body ought to wait the result of that litigation before they proceed to act upon either the one theory or the other.

1169. *Chairman.*] Now, you have been asked a great many questions about this case of Mr. Sheridan's, and you say that you have no recollection of what passed that day at the Board; and it seems to be doubtful even whether you were present at the Board at the time that it came on. But it appears from the proceedings of the Board that Sir Alexander Macdonnell was present, and in all probability his authority would have very great weight at the Board?—Yes.

1170. And you would be very much influenced by his weight of authority?—Yes.

1171. If, therefore, it constitutes a precedent in the case, it is entitled to great weight as having been done under the authority of Sir Alexander Macdonnell?—Yes.

1172. Now, I understand you to disclaim altogether the imputation of any motives to any of your colleagues?—I imputed no motives to any of my colleagues; certainly not; I disclaim it emphatically.

1173. And if you speak of their acting under any ecclesiastical influence, you mean a legitimate influence, which might operate upon one mind though not upon another?—I mean what they considered a legitimate influence.

1174. And which might apply to the Presbyterian Church or to the late Established Church of Ireland?—Yes; and I should object just as strongly to taking the certificate of the General Assembly, or of a bishop of my own church, as I would that of a bishop of any other church; I would not register the decrees of any of them.

1175. But when you speak of ecclesiastical influence, you speak of a desire to increase the general influence of the Board among the community, and to extend the influence of education in Ireland?—It may be so.

1176. Therefore, whether the judgment of the individual be right or wrong, the motive, you consider, has been legitimate and directed to a proper purpose?—I impute no motive whatever; that is no business of mine. I do not draw any inference; I merely state the facts. I am found fault with for calling Bishop Moran's letter a mandate; I think it was a mandate, and a very imperative mandate to call on the Board to accept without hesitation a gentleman whom he appointed as administrator of the parish, not as parish priest, but removable at any moment that he pleased.

1177. I am not asking you about these particular passages, but I wish to know whether I understand you rightly, that, in speaking of ecclesiastical influence, you do not attribute to any of your colleagues the being under the influence of any church, much less of any particular church; or under the influence of any

0.93.   O 2   other

Rt. Hon. Mr.
Justice *Lawson*.

11 June 1873.

other feeling than a desire to promote the influence of the system of national education in the country?—I never suggested, and do not suggest, any improper motive to any of them.

1178. And if you have differed from others on occasions of that kind, it has been a difference of judgment, and not a difference of object?—I am sure that they all have the object to do what is right.

1179. If I collect your opinions rightly, you agree with those Commissioners who have been previously examined, in the statement that there is properly speaking no *ex officio* tenure of any appointment of manager?—I do.

1180. You differ from them in this, that you consider that suspension by the immediate superior ecclesiastical authority is not a conclusive reason for removing a clergyman from the office of manager?—That is my opinion.

1181. If a clergyman ceases to be the clergyman having cure of souls in the parish, I understand you to agree with your colleagues that the appointment of his successor would be *primâ facie* that which you would expect would be recognised?—Yes; or, as a rule, if he went away and left the managership vacant, unless there was a valid objection to it, his successor would naturally be appointed, not always.

1182. I think that we have heard before that a large proportion of the schools are parochial schools: that is, that the clergyman has become the manager of them by succession from those who before him have had the cure of souls in the parish. Is that your view?—My distinct opinion is, that there is no such thing as parochial schools connected with the system at all.

1183. Then if that opinion has been given by others, you do not agree with it?—I do not agree with it; I think it is contrary to the whole system.

1184. Is there anything else you wish to state to the Committee?—I wish to clear up one or two matters which The O'Conor Don asked me about. With respect to this expression that I used, "discreditable litigation," on thinking the matter over, now I recollect that it refers to an action brought by a Mr. Woods against the Commissioners. He was a teacher, and had done his duty before Mr. O'Keeffe was suspended at all, and his action for the salary was defended; and when it came before the Board the matter was very much discussed, and we were unanimously of opinion that he was entitled to be paid, and we instructed our counsel to defend the case on the legal ground that we were not liable in an action; but as soon as the decision was given in our favour, then to state that we were willing to pay him because he had done his duty. That would be the litigation that I referred to. Then the honourable Member for Roscommon asked me whether Miss Keogh's salary had been offered to her. My impression is that it will appear in the papers that it had been offered to her. And with respect to another question, the suggestion that I ought to have embodied the entire of Lord Monck's amendment in my letter, the recitals in that amendment were disputed as a matter of fact, and it will be found upon the records of the Board that Mr. Justice Morris moved a motion in which he expressly contradicted those recitals; so that the part of the amendment which it introduced was what I thought was the material part, namely, the operative part of the amendment, and I did not introduce these recitals in which I did not myself agree, as a matter of fact.

1185. *The O'Conor Don.*] But I suppose we may assume that the majority who voted for that amendment and against you, did agree in those recitals?—I suppose they did.

1186. And they being very important recitals that they were the grounds of their voting, in the way they did?—I suppose so; but still I consider that when I referred to the amendment I did as much as was requisite, and that I was not bound to set forth all those recitals in which I did not concur.

The Reverend *Charles L. Morell*, called in; and Examined.

Rev. C. L. *Morell*.

1187. *Mr. Cross.*] You are a Presbyterian Clergyman, I believe?—Yes.

1188. And how long have you been a member of the Board?— Since May, 1868.

1189. Were you then Moderator of the General Assembly?—I was Moderator a few a few months afterwards; in the month of June I became Moderator of the General Assembly.

Rev. *C. L. Morell.*
11 June 1873.

1190. You I believe, were one of the minority in this case of O'Keeffe at the Board?—Yes.

1191. Would you state shortly your reasons for differing from the majority in that matter?—Well, I thought that Mr. O'Keeffe should be communicated with and afforded an opportunity of offering an explanation before we should take action, more particularly as we had good reason for believing that he denied the fact of his suspension, having brought an action against Cardinal Cullen for calling him a suspended priest.

1192. You have heard of the precedents which have been brought forward of course in this matter; do you wish to state to the Committee the reasons why you think those precedents do not apply?—I think that the case of Mr. O'Keeffe differed somewhat from all those cases that have been called precedents. He not only denied the suspension, but he took action upon his denial and appealed to the civil courts, and then we had the statement on the one hand of Cardinal Cullen, saying that he was a suspended priest, and on the other hand his own statement that he was not; and in addition to this he offered proof that he was not a suspended priest, by appealing to the civil courts. I think, and I thought at the time, that, *pendente lite*, we should have awaited the issue.

1193. In your opinion, you do not take the suspension by the ecclesiastical authority as conclusive, as to the dismissal from a school?—Not as conclusive.

1194. Do you think it right to consider the effect that the suspension of a man would have upon the conduct of a school, and the work of education which the school would carry out?—As a general rule I think it is not desirable that a suspended clergyman should be the manager of a school, but I think that there are cases where there are exceptions to this rule. For example, if a man has established a school himself; for example, I have established a school during the last two or three years, not as a clergyman, but simply as a private gentleman; or, I think that another exception would be where he is manager of a school where a majority of the children, or a large number of them, are members of another denomination; in that case, if he were suspended for heresy or for contumacy, that would not affect the influence that he would have for good over the majority of the children; and, especially, I would say, where the school remains in the possession of the suspended person, and where his moral character is good, and the parents are satisfied that he is the proper person to give religious instruction to the children.

1195. Then you would set considerable weight upon the opinion of the parents in the matter?—I set great weight upon the opinion of the parents in the matter; it has always been considered of great importance by the church with which I am connected; and I think the rules of the Board set great weight upon that; for we have on the second page, No. 1, under the 4th Section, this rule: "Opportunities are to be afforded to the children of all the National Schools for receiving such religious instruction as their parents or guardians approve of." And again on page 3, paragraph 11, "The parents or guardians of the children have the right to require the patrons and managers to afford opportunities for the reading of the Holy Scriptures in the school-room, under proper persons approved of by the parents or guardians for that purpose." I set great weight upon the wishes of the parents as to the religious instruction that the children should receive.

1196. *The O'Conor Don.*] Does not that apply exclusively to vested schools?—The first rule I read applies to all schools, and the second one applies altogether, I think, to vested schools, but the first one, as I have said, to all schools: "Opportunities are to be afforded to the children of all National Schools for receiving such religious instruction as their parents or guardians approve of."

1197. Mr. *Cross.*] Now supposing that a clergyman of any denomination were suspended by ecclesiastical authority, would you recognise the jurisdiction of the Civil Courts in considering the question of suspension, as to its validity or not?—I think there are cases, at least so far as the Board is concerned, where the Civil Courts are competent to declare whether sentence has been pronounced in accordance with the rules of the Church to which the accused had given in his adhesion, and where an adverse decision of the Civil Courts should be received by the Board of Education. I say nothing now about the Church, for I am not competent to express an opinion upon that subject, but should be received by the Board of Education as influencing their action.

Rev. *C. L. Morell.*
11 June 1873.

1198. You draw a distinction as to the validity, so far as affects the Board, and so far as affects the church to which the clergyman happens to belong?—Yes.

1199. Then, in that case, you are not of the same opinion that Dr. Henry was in the evidence which he gave before us the other day?—No, I am not.

1200. Did you hear, or have you read, the evidence given by Dr. Henry as to the conditions upon which the Presbyterian body joined the Board and brought its schools into the Board?—I have read this evidence, but only a very meagre report of it in an Irish newspaper.

1201. May I call your attention to the answers given by Dr. Henry to Questions 589 and 590. In Question 589 he was asked, "Now, did anything take place at that time about the recognition of deposed clergymen?" and he replied, "There was no rule. If it had been proposed as part of the arrangement between the Synod and the Board, or the Government, that their certificate should not be received as stating the ground of deposition of a minister, I am quite certain that my church, the General Assembly, would never have accepted aid from the Board. It would have been a direct interference, I think, with their discipline and internal government." Then, in Question 590, he was asked, "Do I rightly understand you to say that it would have prevented the junction of the Presbyterian Church at that time?" and he answers, "I am quite sure that if it had been put forward as a positive proposition it would have prevented it. I cannot conceive of the case, and I think it is quite right to state that the Presbyterian Church has always stood strongly out for the recognition of the status of their own ministers." Do you concur in the views there expressed?—I never heard of the consideration mentioned in the answer to the first question influencing the Church in connecting itself with the Board. That is a matter of opinion, of course, altogether. In regard to the answer to the second question, I do not agree with Dr. Henry in the statement which he there makes, but it is a matter of opinion entirely.

1202. *Chairman.*] So far as it is a matter of opinion, did you take any part in the negociations that preceded and accompanied the union of the Presbyterians with the National Board in 1839 and 1840?—No; I was only a very young man at that time.

1203. But in the immediately preceding question put to Dr. Henry, he was asked if he had, and he stated that he was called upon to take a very prominent part?—I am quite aware that he did take a very prominent part, and he is more competent on that account to give a valuable opinion than I am, but I never heard such a thing.

1204. Mr. *Cross.*] Do you know the feeling on the part of the Presbyterian body generally on that question?—I know the feeling is very general that the majority of the Commissioners did very wrong in dealing with Father O'Keeffe as they did; and the largest and most influential Presbytery in the Presbyterian Church, that of Belfast, passed upon them a very strong vote of condemnation, almost unanimously.

1205. When was that?—About six or eight weeks ago, I think.

1206. Could you favour us with a copy of that resolution?—I can get it; it would require a day or two, of course, to obtain it. (Vide *Appendix.*)

1207. Then, in your opinion, the majority were quite wrong in cutting off these schools from their connection with the Board?—Yes; I agree with Judge Lawson, that it was really punishing parents and children for what, to say the least of it, was not their fault.

1208. Is there any other matter that you wish to bring before the Committee?—There is only just one other matter. I think there was some question put to Judge Lawson as to whether he ever knew of a case in which a pressure was brought to bear by the Roman Catholic clergy upon the Board, to induce them to do anything that they were not inclined to do; and when I was listening to that, I did remember a case myself that came under my own notice a very short time ago. We had come to a resolution, and made a form of agreement with managers and teachers, and when we had the form drawn out we found, by correspondence that poured in upon us, that it was not a form that commended itself to the bishops of the Roman Catholic Church, and they directed the clerical managers not to sign this form; and we modified that form in order to suit their

their wishes and in order to get the poor teachers the money that otherwise they would have been deprived of.

Rev. C. L. Morell

11 June 1873.

1209. Is there any other matter that you wish to state, either about Mr. O'Keeffe's case itself, or about any of the precedents that we have had before us?—No, I do not know that I have anything to say, except to express my entire agreement with what Judge Lawson has said. That it was an error of judgment on the part of the majority, from no wish or inclination at all to act a subservient part towards the dictates of any bishop, or priest, or clergyman.

1210. Mr. *Bourke*.] I just wish to draw your attention to two or three words of Dr. Henry's, in answer to Question 591: "Let me suppose that in this case we had for the first time departed from our settled practice, and had declined to act upon the certificate of the Roman Catholic Coadjutor Bishop of Ossory." Now do you consider that in taking the course that the majority of the Commissioners did take, they acted according to any particular settled practice?—Well, I think according to these precedents there was a practice in the case; but I have already pointed out the difference between those precedents and the particular case of O'Keeffe.

1211. But I want to know also, supposing that the Board had acted in accordance with the opinions of the minority, would they, in that case, have departed from the settled practice of the Board, in your opinion?—No.

1212. What is your reason for saying that?—Because his case differed from the other precedents in the particulars which I have mentioned.

1213. Mr. *Whitbread*.] You stated that you had on the one side Mr. O'Keeffe's statement, and on the other side Cardinal Cullen's, before you at the Board; now in looking at Judge Lawson's evidence, which he has just given, I see that the only evidence submitted to the Board was a letter from the Bishop of Ossory; was Cardinal Cullen's statement ever before the Board in any official sense?—No, it was never before the Board that I know of. Perhaps, in using the word statement, I was incorrect. What I meant to convey was, that it was generally known, a matter of notoriety, that Mr. O'Keeffe denied the fact of his suspension, and had really taken an action of libel against the man that said he was suspended.

1214. And you heard Justice Lawson's answer, that that order of Cardinal Cullen's suspending him was not acted upon, and never would have been acted upon, but that what was before the Board was the Bishop of Ossory's letter; do you concur in that?—I could not say whether it would have been acted upon or not.

1215. It was not acted upon, at any rate?—It was not acted upon until Dr. Moran wrote to the Board.

1216. Although its existence had been officially notified to the Secretaries of the Board by the inspector four months previously, and no action was taken on it?—No action until Bishop Moran wrote to us, acquainting us with the fact; but I could not, of course, say what the Board would have done if Bishop Moran had not notified the fact to us at all.

1217. Mr. *Gathorne Hardy*.] As a matter of fact, the document which had been submitted to the Secretaries was not brought before the Board until Bishop Moran had written, was it?—I think it was brought before the Board. I may be incorrect in that; it is a mere matter of memory.

1218. Was the question discussed at the Board?—No, it was not discussed at the Board, so far as I remember, until Dr. Moran's letter came.

1219. At the time that it was discussed, were you acquainted through Mr. Justice Morris with the pleadings in the case between Mr. O'Keeffe and Cardinal Cullen?—Yes; Judge Morris brought before the Board the whole circumstances which, indeed, we had a perfect knowledge of from the public notoriety of the case.

1220. *The O'Conor Don*.] I think you stated at the commencement of your evidence, that you were the Moderator of the General Assembly?—Yes.

1221. Are you such now?—No; our Moderators generally only continue for one year; we are afraid of anything like prelacy growing up, and so we keep them in their proper position.

1222. Would you, as Moderator of the General Assembly, feel it your duty to bring before the Board the suspension of any Presbyterian clergyman?—I do not think I would.

Rev. C. L. Morell.
11 June 1873.

1223. Of one who was the manager of a school, I mean?—In particular cases I might; if it were a case of gross immorality or so, I might.

1224. But if it were merely suspension for ecclesiastical reasons, we will suppose, you would not think it necessary, as I understand you?—No, I would not.

1225. If such a suspension were brought before the Board of National Education, by a certificate of the General Assembly to the Board of National Education, do you consider that the Presbyterian body would expect, or that the General Assembly would expect, that that certificate would be recognised?—No; I think they would expect that the Board would consider, on receiving that certificate, the fitness of the man to be a manager, taking all the circumstances into account what he was suspended for, what was his relation to the schools, whether the parents of the children were satisfied with his religious instruction, and so forth.

1226. You consider then that the General Assembly would be satisfied with that, and would not expect that the National Board should act upon their certificate?—Yes.

1227. Now you have referred to these precedents, and stated that they did not correspond with the case of Mr. O'Keeffe; do you recollect the case of the Rev. Mr. Wilson?—Yes, I have read his case.

1228. I understand you to say, that the reasons why you did not consider that the precedents corresponded with the case of Mr. O'Keeffe was, that in Mr. O'Keeffe's case he denied his suspension on the one hand, and on the other hand had taken legal proceedings?—That he had both denied it, and had taken legal proceedings.

1229. Those facts were not officially before the National Board, were they?—Not at the time. I think they were in the debate probably all mentioned.

1230. There was no statement coming from the Rev. Mr. O'Keeffe to the Board, announcing on the one hand that he denied the suspension, and on the other hand that he intended to take, or was taking, legal proceedings?—No; we had only the public notoriety of the case.

1231. But is not this the main difference between Father O'Keeffe's case and Mr. Wilson's, that in the case of Mr. Wilson the Board had before it a letter from Mr. Wilson, in which he distinctly denied that he was deposed, and stated his intention of shortly submitting the case "to the dispassionate consideration" of a jury of his countrymen?—Yes, he both denied it and admitted it in the same letter, as far as I remember now. He says that he was suspended by the Presbytery of Magherafelt, and he says that he was not suspended; and he says that he intends submitting it to a jury of his fellow countrymen, but he never does that thing or takes any steps to do it.

1232. But at the time the Board decided to remove him from the management of the schools, they had before them a statement in which he had denied that he had been suspended, and a statement in which he also intimated his intention of appealing to a jury?—Yes, and a statement at the same time from him, admitting that he was suspended.

1233. But is not that the case very much with regard to Mr. O'Keeffe; does not he admit that he was suspended by Cardinal Cullen?—He admits that he was suspended by Cardinal Cullen just as he might admit that I suspended him if I took the trouble of doing it.

1234. Did not Mr. Wilson do exactly the same; did he not admit that he had been suspended by the Magherafelt Presbytery, but deny their authority to do so?—He did not deny their authority I think; I may be wrong.

1235. "I may here mention, that when the Magherafelt Presbytery found that I was about to join another body they convened a meeting, and in the most preposterous manner, and contrary to all precedent and constitutional principle, did pass a sentence of deposition, just because I continued to preach the Gospel;" that is what I find in Mr. Wilson's letter?—Yes; he says that they deposed him on insufficient grounds, and were actuated by improper motives, but he does not say that they had no power to do it; he could not be a Presbyterian and deny the authority of his Presbytery.

1236. He goes on to say, "We have ceased of course to be under the care of the General Assembly, but our services are to be conducted in future under the jurisdiction, and in accordance with the forms of another church in which we repose all belief and confidence?—Yes.

1237. Does

SELECT COMMITTEE ON CALLAN SCHOOLS.   113

Rev. C. L. Morell.

11 June 1873.

1237. Does not he there dispute the authority of the General Assembly as justifying his removal from the school?—No; he there declares that he escapes from the authority of the General Assembly by joining another communion.

1238. And he therefore disputes, so far as the Board is concerned, their right to remove him from the management of the schools on the ground of suspension?—Yes, he does dispute the right.

1239. Now, do you remember the first case of these so-called precedents, the case of Dr. Keenan?—I have read it.

1240. You are aware that in that case the Board removed Dr. Keenan from the management of the school, although the parents of the children attending the school, and the Committee who had the management of the school, objected to his removal?—Yes; and I think they did very wrong in doing it.

1241. But, so far as the precedent goes, it shows that in that case the Board, which at that time was composed of Dr. Whateley and Archbishop Murray, and other men of eminence in Ireland, did decide, in spite of the protestations of the Committee of the schools, and of the parents of the children, to remove Dr. Keenan from the management of those schools?—They did.

1242. Do you not think that that case, if it differs from Father O'Keeffe's in any respect, is a stronger case than his?—No; I do not find that he appealed to the civil courts in order to prove that he was not suspended.

1243. But do you consider that that makes a greater difference between the two cases, showing that Father O'Keeffe's was the stronger case of the two, than the fact, that in this case of Dr. Keenan, the committee and the parents of the children both protested against the removal?—That is a new element in his case, that makes it strong; but it differs from O'Keeffe's case in the point that I have mentioned.

1244. Do you consider that the fact of a clergyman appealing to the legal tribunals of the country is sufficient reason why he should, under all circumstances, be continued in the management of the schools?—Until the legal tribunals decide; that is to say, decide within the bounds of their own jurisdiction; decide if the man has been suspended in accordance with the rules of the church with which by his ordination he entered into a contract.

1245. I understood you to say, in answer to Mr. Cross, that the Presbyterian body in Ireland have passed strong resolutions, condemning the conduct of the Commissioners in the case of Father O'Keeffe?—I said that the Presbytery of Belfast, one of the largest and most influential of the Presbyteries, had done so. The whole General Assembly has not passed any resolution; it is sitting at the present time, and I would not be surprised if it did, but I would not say that positively.

1246. Do you think that it would have passed a similar resolution if the clergyman who was suspended had been a clergyman suspended by the General Assembly?—It is not likely that they would have been so strong in that case.

1247. I suppose you are acquainted with Mr. Gibson?—Yes.

1248. Is not he the law adviser of the General Assembly?—He is.

1249. And was not he one of the majority?—Yes.

1250. And he is a man who, amongst the Presbyterian body, would have great weight?—Yes, very deservedly, both from character and legal knowledge.

1251. You are acquainted with Mr. Hall, who, I believe was your predecessor at the Board?—Yes.

1252. He was a man in whom the Presbyterian body had very great confidence, was he not?—Yes.

1253. And do not we find him concurring in the removal of clergymen, upon the certificate of their suspension, in these precedents?—I do not know whether he was present in any of those cases or not; if he was, it is likely to have been in the last only.

1254. In the two last cases I find him recorded as being present?—I did not know that.

1255. Do you concur with Judge Lawson, that a suspended clergyman should not be removed from the management of a school, under any circumstances, if the suspension be merely for ecclesiastical reasons?—No, I do not, altogether. I think that the whole circumstances of the case should be considered, as I have already pointed out. A man may have the management of a school, for example, that is upon his own church grounds, and that is attended almost exclusively by

0.93.   P   children

Rev. C. L. Morell,
11 June 1873.

children belonging to his own denomination, and if he is in that case suspended for heresy of any particular kind, I do not think it is desirable that he should be the manager in that school. But if the school, say, was not immediately connected with his Church, and if, as I have said already, it was attended by a large number of children of another denomination, or if the parents approved of him as a suitable person to give instruction, his heretical views would not, in that case, affect his usefulness as manager of that school. I think that every case should be decided upon its own particular merits, after due and careful examination.

1256. But you consider, do you not, that if a clergyman was appointed manager to a school in a parish in which he had the cure of souls, and if he was condemned for heresy, he ought not to be continued as the manager of that school over which he was appointed as having the cure of souls in that parish?—No; I would not go the length of saying that in every case. As I have already said, I have established a school, and was appointed manager of it myself some two or three years ago, not as a clergyman, but as a private gentleman; and if I chose to become a Roman Catholic to-morrow, I do not see why the Board should interfere with me or my school. On the other hand, if the school was upon the ground of the Presbyterian Church, and if it belonged to my predecessor before me, I think it would be exceedingly undesirable, if I separated myself from the communion of the Church, that I should be continued in that school.

1257. Do you consider that there are such schools as parochial schools?—No; I do not think that there are such schools as parochial schools. I would not like to give them that description.

1258. Are the National Schools in connection with the Presbyterian body in the North of Ireland called Presbyterian schools in the ordinary conversation of the country?—Sometimes they are; where there are three national schools, say, in a town, we are sometimes told of the Roman Catholic national schools; of course it is an improper nomenclature.

1259. Are you aware of any single instance since the formation of the National Board, in which the certificate of the ecclesiastical superior, certifying that a priest or a clergyman had been suspended, was not followed by his dismissal from the management of a school?—I never heard of any cases, except those which have been already mentioned as precedents.

1260. And it is your belief, I suppose, that there are no such cases?—I really do not know.

1261. At all events, you are not able to state a single instance in which the certificate of the ecclesiastical superior as to suspension having been formally laid before the Board of National Education, the dismissal of the teacher did not immediately follow?—I am not.

1262. And without any explanation being asked of him?—I am not able to give any case of that kind.

1263. *Chairman.*] You have founded a school yourself, as a private gentleman, quite irrespective of your position as a Presbyterian clergyman, I understand you?—Yes.

1264. Have you any other school or schools which belong to you in your capacity as a Presbyterian clergyman?—No; there were no schools in my parish connected with my congregation or my predecessor's when I came to it. I have established two schools, one for the people of the town, and one for the poor people in the country, simply as a private gentleman, and I have that jurisdiction over them.

1265. Do you know as a matter of history, that in 1839 and 1840, when the junction of the Presbyterians with the National Board took place, there were schools generally attached to the Presbyterian chapels in the North of Ireland?—Yes, there were, and there are still.

1266. And those were received into connection with the National Board, were they not?—They were.

1267. Now if you had happened to have a school or schools of that kind, would you have considered that you succeeded to them in the same way in which, when that unhappy event occurs, your natural successor will succeed to your two schools, and on the same right?—Not as of right, but as being the most desirable person to have charge of the education.

SELECT COMMITTEE ON CALLAN SCHOOLS. 115

Thursday, 12th June 1873.

MEMBERS PRESENT:

Mr. Bourke.
Mr. Secretary Cardwell.
Mr. Cross.
Mr. Gathorne Hardy.

The O'Conor Don.
Dr. Lyon Playfair.
Mr. Whitbread.

THE RIGHT HONOURABLE EDWARD CARDWELL, IN THE CHAIR.

Mr. *William Homan Newell,* LL.D., re-called; and further Examined.

1268. Mr. *Cross.*] I wanted to ask you a question about the *ex officio* appointment of parish priests at these schools; is there such a thing as an *ex officio* appointment?—I never heard that managers were recognised *ex officio.*

1269. Have you got any papers connected with the Ballinspittle School?—I have.

1270. What year was that?—1840.

1271. What is the first paper that you have got with reference to that school?—Since this inquiry commenced, I was, of course, looking up this subject, and the earliest record that I could find in the Education Office on the subject of *ex officio* management is dated the 11th June 1840; it is addressed from the secretaries (the whole case was before the Board at that time) to the Rev. P. M'Swiney, Courcies, Kinsale:—"Sir, We have laid your note of the 20th ultimo before the Commissioners of Education. They direct us to inform you that, from the satisfactory tenor of your communications, and it appearing that you had acted under a misapprehension of the rules of the Board, they will continue the payment of the teachers' salaries, leaving the school under your management as heretofore. With respect to the three rules laid down by you as essential to the working of the system, we are directed to inform you as follows: In the first rule you suggest that the acting parish priest should be, by virtue of his office, a recognised manager of the parochial school. Such a recognition, we are to inform you, would be quite at variance with the rules of the Board, and were it adopted the same privilege should, as a matter of course, be extended to all the clergy of the parish, of whatever denomination." The rest of the letter does not refer to that point; shall I continue it?

1272. Will you please read the whole letter?—"You will, however, bear in mind that the Commissioners require the national schools to be open to the inspection of the public generally, so that every person who chooses may have an opportunity of ascertaining how the school is conducted, but not to interrupt the business. With respect to the 2nd and 3rd Regulations, we have only to say that such are the rules of the Board. No correspondence is carried on with teachers, and the inspector of religion with normal school is a licensed clergyman of the persuasion of his pupils."

1273. Have

Mr. *W. H. Newell,*
LL.D.

12 June 1873.

0.93.   P 2

Mr. *W. H. Newell*,
LL.D.

12 June 1873.

1273. Have you got the letter to which that is an answer?—No; I may observe that in the same year, somewhat antecedent to that, I have discovered another paper.

1274. I was going to ask you, have you got any other paper of the year 1840, bearing upon the same subject?—I have.

1275. What paper is that?—This is a paper which contains an extract from the proceedings which were reported in the newspapers of the day. It will be found in the Report of the Powis Commission, p. 123, "At a general meeting of the Roman Catholic Prelates of Ireland, held in Dublin on the 14th of February 1840, the most Rev. Dr. Crolly in the chair, the following arrangement was proposed and adopted. That in every national school, for the mixed education of Protestant and Roman Catholic children, the Roman Catholic Bishop of the Diocese, the parish priest, or the Roman Catholic curate of the parish in which such school is situated, may be a patron of said school, in order that he may prevent the appointment of any teacher whose moral or religious conduct should be found objectionable, and if necessary direct the dismissal of such teacher from so important a situation." To which his Excellency replied, "The Board has nothing to do with the selection of patrons who are locally chosen by those persons whose funds have been subscribed, or whose land has been given for the establishment of schools." That was from the Lord Lieutenant of the day, who was Lord Ebrington, I think; but on that point, I am not sure.

1276. Do you wish to state anything to the Committee about the four precedents which have been laid before us?—No, I do not wish to say anything; I volunteer nothing.

1277. Mr. *Gathorne Hardy*.] You have no other precedent of any kind that you know of?—I have no precedent but those already put in.

1278. Do you know of any cases where there have been suspended clergymen in which they have not been removed?—There was the case of the Rev. Peter Daly, of Galway; he was suspended for some time; but there was no intimation of his suspension sent to the Commissioners, and he retained the management until the time of his death.

1279. Do you know any case except that of the Rev. Mr. Sheridan, which is one of the precedents, where the removal has taken place without a certificate from the ecclesiastical superior; in the case of Mr. Sheridan, it appears on the papers that there was no certificate at all?—No. The letter in that case was from the inspector of the district. You are speaking now of Roman Catholic clergymen, I suppose?

1280. No, I speak of all; my question was general; if you know of any cases of suspended or deposed clergymen, who have been continued as masters of schools after any notification to the Board of their suspension?—No, I do not, except that in those cases before some of those clergymen remained managers for a time after the notification to the Board. For instance, in the case of Mr. Sheridan, of Ratoath, Mr. Fulham had applied for the schools some two years before, and yet Mr. Sheridan remained on the books until the inspector notified his removal; and in the case of Mr. O'Farrell, of Annaduff, who was removed, he continued manager of another school in the parish of Lisduff, which was a vested school, until his successor was appointed by the Honourable Mr. Keppel, now Lord Albemarle; that was by some oversight of the clerk, I believe.

1281. *Chairman*.] In the case of the Ratoath Schools, when Mr. Fulham repeated the application, it was at once acted upon, was it not?—I think the next intimation came from the district inspector. I am not sure about the dates; they are very close.

1282. Mr. *Gathorne Hardy*.] Can you tell me whether the inspectors had reported upon these schools to the Board?—Yes, regularly.

1283. And in those reports, would they notify in all cases to the secretaries, at all events, or the Resident Commissioner, the fact of the suspension of a clergyman?—They might not, because there is no query in our reports to that effect.

1284. *The O'Conor Don*.] You stated that you have been investigating for sometime

sometime past all the records of the office with regard to the cases of a similar description?—Yes, as points turned up, as I saw by reports in the newspapers, I used to look over them.

Mr. *W. H. Newell*,
LL.D.

12 June 1873.

1285. And do you believe that all the reports that are extant in the office with respect to this case of the Ratoath School, have been discovered and placed before the Committee?—I am sure that the reports have not; they have not been asked for. In some of those years there were three reports upon each of the schools, and none of those have been asked for.

1286. Reports with regard to suspension, I mean?—I think all the reports with regard to suspension have been produced.

1287. Might I ask you what you understand by the term *ex officio*?—I understand by the term *ex officio*, that a man holding a certain position is entitled to (*virtute officii*) discharge collateral duties as it were.

1288. In fact, that he has a right to hold the particular position?—Yes.

The Right Hon. Mr. Justice *Morris*, called in; and Examined.

1289. Mr. *Gathorne Hardy*.] I BELIEVE you have been a Commissioner for some five years?—Yes; I have been a Commissioner of the National Board for about five years; since some time in 1868.

Rt. Hon. Mr.
Justice *Morris*.

1290. Did you serve on the Commission which inquired into the primary education of Ireland?—Yes, I sat as a member of that Commission of fourteen, presided over by Lord Powis, which was occupied with this subject for over two years.

1291. I need not ask you then, whether you became familiar with the rules and arrangements of the National Board?—Yes, I became much more familiar with them sitting on that Commission, which was to inquire into them, than I did even as a member of the National Board; so many subjects turned up upon that inquiry.

1292. Now I need hardly ask you, because it seems to be generally agreed, that you do not believe in *ex officio* managers?—No, I never heard of *ex officio* managers until this "affair O'Keeffe," as it is called.

1293. Do you understand the sixth rule in the same sense as that in which it was interpreted by Mr. Justice Lawson, whose evidence you heard yesterday?—I do understand it as interpreted by Mr. Justice Lawson, but with great respect to him, that is to understand it as it is written, or printed rather. There was never any allegation that I ever heard that any one was patron or manager *ex officio*. (Now, there is some attempted interpretation given, according to which *ex officio* does not mean *ex officio*, but means something else.) It would be incompatible with the rules which provide that the Board should have the decision as to who was the fit person. I always understood that the decision of the Board as to a manager depended upon who was the representative man of the locality best suited for educational purposes, and the person in whom the district would have confidence; that these would be the elements which ought to decide the Board in their decision. And a very short time ago, since this "affair O'Keeffe," we had a question as to who was to be the manager of the schools in Carrick-on-Shannon, and there was an unanimous expression of opinion of the Board that it should be the agent, I think, of the lord of the soil, although the parish priest, a most respectable gentleman, I have no doubt, was a candidate for the office. I therefore confess that I am unable to understand, and it is beyond my comprehension, what the point now is about a managership being *ex officio*.

1294. *The O'Conor Don.*] Was that the case of a new school?—No.

1295. And who had been the manager in the school before?—I do not know.

1296. Mr. *Gathorne Hardy*.] Were you aware of there being any rule or practice as to a suspended priest at the time that the discussion arose on the 23rd of April 1862?—No. I know there was no rule; for I repeatedly asked those who advocated the views of the majority to point me out the rule, and I would be the very first to concur in it. Of course, if there was a rule, *cadit*

0.93.   P 3   *quæstio*,

Rt. Hon. Mr.
Justice *Morris*.
———
10 June 1873.

quæstio, and if there was no rule, surely the thing should be decided as a matter of expediency. I understand that a rule asserts a principle. I knew that there was no rule, and I never heard that there was a practice, or a tradition even.

1297. Were you acquainted with the case of Father Daly?—Yes; I was Member for the town of Galway, and I knew that Rev. gentleman very well.

1298. I believe he was, in fact, suspended, and yet remained the manager of five or six schools?—No doubt he was suspended, to my personal knowledge, and I find by the records of the Board that he was the manager of six schools, and so continued to the day of his death.

1299. But that would necessarily be known, I suppose, to the inspectors and others who had to do with the schools in the district?—Just as well known as that Her Gracious Majesty was Queen. It excited a great deal of attention. He appealed to Rome; there was a great deal of discussion about it. And he was a very remarkable man, I need not say; the Premier of the day, Lord Palmerston, I believe had various interviews with him.

1300. Now, in the case of a suspension being brought to the notice of the Board, what, in your judgment, is the duty of the Board?—I consider that the suspension of a priest, *primâ facie*, would be so grave a matter as that it should at once be brought under the notice of the Board and dealt with under the circumstances of the case. In nine hundred and ninety cases out of a thousand I suppose a priest is not, and would not be, suspended for any cause such as would not be also a sufficient cause for the National Board to cease recognising him as manager; for instance, if there were allegations of misconduct, social or otherwise, I think that we should then inquire as to what were the reasons why he was suspended. These are very often given verbally, as Mr. Justice Lawson stated yesterday, by somebody who knows the facts of the case. And then *primâ facie*, I would be disposed to remove him, not upon any rule, not upon any settled *ipso facto* principle, but as a question of expediency. If, on the other hand, on full inquiry, I found, as I understood in this O'Keeffe case, that the original ground of his suspension was for having resorted to the tribunals of the country, I would consider it rather startling that a Government Board acting under a letter merely from the Viceroy, should remove a man solely on the ground that he was suspended, knowing, or having the full means of knowing, that that suspension was, because he asserted the right of every subject of the Crown to go to law in Her Majesty's High Court of Queen's Bench. I would not for that simple reason dismiss him; I would require the whole circumstances of the case to be brought before me, on notice to him.

1301. With respect to giving him notice, I presume you are now of the same opinion as you were then, that notice should have been given to the suspended priest, in order that he might, if necessary, offer any explanation?—Certainly; when I moved my amendment of the 23rd of April 1872, I really thought, and a gentleman who was sitting by me thought, that there was no use in moving it, for that everybody would agree to it. The well-known legal maxim, as well a maxim of morals, *Audi alteram partem*, I thought should apply to that case as well as to every other case. It was suggested here yesterday that *Audi alteram partem* means to give a man notice, but not to hear him; the translation of it, given in a legal and a moral sense is, "No man should be condemned unheard." And going back to the days of Seneca, which is a long time ago, he lays down, *Quicunque aliquid statuerit parte inauditâ alterâ, æquum licet statuerit, haud æquus fuerit*; and Justice Fortescue says, that both by the laws of God and man, a party is entitled to an opportunity to make his defence, if he has any. Now, it was stated that there were some precedents in which some persons had not got notice. That was dealt with in the case of Williams and Lord Bagot, in 3rd Barnwell and Creswell, in which it was declared that immemorial custom cannot avail in contravention of this principle. I think that on all these grounds, as well as the natural reason of the thing, *audi alteram partem* should be applied in such a case, and I, being strongly of that opinion, moved my amendment, which was negatived only by a majority of one. I think it right to say that the Chief Justice of my court, Chief Justice Monahan, who has voted with the majority in all subsequent matters, on that occasion expressed

expressed himself rather emphatically that really he could not vote against that amendment of mine, and so he voted with it.

Rt. Hon. Mr. Justice Morris.

18 June 1873.

1302. Now, with respect to schools not in immediate connection with the chapel or church of the suspended clergyman, should you think it right to act in a different way with respect to them, as compared with schools which are immediately connected with the chapel or church?—I would not act at all if I found out that the manager was suspended simply for a cause which I could not, as a mere citizen, take notice of. He might be contumacious in an ecclesiastical sense, and from that standpoint, possibly, be in error. I have nothing to say to that. As I argued, if his schools were eminently successful, if he was, socially, a proper and fit man, and if he obeyed the rules of the Board, and if it would be for the interests of education, I considered that our power ceased there to interfere with him.

1303. Did you yourself bring before the Board at that time the proceedings that Mr. O'Keeffe was taking against Cardinal Cullen?—I did. I should like to go back to an earlier meeting than that at which Mr O'Keeffe was dismissed. At page 17, in Paper 244, you will find the meeting of the 9th of April referred to. That was the first day that the matter came before the Board. I found on the programme this matter of Mr. O'Keeffe, and a letter from the Bishop of Ossory, Dr. Moran, and I attended that day perfectly innocent of this alleged rule and practice to dismiss a suspended clergyman at once, and without any inquiry of any sort, but merely that the certificate of the bishop was to be thrown down something like an incumbered estates court conveyance, and that it should be said, that settles everything. Mr. Justice Fitzgerald upon that occasion (there being 10 Commissioners only present, the body consisting of 20) moved "That the consideration of the Rev. W. Martin's letter be postponed to this day fortnight, and that no reply be given in the meantime." There was a letter which you will find at page 17, written on the same day that the Bishop's letter was written to Mr. Keenan, and I have no doubt, of course, that they were substantially compared together, in which the Rev. Mr. Martin rather curtly writes to the Commissioners:—"I beg to inform you that I have been appointed administrator of the Roman Catholic parish of Callan; I, therefore, request you to forward to my address the moneys payable to the manager of the various national schools of this parish." Now, at the time that he wrote that letter, the Rev. Mr. O'Keeffe had been manager for many years, and this gentleman, because he says he is appointed administrator, requests that there should be forwarded to his address the moneys payable to the manager. Now, if that is not claiming to be manager *ex officio*, I do not know what is, because, with regard to Mr. O'Keeffe, who was in office *de facto* (and *de jure*, even until he was removed on the 23rd of April), Mr. Martin requests that his existence should be ignored, and that he himself should be taken up as manager. When Mr. Justice Fitzgerald moved that the consideration of that letter should be postponed till that day fortnight, I then, for the first time, saw that it was evidently going to be postponed as if to be acted upon. I moved on that occasion my first amendment, "That a copy of that letter be sent to the Rev. Robert O'Keeffe, the present manager of the Callan National Schools." I thought it was one of the most obvious things in the world that when one man was *de facto* and *de jure* the manager, and another mildly applied that he should be dealt with as if he was manager, and another ignored, the other should be told of such an extraordinary application. On that occasion there was a division, and I was beaten by a majority of only one. There were for my motion the Lord Primate, Mr. Waldron, Mr. Justice Morris, and Mr. Jellett. Against it, there were Lord O'Hagan, Lord Monck, Mr. Murland, Mr. Justice Fitzgerald, and Mr. Keenan. Mr. Justice Fitzgerald's motion was then put, and carried by a majority of three, that the whole question should be postponed for a fortnight, in the meantime Mr. O'Keeffe getting no notice of any sort or description. If he had even got Mr. Martin's letter, he would be on the *qui vive*, to say the least of it, for that day fortnight. Now, I think as hearing upon a portion of Mr. Justice Lawson's evidence, that it does not necessarily follow, because a Commissioner's name is taken down that he was present, even when an important subject was dealt with that day, I may state that I are on that day, the 9th of April, Dr. Henry is stated to have been present. He had left, I believe. This I consider important; because, though Dr. Henry was not present at the division,

0.93.   P 4

Rt. Hon. Mr.
Justice *Morris*.
12 June 1873.

division, if there had been no division there, or if it had been carried *nem. con.* by those who were present, Dr. Henry would have been taken, at some future period, some 20 years after, by any man looking over those minutes, as having been there present, and as agreeing in the whole thing. He certainly would not have agreed with the minority, from the views which he took afterwards.

1304. Were the precedents which have been before us produced at the meeting of the 23rd of April?—The four precedents referred to in the Return moved for by Mr. Pim were, if not produced, referred to especially by the Resident Commissioner, who would be most intimate, I presume, with them. I had never heard of one of them before, and I declined, to a great extent at the time, even to concern myself much about them; because, I said, "If they are precedents that a man is not to be heard before he is dismissed, as I was not a party to them I am very glad to say I decline now even to look at them, because I will follow no such precedents as contrary to every principle, either of law or justice."

1305. Those were the only precedents at that time before you?—These were the only precedents at that time before me. I have since looked into them to consider them, and I believe that no Commissioner that has been examined has any personal recollection about them, but that they have merely given evidence on them after looking over the papers there and drawing their own deductions, which I am vain enough to think that I am as competent as some of the other Commissioners to do, I do not say as competent at all.

1306. Do you think that they are really precedents in support of this case?—On the contrary, I do not think so. I see most material distinctions between them in my opinion, and I see matters of very grave importance in my opinion on the very face of them.

1307. Will you point out what you consider the material distinctions between the case of Mr. O'Keeffe and those cases?—On the first case of Dr. Keenan's, which occurred as long ago as the year 1845, as I understood this so-called rule (for it was sometimes called a rule, although I demanded to get a look at it if it was one), so-called practice, so-called tradition, it was alleged that the certificate of the bishop or his letter, stating that a priest was suspended, settled the question. Now I find on page 4, of Paper 138, that the Right Rev. Dr. Blake on the 8th of May 1845, wrote to the Most Rev. Dr. Murray, the much lamented and highly respected Archbishop of Dublin, in these terms: "In the month of February last, I addressed a letter to the Commissioners of National Education, to apprise them of the disorderly conduct of the master of the Magheral School in this diocese, and as I did not think it necessary to render an account to them of my reasons for suspending the Rev. John Keenan, and appointing another administrator in his stead over the parish of Anaghlone, I respectfully begged to inform them that the Rev. John Macken is now the administrator to whom I have committed the case of the Catholics of that parish, and that he is the fittest person to be patron and manager of the aforesaid school," &c. "The Commissioners have not condescended to honour me with an answer, but their secretaries have written the letter herewith enclosed to the Rev. Mr. Macken, from whom I received it this morning, and I learn from it, not only that the master, whose indiscretion and turbulence are acknowledged by the Board, is to be continued over the Magheral School, but also that the refractory clergyman, to whom I cannot conscientiously confide the case of the children, is to be their patron and manager." Why I thought that the case was, that upon throwing down that letter of Dr. Blake's *cadit quæstio*. So far from that being the fact, if this letter of Dr. Blake's, which I have no doubt properly represents the story, be correct, it appears that it was not a *cadit quæstio* at all, but that his letter was ignored, and that this Rev. Mr. Macken, who would, *mutatis mutandis*, be the Rev. Mr. Martin in this case exactly, was informed that Dr. Keenan was to be continued the manager. I confess if that case was cited to me in a court of law, as being a case bearing upon the important fact that the certificate was to be conclusive upon the matter, I should be rather amazed at the counsel who brought it forward.

1308. *The O'Conor Don.*] Did you refer to the letter stated to have been written by the Bishop in February?—No.

1309. You

1309. You do not know what that letter contains?—No, I have a little memorandum on the back of it, "See this," with three notes of admiration of my own, showing that the same idea occurred to me as to you.

1310. Have you read the evidence given to this Committee?—I got it from the Committee Clerk only yesterday, and have not had time since to read it.

1311. You are not aware that that letter has been before the Committee, and that Dr. Keenan's name never appears in it?—I certainly am not aware of it. This I am aware of; I did see a letter from Dr. Keenan in the month of March stating his case, in answer to some letter I presume from the secretaries of the Commissioners; and that also, I think, disproves another allegation of this tradition, namely, that a man should not be noticed and heard; for Dr. Keenan wrote in March stating his case to the secretaries, or to the Board through the secretaries. This proves, in my mind, that he was noticed, and that he was heard, and the letter of Dr. Bluke, the bishop, appears to me to establish that he was successfully heard, and that Mr. Macken was informed that Dr. Keenan was to remain in the management, although suspended; and that Dr. Keenan's own letter was before the Board in March. If it were necessary to deal with the case as a precedent, I would have brought it forward as a precedent, to show that there was no such a rule as alleged.

1312. Mr. *Gathorne Hardy*.] So far as that precedent on the paper is concerned, it was all brought before you at the time of the meeting in April 1872, was it not?—It was not brought in its detail before us at all; it was mentioned, and I daresay there were papers on the table. I said, in an astonished sort of way, "Is this unheard of proceeding to take place? It was said there were precedents; I have neither time nor inclination to look into them," I said. "If there are 400 precedents, I would not look into them, if they were to establish the principle that a man is not to be heard."

1313. Then your objection was to the principle of condemning a man without hearing him at all?—Yes. I have referred to high authorities already, and there is a very remarkable case in 7th Moore's Privy Council Cases which bears upon this case.

1314. The fact is, that we want rather your opinion upon the question?—My opinion is a very humble opinion, compared with that of Lord Lyndhurst, Lord Brougham, Lord Kingsdown, and Mr. Gladstone, who in that case of "Willis v. Gipps," decided that a judge who was removed was properly removed if he got notice; but that, not having got notice of his removal, he should be restored.

1315. Have you any other remarks to make on any other case besides Dr. Keenan's?—As regards Dr. Keenan's, I should say further, that there is another point. The Board of that day, a very small Board, consisting of only four persons, it appears, did appoint Mr. Macken. The committee protested against that, as you will find, by a long correspondence. It does not appear upon this paper, but I have inquired at the office since this investigation began, and I went over there a day or two to post myself up in the facts, and I find that the committee were successful in their opposition to this most illegal appointment, in my opinion, of Mr. Macken, because a Mr. M'Gort, a layman, I believe, was appointed manager in January 1848; on the appointment, or on the nomination rather, of the committee, he was ultimately appointed, they contending all through against Mr. Macken; and the Commissioners appear to have given up the contest, and thereby, I think, in the most practical manner, admitted that they were egregiously wrong in appointing Macken, because they withdrew his appointment and appointed Mr. M'Gort, a layman; so they had a victory.

1316. Do you think that the appointment of a new manager, while there is a manager *de facto* in possession, tends to the peace and harmony of the place in which it is done or to the advancement of education?—I think if you appoint two men to the same place in any position in life, the inference is obvious; it depends upon the pugnacity of the parties altogether.

1317. Will you proceed to the other precedents?—The next precedent has been trotted out as a Presbyterian precedent; that of the Rev. Mr. Wilson. The first paper I see upon that is, "Read letter from the Rev. G. Kirke Wilson, complaining of having been superseded in the managership of the Glenvale

Rt. Hon. Mr.
Justice *Morris*.
12 June 1873.

National School." Now, I do not find how he was superseded. I find no minute at all of his being superseded; but only that there is an order that he "be informed that the Commissioners, having learnt that he has been deposed from the ministry, are under the painful necessity of declining to recognise him as manager of either the Glenvale or any other national school." Now, the first question I ask is, when was he really superseded? for he complains, by letter of an earlier date than that order, of having been superseded; and, in the next place, who informed the Commissioners that he was deposed? I have looked into the papers, and I find, by a letter of Mr. Doherty, who was the parish priest, that, previous to this, he informed the Board that this gentleman, this Mr. Wilson, was disordered in his mind; I do not know whether that was from temporary causes or not; that, at all events, was before the Board, I presume, or within their knowledge. Another inference to be drawn from this case is, that it was not Mr. Wilson's successor in the ministry at all that was appointed as I understand, but it was the parish priest. I am informed of that, and believe it to be the fact *non obstante* Dr. Henry.

1318. *Chairman.* Do you wish to give evidence that the person appointed in succession to Mr. Wilson was the parish priest of Glenvale?—No; I only wish to give evidence that I am under the impression that it was so. Mr. Newell now informs me that I have confounded one case with another. The case in which the parish priest succeeded was that of another Presbyterian clergyman, at the very same period, that of a Mr. Macpherson.

1319. Mr. *Gathorne Hardy* (to Mr. Justice *Morris*).] I observe in that case of Mr. Wilson's that a removal is not only a removal from the schools of which he was manager, but a prohibition from becoming manager of any other national schools?—"That they are under the painful necessity of declining to recognise him as manager of either the Glenvale or any other national school."

1320. Do you think that a suspension in itself, however much it might affect the question of chapel schools, should affect those schools which a man holds as manager quite irrespective of his position as a priest?—If I had learned on that day at the Board that Mr. Wilson was disordered in his mind, either from temporary causes or otherwise, I would at once have voted for it. I should have entered into the real facts of the case, and, as a question of expediency, and looked to the interests of the locality and the whole circumstances. I would not keep as manager a man who was suspended for unpleasant causes

1321. As to Mr. O'Farrell's case, have you anything to say?—That he was for 10 years (the bishop says for several years), suspended, and that he was manager all the time of certain schools. He was removed on the 22nd of August 1862, from being manager of a particular school, called Annaduff; but he remained manager of another school called Lisduff, for two years and nine months, when it was well known by all the correspondence that he was suspended, and must have been known; because he was removed from one of the schools, and I believe it was notorious at the time that the grounds of his suspension were not pleasant.

1322. Have you anything to say with respect to Mr. Sheridan's case?—As regards Mr. Sheridan's case, in 1865, which I believe is the latest, at that time you would have thought the practice and the tradition were settled; but I find a very intelligent inspector writing to submit the point to the Commissioners, whether or not a suspended clergyman should continue as manager of the schools.

1323. That was at the date of 1864?—The 15th of November 1864. At page 20, it will be seen that the inspector submits, as a nice point for the Commissioners, "whether or not a suspended clergyman should continue as manager of the schools." And it appears (this has been already referred to, for I was present yesterday, when Mr. Justice Lawson was examined) that by the letter of the 4th of November 1864, that gentleman, Mr. Sheridan, admitted his suspension, and was in hopes of a speedy restoration, as an act of grace; showing that he was in error, I presume. Well, the Board, by their order of the 27th of January 1865, after refusing to recognise Mr. Sheridan any more, declared to Mr. Fulham, the newly appointed administrator, "that as the schools are nonvested, and under the directions of committees, it is necessary that he should be nominated by them, before the Commissioners can recognise him as manager."

Well,

SELECT COMMITTEE ON CALLAN SCHOOLS.   123

Well, I have inquired at the office whether there was ever any nomination of Mr. Fulham by the committees, and (I am only, of course, giving my impression, because these are not matters on which I can give positive evidence), I am under the impression that there was none.

Rt. Hon. Mr. Justice *Morris*.

12 June 1873.

1324. You are not, perhaps, aware that we have got the facts of that case before us already?—No; what I understand was, that Mr. Macdonnell, then the Resident Commissioner, made an order himself to recognise Mr. Fulham in the month of June, 1865. Now, if that he so (of course, I can only say if), it certainly would be most irregular in every way that one Commissioner, even the Resident Commissioner, should appoint a manager, and that after an order of the Board made the previous January, that it should be done by the Committees. Therefore, now having considered the precedents really for the first time, I am under the impression myself, probably taking no sanguine view of it, that I could clearly establish that they were no precedents. Then, what precedent were they for the O'Keeffe case? It appears that Mr. O'Keeffe had in the February before he was removed (he was removed on the 23rd of April 1872), commenced an action in the High Court of Queen's Bench to test this very question, that action had been pleaded to by his Eminence, Cardinal Cullen, thereby, I presume, recognising that the Court was competent to deal with it, for otherwise he would have either demurred to it or allowed judgment to go by default, and not submitted himself to a lay tribunal; but wisely advised, I presume, by the eminent counsel who, I find, represented him upon the occasion, namely, beginning with the present Attorney General, he did plead to it on the 11th of April, as you observe, some days before the matter came before the Board, which was on the 23rd of April. At the previous meeting on the 9th of April, at which I moved that Mr. O'Keeffe should get notice of Mr. Martin's letter, I mentioned that, as I saw in the newspapers as matter of public notoriety this action was pending. Knowing that it is always better to be fortified with a document than to have merely general talk, on the 23rd of April I came with those very identical pleadings in my pocket, which I wrote for to one of the counsel, who, I saw from the newspaper, was concerned in the case, without telling him the purpose for which I wanted it. I produced those pleadings on that 23rd of April 1872, and I said, "Is there any precedent for acting in this manner with a case pending in a court of justice, the highest court of common law in the country? I may be called upon hereafter, although I am not a judge of the Court of Queen's Bench" (but there was a judge of the Court of Queen's Bench present) "on appeal before me to decide this very identical question." I should state in fairness that it was argued that the question was not decided by our dismissing him, because the certificate of the bishop was just to be taken for granted, and there was to be no inquiry on it. I said, "That is a very nice way of putting it; but what will the world at large say? That you have dismissed this man as a suspended priest, and that you are deciding it. At that time I thought that the case of O'Keeffe and Cullen might be tried in the following month of June. As a matter of fact, it was not tried until this very year; but that arose from the great press of business occurring in the Court of Queen's Bench, from cases attendant on the Galway judgment.

1325. Is there any other point to which you wish to call the attention of the Committee in reference to your proceedings in this matter?—I should say that upon that occasion also I got what was previously sent by post to, I believe, every Member of Parliament, and Judge, and Privy Councillor found in the almanac. I was sent a pamphlet, entitled, "Cardinal Cullen and the P. P. of Callan;" and I looked at that, as this thing was pending at the National Board, and I found in it that Mr. O'Keeffe, by a letter of January the 18th, 1871, nearly a year and a half before the time that we were in action, in April 1872 himself informed the Board of his then fifth suspension.

1326. We had those letters before us yesterday; perhaps you are not aware of that?—I am not. I called attention to the fact that these appeared to me to be rather queer suspensions, because if one was a good one you would think that the others were unnecessary, and that altogether, taking all the circumstances of the case, we ought to hold our hand; particularly as I thought the case would be then tried at the Trinity after sittings, and then that we would be more free to deal with it, and know more about it. As I say, Chief Justice Monahan, who thought afterwards that Mr. O'Keeffe ought to be removed, thought that we ought to do so. Mr. Waldron, a brother Commissioner, had an amendment upon that occa-

0.93.   Q 2   sion:

Rt. Hon. Mr.
Justice *Morris.*

12 June 1873.

sion: " That inasmuch as the Rev. Mr. O'Keeffe has in no way infringed the rules of the Commissioners, he cannot be arbitrarily removed from the managership of the Callan National Schools " I had intended to support that amendment, and so had Mr. Waldron, of course, who was to move it; but when we were beaten on what we thought the strongest point, the notice to him, that amendment was not put, and the division was then taken upon the general resolution.

1327. *The O'Conor Don.*] Does that amendment of Mr. Waldron's appear on the minutes?—No, because it was not put; but I distinctly recollect it, and I have a letter from Mr. Waldron, stating it; but it does not appear on the minutes, nor was it put; because when the man was not to be heard, what was the use of going deeper into it?

1328. Mr. *Gathorne Hardy.*] The action of the Poor Law Board has been referred to; do you make any distinction between your action and that of the Poor Law Board?—The distinction between the cases of a Board of Bequests and the Poor Law Board, and the case of our Board, are so obvious that, as I said on that occasion to the Board, I was rather amused at their being cited. The Poor Law Commissioners employ a clergyman, *quâ* clergyman, for sacramental and clerical purposes; and, of course, if there is any question about his being able canonically or ecclesiastically to administer certain functions, the Poor Law Board may think that he ought to be like Cæsar's wife, and above even suspicion. As for a Board of Bequests, in the case of any bequest to a parish priest, they would be very particular, I presume, in finding out who the parish priest was. But surely the whole superstructure fell when our manager was not appointed *quâ* parish priest at all. If he was appointed *ex officio* as parish priest I could understand the application of the Poor Law Board case, and the Board of Bequests. If he was not appointed *ex officio*, as he indisputably was not, because I understand that point has now been abandoned, although it was then the substratum on which the whole thing was built up, how does the fact of his ceasing to be parish priest make it a similar case to that of a Board who employ him solely as parish priest. We did not employ him as parish priest at all. In fact, if he had administered mass, or performed services at certain hours, he would have been dismissed for violating the rules of the Board. Therefore I could not see the application of those cases.

1329. Dr. *Lyon Playfair.*] In some evidence given to us by Mr. Keenan with regard to what is called the Ballyna case, he states in his answer to Question 66 about Mr. Madden succeeding Mr. Malone: " The first time that the name of the successor appeared before them was when the application was made for the books; it was clearly a disrespectful thing for a new clergyman who had assumed the management to begin his communications with the Board by assuming that he had been actually appointed, and the Board felt that they could not tolerate such a proceeding, and sent him back the money, and told him that they could not recognise him" Now, you state that Mr. Martin's letter was a very curt letter; do you find anything in that letter which requests the Board to appoint him, or was there the same sort of assumption which existed in the case of Mr. Madden?—It appears to me to be an assumption, that because he was appointed administrator, *ergo* he necessarily became manager, and that I thought was to be the great contention that he, *ex officio*, became manager. It had been before the subject of discussion, and I believe that a circular of July 1857 has been read here, which was sent to the district inspectors, as far as I remember it, substantially to caution or notice parish priests, that they were not to take this for granted at all; and I find that so long ago as the year 1840, on the 11th of June in that year, in the Ballinspittle case, which has been referred to, that clergyman seemed to be under the same impression, and that he received the answer which has been read this morning.

1330. In the Minute of the Board on the 23rd of April 1872, stated at page 18 of Captain Archdall's Return, the following passage occurs: " Read letter from the Rev. W. Martin, administrator of the parish of Callan, asking the Commissioners to recognise him as manager of the National Schools in the parish, now under the management of the Rev. R. O'Keeffe, P.P." Is there anything in Mr. Martin's letter that justifies such a description, that it asked " the Commissioners to recognise him as manager of the National Schools in the parish

now

SELECT COMMITTEE ON CALLAN SCHOOLS.

now under the management of the Rev. R. O'Keeffe, P.P.?"—I think there is, but by implication.

Rt. Hon. Mr. Justice *Morris.*

12 June 1873.

1331. Or is there by assumption?—There is by assumption, indisputably.

1332. But is there any direct request that he should be recognised as manager, or is it not assumed that he succeeds as manager?—It is assumed that he succeeds as manager, and therefore, by implication, that he is to be recognised as such.

1333. But in this case, was there any resentment of the assumption as in the case which I read to you just now?—No; they appointed the Rev. Mr. Martin on that very day, and by the motion moved by Mr. Justice Fitzgerald, "that the certificate of the Roman Catholic Coadjutor Bishop of Ossory he received and acted upon;" he was appointed, by letter from the secretaries, manager of the schools which were not under a committee, and he was informed that there should be a nomination from the committee to those which were.

1334. Do you think that by the term of your rules, "appointment" and "recognition" may be taken as convertible terms; have you, as a Board, any right to appoint the manager to a school not vested in the Board?—Distinctly, in my opinion, not; and I argued that point (I am afraid I said it too often) that we assumed a most ridiculous position to appoint a man manager over three non-vested schools, over which we had no right of property, which we had no more connexion when they ceased to be brought under our system by whoever was the owner of the structure than with a house in the City of London.

1335. Then you do not agree that, when the secretaries used the term "appoint" in their letter that means recognised?—Probably they meant the same thing; but I thought it equally impossible to do either when we were aware that the Rev. Mr. O'Keeffe was in possession of the schools. I do not know who has the legal title, if anybody has, and, of course, if nobody else can show a better title, then the man in possession must have it; therefore I did not know how we were to appoint or recognise Mr. Martin as manager over schools which he could not even enter; and if you look at the resolution which I subsequently moved in the month of January in the present year, I brought the thing to a crisis then, because I moved a resolution then substantially to this effect: that as Mr. Martin was unable to perform the duties of manager, to which the majority of the Board had assumed to appoint him, such pretended management should at once cease. The majority then were obliged, after an interval of eight months, to follow out the logical results of that which they had done in the month of April, namely, to cut the Gordian knot and strike the schools off altogether, which I thought was a very disastrous conclusion; but the inevitable result of purporting to either appoint or recognise a manager over schools in which it was notorious that he had no more right of entry than I had.

1336. Are you aware that in 1841 the Propaganda addressed a letter on the subject of national education in Ireland to the Roman Catholic prelates, in which they recommended them not to vest schools in the National Board, but to make the legal owners the parish priests?—I recollect it, and I think it is in the Report of the Commission upon which I sat.

1337. If that recommendation of the Propaganda has been generally acted upon, may not that explain the fact that so many of the patrons of non-vested schools are clergymen?—I think what explains the fact of so many patrons or managers of national schools, particularly in my Church, the Roman Catholic Church, being clergymen, is that we recognise, at all events, more than any other denomination of Christians, the right of the clergy and episcopacy to interfere in education; and accordingly, as the clergyman is desirous to be, and for a variety of reasons nearly always is, a manager, no person will be foolish enough to get into competition with him as regards an appointment which gives no emolument, but involves much labour. I think that clergymen of all denominations are, in the abstract, the most suitable persons to have these appointments, and for my own part, *cæteris paribus*, I would desire that they should get the preference. Those, I think, are the reasons which have led to so many Roman Catholic clergymen being the managers; that they always wish it, and that other people do not wish it, or if they do, will not get into a contest which must be very troublesome, for the position.

1338. If the parish priest is presented to you as the legal owner of a non-vested school, if you take it into connection, you view him as you would any

0.93.   Q 3   other

Rt. Hon. Mr.
Justice *Morris*.

12 June 1873.

other patron, lay or clerical?—Yes; whoever brings a school to the National Board, and says, "Here I am, a respectable man with a school, which the inspector will say has all the requisites, sanitary and otherwise, to be a national school; I am ready to obey your rules, and I have a proper attendance." In my opinion we always take any school from all quarters into connection that obeys those rules, and that is the very point which I draw attention to. "Why should we get into this conflict between Father O'Keeffe and his bishop," I said. I always said, "Do not drag me into the contest at all; I do not want to side with either party, and I object to being drawn into the fight."

1339. Is there anything in your rules that would displace a patron of a non-vested school, if it did not become vacant by death or by resignation?—I believe not. The rule is No. 7 in the case of a vacancy which has been already referred to, and I have relied most strongly upon that rule in all this discussion in the O'Keeffe affair, on the ground that *expressum facit cessare tacitum*; that we had expressly there what was to be done, and by implication that the other was not to be done; and I said, "Having these rules at various times before you" (and the last revision was comparatively late, I believe in 1869), "why did you not add on to the rule, 'and in all cases in which a priest shall be suspended, the certificate of the bishop shall be taken, and he shall be removed,' just because you know that that rule would never be allowed, and you would find it very difficult to get from Parliament a grant of 400,000 *l.* with such a rule; and now you want to carry out by a practice what you cannot do by a rule."

1340. *The O'Conor Don.*] I understand that you do not undertake to state in answer to a question asked you by Dr. Lyon Playfair with respect to this order from the Propaganda of your own knowledge, that the greater number of the schools are the legal property of the parish priests?—No, I believe the great majority are not, and that is the reason why I rather excepted to his idea of what led to so many managers being parish priests, and gave my own reason. The property has very often been obtained by the subscriptions of the parishioners, and by the landlord giving his own land (I have a school in my own property); and so on, and if the priest comes forward as manager, if you do not pull with the clergyman he would have the power of preventing your having a school at all; and I do not think that anyone ought to compete with the priest or any clergyman, except for good reasons.

1341. With regard to these precedents to which you have alluded, I understand that you have given the Committee your impressions upon the reading of these precedents; but you have not read all the documents in connection with them so as to give any evidence beyond what is before the Committee?—I read some of the documents connected with them, and I have the precedents in the Parliamentary Papers. Mr. Keenan became a Commissioner only a year and a half ago, and he gave his account, and his idea from reading them there. I thought therefore from five years' experience on the Board, and two on the Primary Education Commission, I might take the liberty of giving my idea.

1342. But you have not read the other documents, besides those which are in the printed Return?—I read as many as I could. My impression is, that when I went to the office last week, and asked to see that letter which you referred to, I was told that it was over in London. I believe I have read all the material documents.

1343. With regard to this case of Mr. Sheridan's, I only want to ask you one question. You have pointed out that in the letter of the inspector, he uses the words, "I submit the point to the Commissioners whether or not a suspended clergyman should continue as manager of the school?"—I did, I referred to that as being in the last case, when I was told that there was an invariable rule, as Dr. Longfield says in his letter.

1344. But are you not aware that in that case of Mr. Sheridan's, the committee who had the appointment of the manager to the schools, having been applied to, the majority of that committee declined to appoint the Rev. Mr. Fulham, the administrator, as the manager?—Yes, and I noticed that point of how he became to be appointed manager afterwards; but I do not see the connection between the removal of Mr. Sheridan and the alleged rule. If it was admitted that he was suspended, then whoever became the manager, he ought to have ceased, at all events on his suspension, according to the alleged rule.

1345. But

SELECT COMMITTEE ON CALLAN SCHOOLS. 127

1345. But you are not aware that the secretaries, without having brought the matter before the Board, had written to this inspector to ask him to get information which might be submitted to the Board as to the opinions of the Committee upon the continuance of Mr. Sheridan in the management of the schools, and upon the appointment of Mr. Fulham to the office of manager?—I read such a document.

Right Hon. Mr. Justice Morris.

12 June 1873.

1346. If such a document existed, would not that account for the inspector in reply, submitting the point whether, no matter what was the opinion of the Committee, this suspended clergyman should be continued as manager?—No; I think it most remarkable that he puts that as a sort of abstract question, and as being a new case, in order to get orders. I think that is how anyone would interpret it, but you have, of course, the same elements that I have to enable you to interpret it.

1347. Mr. *Whitbread*.] With regard to an answer that you gave to one of Mr. Hardy's questions, that you thought that a man ought to be allowed to make a defence if he had one to make; I want to know how far you carry that principle in this particular case; did you wish Mr. O'Keeffe to go into the whole matters between him and his ecclesiastical superiors?—I wished nothing at all personally; but I consider that I could not tell how far I would go until I heard from him, or from the party accused, what his case was. After a man is convicted by a jury, before he is sentenced to be hanged, he even is asked, has he anything to say why judgment should not be passed upon him, although he never has anything practically to say.

1348. That is the sort of position that you thought Mr. O'Keeffe would have been put in, is it?—No, quite the reverse; what I consider (perhaps I put too strong a case) is, that at all events a man only accused of being suspended, ought to get an opportunity of making whatever defence would occur to him in his better judgment; I was not his adviser; I never saw the gentleman; I only knew of him as a public character.

1349. Would not that involve the necessity of hearing the other side too?—Most indisputably; and if there are two sides in a quarrel, I do not know how you can dispose of it without hearing them both. I would have made the same objection to not hearing the bishop, but how could I tell what would happen if the man got notice.

1350. You would have been prepared to hear both sides fully out, would you?—I do not know that I would. If I heard Mr. O'Keeffe's case, and found it was a blind one, and that he said nothing that would occur to reasonable people as showing any ground why he should not be dismissed, I would not call on the other side. The whole thing is a question of "if," and under "if" you can arrive at any conclusion.

1351. And do you think that that would be a proper course for a mixed board, like the Board of National Education, to pursue?—I do not see what its being a mixed board has to do with it. I am of the same religious denomination as the parties litigant; but if Mr. Wilson's case had been before me, I do not think it would have made any difference. I would never get into a wild inquiry into canon law, which I do not understand. But if I found that this gentleman was only suspended for resorting to a civil right, I would say, "Are we, a tribunal here under the Executive Government, to dismiss a man for resorting to his civil right?" If it turned out that Mr. O'Keeffe was an improper person, that would be another thing.

1352. You think that, having once given him an opportunity of making his defence, you could stop him when you pleased?—Yes, that is the right of every tribunal subject to public opinion, and to natural justice, and to right.

1353. To go another part of the subject, I gathered from you, I think correctly, that you thought that the suspension of a priest was so grave a matter that, on the whole, it would give you a leaning against him; but that you thought that in all these cases the whole circumstances of the case should be considered, and that if the man was as a manager eminently successful, and if his schools were conducted according to the rules of the Board, you ought not upon mere suspension to remove him. Now, what I want to ask you is, whether, considering all the circumstances of this case, and the official reports that were before you, you considered that the schools were so eminently successful, and carried on so much in accordance with the rules of the Board, as to convert your

0.93. Q 4 leaning

Right Hon. Mr. Justice Morris.

12 June 1873.

leaning against him on account of suspension into a leaning in his favour?—You have exactly missed the point. I was always most anxious that Mr. O'Keeffe should be tried on his general merits, and I repeatedly said, "Let the case be tried on all its merits; on his trial, if he has misbehaved himself, and if there is a want of success of his schools, if they are unsuccessful, and I will be the first to join you, if it becomes necessary, in removing him." But they took high ground, and say, "We will not enter into those questions at all, but will act upon the mere certificate of suspension." And the strength of the case against Mr. O'Keeffe on these subjects which you have mentioned, the worse the principle that was asserted in this case, in my opinion, was, for it was ruled not that he should be removed upon general merits, but upon the mere certificate of suspension, *ipso facto*. Therefore all the elements which you have mentioned, in my opinion, ought to have been considered, if they existed.

1354. But were they considered?—Distinctly not.

1355. Then these circumstances were not taken into consideration?—Distinctly not. The case was, in the views of the majority, that this suspension by Dr. Moran, being certified to us *cadit quæstio*, "Mr. O'Keeffe walks out."

1356. And there was no attempt to enlarge that view on the part of the minority?—Certainly there was; we were anxious that it should be discussed on the other ground, and if you refer to Mr. Justice Lawson's letter, you will find that he said that he was always most anxious that Mr. O'Keeffe's case should be treated on the general merits.

1357. Was any motion ever made to that effect?—No; what was the use of any motion when the man was not to be heard? We could not enter on demerits of a general character without hearing him.

1358. But there was no refusal to hear him upon these general questions of management, was there?—But they were not the subject before the Board. The majority of the Board said, "We want to dismiss Mr. O'Keeffe, because the bishop says that he is suspended." I said "No" to that. "I must go into a general inquiry into the cases." The majority say, "No, that is enough for us that he is suspended."

1359. I think I understand that, according to your view of it, the majority limited the action to this question of one suspension; but that there was no motion made on the part of the minority ever to extend that, so as to embrace considerations of school management?—No, because it would be a wholly irrelevant inquiry. One matter was being inquired into, and you should dispose of that. If we succeeded in our contention that he was not to be dismissed merely on the ground of his suspension, then, I should say, would be the proper time for bringing forward the question, will he be dismissed on general merits; and when, after this case received considerable public attention, there was a motion upon Mr. O'Keeffe's renewed application to be reinstated, I really thought that it might be dealt with upon that ground, and I might have some difficulty as to what conclusion I should come to. I would have had to investigate the case; but the majority, I must say most consistently, took their stand again upon the certificate, I mean in this present year, and not upon events which had occurred, which might have, or would have raised, a case against Mr. O'Keeffe upon grounds independent of the suspension.

1360. I am not misconstruing you in saying, that in voting upon the question whether suspension should be sufficient to cause the removal of Mr. O'Keeffe you did not bear in mind any charges of mismanagement, or of breaking the rules of the Board which had been officially made against him?—On the contrary, I always argued the case on the principle as if the schools were eminently successful, as if he were one of the most excellent men in the world, apart from his having been suspended, and I was met with this: "With all that, even if he turned out to be an Admirable Crichton, he must be dismissed, because the bishop has certified that he is suspended."

1361. Mr. *Cross.*] Will you listen, if you please, to one question that I put to the Resident Commissioner, and his answer, and say whether you think that expresses the view of the majority. The question I put to the Resident Commissioner was this: "You view it in this way, that when you have the certificate of the ecclesiastical superior, the function of the National Board becomes purely ministerial": and he answers, "Purely ministerial?"—And that answer answers all the questions that were put by the Honourable Member for Bedford.

1362. *Chairman.*]

1362. *Chairman.*] The answer that you have just given to Mr. Cross shows your view of what was the contention of the majority from which you expressed your difference; is that so?—Quite so.

1363. You do not consider that the case which has been decided by a majority of the Board is the question of whether Mr. O'Keeffe shall be manager of the schools, but the question whether he shall be displaced on the simple certificate of the bishop that he has been suspended from his cure?—Quite so.

1364. I understand you to say that you would not in any case wish the Board to become interpreters of the canon law; is that so?—Quite so.

1365. Nor to decide in any case, either of a Roman Catholic, or a Presbyterian, or any other clergyman, whether he has been, or has not been, properly suspended from his clerical functions?—That would be the tendency of my opinion.

1366. But you hold that a man may have been properly suspended from his clerical functions and yet be a proper person to continue a manager of a school under the National Board?—Properly suspended, from an ecclesiastical point of view.

1367. I say, properly suspended from his clerical functions; you hold that he may be that, and yet not necessarily an improper person to continue the manager of your schools?—Yes.

1368. You would, therefore, in any such case, proceed to examine whether the suspension had or had not that effect in an educational point of view?—Yes.

1369. And that you consider has not yet been done in the O'Keeffe case?—I consider that it has appeared that it was very disastrous in an educational point of view, because the inspector reported a very large attendance at the schools that were struck off our roll.

1370. I understood you to say a little while ago that *primâ facie* you consider the suspension of a clergyman a grave matter, and one which requires inquiry by the Board?—I do distinctly; as in 999 cases out of 1,000, probably the suspension would be for causes which any tribunal sitting such as we are, looking at it from an educational point of view, would consider to incapacitate a man to some extent for the position which he held; but that there might be a thousandth case in which it might appear that he was suspended for a variety of reasons which I do not want to go into examples of, because they would be so numerous, with which we should have no concern.

1371. I understood you just now to say to the honourable Member for Bedford, that you did not propose an examination on educational grounds into the O'Keeffe case, because it had been already decided that Mr. O'Keeffe was to receive no notice?—Quite so.

1372. But if Mr. O'Keeffe had been permitted to receive notice, then you would have been prepared to go into an examination of his case upon educational grounds?—Upon educational and social grounds.

1373. And to decide upon those grounds, and not upon any grounds of the canon law, whether he ought or ought not to be continued manager of the national schools in Callan?—Quite so. As we did not employ him *qua* priest, I considered that a mere suspension of him *per se* was not sufficient to settle the question. If we employed him for priestly purposes, it would raise a different question.

1374. Then with regard to the precedents, I have understood you to say that however many the precedents had been, you would have considered them comparatively irrelevant, inasmuch as no amount of precedent would have guided you in a case which you thought in itself plain and simple?—That would have been my view. I have already referred to the fact that immemorial usage has been held not to be sufficient to avail, in contravention of the principle that a man should have an opportunity of making a defence if he has any, and properly so held, upon the grounds of natural justice, and not of mere strict law, because that decision in the Queen's Bench here, was founded upon this, that it was contrary to natural justice that a man should not be heard.

1375. Do you understand that the main difference between the majority and the minority, including yourself, is that they have acted upon what they contend has been the uniform practice of the Board, namely, that a suspended clergyman shall cease to be manager, and that you decline to recognise that fact?

Right Hon. Mr. Justice *Morris.*

12 June 1873.

Right Hon. Mr. Justice *Morris*.

12 June 1873.

—That is not the whole difference between us. I think it is part of it; only a part.

1376. What is the rest of it?—The rest of it is, that I did not think that the precedents were applicable; I considered that they were not precedents, in fact.

1377. I understood you to say that the precedents were not applicable, and to draw various distinctions; but also to say that if they had been ever so applicable and ever so numerous, they would not have availed to guide your judgment?—They would not have availed to guide me individually; but I think it is unnecessary to inquire into that if you do not find this invariable practice. I deny that there was an invariable practice; and I assert, in the next place, that I would not follow it as being in my judgment contrary to reason. Eminent and able men have taken a different view; but I cannot help that.

1378. That being your opinion and the opinion of the minority, the majority have held the opposite opinion, have they not?—I presume so from their actions. I do not attribute motives, and never have any desire to investigate intentions.

1379. That is a point on which your opinions and theirs were entirely at variance?—Entirely antagonistic; in a word, I considered the determination of the case should be dealt with as one of expediency, and they asserted it to be a principle to dismiss on suspension.

1380. Or, to put it in another form, you would consider that the continuance of the manager was to be determined upon educational grounds?—Not alone upon educational grounds; cases might occur in which he might be very advantageously retained on educational grounds; and still I would not wish to keep him on. That is one of the reasons why I should like to hear the facts of the case. I do not lay down here now a case which would make me act against a man; but I controvert the proposition that I am not to hear anything at all about it; there is where I may take my stand, that I am not merely (to use the language of Mr. Justice Lawson) to register an edict, like the old French Parliaments of Louis the Fifteenth, who were sent to the Bastile if they refused; we are not sent to the Bastile.

1381. You claim for the National Board a decision on the circumstances in each case, all the merits of it having been before you?—Distinctly; otherwise why do we assert by our rules that we are to say for ourselves who is to be considered a fit person? I cannot help expressing myself decidedly, because it has always struck me as being so plain.

1382. And in no case would you consider a construction of the canon law or a decision as to the propriety of a clerical suspension, *qua* clerical, to be any part of the duty of the Board?—I do not wish to give any definite opinion upon that; but at all events that did not arise in this case; sufficient unto the day is the evil thereof.

1383. Mr. *G. Hardy*.] In addition to the grounds put before you by the Chairman, in this case did the fact that there was an action in the Civil Courts testing the very question of suspension influence your mind?—Most distinctly; when I thought that it would be decided in a couple of months at the outside, and we had notice in the month of November previous that this gentleman was suspended, I did not see that any great harm could come from waiting for another couple of months.

1384. *Chairman.*] Your view has been that in whatever respects the other precedents may have borne upon this case, one of the main distinctions was that there was a suit pending in this case which had not been the case in any other instance?—Yes, I think that that is a most important difference; it will not do to say that there have been other suspended priests dismissed. If it is a question of expediency, surely the man must be heard. If it is a case in which you are to hear nothing, that is a different stand-point.

1385. Mr. *Bourke*.] I believe Mr. O'Keeffe, at the beginning of this year, made a renewed application to become manager of his own private school?—He made a renewed application to become manager of certain of the schools, I forget which, and I do not understand why that application was not entertained and decided on its merits. As I said, suppose Mr. O'Keeffe, of course from mere conscientious conviction, was wrong enough, in my opinion, to become a Protestant, is there any rule that a man cannot become a Protestant and be the manager of a school; and would not that, I said, be doing much worse than being suspended.

1386. After

1386. After that renewed application, was an inspector sent down?—Yes; I stated that at the Board; I put that as a test. If the gentleman was ill-advised enough to become a Protestant, was not he entitled to continue to be in possession of the five schools, and I do not know what the answer was; I never could find it out, except tradition, which I take when it is on a proper subject-matter, but I do not believe in it in the National Board.

1387. In consequence of that renewed application of Mr. O'Keeffe made at the beginning of this year, was there an inspector sent down?—Distinctly; I thought according to the principles of the majority if a suspended priest made an application, he ought to have been told that he was a very audacious sort of man, but instead of that an inspector was sent down, and the inspector made a report, which report, for the purposes of argument, was accepted, and be said in a note, "If this was an ordinary case, it would pass in the office." It was brought before the Board, and this gentleman was turned out because he was a suspended priest. I said, "Does that mean that he is a pariah?" I understood that he lost his privilege of being a priest; but there are all the intermediate castes, from a Brahmin to a pariah, and I said he ought to be allowed in upon some of them.

1388. Did the inspector upon that occasion, when sent down to report upon this renewed application, report in favour of the school?—He reported, I believe, that one of them at all events would be, under ordinary circumstances, passed, and the majority of the Board did not deal with it (I give them credit for that) on any small points; they said, "If it was the finest school since the beginning of time, you are a suspended priest, and must go away."

1389. *The O'Conor Don.*] In answer to Mr. Bourke, you have just stated that the inspector was sent down to visit those schools, and that you considered that in that the principle was given up?—I really did. I may be wrong in thinking it, but I did think it.

1390. Are you aware what was the order of the Board in sending down the inspector?—I think the Chief Baron drew it up; it reserved our rights, but I think the principle was abandoned at the time, for what was the use of sending him, when you knew that the whole thing on a higher ground was gone? If a man is an outlaw, what is the use of discussing anything more about it in going to any expense; for on the finance ground, it was an absurdity for the inspector to be inquiring into a thing that could never be investigated.

1391. As a matter of fact, did the Commissioners make any order that the inspector should go down?—No, but "that it should be dealt with in the office," and that is the way that it is dealt with in the office.

1392. Was not the order this: "That the Commissioners decline to make any order in this case until such time as the application, with the usual papers, comes before them, after having been dealt with in the office in the ordinary way"? — That is the ordinary way; I am giving you the details of the ordinary way; it is to send the inspector down, and he examines the schools as if it were a *de novo* application, and he calls in the neighbourhood, and asks, "Is there any objection?" he says, "Are they proper schools in size and in sanitary respects;" and there are such a long string of questions as would reach to the door. And he said, if this was an ordinary application the schools would be taken into connection; but the majority of the Board then say they cannot be taken into connection, because you, O'Keeffe, are a person that cannot be taken as manager. Why did they not tell him that at once, instead of letting the inspector go down on his application.

1393. I want to ask you a question with regard to the case of the Rev. Peter Daly, which you referred to?—I did not refer to that case; we were not very good friends in public life, and as Father Daly is now dead I should not like to be supposed to have referred to that case.

1394. Was he long under suspension?—He was under suspension long enough to have gone to Rome and come back again.

1395. Was he under suspension when he died?—No.

1396. The suspension was removed?—Yes, I am very glad to say that it was. I did not agree with him in public matters, but he was a very estimable man in many ways; he had a hot temper, but many excellent people have that.

The Right Honourable Mr. Justice *Fitzgerald*, called in; and Examined.

Right Hon. Mr. Justice *Fitzgerald*.
12 June 1873.

1397. *Chairman.*] WILL you kindly state to the Committee what your position is as regards the National Board?—I am one of the Commissioners of the National Board; I have been one, I think, since 1864; about nine years.

1398. Are you also a Commissioner of other Boards?—I have been also a Commissioner of the Board of Endowed Schools for some years; and I think since about 1861 I have been a Commissioner of the Board of Charities.

1399. Having introduced the motion to suspend the relations of the Board with Mr. O'Keeffe, are you desirous of making any statement upon the subject to the Committee?—Certainly; and in the first instance mentioning to the Committee that for the motion, I mean for the shape of the motion, I, and I alone, am responsible; I was the party introducing it, and brought forward that motion without any concert with any one; in fact the resolution was written by me at the table of the board-room at the moment as what I conceived to be the best mode of meeting the case. It is in my language; it was shown to no one; and, therefore, it is that I say that I, and I alone, am responsible for it; and I wish to state, for the information of the Committee, my action in reference to the carrying of that resolution. The Committee upon looking back to the documents will see that the suspension first came officially before the Board of Education on the 9th of April; prior to that, I had myself no acquaintance with the case of Father O'Keeffe at all, I mean as a Commissioner; I had as one of the public; I knew, of course, from the public papers that it had been before the Poor Law Board, and I had knowledge of previous litigation in the Court of Queen's Bench (I do not allude to the litigation between Father O'Keeffe and Cardinal Cullen at all). My presence at the Board on that day was entirely accidental. I was not aware that the case was on the programme; I had not seen the programme, but by pure accident I was at the Board on the 9th of April, and when I went into the board room I found the case of Father O'Keeffe then being mentioned, the certificate of the bishop, and the letter of the Rev. Mr. Martin; that was my first acquaintance with the proceeding before the Board. Although there had been a previous letter, I think in the month of November previous, from the inspector, mentioning the fact that a decree of suspension had been published at the Roman Catholic Chapel, at Callan, I do not recollect that that was ever brought before the Board; it may have been, but I do not recollect it. When I went in I found that a motion was then being made that notice of the proceedings should be given to the Rev. Mr. O'Keeffe. The case struck me as one of very great importance as to the course to be taken. The Resident Commissioner was there, and he mentioned, at the request of the Board, some of the precedents; and it struck my mind at once that it was, in reference to educational purposes, a matter of very grave consideration what course was to be adopted; and, accordingly, if the Committee will look to the proceedings, they will find that I suggested a postponement for a fortnight. In the ordinary course we meet once a week, but my suggestion was a postponement of this case for a fortnight, to give time for consideration. Looking to the proceedings of that day, you will see that my suggestion, which I thought a limited and reasonable one, was opposed; and my motion for postponement was met by a proposal that a copy of the letter of the Rev. Mr. Martin should be sent to the Rev. Mr. O'Keeffe; however, by a narrow majority my view was taken, and the case postponed, and that gave an opportunity for consideration; and I wish, as there is some error, I think, prevailing, to state to the Committee, for myself, at least, the information which I had, and the matters which weighed with me and determined me to take the course which I subsequently did. Now, I was not at all aware of the action in the Queen's Bench of the suit of Father O'Keeffe against Cardinal Cullen till it was mentioned on that day by Mr. Justice Morris, who seems to have had much earlier knowledge than myself of the proceedings; and I think he produced a copy of the declaration. And accordingly before the next day I had apprised myself of what that action was. Now there is an error which I think Mr. Justice Lawson fell into yesterday that I would wish to have corrected, and it is an error that is of some importance. As I understood Mr Justice Lawson's statement upon the

the second day that we met, not only were the pleadings referred to in detail in the case of the action and suit of Mr. O'Keeffe against Cardinal Cullen, but his language was that the very issue was stated which had been "knit between the parties, and which was then for trial, namely, the one side alleging that he was legally suspended, and the other side denying that he was legally suspended." Now there is a misconception there which might tend to mislead either the public or the Committee that I wish to correct at this early stage. I have brought with me a copy of the pleadings, and I can give the dates exactly when issues were joined. The action was commenced on the 26th of February 1872, that is, the writ of summons and plaint was issued on the 26th of February 1872. When it was served upon the cardinal I have no means of knowing. That is an action in which the Rev. Robert O'Keeffe complains that the cardinal published a sentence of suspension against him, in which he described him as suspended from all ecclesiastical functions; meaning thereby that he was unfitted to discharge the duties of parish priest; and there is also in it a complaint for issuing an interdict prohibiting the celebration of sacraments in the parish chapel, and concluding with a claim for large damages. When we first met on the 9th of April there had been no appearance or defence to that action at all; it was only that the writ had issued; when it was served I do not know, but there had been no appearance or plea. But on the 11th, two days afterwards, it appeared that the cardinal filed defences; the appearance and the filing of pleas are simultaneous, and accordingly he appeared and filed his defences on the 11th of April. The defences are of a very varied character, largely consisting of traverses; and, among the rest, an allegation that the publication of the suspension was no libel; and there are also special defences in which the cardinal urges, first, in the shape of a justificatio, and afterwards of a plea of privilege, that he had, under rescript from the Pope, authority to try the Callan case, that he had cited Mr. O'Keeffe before him, that he had heard him and pronounced sentence, and that he published that sentence as he lawfully might. And in another set of defences, it is alleged that having that authority and Mr. O'Keeffe having appeared before him, and believing that he had jurisdiction, and having heard the case, he pronounced the sentence that he believed was right, and he published that sentence; and he said, "Whether I really had jurisdiction or not, it was a privileged communication." These were the defences that were put in, and these would by no means disclose at all (for they are very complicated) what the issue would be eventually. The next step in the case I do not recollect; certainly I had not seen these defences at the time we met on the 23rd of April. The next step in the case is on the 11th of June 1872, that is after an interval of two months had occurred; the Rev. Mr. O'Keeffe's replications to the pleading were put in. But the pleadings did not terminate then, and on the 19th of June rejoinders were filed to these replications, which do raise issues. And again on the 31st of July 1872 a demurrer was filed, both further pleadings and a demurrer, which raised issues in fact and issues in law, which eventually came before the Court of Queen's Bench. So that it was not until a late period in June that anyone could indicate from the proceedings what the issues was to be, either in law or fact; I merely wish to correct an error which Judge Lawson fell into.

Right Hon. Mr. Justice *Fitzgerald*.

12 June 1873.

1400. You consider it important?—I think it very important; in one point of view it might be very important. It is a matter of fact on which there ought to be no misconception; no issue was joined in fact until July, and no issues were capable of being estimated until late in June. Now, having got the fortnight's time for deliberation, and learning what the case was, I had ascertained, for myself, that the schools in question were what I would call parochial schools, that is, the three schools in Callan were schools which have been built by public subscription, that they were not the schools of the parish priest at all, but had been built by public subscription; and there were two country schools in the same parish; one of these in the country district was actually built in the chapel ground; I am not quite certain whether both were not; but in my judgment they were all five properly described, though not technically so, as parochial schools, as schools to which the Rev. Mr. O'Keeffe had succeeded as manager in his character of parish priest; I do not mean to say at all *ex officio* (there is no such thing as an *ex officio* under our Board), but that he had succeeded as parish priest; and I found also, and knew, that he had succeeded his predecessor, who had not died, but had gone elsewhere, who had again succeeded his predecessor who had succeeded

Right Hon. Mr.
Justice Fitzgerald.

1s June 1873.

ceeded his predecessor; in fact, there were four successions from one parish priest to another from the time that they were originally brought by the parish priest in connection with the Board down to the Rev. Mr. O'Keeffe. I had also requested on the 9th, the Resident Commissioner that he would look into precedents, and with these means of information we met on the 23rd. And I beg particularly that the Committee would carry along with them the fact that these were not schools established or brought into connection with the Board by the Rev. Mr. O'Keeffe; but what I call clerical parochial schools, of which in his character of parish priest and no other, he had succeeded to the management, and been recognised by the Board as manager. We do not appoint, but recognise; "appoint" is popularly used, but is an erroneous term. Under these circumstances the case came before us on the 23rd, and upon the best consideration that I could give the case, I came to the conclusion that with the difficulties surrounding it, and finding a course of precedents all going in one direction, the best course for us was not to enter into discussion of the suspension itself, but to follow what appeared to me to be the established usage, and simply to act upon the bishop's certificate, and just as if we had a copy of the judgment of any Ecclesiastical Court before us; to act upon it in this sense, that as Mr. O'Keeffe who had succeeded to these schools as parish priest had been suspended by his ecclesiastical superior, the safest and best course was for us to suspend him from his relations with us as manager as long as the ecclesiastical suspension continued to exist; and, accordingly, at the table of the Board, I wrote the resolution which is before the Committee, and certainly my intention was not to decide anything, but to act simply on the suspension of the bishop by suspending Mr. O'Keeffe from his relations with us, until by some competent Court the ecclesiastical suspension had been overthrown or declared to be null and void; that was the course of action which I was anxious to explain. I have adverted to the precedents; I do not pretend to any special acquaintance with them myself; I have been nine years at the Board, but I have not been a very constant attendant, having other and more pressing duties to perform. I generally only go when I find on the programme some weighty case or question of principle involved; therefore, on these precedents I cannot give the Committee more, or probably so much, information as they have already. When we met on the 23rd the precedents were brought before us by the Resident Commissioner and considered; and it occurred to my judgment then, and I remain of that opinion, notwithstanding all that I have heard and read on the subject, that there were, running through these precedents, two rules of practice; one, that in reference to clergymen who as such had been recognised as managers of national schools, if they were suspended as clergymen, the suspension was a matter which we were bound to take notice of; secondly, that in reference to that limited class of cases, we did not profess to inquire into, and constantly declined to inquire into or investigate, the grounds of suspension; in other words, that we acted upon the suspension as it came before us, until it was in some way or other removed; I confine my observation to cases in which the manager with whom we were in communication had been as a clergyman of a parish or congregation, no matter of what church adopted by us, as our correspondent. Those were the motives influencing me on the 23rd in bringing forward that motion, and the Committee know the fate it met with. I desire to observe, too, that in reference to the proceedings of the 23rd, my memory does not entirely agree with Mr. Justice Lawson's in one particular. Where we are dealing with conversations which took place at a public Board, you will always have a difference of recollection; there will be to-morrow a difference as to what has occurred here to-day. I understood the controversy at the Board not to turn on the question whether notice or no notice should be given to Mr. O'Keeffe, but whether there should be an investigation. I think that notice without investigation would have been an absurdity. I understood, then, the question to be whether there should be an investigation; but Mr. Justice Lawson stated yesterday, that he thought the question was simply one of notice or no notice. Now, I think, if I recollect right, Mr. Justice Morris's amendment to my motion in the first instance was, that notice should be given to Mr. O'Keeffe of the charges made against him. It was pointed out that there were no charges against him that we had to deal with; that the only fact was, that on the certificate of the bishop he had been suspended; and then his motion was modified, to meet that new view

of

of the case; but the Chief Baron did suggest that notice should be given to Mr. O'Keeffe, with an intimation, however, that the Board would not be competent to inquire into the causes of suspension. I was perfectly ready to adopt that; but what we were discussing was not the mere expediency of giving this gentleman a dry notice that such and such was before the Board, but one with a view to investigate. Accordingly, the motion which I mentioned was proposed; I wished first to explain, in the way that I have done to the Committee, the course which I pursued, my action in the case, and my entire individual responsibility for what occurred.

Right Hon. Mr. Justice Fitzgerald.

12 June 1873.

1401. Do you wish to make any observation with regard to any of what are called in the memorial "mis-statements" that had been made with respect to the action of the majority of the Commissioners?—Yes. If I did not think that there had been very grave mis-statements, I for one would not have concurred in demanding the inquiry by this Committee; and I shall mention what the mis-statements are. Now, I think the mis-statements are to be found principally in the points to which I will refer. Possibly I should use too strong a term in using the word mis-statements, for I wish not to say one word that could lead to any further angry feeling in reference to this unhappy case; but there is language, principally in the letter of Mr. Justice Lawson, which has received also the sanction of Mr. Justice Morris, as I learn to-day, that is calculated to create great misapprehension, both of the action of the Board and of the conduct of the majority. I quite accept what Mr. Justice Lawson said yesterday, and I am sure with great accuracy, that he did not intend to convey any imputation upon anyone; in other words, that the language used was used somewhat in a Parliamentary sense; I am sure that was correct in his mind; but what I had to look to was, not what passed in his mind, but what the public or Parliament would understand from his language; and I do not think that anyone reading that letter with candour and fairness will come to the conclusion that that does not impute, or at least is not calculated to convey to the public, that the majority of the Board were acting in subserviency to ecclesiastical dictation (and upon this I am anxious to be clear and specific). Also, as I conceive, reading it as one of the public would read it, it imputes that there was on the part of the majority of the Board a reprehensible anxiety to insist on "immediate execution of the mandate conveyed in the bishop's letter." Now, these are very strong terms, "immediate execution," and obedience to a "mandate;" and I mistake the meaning of language if that does not impart to any unprejudiced mind that there was a reprehensible anxiety on the part of the Board to yield, and be subservient to ecclesiastical dictation. Again, he speaks of the "grave impropriety of prejudging a case which was actually in litigation;" and point is given to that charge against the majority of the Board by a subsequent statement lower down, that that was specially improper in the case of judges before whom the matter might come judicially, and I read this as specially pointing to myself (I do not say it in the least degree with anger or feeling at all, but simply as defending myself). And, again, he speaks of our "not very creditable litigation" (I will advert to that presently), and the "disastrous consequences" that we had provoked, and the strong expression of public opinion against us. Again, that we presented the appearance of "starving" the teachers into ecclesiastical submission. Again, that we issued an "educational interdict" in consequence of Mr. O'Keeffe's contumacy towards his ecclesiastical superiors; and, finally, that all this had arisen (I again give the language of the letter) "from the Commissioners mixing themselves up in a quarrel with which they had nothing to do; as long as the schools were managed in accordance with the rules of the Board, the Commissioners should not have interfered." Well, I learned from Mr. Justice Lawson yesterday, that this letter, so far from intending to impeach any individual, was, to use his words, "expressed in language of studied moderation." All I should say is, that if that represents studied moderation, I should be very sorry to be exposed to the full force of Mr. Justice Lawson's pen. Let me take these charges in detail. Now I wish on my own part, (I speak now for myself only, but I have no doubt I speak the opinions of all the rest of the Board) to express the strongest objection to be subjected even to the suspicion of any subservience to ecclesiastical dictation in any way or shape; but above all, to allow ecclesiastical dictation to interfere with us in conducting national education, or to put us in any way in conflict with the law of the land. That is a thing that I should never yield to, and I do not believe

Right Hon. Mr.
Justice Fitzgerald.
12 June 1873.

believe any other member of the majority would. And I must also observe on the injustice (I am sure it was not so intended) of imputing that we were anxious to insist upon immediate execution of the mandate conveyed in the Bishop's letter." I am not aware of there having been anything in the shape of a mandate before us. I desire on my own behalf to meet the charge of impropriety in pre-judging the case, and especially as I was a judge of the Court of Queen's Bench, before whom the case might come. I desire to say that in my humble judgment we neither judged or prejudged anything; and I recollect all through being most specially cautious not to let drop from my mouth a syllable to convey to any one that I entertained any opinion adverse to the Rev. Mr. O'Keeffe on the questions that could arise or were likely to arise; and one of the things that pressed upon my mind in the course that we took was, that we should not be drawn into an inquiry on matters in which we might be afterwards judicially engaged. I was the only judge of the Court of Queen's Bench; but there were three judges of the Common Pleas, and the Chief Baron of the Exchequer, on the Board; and though it is true that the case would come before the Queen's Bench first, there was no doubt that the real appeal would go to the Exchequer Chamber of which the judges of Common Pleas would form one-half; and one of the matters pressing on my mind was, that it would not be desirable that we should enter into any inquiry in which our judicial minds might be prejudiced either for or against the Reverend plaintiff. The other matters I shall not advert to now, as they will more legitimately come in answers on some other subjects of inquiry before the Committee; but I was specially anxious on the subject of ecclesiastical dictation.

1402. Your view was that the mere fact of ecclesiastical suspension, according to the practice of the Board, was a reason for suspension from the office of manager?—Yes, in that particular case, or any similar case.

1403. In the case of a parochial school, I mean?—In the case of a parochial school, where the manager had become such, and was recognised by us in his character of parish or congregational clergyman.

1404. Assuming, therefore, for the moment, that the suspension itself was altogether invalid, and might ultimately be proved to be so; according to that view, until it had been decided to be invalid, it was in your judgment a reason for suspending the function of manager?—For suspending our relations with him.

1405. What I understand you therefore to say is, that it was not inconsistent for the same person to decide as an Ecclesiastical Commissioner of the National Board that in the interim the relations should be suspended, and yet afterwards as a judge of the Queen's Bench, after hearing the case, to decide either way with regard to the validity of the suspension?—Quite so.

1406. Do you wish to make any other observations?—Upon the subject of notice I would certainly wish to add something, as the point has been very much urged of not giving notice to Mr. O'Keeffe, and it is important that it should stand on its right grounds, as it has formed the subject of popular declamation. There is no doubt that you ought not to decide anything judicially which can affect the rights or position of the party, without giving him notice; *audi alteram partem* is a maxim of the law; not of universal but of general application to all judicial proceedings; but it imports that there is something which you are to inquire into; that there is some imputation which can be displaced; some matter of controversy which is to be investigated. Now the Committee will observe that as to the fact of a decree of suspension, there never had been any controversy, for the action brought against Cardinal Cullen was in consequence of the publishing of the decree of suspension. Of the fact of suspension, I mean that his ecclesiastical superior had pronounced a decree of suspension against him, there never had been any controversy, and that there had been (but I was not aware of it at the time) a previous episcopal suspension contradistinguished from the larger one pronounced against him by the cardinal. As to that there never was any doubt or controversy. We also knew, as members of the public, that this matter had been in the previous January, and extending down to February, before the Poor Law Board, where an inquiry had been instituted, and that that Board had determined on the removal of Mr. O'Keeffe from his office of chaplain to the workhouse. As to the fact of the suspension, therefore, unless we determined that we would

investigate

SELECT COMMITTEE ON CALLAN SCHOOLS. 137

investigate its clauses, there would be nothing whatever to give notice for.   Right Hon. Mr.
For instance, if we had given notice to the Rev. Mr. O'Keeffe, probably we   Justice *Fitzgerald.*
should have got the answer which he gave to the Poor Law Board, that is to   12 June 1873.
say, " that the Cardinal Archbishop had as much right to suspend him as the
Archbishop of Vienna," and that would have been a denial, not of the fact of suspension, but of the authority of the judge, or that he properly exercised his
jurisdiction. You will find that answer given in one of his letters; it did occur
to me, that under such circumstances, unless we were prepared for an inquiry,
the giving a notice to Mr. O'Keeffe would only be involving us in a correspondence, possibly, of considerable length, and doing no good whatever, and that
unless we were determined to inquire into the case, it would be a hypocritical
pretence to give him notice. The real question, and the question before us was,
not on this question of notice, but whether we ought to inquire into the suspension and its foundation, because if we ought, undoubtedly we ought to have given
notice. The question really is, ought the Commissioners to have inquired into
the decree of suspension before acting on the certificate of the bishop. If we
ought to have done so, then we ought to have heard Mr. O'Keeffe against it, and
the Archbishop for it, no doubt we ought not, in such a case, to have gone one
step without notice to both parties, and giving them an opportunity of being
heard; I thought then that we should act upon the certificate of the bishop without more; and I thought, and I still think, that notice would have been useless.

1407. Your contention was, that the practice required you to proceed upon
the certificate?—Yes.

1408. And that therefore there was nothing else to hear?—Yes, and no imputation that we could deal with. If we were wrong in not hearing him, we are
wrong in all.

1409. Your contention was, that upon that certificate practice required you
to act, and that nothing you could hear upon any inquiry would vary that conclusion?—Yes; and then the next question would be, ought we to have investigated the suspension and its causes.

1410. You had the precedents before you?—The four precedents only that
have been given here.

1411. And do you agree with the majority of the Board in the interpretation
which has been put upon those precedents, or with the minority?—I agree with
the majority. I think that two rules are to be deduced from them; that is, that
you act upon the judgment of the Ecclesiastical Court, and then that you do
not inquire into its foundation.

1412. Is there anything else that you desire to say?—In reference to whether
we ought to have gone into the case, and investigated the foundation of it, either
as a whole or partially, as suggested by Mr. Justice Lawson, the opinion which
I arrived at was that the best course was not to investigate. I thought that the
precedents were that way, and that that was the wisest course under the circumstances. First of all I may observe, that we had not the means; we are not a
tribunal for the investigation of such cases as this (I am now applying myself to
Father O'Keeffe's case), and we had not the means of investigation. There are
certainly some men on the Board who are accustomed to judicial action, but the
majority are not so; the minority there are laymen; there are five judges out
of the 21, and the remainder are laymen. But we have no power of bringing
parties before us; we have no means of examining witnesses; if we wanted the
presence of the Cardinal Archbishop we have no means of bringing him before
us; and we cannot administer an oath.

1413. All the Commissioners, the majority as well as the minority, are agreed
that an inquiry into the validity of ecclesiastical suspension would be *coram non
judice*, are they not?—I cannot answer that.

1414. Do you think that any motion of the Board could be discussed
before the Board, whether or not a clerical suspension, Roman Catholic
or not, is valid?—I understood Mr. Justice Lawson to say, yesterday, that, to a
certain extent, it could and ought; that we could have examined him to this
extent, that you could ascertain first whether there was a charge, and what
the nature of the charge was, whether there had been a citation, and
whether he had been heard in his defence; whether there had been
a judgment by the Ecclesiastical Court, and what was the foundation
of that judgment; not to inquire into the cause of suspension, but to see
whether it was a charge of immorality, or merely some ecclesiastical matter;

0.93.   S   that

Right Hon. Mr. Justice Fitzgerald.

12 June 1873.

that is what I understand Mr. Justice Lawson to say, but I may have misapprehended him.

1415. I understand Mr. Justice Lawson to say, that a clerical suspension might be good for an ecclesiastical purpose, and yet might have nothing in it which should justify you, as Commissioners of the Board of National Education, in refusing to recognise a suspended clergyman as manager of a school?— And I entirely agree with him in one sense. I have already shown that we had no power at all to inquire into this, or to investigate, or to go into these questions at all: for instance, if we were to inquire into whether there had been a citation or not, that is often a question of very considerable difficulty; and it happens, I believe, in the very present case, before the Court of Queen's Bench, one of the points reserved for the Court is whether, in certain cases, the citation may be waived; and I thought it was best not to enter into these points; and finding a course of precedents in that direction I thought we should follow it.

1416. You think the course of precedent pointed out that course, and your own judgment as to what is wise agrees with that course of precedent?—You will observe, considering there are about 7,000 schools altogether, we have had very few of those cases. This is the only one, that I am aware of, that has occurred during my nine years there; and our whole precedents, I think, during the whole period of the existence of the Board do not go beyond six or seven, so that it is a very rare case.

1417. Have you anything else to state to the Committee?—Again, there is an allegation brought against the majority of the Board, that if we did not investigate the case, and there were pending litigation, we ought to have waited until that litigation was over; that, *pendente lite*, we ought to have done nothing. That is a matter which I have considered, and upon which I wish to make some observations. Now I think if it was shown to us at all that within a very limited time this question might have been determined by some legitimate tribunal, as by appeal to an ecclesiastical superior, or question raised in one of the superior courts, possibly there might have been something in that; but I recollect bringing before the Board the course of procedure that was likely to arise in the particular case; and everything that I said then has been justified. This action was commenced in February 1872, I think, and we are now in June 1873, that is a year and four months afterwards. I knew the course of pleading would be very long, that it might be exceedingly doubtful whether the real question which ought to affect our judgment could ever arise in that action, and that some years would elapse probably before even you would get the judgment of that court, and in that I was right. The case stands, at present, thus: upon the issues in law raised by demurrer, the Court of Queen's Bench has given its judgment, and that judgment has been in some very main points in favour of the Rev. Mr. O'Keeffe; but then the Committee should know that every part of the record is covered by issues, in fact; and amongst the rest, the Rev. Mr. O'Keeffe alleged that he was suspended solely for bringing an action against the curate or bishop; the answer to that is, "You were not suspended for that cause alone." That is one of the issues, and there are other issues, in fact, of very great importance: and they were tried the other day before the Chief Justice, and they resulted in a verdict for the plaintiff with a farthing damages. It came before the Court of Queen's Bench again last week, upon an application for a new trial, and a rule nisi was given; and that rule cannot come before us until November next. That rule will probably be decided either late in November, or, if not, in January 1874. I really do not know myself all the questions in the case, but supposing that the Court should decide in favour of a new trial, the whole thing has to be done over again, and it is not until you have an ultimate and final decision on the issues, in fact, and judgment made up, that it can be taken to the Court of Exchequer Chamber. I will not venture to predict what will happen when it gets there. Judging by the state of business heretofore in that court, and the delay in causes of not equal magnitude, a delay of a couple of years may probably ensue before it is heard, and at the end of that time a judgment may be given there one way or the other; but the issues in law are so grave, and involve rights so large, that it is a case that will either go to the House of Lords, or to whatever may then be the ultimate court of appeal.

1418. As

1418. As we heard just now from Mr. Justice Morris that it might possibly be decided in June, and that it was better, *pendente lite*, to take no steps; I understand you to wish to make some answer to that?—My answer to that is, that from the very nature of the pleadings it could not come to any short termination; a very long period must elapse before it is finally decided, and the issues in it are so large and of such very great importance, that such a case can only be finally decided by the House of Lords of the final Court of Appeal.

Right Hon. Mr. Justice Fitzgerald.

12 June 1873.

1419. What you are directing your observations to, I think, is the remark of Mr. Justice Morris, that it might possibly have been decided in June 1872, and that it would have been better for the Board to take no step *pendente lite*, and in answer to that, you say that it is not finally decided even in the Queen's Bench, in June 1873, and that it may have ulterior steps to pass through after it has left the Queen's Bench?—Yes, if it could have been shown to me that, say in six weeks, this question would have been decided, I should have said that masterly inaction would be the proper course; but seeing that a very great length of time must elapse, was one of my reasons for not taking that view. But I have others that pressed upon my mind. I cannot agree in the conclusion of Mr. Justice Lawson's letter that this was a matter which we had nothing to do with but to stand by and look on. I think it would really have amounted to this, that in the case of any suspended clergyman who challenges the suspension, and institutes proceedings *bond fide* to question it, we should wait, no matter what the time, till these proceedings were determined, before we take any action on that. I do not think that that is the proper view to take of it; and I think it would be productive of the worst consequences; you would have in many cases years of turmoil interfering with education if you adopted any such rule, and if we are to be called upon to investigate these cases of suspension, or to stand by and look on *pendente lite*, it seems to me it would be better to say at once that you will not appoint a clergyman, especially a priest, or recognise him as manager of a school, because we know that he is appointed by his bishop, and that in that position he is liable to be suspended by a summary process for a canonical cause. I should say if we were to wait till litigation has been determined, the wiser course would be to say that we should not appoint a priest as manager of a school in his character of priest.

1420. Is there anything further that you wish to add?—I wish shortly to state my reasons for not quite concurring in Judge Lawson's evidence yesterday, as to what I call a partial inquiry, as I understand him, that is to say, an inquiry into the procedure which had taken place which led to the suspension, whether there had been a citation, a hearing, and a judgment, but not an inquiry into the causes whether the causes of the suspension were well founded; but as to what they were, whether it was for some alleged immorality, or some breach of ecclesiastical discipline. I should say in reference to that, that it was not suggested to us before in any way or shape that a partial inquiry of that kind should take place; but I think myself that there are very grave objections to that, the same that would exist in some sense to a full inquiry. I have pointed out already the importance of the technicalities that beset a citation and other matters of procedure which we were quite incompetent to deal with. But I do not understand how you can stop short when you get at the facts of citation and decree, and that it has been for some ecclesiastical cause, without going further and inquiring into that ecclesiastical cause, and its nature and character; because a man may be suspended for a purely ecclesiastical cause of a character which would involve no moral delinquency, but which would quite call upon us if we had recognised him as manager in his character of clergyman to act upon the suspension. I will illustrate that by an instance. A priest may be suspended for various ecclesiastical causes not involving any moral delinquency. Supposing, for instance, the Rev. Mr. O'Keeffe had changed his religion and become an Unitarian, that would involve no moral imputation, but would be a very good ecclesiastical cause for suspending him from his position as parish priest; I believe that would not be doubted; it would appear to me to be equally a case in which, as he had been recognised as priest as the manager of a Roman Catholic parochial school, he should not be allowed to continue in that character; there is no doubt whatever that the manager of a non-vested school has entirely the religious instruction to be given to the pupils in his own hands. I mention that as an illustration that there are a great many ecclesiastical matters you might have to enter into. Again, suppose a priest was suspended for the ecclesiastical

0.93   s 2   offence

Right Hon. Mr.
Justice Fitzgerald.

18 June 1873.

offence of disclosing what had occurred at the confessional, it would, in the eyes of the Roman Catholic church, be a very grave offence; and I should say that if he had been suspended for that, and if he had been recognised as manager in his character of parish priest, it would be a very good ground for removal. I wish to point out that you cannot stop short and say, "We will ascertain merely whether it is for some immorality or for an ecclesiastical cause;" you must necessarily go into the cause, and, in my judgment, as you cannot have a partial inquiry, you must either have a full inquiry into all the causes of the justice of the suspension, or no inquiry at all.

1421. Dr *Lyon Playfair*.] I think you said that you saw the very important issues raised in this case the first time that it was brought before the Board?—I saw from its character that the issues would probably be of very great importance; that is all that I meant to say.

1422. And you then inquired what precedents existed bearing upon such a case?—Yes.

1423. And you understood that these precedents made rules for the practical guidance of the Board?—That they established a practice which we ought to follow.

1424. Which you followed as rules; I think you used the expression "two rules".?— I thought that there ran through these precedents two rules; first that we acted upon a suspension without inquiry, and that the suspension of a clergyman, who as such acted as manager, would be a ground for removing him.

1425. Did your Board, in any of its annual reports laid before Parliament, ever tell Parliament, or the public, of the existence of these precedents?—I cannot answer that, as I am not myself much acquainted with details.

1426. You are not aware whether Parliament was ever informed that the Board considered these precedents as sufficient for forming a definite rule of action in such an important case?—Certainly not.

1427. *The O'Conor Don*.] I understand that you take the view that in the course that was adopted by the Board, the members of the majority expressed no opinion whatever upon the merits of Father O'Keeffe's suspension?— Certainly; I speak for myself particularly; I was most cautious to avoid giving utterance to a single word on the merits; I recollect using the expression very well upon the first occasion, or upon one of those two occasions, that so far from expressing any opinion, if I had any sympathy at all in the case, or would permit sympathy to guide my judgment, my sympathy was with Father O'Keeffe at that time.

1428. And you believed that the course which the Board followed, in acting simply upon the certificate of the bishop, was the only course which would leave your hands free, and enable you not to form or come to any conclusion upon the merits of the case?—I think, myself, that if we had been called upon to carry out, and the Board had determined that we should carry out, a thorough investigation into this suspension, it would virtually have disqualified five members of the Board from taking any part in it; and I, for one, would have withdrawn immediately.

1429. You believed that, as a judge before whom the case might eventually come, the course you adopted was the course which you must adopt if you acted rightly in the matter?—I thought it did no real mischief, and that it was the best.

1430. And whereas you hold that opinion with respect to the conduct of the judges, who might have had to try the case, I presume that you would hold the same argument with respect to any person who might happen to be a counsel in the case?—I think there is much less objection in the counsel's taking such a course. There was one gentleman counsel in the case, a member of the Board, a gentleman of the highest character, and of the nicest honour, and if he or any member of the Board had entertained a doubt as to the propriety of his action, he would have withdrawn at once.

1431. But you are aware that since then imputations have been cast upon him for having voted on the first occasion?—Yes, and I think most unjustly; it has been a common and popular idea that we decided the case against Father O'Keeffe. We decided nothing, emphatically nothing, either for or against him.

1432. I understand you not to agree with Mr. Justice Lawson. He stated, yesterday, "I have no hesitation in saying that I would not consider the fact of a clergyman

SELECT COMMITTEE ON CALLAN SCHOOLS. 141

a clergyman changing his religion any ground for removing him from the schools, if the schools were carried on as before, and if the scholars attended them, having reference to the fact that our schools are undenominational"?—I take rather the distinction that Dr. Morell mentioned yesterday. If an independent person established a school; a clergyman, for instance, if he established a school of his own, and afterwards changed his religion, I think it would not be matter at all for us to enter into. But it is a very different thing, for instance, if the Protestant rector as rector is recognised as manager of the school, to give religious instruction to the Protestants of the parish, and he becomes a Roman Catholic afterwards; I think that is a matter to be taken into consideration.

Right Hon. Mr. Justice Fitzgerald.

12 June 1873.

1433. You consider, then, that there are such schools in connection with the National Board as are practically congregational or parochial?—Decidedly; I have no doubt about that. I think that the majority of the schools in connection with the Board are practically parochial schools. We have what are technically and legally called parochial schools; namely, the Protestant National Schools. There is a difficulty in calling the Roman Catholic schools parochial, because, in law, we do not recognise the Roman Catholic parish; but I have no doubt that they would, in this case, be properly called parochial schools.

1434. They might be better called congregational schools, perhaps?—Yes.

1435. Are you aware that in the Report of the Royal Commissioners on Education it is stated that, "some of the non-vested schools being the property of congregations are as exclusively set apart in practice for educational purposes as are the vested schools;" that the Commissioners on reporting upon primary education distinctly name the schools as congregational schools?—I was not aware of that.

1436. You are not aware that in that report is to be found a table, from which it appears that 52 per cent. of the non-vested schools in Ireland are specially named as parochial or congregational?—I am not aware of that. I have no doubt the fact is so. I have seen the name up over a parish school.

1437. And you consider that these particular schools with which you have to deal in this case were of that character?—All of that character. Two of the schools there could be no question as to; one, as I mentioned, was built by the predecessor of Father O'Keeffe in the chapel yard. And the three in the town of Callan were erected by public subscription for the town as a portion of the parish, and it was in consequence of that that Father O'Keeffe's predecessor became in connection with them.

1438. Regarding them in that light, you would consider that the fact of the suspension of the priest, no matter whether for ecclesiastical or other misconduct, was sufficient ground for removing him?—I think that when he became as priest, the manager, and was recognised so, when he ceased to fill that character we ought not to recognise him further.

1439. And you consider that the Bishop's certificate or that of the ecclesiastical superior, ought to be sufficient, without further inquiry in such a case as that?—Yes; for instance, if in place of being a decree emanating from a Roman Catholic Bishop, it had been a decree from a bishop of the Established Church, I would equally take the copy of that just as we do receive the certificate of a judgment of the Inferior Court. In the court of the county chairman, we take the certificate of his judgment until it is impeached.

1440. Now, with respect to Cardinal Cullen's assumed interference in this case, you have been a member of the Board for nine years, I think you stated?—Yes.

1441. And during the whole time that you have been a member of the Board, has Cardinal Cullen directly or indirectly interfered in any matter, or had any communication with the Board that you are aware of?—I am not aware that he has ever communicated with the Board in any way or shape; on the contrary, I have always regarded him as one of our chief opponents; we have had a great deal of difficulty to encounter on all sides, but on the Roman Catholic side I have always understood that Cardinal Cullen led the opposition against the Board, and I am not aware that we ever had, from the time that I had been there, any communication from him or with him.

1442. Something was said yesterday by Mr. Justice Lawson with regard to the course commonly or occasionally pursued by the late Resident Commissioner, Sir Alexander Macdonnell, in making non-official statements to the Board, upon

0.93. s 3 which

Right Hon. Mr. Justice *Fitzgerald*.
19 June 1873.

which the Board were supposed to act?—I was present when that evidence was given yesterday.

1443. Do you concur in that opinion?—In one sense, I concur in it; we paid the utmost deference to the judgment and the experience of the Resident Commissioner, and he deserved it all from us; but I think that Mr. Justice Lawson was in error in saying that we took statements of facts from him as facts merely within his own knowledge. What frequently occurred was this: when we had a complicated case coming before us, the Resident Commissioner would take the trouble beforehand of preparing an analysis of the evidence for the Board; sometimes it depended upon an analysis of a great number of documents, going over a period of years; and he would read to the Board that analysis of the evidence, and we would take it from him upon his credit; but I never knew the Board to act upon statements from the Resident Commissioner of matters not in evidence before them.

1444. Sir Alexander Macdonnell's action, so far as you are aware, was confined to placing before the Board, in a concise form, what he had learned from official reports on the table of the Board?—From the reports and documents in evidence before the Board.

1445. As regards any facts upon which the Board had to decide, you were not aware that he ever asked the Board to decide upon facts that were not contained in the official reports?—And not alone that, but which each member of the Board could, if he thought fit, ascertain for himself.

1446. Now with respect to this litigation that the Board had with some of the teachers for the non-payment of salaries, which has been called discreditable, would you explain to the Committee what was its nature?—As far as I recollect, there were five actions brought against the Board. Some of them, if not all (I forget whether all were), though in the names of others, were instituted by Father O'Keeffe. In one of them he was certainly the plaintiff himself; and two others were instituted by him for teachers who had left the country. And the Board were entirely successful in establishing that the actions could not lie. They could not avoid the litigation; but as I understood Mr. Justice Lawson yesterday, it was in reference to the case of a person named Woods that he used that expression. Certainly, that would not have been the interpretation that I would have put upon his letter, that in one case there had been litigation which the Board ought not to have entered into. I read that as imputing a course of discreditable litigation in the five actions; in all they were successful. Now as to Woods' case, there was nothing discreditable.

1447. Perhaps you will allow me to read Judge Lawson's exact words to the Committee: he was asked, "Is there anything else you wish to state to the Committee?" and he replied I wish to clear up one or two matters which The O'Conor Don asked me about. With respect to this expression that I used, 'discreditable litigation,' on thinking the matter over, now I recollect that it refers to an action brought by a Mr. Woods against the Commissioners."?—In Woods' case the Board of course were obliged to defend the action, because they could not carry on if they admitted liability to these actions at all. Accordingly they were obliged to assert the principle that they were not liable at all. They do not deal with the teachers at all, either appoint, or dismiss, or pay them. But in Woods' case they would not pay a salary for any teacher until he had been recognised by the Board, and Woods never had been recognised by the Board. After the Recorder had decided the case in favour of the Board, and there was an appeal, upon further investigation, it appeared that though Woods had not been recognised, the reason of his non-recognition was a delay in the office, and the instant that that was discovered to be the case the Board said, and so instructed their agents, "Though we must deny any liability, yet as soon as the case is settled we authorise you to pay for him to the Rev. Mr. O'Keeffe the amount of his demand," for Woods himself had emigrated.

1448. Before the Board were in a position to pay him he had emigrated?—Yes.

1449. And the action was not taken by Woods against the Board, but by Mr. O'Keeffe?—Mr. O'Keeffe alleged that he had the authority of Woods to bring the action; it was for the small sum of 12 *l.* 10 *s.*

1450. Are you aware that a diminution in public confidence has been in any way shown in the National Board by the withdrawal of schools from under the Board, in consequence of your action in this case of Mr. O'Keeffe?—Certainly not;

not; and, on the contrary, I believe the fact to be, which we can have from the Resident Commissioner if I am erroneous, that during the year that has occurred since, that is 1872, we have had more new schools added than in either of the two years that preceded his removal. That is a very speaking fact; we have now a greater number of schools than ever.

Right Hon. Mr. Justice Fitzgerald.

12 June 1873.

1451. In fact, in the last year there has been a greater proportionate increase of applications to join the Board than in any preceding year?—No, not than in any preceding year, but the two preceding years.

1452. More than the average you mean?—Yes, more than the average. In the year 1872-73, that has occurred since Father O'Keeffe was removed from the management; we have had more new schools than in either of the two preceding years.

1453. One word, now, as to your opinion of the *ex officio* question. You stated expressly that you did not consider that there were any *ex officio* managers. Would you explain to the Committee what you understand by "*ex officio*"? —I think that there has been rather a wordy dispute about that. By "*ex officio*" would be meant a person who succeeds, as a matter of right, in respect of an office; that, being appointed to the office, he succeeds, as a matter of right, to something else. For instance, if you find in a Act of Parliament, "Be it enacted that the Lord Chancellor shall be *ex officio* a member" of a certain board, that is an appointment that cannot be questioned; but there is no such thing with us.

1454. But the recognition of a clergyman as a manager of a school in consequence of his being a clergyman is a practice which you constantly follow?—It is almost universal. We look upon the fact of his being appointed as clergyman as such a recognition of his private character that we do not make inquiry, unless there is some imputation or charge, and then we would inquire into his fitness.

1455. You mean that there is no such management recognised as would give a right to the holder of any office to claim to be appointed manager of a school? —To claim to be appointed, but not a right to be appointed.

1456. Mr. *Cross*.] That is, that the Board would always keep in their own hands what their judgment was as to the fitness of the man that was appointed? —Yes, always exercise supervision in that way, if there was any question as to his fitness.

1457. Whether parish priest or not?—Yes.

1458. Therefore, though a gentleman may have succeeded as a parish priest, still it would be subject to the approval of the Board as to his fitness?—Clearly, at all times.

1459. There is nothing of the kind of an *ex officio* appointment?—Nothing whatever.

1460. Then the question of the fitness would be the same in the mind of the Board as to what you have spoken of as parochial schools, and as to general schools?—With this distinction; that where a person comes as a successor to a clergyman in his character as clergyman, we consider that sufficient.

1461. Naturally you would allow the man appointed as parish priest to be manager, unless there was something against him, you mean?—Yes.

1462. But still in the abstract the question of fitness is the same in both cases, whether the school is what you call parochial or not?—Yes, we are always bound to consider fitness.

1463. You have stated that all these schools were succeeded to by Mr. O'Keeffe as parish priest?—Yes.

1464. But in the case of the infant school, that was established by Mr. O'Keeffe himself, was it not?—That was the one exception that I referred to some time back. I do not think that is exactly as you put it. That school was established by a public subscription, under the guidance of Father O'Keeffe, but it is partly on the parochial school premises. What has been done is this: there was a portion unoccupied of the old school premises, and to that a small external building has been added, but you enter into the infant school through the other schools; there is only one entrance to them, and it stands partially upon what is called the Callan School ground.

1465. Still Mr. O'Keeffe was the gentleman who got up the subscriptions, and got it built, and offered it to the Board?—Yes. I do not think that there can

Right Hon. Mr.
Justice Fitzgerald

12 June 1873.

he any solid distinction between that and the other. We may be wrong as to all; but if we are right as to the others, we are right as to that also.

1466. I presume you simply know as much about the precedents as the Committee can find out themselves by looking at the reports of the office, and no more?—I do not think that I know so much. I know nothing beyond what you will find in the Parliamentary Papers, and I draw my own conclusions from that.

1467. Just as much and nothing more than we can draw our own?—Yes; and very probably the Committee can draw them much more wisely.

1468. I understood you to say, that in the case of Mr. O'Keeffe you decided nothing at the Board?—I mean in this sense, that we did not attempt to decide whether the suspension was a good one or not.

1469. But you decided that he was an unfit man to manage the school?—I do not think we did that either. What we decided was, that having as parish priest become and been recognised as our correspondent, we had before us *primâ facie* evidence that he had ceased to be parish priest, and therefore he ought to cease to be our correspondent.

1470. And therefore you did decide, at all events, that you ought to cease corresponding with him?—To that extent we decided on the course of precedent.

1471. Never mind the precedents for a moment; therefore that decision for your part practically deprived him of all assistance from the Board, so far as the schools were concerned?—Certainly, if he did not recognise the order of the Board appointing a new manager. We do not deprive him of anything.

1472. You declined to correspond with him?—Yes.

1473. The consequence of your declining to correspond with him was that no teacher in the school could have any assistance from the Board?—Yes.

1474. Therefore you did practically decide that no Board assistance should be given to the school?—I do not think we did any such thing. It never entered into my mind that Father O'Keeffe would adopt the course that he has done.

1475. The practical result of your decision was that you stopped the supplies?—Eventually, in consequence of Father O'Keeffe resisting the suspension of the Board as our correspondent. I wish to correct one misapprehension in reference to what the honourable Member has just mentioned; it is supposed that we have deprived Father O'Keeffe of something. Now I find this in a passage, that I will read from a work, that both in and out of Parliament will exercise a great and deserved influence from the character of the writer. "Father O'Keeffe, a Roman Catholic priest, has been caught in one of the many snares which the Jesuits of Rome have prepared, and he has lost upwards of 300 *l.* a year by being deprived of the management of the schools of Callan." Now there is no such thing as that; he loses nothing.

1476. Practically you stopped the supplies of the schools; that was the result of your decision?—Eventually when we struck them off.

1477. You say that you decided nothing judicially, because that remark implies that there was something to inquire into?—Yes.

1478. Then the mere fact of the bishop's letter would make in your opinion the action of the Board a necessary consequence?—According to our precedents.

1479. According to your practice you mean?—Yes.

1480. That is, that when the bishop's letter suspending a clergyman comes you act purely ministerially, and an order of the Board follows as a matter of course?—With this qualification, that it is in a case where the manager has become such as clergyman of a parish or congregation.

1481. But not for the purpose of performing ecclesiastical duties as clergyman?—I think he does.

1482. In national schools?—It may be in them, but after the hours for secular education. I think when we appoint a priest or a Protestant clergyman as manager, we commit to his hands entirely, and with the view that he should exercise it, the power of giving all the religious instruction.

1483. What was acting upon your mind at the time; was the fact of the suspension by the bishop, and not the effect upon the education of the children who would be brought to the school?—I think we had both before us; for I considered that if we waited till the question had been finally determined by some court, the ultimate result probably would be a scene of confusion as a general rule

SELECT COMMITTEE ON CALLAN SCHOOLS.   145

Right Hon. Mr.
Justice Fitzgerald.

12 June 1873.

rule (I speak not of this particular case), and of altercation which would be very prejudicial to the cause of education.

1484. Still, the moment that the suspension of the bishop is thrown down upon your table, you upon that decline to correspond with the gentleman, and enter into the case no further?—In the one class of cases. I am far from saying that we do so, or ought to do so, in an independent class.

1485. Allow me to put an extreme case to you. Supposing the case of any ecclesiastical body, Roman Catholics or Presbyterians, or the Disestablished Church, choosing to suspend a clergyman because the clergyman acted upon one of your rules, such as a time-table conscience clause?—I should not for one moment hesitate to say that we would not act upon that.

1486. Supposing it did not appear upon the face of the suspension, but was the fact, do you mean to say that the Board would then not inquire into that fact?—I do not know how that fact could be brought before us.

1487. It would be brought before you in the report of your own inspector?—I cannot imagine such a case.

1488. I want you to imagine it for one moment?—I cannot imagine such an absurdity as that a Protestant clergyman or any clergyman was suspended from his clerical functions because he chose to act upon the rules of our Board.

1489. Now, I will put another case, the case of a clergyman of the Disestablished Church suspended by the Disestablished Church, as put by Mr. Justice Lawson, because he chose to preach very High Church doctrines, but that the schools were flourishing, and that all the parishioners or the great body of them accepted his doctrines and liked them, and that he was doing good educational work. Would you, upon the receipt of the suspension from the alleged ecclesiastical authority, at once cease to correspond with that man, or would you allow him to go on doing his work, and correspond with him?—My answer is that, if he had been appointed to that school as the rector of the parish, we will say, and was suspended by his ecclesiastical superiors from being rector, we would act upon the judgment of the court that removed him.

1490. However much good work he might be doing in an educational point of view?—No matter what his qualifications were in an educational point of view, or the work that he was doing. We would act *primâ facie* upon the judgment of his ecclesiastical superiors who removed him from the office in respect of which he had been recognised as manager.

1491. You use the word *primâ facie*; what do you mean by that?—I mean that we would recognise it in this sense, that we would hold it to be conclusive until it had been in some way or other removed.

1492. Removed by a "competent ecclesiastical authority"?—You are now upon the meaning of the words "competent authority." I do not confine it at all to a competent ecclesiastical authority.

1493. Do you think that if the law of England stated that that suspension was wrong, you, the National Education Board, would then be bound to follow the law of England?—In my own view. I set no law above the law of the land, and I shall always be prepared to yield obedience to, and assert that law.

1494. Supposing that a clergyman is suspended by ecclesiastical authority, and in the Irish courts of law disputes the validity of the act of suspension, and the Irish courts of law decide that the suspension was invalid; but supposing that the ecclesiastical body still maintained the validity of the suspension, in that case how would you act?—I shall always myself (I am speaking now as an individual) yield obedience to the law of the land, and I shall never consider any law above it. It is part of our constitution. We allow no rivalry; the law of the land is supreme, and overrides every other, and there is no law superior to it, or equal to it, that we can recognise, and therefore I would always be prepared to give effect to the decision of the law of the land. But that may leave behind it another and a different question. If the decision of the court of law had been that, according to the law of the church, the party had not been validly suspended, I should be prepared to give full effect to that. But if, upon other grounds, it may leave behind a question as to all voluntary churches, as to whether the suspension may not be a good and valid suspension according to the contract and agreement of the parties, and as between themselves, although it would not be enforceable by the law of the land.

1495. And in that case you would suspend him?—I do not say that at all. I could illustrate my view upon that subject best by what has occurred. The right honourable

0.93.   T

Right Hon. Mr. Justice Fitzgerald.

12 June 1873.

honourable and learned Member for the University of Dublin has put a case twice in the House of Commons. Supposing in the particular case here before us, the case of the suspension of Mr. O'Keeffe, that Cardinal Cullen had as archbishop professed to suspend him? he is Archbishop of Dublin, and in that sense the diocese of Ossory is a suffragan diocese. The case put by the right honourable and learned gentleman was, that an archbishop has no jurisdiction within the diocese of his suffragan. I believe that is right, and according to common law, and the law of the Church, if that had been the case, and if it had been decided by one of the superior courts that the archbishop had proceeded to decide a case that did not come before him properly at all, according to church law, and if it had annulled his decree on that ground, I would be prepared to give the fullest effect to that; it would be a decision by one of the superior courts that, according to church law, he was not a suspended priest.

1496. Now, supposing that the priest in this case, who was suspended, made that defence in an action, and wished to bring it before you, he ought to have an opportunity of doing so, ought he not?—I do not think that the Board of Education were competent to inquire into that, or entertain it.

1497. Supposing that the parish priest who had been suspended fought out that defence in a court of law, and won the action, and was prepared to bring that defence before the National Board?—He would bring before us the judgment of the court of law.

1498. He ought to have the right to bring that defence before you, ought he not?—To bring before us the fact, that a court of law had annulled the suspension.

1499. He ought to have the right to do that?—Certainly.

1500. If he is to do that, he ought to have notice, ought he not, from you, of the action which you are going to take on the matter?—If you mean notice of our acting on the suspension, I think not. I have stated my views on that; but it would be a delusion to give him notice if we were not prepared to hear him.

1501. But I understood you to say that if the parish priest had contested the validity of a suspension, and had had judgment given in his favour, he ought to be allowed to bring that fact to the notice of the National Board before they decided anything?—Yes.

1502. But how could he bring that fact to the notice of the National Board before they decided, unless he had had notice of the action that you were going to take?—If there had been any such case as that, of course we would have heard him; we would have given him notice, and heard him, but we knew that was not the case.

1503. You do not know anything except officially?—But we knew what had not occurred.

1504. I am speaking of the actual official practice of the Board; officially you would know nothing of the suspension being set aside until it was brought before you?—Certainly not.

1505. Then ought you not, as a matter of practice in such a case as that, at all events, if not in all cases, to give the person whose case you are treating, notice of the action which you are about to take?—If we had the slightest idea that there was anything of that kind, you are quite right.

1506. *Chairman.*] We have been told that you had in this case the inchoate proceedings actually before the Board?—Yes, we had everything in that sense before us, and we knew that it had been all before the Poor Law Board.

1507. But you had the declaration, had you not?—Yes, and the defences.

1508. Mr. *Cross.*] And you had all that had been before the Poor Law Board?—Only as members of the public.

1509. That is precisely the way in which I understood Mr. Justice Lawson to state yesterday, information was often given by the Resident Commissioner upon facts which did not appear on the official documents?—I do not recollect any instance.

1510. You have given the instance of the action of the Poor Law Board which was in the cognizance of members of your Board?—As members of the public.

1511. And which no doubt influenced some of their minds?—It merely satisfied us that there was nothing that we could inquire into, before we entered into any full inquiry.

1512. Mr.

1512. *Mr. Bourke.*] With regard to the document of the defences which were produced by Mr. Justice Morris at the Board, to show, as he thought, the matter in issue between Mr. O'Keeffe and the defendant, I think you said that, according to the technical way in which the things were placed, it was impossible at that early stage and at the time Mr. Justice Morris produced it, to say what issue would be knit afterwards?—Yes.

1513. And you went on to say that, although that technically was so, yet practically it was before the Board what the real issue was?—Yes, that we could very fairly conjecture what it would be.

1514. *Mr. Whitbread.*] You have stated that you admit that the Board, on the 23rd of April, were aware that a suit had been commenced by the Rev. Mr. O'Keeffe; I want to ask you whether any motion was ever made by any member of the Board to wait the result of that trial?—No such motion was ever brought before us.

1515. The motion was, was it not, to give Father O'Keeffe a hearing before the Board, or an opportunity of giving explanations?—The motion was to give him notice, and, as I understood it, with a view to an explanation and a full hearing; that is, at least, what was conveyed to my mind.

1516. The words being, that the Rev. Father O'Keeffe should get notice, and have an opportunity of offering an explanation to the Board?—I have no doubt you state correctly the terms, and I may have misinterpreted it; but I interpreted it to mean, notice with a view to an explanation and a final full hearing of the case.

1517. But no notice was ever made to wait the result of the trial at all?—None. That may have been indicated in argument or discussion; but no such matter was ever brought before us.

Right Hon. Mr. Justice *Fitzgerald.*

12 June 1873.

The Right Honourable Mr. Justice *Lawson*, re-called; and further Examined.

1518. *Chairman.*] Do you wish to add anything to the evidence which you gave yesterday?—I wish, in consequence of something that fell from Mr. Justice Fitzgerald, to make an explanation. He stated that I made an error, which he was kind enough to call an unintentional one, when I stated that on the 23rd of April the matter in issue between Mr. O'Keeffe and Cardinal Cullen was pointed out to the Board. I beg to say that I made no error of any kind; the statement in my letter is this, that Mr. Justice Morris "pointed out that Mr. O'Keeffe denied the allegation that he had been suspended, and he read the pleadings in an action then and still pending in the Court of Queen's Bench, in which the very question whether he was suspended was in issue." Now, I have the pleadings before me which Mr. Justice Morris read on that occasion. The declaration is, that the Cardinal untruly stated that Mr. O'Keeffe was a suspended priest, and the plea which Mr. Justice Morris read upon that occasion was in this language: "The defendant says that, by reason and force of the said judgment and sentence, the plaintiff became, and was legally suspended from, and deprived of, the said office of parish priest." Therefore, the plaintiff was asserting that he never was suspended, and the defendant was asserting that he was legally suspended. It is quite true, that in the technical sense of the term, issues had not been settled, because that is not done till notice of trial is served; but it was plain to everyone that that question was involved in the litigation, and must be disposed of. Therefore, I did not make any mistake of any kind. If I used the words "issue knit," I did not mean in the technical sense of the term; I meant that the plaintiff alleged one matter, and the defendant another; perhaps the Committee will allow me to say that Mr. Justice Fitzgerald has made certain criticisms upon my letter, which I do not mean to notice, except to say that the letter is in substance a narrative, and a correct narrative, of the observations which I made at the Board; and as to the language which Mr. Justice Fitzgerald objects to about the "grave impropriety" of our pre-judging a case actually in litigation, and my statement that, according to my view our action had received "universal condemnation" from public opinion, these were matters which I stated at the Board, and which I allege in this letter, that I stated at the Board as my opinion, of course, but

Right Hon. Mr. Justice *Lawson.*

Right Hon. Mr. Justice *Lawson*, 12 June 1873.

but I did not expect the majority to agree in those opinions. I had a right to state them there, and I did so; and I had a right to state in this letter that I did state them; and I shall only say that I do not recede from any single observation contained in that letter.

The Reverend *Robert O'Keeffe*, called in; and Examined.

Rev. *R. O'Keeffe*.

1519. Dr. *Lyon Playfair*.] WHEN did you become Parish Priest of Callan? —In February 1863.

1520. At that time how many national schools had been under the management of your predecessor?—There were four national schools under the management of my predecessor, the Rev. Mr. Salmon.

1521. Were all of these non-vested?—No; two of them were non-vested, and two others were under a committee, or said to be under a committee.

1522. Who are the legal owners of the non-vested schools?—The parish was the legal owner of all the schools, and I, as representing the parish, on being appointed parish priest, took possession of all the schools on my coming to Callan, in the same way exactly as I took possession of the chapels of the parish, and the parochial house in which I live, in right of my being parish priest.

1523. Were you recognised by the Board of Education as the manager of these schools?—I wrote to the Board of Education on my arriving at Callan, and I said to the secretaries that I had been appointed parish priest, and I requested to be named in the office as the manager of the four schools of the parish, particularising their names, and the secretaries wrote to me that they had, in accordance with my wish, entered my name in their books as manager of the school at Coolagh and the school at Newtown; and they said, "With regard to the Male and Female Schools at Callan, as they are under a committee, we must request you to send us a request from the committee before we can name you as manager of these schools."

1524. And did the committee send a nomination on the 28th February 1863, nominating you to the Male and Female Schools of Callan?—On the receipt of this letter from the Education Office, I wrote a recommendation in these words: "We, the undersigned, recommend the Rev. Robert O'Keeffe to be named manager of the Callan Male and Female Schools;" and I signed that recommendation first with my own name, and I took that recommendation round to all the gentlemen that I thought were members of the school committee, and every gentleman to whom I applied for his name, and whom I found in his house at the time I called, gave me his name.

1525. Is that the document that was sent in to the National Board (*handing a document to the Witness*)?— Yes, that is the paper that I sent to the National Board.

1526. Is there any authority for this statement in the letter signed "Patrick Cody, J.P.," the secretary of the committee, on the 23rd of April 1873, addressed to the National Board, "We beg to inform you that that document is not genuine, the signatures to it are forgeries, and the committee never forwarded the Rev. Robert O'Keeffe's name to be recognised as manager by the National Board." Is there any truth in that statement?—There is no truth in it; it is entirely untrue.

1527. Look at the second signature (*handing the document to the Witness*)?— "Patrick Cody, J.P."

1528. That is the Patrick Cody who writes this letter?—Yes.

1529. Can you recognise that as the signature of Patrick Cody?—Yes; I am acquainted with his handwriting.

1530. Mr. *Bourke*.] Who forwarded that paper to the Education Office?—I sent it to the Education Office. "The above is forwarded in accordance with the directions in your letter of the 24th instant.—Respectfully, *Robert O'Keeffe*." That was after getting the signatures of these gentlemen, and they were all put down in my own presence.

1531. Dr. *Lyon Playfair*.] Did you yourself found any school after your appointment as parish priest?—Yes, about four months after my appointment to the

the parish of Callan I established a school, and it was chiefly a work school for the purpose of giving employment to grown females in knitting and netting. I gave a great deal of employment through that school for some years.

Rev. R. O'Keeffe.
18 June 1873.

1532. Was that school recognised as a national school?—That school was recognised from the beginning, on my application to the National Board, as a national school, and I was recognised as the patron and manager.

1533. And it became afterwards an infant school?—When the head teacher died, I changed it into an infant school for males and females under seven years of age.

1534. How long did you continue as manager of these schools in connection with the Board?—Up to the 25th of April 1872.

1535. At that date you received information, did you not, that your services as manager were no longer recognised?—Yes, they informed me that I had been removed from my office as manager, and that another gentleman had been appointed in my place to three of my schools, to the infant school as well as the two other schools.

1536. Before you received that dismissal, had you any intimation from the Board that such an act was in contemplation?—None whatever.

1537. Were there any grounds stated in the order of the dismissal as a justification for it?—There were no grounds except that the Board said that they had received a certificate from Dr. Moran, the Roman Catholic Bishop of Ossory, stating that I had been suspended from the exercise of all clerical functions, and that I therefore was unfit to be the manager.

1538. We do not want to go into the clerical part of it, but was it your contention that you never were suspended, and that you are *de jure* and *de facto* parish priest of Callan?—I have never been suspended, I am *de jure* and *de facto* parish priest of Callan, and have been for the last ten years.

1539. Do you admit that if you had been validly suspended, the Commissioners of Education would have been justified in removing you from the school?—No, not at all; they had nothing to say to my being suspended, or not suspended.

1540. How do you establish that?—I say that the Commissioners of Education had no right or power to remove me, whether I became a suspended priest or not. I received no office or appointment from the Commissioners, and therefore there was no office from which they were competent to remove me. I held possession of four of my schools, and their contents, in right of my being pastor of my people, exactly in the same way as I held possession of my parochial house, of my chapels with their contents, such as furniture and apparatus for public worship; and the Commissioners had no more right to dispossess me of my schools and put another manager in my place, than they had to put me out of my house, and place it at the disposal of the pretender to my parish. In fact, the Commissioners in their annual reports constantly inform the public, that the possession of all non-vested schools like mine remains in the hands of local parties, such as committees or individual patrons. In no case whatever, is it competent to the Commissioners to change the patrons or managers of non-vested schools; and their attempt to do so in the case of my five schools, was a gross blunder, and betrayed the most inexcusable ignorance of their own rules in the matter of the patronship and managership of schools. These rules, with great logical clearness, provide for all cases of recognition of patrons and managers, and of the subsequent changes which may take place by resignation or death, the only two ways in which any such change can take place.

1541. Do you contend that a patron cannot be dismissed?—I can show this clearly. A patron is a person, or a local body, who first, after providing a school and putting it into operation by appointing teachers and supplying the school with all necessary working apparatus, applies to the Board to be recognised as holding this position, and to be recorded in the office as the correspondent through whom salaries are to be transmitted, books and other school requisites supplied from the office, and returns made to the office from the schools. Assuming the patron to be unobjectionable, it is a matter of course that he is recognised at the Education Office as holding this position, and this recognition can never be cancelled unless the patron himself may choose to transfer his position and the possession of his schools to another party, or that the hand of death may separate him from it. From the day the patron is first recognised in the Education Office, his school must be at all times open to the district inspector, or any other officer of the Board

Rev. R. O'Keefe.
12 June 1873.

whose duty it is to see that the teachers are duly qualified for their office, that their character is good, that the school is supplied with suitable furniture and all necessary apparatus, that the school accounts are properly kept; and, in one word, that the school is in every way conducted in accordance with the rules of the Board. While this state of things continues, and the average daily attendance at the school is sufficient to entitle the teachers to payment of salaries, these salaries must be paid, whatever change the patron may personally have undergone in religion or morals. From being a Roman Catholic priest he may have become a Protestant clergyman, or *vice versa*; from being temperate and moral, he may have become intemperate and immoral; still, his change of personal condition can only be noticed by the Board when it is found to affect the school so as to cause the withdrawal of the children from the school, or otherwise produce irregularities in the school or teachers which would warrant the Board in visiting the teachers with fines, suspension, withdrawal of salaries, or perhaps erasing the school from the roll of the Board. The Board, in one word, has full power to deal with any irregularities appearing in the school or teachers; but it has nothing whatever to say to the morals or conduct of the patron. In truth, no man of honourable feeling would have his name recorded in the Education Office as the patron of a school if he thought that he was thereby subjecting his morals to the supervision of a public Board that could, as has been done in my case, publicly pronounce him degraded without leaving him any means of defending his character. All this reasoning applies in spirit and in letter to the case of my infant school, which was established by myself four months after my appointment to Callan. It was originally established as a work school for adult females, and I gave, through this school, much employment to grown girls, chiefly in knitting and netting; but after my principal teacher died in 1865, I converted it into an infant school for males and females under seven years of age. The average daily attendance continued at about the same figure, say 60, and three teachers were continued in pay, a principal, an assistant, and a monitor. By the rules of the Board I was both patron and manager of this school, and could at any time have retained the patronship, appointing a manager to correspond with the Board; and this manager might be either one of my own curates or any other gentleman, lay or clerical.

1542. Would the same principles that you contend for as to the Infant School apply also to the Callan Male and Female Schools?—No; I shall state the circumstances regarding those schools; the case is very different. I took possession of the Callan Male and Female Schools, as parish priest, on my appointment to the parish; but before I was recognised in any way by the Education Board, I had to send to the office a recommendation from the schools' committee, it being a rule of the Board that when schools are under a committee, such committee must name an individual to act as manager and correspondent; and if the person thus named be unobjectionable, he must be recognised by the Board, and can only be removed from his position by an act of the committee, his condition being, in relation to the Board, exactly the same as that of a manager appointed to the office by an individual patron. When the Commissioners, therefore, undertook to remove me from my position as manager of these schools, they acted in opposition to their own rule, and in violation of the acknowledged right of the Committee to continue or remove me at pleasure. That is the case with regard to Callan Male and Female Schools.

1543. Have you any remark to make with regard to your schools at Coolagh and Newtown?—Yes; theirs is a different case altogether. I shall state very briefly the circumstances of those schools also. I took possession of these schools, the Coolagh and Newtown Schools, also as of the Callan Schools, as a matter of right, on my appointment to the parish, and having their possession, I applied to the Board to be recognised as holding this position, and I was, as a matter of course, so recognised as manager of them, in accordance with the 7th Rule of the Board, which compels the Commissioners to recognise the successor of a deceased clerical patron, without any inquiry as to his social position, the presumption being that no such inquiry can be needed. Both these schools were provided by a former predecessor of mine, and put by him, in connection with the Board, just as my present Infant School was by me, and he (the Rev. John Mullens) was patron as well as manager, but in these cases it is the practice of the Education Office to designate the person simply as manager, treating him as both manager and patron. I was really, therefore, patron

patron of the Coolagh and Newtown Schools in succession to the founder, and could, as in the case of my infant school, have continued patron, and have appointed at any time any other unobjectionable gentleman, lay or clerical, as manager. The irregularity of the Board's proceeding in all the five cases of my schools has arisen from a want of sufficient acquaintance with its own rules, and the unfounded belief that non-vested schools, as well as those vested in the Board, were all equally in its possession, and that this possession could be transferred, at the will and pleasure of the Board, from one gentleman to another.

Rev. R. O'Keeffe.

19 June 1873.

1544. Does the case of your removal from these schools differ in any way from the precedents which have been laid before Parliament, as having guided the Board on former occasions?—Yes, the circumstances of my removal differ very materially from the circumstances of the cases in which other gentlemen are said to have been removed. In all the cases quoted as precedents to justify the action of the Board in my case, it would appear that the clergymen suspended acknowledged the validity of the sentence passed on them, though denying its justice; whereas my case is that the censures passed on me were not only unjust, but completely null and void. They were so manifestly invalid that I could not properly take any notice of them.

1545. But, assuming for the moment, that in the opinion of the Board you were validly suspended, was not the Board justified by these precedents in removing you from the managership of these schools?—Not at all. I will explain the difference. In all the cases quoted as precedents, the Board acted plainly *ultra vires*, and in clear opposition to its own rules. And from these rules the Board cannot depart without breaking faith with all the patrons and managers of schools who have connected their schools with the Board in the belief that these rules which have the sanction of the Government would be always adhered to.

1546. Does not the Board, by its rules, reserve to itself the right of refusing to recognise any unfit or objectionable person?—The Board reserves to itself the right to judge of the fitness of a person to be patron of a school, when that person first applies to have his school taken into connection; but if his position be once recognised, no question of his fitness can afterwards arise. In the same way, whenever a committee or a patron recommends a manager to be recognised as such for the first time, the Board has the right to entertain the question of his fitness, but not afterwards. If a manager should be once recognised as a fit person to represent a committee, or an individual patron, he can only be removed from that office by the committee or patron that appointed him to it.

1547. Do you think that the same thing holds good when a person applies to the Board for a recognition as the successor to a previous patron or manager?—Yes; the successor of a clerical patron, or the legal representative of a lay patron, is assumed as a matter of course to be fit to act as patron, and no right is reserved to the Board under its rules to pronounce an opinion on the fitness of a patron so succeeding.

1548. But if you look at Rule 7 you will see the words, "if no valid objection exist;" how do you explain these terms?—I can best explain this by an example. I was 11 years patron and manager of two schools, while I was curate in the parish of Ballyragget, in the county of Kilkenny, and in 1860 I recommended my successor for recognition at the Education Office. Before doing so, however, it was necessary for me to get the approbation of the parish priest, as without it I could not transfer the possession of the schools to the curate who succeeded me, nor could he be recognised at the office. The person who applies to be recognised as patron of a school, either when first putting it into connection with the Board or in succession to another patron, is always supposed to have the school in his possession, and to be in a position to guarantee that the school will be always open to the visits of the Board's officers; and if he have not such possession, a most valid objection to his recognition would exist. That is the meaning of the clause.

1549. How many of these five schools are now open?—Four of the schools are still in operation.

1550. And under your management?—Under my management; they have always been under my management.

1551. Is there any ground for stating that, previous to your dismissal, these schools

Rev. R. O'Keeffe.
18 June 1873.

schools were in a less efficient state than ordinary national schools?—No; on the contrary, they were in a most highly efficient state.

1552. Is it not a fact, that in the case of the school which was for some time struck off by the Board the objection of the Board or the inspector chiefly was, that it was educationally too good, and not that it was too bad?—Yes; the great fault was that I was teaching the boys to talk French, in school and in play hours.

1553. And their exercises were conducted in French, were they not?—Some of them. I connected the school with the Science and Art Department at South Kensington. I may say, for the information of the Committee, that I established Christian Brothers in Callan in the year 1868; and when I was doing that, I did not anticipate that the Christian Brothers would treat me as they did subsequently. They set themselves up in opposition to me and national schools, and succeeded in drawing away all the children from my male national school, except seven, in a spirit of opposition to me and national education, and I felt that I had been very badly treated, and I exerted myself to re-establish the school, and to improve the course of instruction given in it so as to attract children to it; and I was most successful. Amongst the means which I adopted for improving the character of the teaching and the school was, first, to engage a very competent teacher, who had been a teacher under the National Board, and was entitled to receive salary under the National Board; but I made him a large addition to the salary payable to him from the National Board; and shortly after that, the teacher being competent to teach abstract science, algebra, geometry, mechanics, and so on, and physical science, I formed a local school committee, and connected the school with South Kensington, and I improved the school in many ways. I will mention one particular. In the year 1871 Colonel Hassart was sent from the Curragh Camp to make an inspection of the science class. He was met at the school by me and some other members of my committee; he examined that class, and it so happens that the boy called up to the board to demonstrate a proposition in Euclid was asked to write down the proposition on the board in chalk, and he did it in the French language. the 47th of the First Book, and made a diagram, and demonstrated the proposition, and while doing that used no language but French. The other boys merely wrote down the proposition on their own slates, and listened to the demonstration given by the boy called to the board.

1554. It was practically not because the education was had, but because it was higher than that of National Schools, that that school was removed by the Board?—As far as I was able to learn, that was the objection to it.

1555. And was it not the fact, that afterwards, upon your complying with the rules of the Board, and the standard of education, that school was taken into connection again?—When they informed me that it was necessary to make some change, and that I should not require boys to say lessons in French, I met their requirements.

1556. *The O'Conor Don.*] So far as you are aware, the only ground upon which this school was struck off the Board was your using the French language?—There were several other objections made which did not come to my knowledge, they were made behind my back, and I was never given an opportunity of contradicting them.

1557. The only one ever brought before you was the one with reference to the French language?—There was a very natural objection raised in the beginning, after I had appointed this teacher, who was a very competent man to give instruction, but was a person who had incurred censure with the National Board previously. When I intimated to the Resident Commissioner that I had appointed this person (his name was Walter Hawe) as teacher in my national school he made some objection about my naming him to a position under the Board; but after some reasoning with him, it was agreed with the Resident Commissioner, Mr. Macdonnell, that I might employ this person, Mr. Hawe, even though he had been censured by the Board previously for some misconduct, because I certified to Mr. Macdonnell that, during the interval between the censure passed upon him at the office of the National Board and the time I engaged him, his conduct had been good.

1558. The Committee would not care to go into detail upon that point; will you state, in a general way, what were the other objections?—That man, who was several years out of the employment of the Board, was called for examination

nation before the inspector, at Kilkenny, and it turned out that he appeared before the inspector, at Kilkenny, under the influence of drink, and the inspector reported this to the Education Board, and the Commissioners of Education informed me that they would not allow me to engage the services of this man at all, and required me to dismiss him. However, I did not immediately dismiss him, because I relied after all on being able to offer some excuse for the misconduct, and I still held him on; and after he had been teaching about nine or ten months, when they considered that he had gone a sufficient time to do away with the effects of the fault that he had committed, or make reparation for it, they agreed to take him into pay, but they fined him 42 *l.*, and I paid that fine for him.

Rev. *R. O'Keeffe.*
19 June 1873.

1559. Was there no information ever given to you that the inspector had reported to the Board that a great number of the Board's rules were broken, "That for a long time no record of the daily attendance was kept. The teacher, Mr. Hawe, was prevented by the manager from keeping the school accounts, which prohibition was maintained to the end, notwithstanding that repeated letters were written to the manager on the subject. When the accounts of the attendance were kept, they were kept either by the Rev. Mr. O'Keeffe himself, or by a young lad deputed by him for the purpose. That when the head inspector visited the school on the 19th of November 1869, he found that from the 1st of the preceding January up to that date, no record whatever had been made of the attendance in either the roll book or report book, but that when the district inspector visited in September 1870, he found the report book filled up for the entire 12 months of 1869, but the numbers on rolls and in attendance were in every case identical, and appeared to have been written off at the same moment of time. That in November 1869, the head inspector recommended that a progressive salary should be awarded to Mr. Hawe, the teacher, on certain conditions, one of which was, that the school should be organised and conducted as a national school, and in strict accordance with the rules and regulations of the Commissioners; the district inspector having reported in September 1870, that this condition had, up to that time, been totally disregarded, the school was struck off the roll, and all grants cancelled by the Board order." Was none of that information afforded to you, or was this report communicated to you?—It was communicated to me about half a year ago.

1560. But none of these reports were communicated to you when they were made to the Board?—Here is all that was communicated to me (*handing in certain returns*); those are the only two reports that the inspector made in reference to the school in the years 1870 and 1871; there were some trifling irregularities about the keeping of accounts.

1561. Is it not stated in this report "that the index register and rolls do not exactly balance"?—Yes.

1562. That "accounts were not properly kept"?—Yes.

1563. That "the report book is incomplete"?—Yes.

1564. In this statement therefore furnished upon the 19th of December 1870, there are those complaints made against the school which you have not mentioned?—These are the complaints I received; but will you allow me to explain the nature of those papers. I have taken this from what is called the district inspector's observation book which is kept in the school; whenever the district inspector comes to make an inspection of the school, and to make an examination of the children, if he finds any matters that require to be corrected, any irregularities, anything wrong about the teachers, or about the accounts, or anything else, it is his duty to note those irregularities in his observation book for the information of the manager; the manager then, in course of time, looks into the observation book, and sees what remarks the inspector has made, and then if there be anything that requires correction, it is the duty of the manager to see that it is corrected.

1565. I only want the fact, not the reasons, but the fact that it was communicated to you by having been written in the way you describe that these irregularities existed?—That contains the observations of the inspector during two years, and he made none others, and whenever he made an observation it was attended to by me; I most carefully attended to it.

1566. Outside this statement, and the matter about the French language, was there no information given to you by the Board that there was anything against the school?—At one time there was something; the inspector said that when he

0.93.   U   came

Rev. R. O'Keeffe.
12 June 1873.

came into the school the teacher refused to let him see the account-book, and I was written to and informed that that would not be allowed, but I never prevented his seeing it.

1567-8. Were there not several complaints outside what you have mentioned, against your management of the school, which complaints were reported to you either by letter, or by order, or by minute from the Board?—No, there was never anything against my management of the school; there could be nothing against the management of the school. You mistake the duties of the officials at the Education Board. It is not their business, or the business of an inspector, to say anything about a manager at all. If they find any irregularities in a school, the inspector, on finding these to exist, will write to the Education Office, and the Education Office will write to the manager, asking the manager to direct the teacher to correct the irregularities; but they would not take the liberty of saying that I was irregular in any manner. It is not their duty to look after the character and conduct of the manager at all, but after the conduct of the teachers and the officers of the school.

1569. Were there complaints made, outside the complaint embodied in this report, and the complaint that the language used in the school was French, of the way in which the school was conducted; or were such complaints made to you in any form whatever from the Board?—I do not know that they have complained that the language used was French; but one of the inspectors informed me personally that that was the objection to my school, that French was used as the language of the school, and that instruction was given in the French language. I told that to another inspector, and he said it was a gross mistake on the part of the Education Commissioners to suppose there was any violation of the rules in the boys talking French in a national school. There was a complaint made to me, intimated in writing, that upon one occasion when the inspector came to visit the male and female schools in Callan, he was told by the teachers in both schools that he could not see the school records. There was a very good reason why he could not see the school records of the female school on that day, because the school records were in the Education Office on that very day. I had sent them a few days previously to the Education Office, because some time previously to that the district inspector of the school had reported to the Education Office that my female teacher had falsified her accounts, and in order to show to the Education Office that she had not, I sent up the accounts to the Education Office, and pointed out that it was a false and malicious charge to make against her. The inspector went upstairs then to the male schools, and he was told by a monitor in the school that he, the monitor, was directed not to show him the accounts, and the inspector then said to the principal teacher, "Do you refuse to give me the accounts, I am the inspector of the district," and the teacher then at once went over to the desk and handed him the accounts; so that he was never refused permission to inspect the school accounts except when they were in the Education Office.

1570. I do not ask you as to whether any of those facts were proved, but whether statements were not made by the Board as to certain irregularities being committed in your school, outside of the one of using French as the language of the school?—The district inspector reported to the Education Office that he was told by the master in the school (this person who had been removed for the act of intemperance) that I would not allow the master to keep the accounts, and that I wished the accounts to be kept by a monitor of the school.

1571. Now, with respect to the alleged falsification of the accounts, of course you hold that that allegation was never proved; but is it or is it not the fact that the Commissioners, so far as their decision goes, decided that it was proved?—That was with regard to the first five or six months of the year 1869, when the school had gone down, and when the children had been all drawn away, and there were only a few, namely, seven, scholars in attendance. It was then that I appointed this able and competent man to give instruction, and I intended to raise the character of the school for giving a good class of education; preparing boys, in fact, for the Civil Service and for the learned professions, with the aid that I myself intended to give the teacher in teaching in the school. For the first few months, say for the first six months, the accounts were not kept at all, that is to say, the entries were not made every day; and then the inspector, in allusion to that, states in this report of his, "From my observation these entries

can

can be supplied." It was easy to supply the entries, because there were only a few boys; six of them were boarders, belonging to Mr. Howe, and 8 or 10 of the others (there were about 20 altogether at that time) were boys that came in from the country to live in town, in order to have the benefit of Mr. Hawe's instruction and mine to prepare them for something above the ordinary course of education of small farmers' children; those boys came as scholars every day to the school; so that there was no necessity of entering their names in one place as on the roll, and in another place as in actual attendance; but when the inspector desired, for the sake of regularity, to have these defects supplied, the thing was done.

Rev. R. O'Keeffe.

12 June 1873

1572. Was there never any charge then of falsification of the accounts on the part of the female teacher?—Mr. Harkin, the district inspector, came to the school one day, and it was after roll-call, the children had been called, and the attendance was entered regularly in the books; he counted the children, and found 65 present; he said to the teacher, "You have 78 entered in the Daily Report Book; how is this that you have 15 children entered who are not in school?" "I do not know," she said, "except in this way, all those that I have entered answered their names when I called the roll: the children were permitted to leave at play hour, and 15 of them must have remained away, gone home, and not come back;" and immediately the principal teacher directed one of the monitors to go round with a slate and to try and ascertain the names of the children who had gone away, and this monitor brought back immediately on the slate the names of six of the children, and the teacher handed the slate, with the names of six of the children written upon it, to the inspector, and he said, "You are too late now." Subsequently, during the day, the names of the other children who had been missing when the inspector called, but whose attendance had been recorded in the rolls of the school, were ascertained; and notwithstanding that, the inspector reported to the Education Office that the female teacher, on the occasion of his visit that day, had exaggerated the attendance by 15.

1573. And the Board ratified that report of the inspector?—They never told me that they ratified it. The Board on that report of the inspector, depressed my female teacher a step. Of course I resented this, and I wrote a very strong letter to the Board, and I charged the inspector with making the deliberately false and malicious charge against my teacher of having falsified her accounts. There was no investigation afterwards into the charge which I made against the inspector, and I was never informed what the result of the investigation was. I may say that the teacher has taken an action now against the inspector. When she could get no redress from the Education Office for the injury done her, she has served a writ upon the inspector, and the case is to come to trial at the next Assizes at Kilkenny, next month; her action against the inspector is for maliciously representing her at the Education Office as having falsified her accounts.

1574. Now I understand you distinctly to state that these schools are parochial schools?—Well, I do not know what you mean by parochial schools; you are using a technical term. The four schools are schools that I hold in my possession, and I took possession of them the day I became parish priest, as being the property of the parish, I representing the parish.

1575. Two of the schools you took possession of when you became parish priest were under the patronage of a committee?—They were said to be under the patronage of a committee. I do not believe that they are. I did not want to get into a controversy with the Education Office, but I knew very well they were not; but when they said, "You must send a recommendation from the committee," I said, "I will go and get a recommendation, and send it up to you; you may think what you like, but I will have my own thoughts about it."

1576. You got the nomination at least of the committee?—I got those seven names with my own to that paper, and in virtue of that I was recognised by the Education Office; but I took possession of the schools, not by leave of the committee nor by anybody else's, but as I did of my parish chapel, because I was the representative of the parish.

1577. I see the first name attached to these signatures of the trustees is your own?—Yes.

1578. Were you one of the committee?—These gentlemen say that there is a committee, and if there is one, the parish priest ought to be a member of it, and

0.93.   U 2   *ex officio*

Rev. R. O'Keeffe.
12 June 1873.

ex officio chairman; he ought to sign his own name first to any recommendation of a manager for recognition by the Education Board.

1579. You thought that the parish priest had an ex officio right to be a member of the committee?—Yes. Of course by my taking that letter to those gentlemen I was appointing them members of the committee, if they were not members of it before. The parish priest names the committee, every one of them.

1580. You had a teacher of the name of Mary Ann Phelan?—She was in one of the schools when I went to Callan.

1581. How long had she been there?—Over 20 years.

1582. Was she a very good teacher?—Yes.

1583. First division, first class?—Yes, for a good many years.

1584. And you dismissed her?—Yes.

1585. On what ground?—Because she disowned my authority; she became, as we say at Callan, a schismatic.

1586. How did she disown your authority?—She disowned my authority as parish priest; she went over to the side of the curates and the bishop and the cardinal.

1587. In what way?—By absenting herself from my church and going to the church of the opposition.

1588. You dismissed her for absenting herself from your church?—I dismissed her. I sent for her, and asked her, "Miss Phelan, you are aware that Paschal time has now ended; have you been at communion during Paschal time?" "Yes," she said. "You are aware that people give disedification if they do not receive communion during Paschal time; and where have you received communion?" "In the city of Kilkenny." "Why did you not receive communion in your parish church?" "Why," she said, "one does not know what to do; one says one thing and another another; and one does not know whom to acknowledge as parish priest." "Well," I said, "that is nice language to come from you, and I request that you will consider yourself as teacher of the school no longer."

1589. You dismissed her at once, although she had been over 20 years teaching in the school, because she had gone to communion not in your chapel but in Kilkenny?—Because she had not received communion in Paschal time in her parish church, in compliance with the canon of the General Council of Lateran, which requires all the faithful of both sexes to receive communion at Paschal time in their own church. That we consider a very gross violation of duty.

1590. The cathedral church of the diocese is not a sufficient place?—No, the faithful are bound to receive it in their own church, or by permission of the priest in another place.

1591. With respect to the Coolagh National School; that for some time was under the management of Mr. Martin, was it not?—No, it was not; they thought it was. I suspected that they had that on their own minds; but I did not care about interfering until it answered my purpose.

1592. Were not the quarterly returns furnished through Mr. Martin?—I will tell you how it happened: after I was removed from the office of manager of the schools, I still sent up the returns in the usual way, when the quarter became due, the 1st of July 1872. The papers were all sent back to me; I got them filled up in the usual way, giving the average attendance for the quarter, and the receipts signed by the teachers, and then I counter-signed all these documents to certify that they were correct, and sent them up to the Education Office for my five schools, and they all came back to me, and I was told, "You are no longer manager of those schools, and we can pay you no salaries." The papers lay over, and I paid the salaries out of my own pocket. In the meantime, this Mr. Martin was calling upon them to send up returns and receipts through him. Of course I told the teachers that they were to do no such thing. As long as they could not get it from the Education Board, I guaranteed payment to them, and that understanding prevailed with all the four teachers, and also the Coolagh teacher, for a considerable time; but after some considerable time I had reason to suspect that he was going over to the other side, and I brought to him the returns that I had sent up to the Education Office just for the sake of trying whether he was faithful or not. "Now," I said, "perhaps it is as well after all that you should get paid from the Education Office; I am running short of money, and I may not be able to pay you next time; send up those papers returned to me to the Education Office, but erase my name,

SELECT COMMITTEE ON CALLAN SCHOOLS. 157

Rev. R. O'Keeffe.

12 June 1873.

name, and write down, 'William Martin' in my place, and then when the papers go up to the Education Office a Post-office Order will be sent down for you to Mr. Martin; go to Mr. Martin this evening and tell him I have told you to do this." The teacher did what I said, and when the papers went up to the Education Office, I found that the man proved false to me, and that he had underhand given his sanction to Mr. Martin as the manager of the school. So I wrote at once to the Education Office; I said, "Now, as you do not choose to recognise me as manager of the Coolagh Schools, I gave permission to the teacher in those schools to receive the salary through Mr. Martin, but I have not allowed him to acknowledge the authority of Mr. Martin in any other way, nor have I allowed the interference of Mr. Martin with my managership in any way whatever, except to that extent, and if you refuse now to recognise me as manager of the schools as before, I will have the schools closed."

1593. So you got this teacher to sign Mr. Martin's name to this return without consulting Mr. Martin at all?—You do not understand it. There were at the time three quarters' salaries due to the teacher; the papers for one quarter's salary had been filled up and sent by me to the Education Office; they came back to me, and I took out these papers to the teacher at Coolagh, and said, "You have nothing to do but to erase my name and write 'William Martin.' With reference to the other papers, you have to fill them up and sign your name to them, and take them in to Mr. Martin, and he will certify that they are correct, and countersign the receipts; then Mr. Martin will be sent a Post-office Order for all the money due to you, and that due to me; and when you get this bring me the amount which I paid to you and keep the other part."

1594. *Chairman.*] Do I correctly understand you that you desired him to erase your name and insert that of Mr. Martin?—Yes; on the face of the paper.

1595. Thereby saying, in fact, that Mr. Martin verified the accuracy of the return?—That was with regard to the one already certified, and found to be correct; but I told him, with regard to the other two, that he was to bring them in to Mr. Martin.

1596. I want to know about the first one that was actually certified by you to be correct?—The first one was certified by me nine months before, and lay over.

1597. To be correct; that the account was correct?—Yes.

1598. Then do I understand you rightly to say that you authorised the teacher to erase your name and substitute that of Mr. Martin?—And to go and tell Mr. Martin.

1599. But not to tell the Commissioners?—To let Mr. Martin forward it for the sake of getting the money that was due; that I wished, in one word, for my own sake, and for the sake of the teacher (for my own sake, because I had advanced to him a quarter's salary, and I wished to get it back), and then for the sake of the teacher himself, to get the three quarters' salaries, I gave him permission to get the money through Mr. Martin, and told him to take in the two additional forms to Mr. Martin to have his signature; but with regard to this form returned to me, I said, "You have nothing to do, in reference to that, but to erase my name and substitute Mr. Martin's."

1600. All this time did Mr. Martin know anything about the accuracy of these returns, or was it you only who knew about it?—The accuracy of the returns, where the paper was already filled, was undoubted; I knew no more about it than Mr. Martin. The universal practice is this in those cases: the teacher is in a country school two or three miles off; when the quarter comes round the teacher makes out the returns and he brings them in to the manager, and the manager, as a matter of course, just puts his name only to the returns; and if there is any flaw or error it is the teacher that furnishes the return and is accountable; the manager is not accountable for anything that is wrong, it is the teacher of the school.

1601. *The O'Conor Don.*] Does not the document to which you, according to your own admission, got this teacher to write Mr. Martin's name without his knowledge, conclude in this way: "I certify the above to be correct, having examined and checked the class rolls, register, and report book"?—I told him to go at once to Mr. Martin.

1602. *Chairman.*] Will you say whether you did not desire the teacher to put the

0.93. U 3

Rev. *R. O'Keeffe*.
12 June 1873.

the name of Mr. Martin, who had not been manager and could know nothing about it, in the place of yourself, who had been manager and did know something about it?—I told him to go to Mr. Martin and to get him to sign the two forms not yet filled; but with regard to this form that had gone up to the Education Office already, and that had been returned to me to put Mr. Martin's name on it, and on the receipt, " Nothing is to be done with regard to this, but erase my name and put Father Martin's on it, and tell him that I told you to do so," I said.

1603. *The O'Conor Don*.] You do not know whether the teacher ever told the Rev. Mr. Martin about it?—Father Martin says that he did not.

1604. Does not Father Martin write, upon this return being sent down to him, "Gentlemen, I beg to return you the enclosed quarterly return, and, in reply to your letter of the 18th instant, inquiring if the signature affixed to it is mine, I beg to say that it is not, but is a forgery. I visited the above school on to-day, and asked the teacher (Pierce Funchion) if he knew anything about it, and he said not, and never saw the sheet signed by anyone since he gave the return to Rev. R. O'Keeffe last June. I am, &c. (signed) *William Martin* "?— That is a complete untruth; he did it in my own presence, and in the presence of several of the children. I do not know what he told Father Martin afterwards.

1605. But in your presence, and under your direction, he signed the name of the Rev. Father Martin to a certificate, by which he professes to have examined and checked the class rolls, register, and report book?—Yes, but it was a certificate that had gone to the office nine months before, and had come back and was lying over. It was just to save the trouble of making out a new form. I said, " This is done already, but make out two additional forms for the other quarters, and tell Father Martin I told you to put his name in place of mine on this one, and then the post office order will come. Then pay me what I advanced to you and keep the rest; you will get the money."

1606. With regard to the case of Woods, the National Board it appears after some litigation granted to Mr. Woods his arrears of salary equal to 12 *l*. 10 *s*., and you applied to the Board for the payment of that salary to you, Woods having gone to America; is not that so; the result of the action was, that the Commissioners agreed to pay those arrears of salary, amounting to 12 *l*. 10 *s*., to Woods?—When Woods was going to America in April 1872, I was at the time the recognised manager of the school; Woods had been 10 months acting as assistant teacher, and the Board of Education should have paid Woods' salary as assistant teacher. I was entitled to appoint Woods at the time that I did, and in the appointment of Woods, and in the discharge of duty by Woods during the time that he was assistant teacher, the Board's rules were complied with in every particular, and still the Board would not pay Woods; and I said to Woods when he was going to America (he was obliged to go, because he had no means of support; he was living by his employment as assistant in the school; I helped him to go to America, and he had some engagement from the other side), " I will make these Commissioners of Education pay you this salary that is due to you: they have treated you very badly;" and he was very thankful to me for saying so, and I took authority from him to proceed against the Commissioners of Education for the salary due, and he filled a receipt in blank, in order that I might have a proper voucher to pass to the Education Office, whenever they would agree to pay the salary due to Woods. He was 10 months doing the duty of a second assistant teacher at the time, and there was no question at the time that the salary was due to him; the Board were bound, though not in law it appears, yet in honour and justice, to pay Woods, because I complied with the requirements of the Board in reference to his appointment, and Woods did his duty in every way in compliance with the rules. I took this receipt in blank from Woods, and I proceeded against the Education Commissioners before the Recorder of Dublin, and the Recorder of Dublin dismissed the case of Woods, on the ground that the Commissioners are not bound to pay salaries to any teachers.

1607. I want to ask you, not the grounds upon which this litigation took place with Woods, but whether Mr. Woods, having been awarded 12 *l*. 10 *s*., as the salary due to him, an application was made by his mother to have 7 *l*. 10 *s*. of that 12 *l*. 10 *s*. paid to her?—It would appear from this return, that a letter was written by some one in Callan; that, I suppose, was his mother.

1608. Did

SELECT COMMITTEE ON CALLAN SCHOOLS. 159

1608. Did you upon the 1st of May 1873 write this letter to the Commissioners: "Gentlemen,—I have received from you a copy of a letter which you say you have addressed to Stephen Woods, late assistant teacher in my Callan Male School, and in which you say that I claim the whole amount due to him, although you knew very well that Woods signed the receipt I sent you, simply for the purpose of enabling me to pass a proper voucher for the money whenever you could be got to pay it. Your statement is an infamous lie"?—Yes, it was an infamous lie. The infamous lie was their representing to Woods that I wanted to keep the money for myself, when I swore in a court of justice that Woods gave me his name on a blank form, in order that I might have a proper voucher to give. They wanted to make out that I wanted the money for myself personally. I had a distinct understanding with Woods that I would send to Woods the balance of the money due to him after paying myself the money I had advanced him for going to America.

Rev. R. O'Keeffe.

12 June 1873.

1609. Did the Commissioners ever make that statement of which you have spoken?—Yes; on page 28 I find this letter of mine: "I have your letter of yesterday's date, and am to inform you that the receipt was duly signed by Stephen Woods on the 1st of April last, when I was the recognised manager of the Callan Male School, and passed to me as a voucher for your office in the event of your consenting to pay the money due." And I swore this in a court of justice on the occasion of the trial: "This was done on the occasion of my getting authority from Woods to sue you for his salary, and my making him an advance to enable him to emigrate from a country where your infernal injustice rendered him unable any longer to live. I will bring the case before a court and jury if you will not send me the 12 l. 10 s." They wanted to make out that I wanted to keep 12 l. 10 s. for myself; they wrote to Woods to tell him to withdraw the authority which he gave me for receiving the money.

1610. Have you any authority for that last statement?—I have their letter to Woods.

1611. Mr. *Whitbread*.] Your contention is that you took possession of the schools of right the moment that you became parish priest of Callan?—One of the schools I established myself, and have always paid the rent of it, and it is my own private school that I can hand over to whom I like. But with regard to the other four schools, I took possession of these four schools in right of my being the parish priest, and thereby representing the parish to whom the schools belonged as public property, exactly in the same way that I took possession of my chapels, and the contents and apparatus for public worship, and everything else that was parochial property.

1612. And your view is that the parish priest, and no one but the parish priest, had a right to those four schools?—Had a right to the possession. The Commissioners of Education do not at all distinguish between managers and managers under the Board, and patrons and patrons under the Board. I became the manager of these schools by the fact of taking possession of them. I was the manager the same as I am now, and the legal owner for the time being the same as I am at present.

1613. And if you had gone to another parish, your successor would have of right succeeded as parish priest to the legal ownership and patronship of those schools?—No, that is not it; only when I transferred the possession to him. By leaving the parish I do not abandon the possession; and when the new parish priest comes in during my lifetime, if that is the case you suppose, he does not, as a matter of course, walk into possession of all the holdings that I possessed; I must give him possession; I must transfer possession.

1614. Then you must modify the statement that you made in reply to my first question, must you not?—No.

1615. I think you told me that when you became parish priest you entered as of right into the position of manager?—Because the late man was dead, and had lost possession by his death.

1616. Did you succeed upon his death?—No; there was a curate in the meantime that was manager of the four schools for six or eight months, Mr. Rowan; he was temporary manager; the Board always in those cases, in order not to interfere with the ordinary course of business where the person entitled to the management of the school is not forthcoming, appoint a temporary manager, and he is supposed to cease the duties of his office when the person who is entitled

Rev. R. O'Keeffe.
12 June 1873.

to become the manager of the schools under the Board applies for their management; the other party resigns.

1617. Then is your position this; that having succeeded upon the death of your predecessor as parish priest of Callan, you became possessed of the property of those schools, which could not, even if you had been removed to any other parish, have passed by right to your successor at Callan, unless you transferred them to him?—Yes; during my lifetime it is supposed I divest myself of possession in favour of the party who succeeds me; but if I am dead, the person who succeeds me takes possession of all the property in my hands as representative of the parish, and that includes the parochial schools.

1618. Do you mean that you could have transferred the property of those Callan Schools to anyone else but your successor in the office of parish priest?—I do not mean to say that I could do it properly; I should be doing wrong. When I was transferred from the parish of Rathdowny to the parish of Callan, the clergyman who succeeded me in Rathdowny as parish priest could not be recognised in the Education Office until I resigned in his favour, and I was six months manager of the schools of Rathdowny, in the parish that I had left, after I had gone to Callan, before I resigned in favour of the clergyman who succeeded me. In the case of parties who are living, and who are once recognised at the Education Office as patrons of schools, their names cannot be erased from the rolls of the Education Office while they live, except by their own act of resignation.

1619. *Chairman.*] I understood you to say in the earlier part of your examination that you succeeded to these schools the moment you became parish priest?—You do not distinguish between the two things. I had nothing at all to say to the Education Office, the day I became parish priest; it rested with me after I became parish priest and took as a matter of right the schools as well as the chapels to say, "Shall I unite these schools with the Education Office."

1620. I did not ask you anything about connection with the Board; I asked you about possession of the schools, and I understood you (and I believe rightly) to say, that the moment you became parish priest of Callan, you entered as of right upon possession of the schools?—Yes.

1621. And you said so because they were parochial property?—Yes.

1622. Then I suppose, if you ceased to be parish priest of Callan, the school being parochial property would pass to the person who succeeded you as parish priest?—Yes; but if I were alive, I should transfer possession.

1623. I am not speaking of the Board at all, but when you left Callan, and somebody else was legitimately appointed to be parish priest at Callan, that somebody else would be in the position in which you were when you came to Callan?—Yes; but I hold everything parochial until I put it into his hands.

1624. Supposing you had gone to a different country, and had left Callan altogether, and somebody else had been properly appointed in your place, would not that somebody else have taken possession of the parochial property?—Because in that case the property would be abandoned; but if I was living, and in the locality, I should be in possession of it till I handed it over to him, or a caretaker on his part.

1625. You hold that you are *de jure* and *de facto* parish priest of Callan at this moment?—Of course I do.

1626. But suppose that you were not, but that somebody else were *de jure* and *de facto* parish priest at Callan, would not that somebody else have a right to the possession of the schools?—Then I think I ought to cease having any right to the possession of anything parochial in conscience; I would be doing wrong if I claimed the exercise of any authority over parochial property after I had ceased to be parish priest.

1627. Is there anything else that you wish to state?—Would you allow me to say a word in reference to the circumstance of my being suspended, chiefly with regard to how I stood before the Poor Law Commissioners, because you asked certain gentlemen whether my case was the same before the Poor Law Commissioners and at the Education Board; there is a great difference. The Poor Law Commissioners could not have properly or legally dismissed me from the office of chaplain of the Callan Union Workhouse, unless I had become suspended at least *primâ facie*; but I will admit that even in the case of suspension only *primâ facie*, I should be removed. It was the duty of the Commissioners to see

that

that my spiritual ministrations to the paupers confined in the workhouse were above all exception. If, however, I could in no sense be considered a suspended priest, then my removal, even though holding office at the pleasure of the Commissioners, was improper and illegal as long as I was the officiating priest of the district, who by law is entitled to a preference. My suspension by Cardinal Cullen was evidently invalid for two reasons, each of which is sufficient alone to show the clear invalidity of the suspension. First, Cardinal Cullen had no jurisdiction over me (no one knows who suspended me; I do not know myself); and to say that a priest can be suspended canonically by one who has no jurisdiction over him, is simply absurd. It is admitted on all hands that the Cardinal had no jurisdiction, either as Archbishop or as Cardinal; and he only claimed jurisdiction as special delegate of the Pope in my case.

Rev. R. O'Keeffe.

12 June 1873

1628. Mr. *Bourke*.] You say, as I understand you, that the bishop only conveyed sentence of suspension to you?—He never conveyed a sentence of suspension to me. I do not know what bishop. The Bishop of Vienna?

1629. Your own bishop?—I have a great many bishops. Dr. Moran is my bishop at present; he never conveyed any sentence of suspension to me, nor did Cardinal Cullen.

1630. *The O'Conor Don*.] Did not he send it to you in a registered letter?—A registered letter came to my house through the post, and I sent it back; I do not know what it contained.

LIST OF APPENDIX.

Appendix, No. 1.

PAPER handed in by Mr. Keenan, c.b., 26 May 1872: PAGE
    Rules and Regulations of the Commissioners of National Education in Ireland - - 163

Appendix, No. 2.

Paper handed in by the Reverend O. L. Morell, in answer to Question 1206 :
    Resolution of the Belfast Presbytery in the O'Keeffe Case, passed on Monday, 10th of February 1873 - - - - - - - - - - - - - - 191

Appendix, No. 3.

Report of Mr. Robertson, referred to at Question 263 in Mr. Keenan's Evidence - - 192
Letter referred to at Question 313 in Mr. Keenan's Evidence - - - - - - 193

Appendix, No. 4.

Letter from Sir Alexander Macdonnell to Mr. Cardwell - - - - - - 194

APPENDIX.

Appendix, No. 1.

PAPER handed in by Mr. *Keenan*, C.B., 26 May 1873.

RULES AND REGULATIONS OF THE COMMISSIONERS OF NATIONAL EDUCATION IN IRELAND.

CONTENTS.

PART I.
GENERAL NATURE OF THE SYSTEM OF NATIONAL EDUCATION.

	Page
SECTION I.—Its Object and Fundamental Principle	164
„ II.—Description of Schools to which the Commissioners grant Aid	164
„ III.—Use of School-houses	164
„ IV.—Religious and Secular Instruction	165
„ V.—Use of Books and Tablets	167
„ VI.—Management of National Schools	168
„ VII.—Inspection by the Commissioners or their Officers	169
„ VIII.—Admission of Visitors	169

PART II.
EXTENT OF AID, AND CONDITIONS UPON WHICH GRANTED.

SECTION I.—Kinds of Aid	170
„ II.—Towards Building School-houses (Vested)	170
„ III.—Towards Support of Schools previously established (Non-Vested)	171

PART III.
DIFFERENT CLASSES OF NATIONAL SCHOOLS.

SECTION I.—District and Minor Model Schools	172
„ II.—Ordinary Literary Schools	172
„ III.—Agricultural Schools	172
A.—School Farms of the First Class under the exclusive control of the Commissioners	172
B.—School Farms of the First Class under Local Patrons:—	
1. Where the Premises are Vested	173
2. Where the Premises are Non-Vested	173
C.—Ordinary Agricultural Schools	173
D. School Gardens	173
„ IV.—Industrial Schools	173
„ V.—Convent Schools	173
„ VI.—Workhouse Schools	174
„ VII.—Schools attached to Prisons, Asylums, &c.	174
„ VIII.—Evening Schools	174

PART IV.
TEACHERS.

SECTION I.—Their Qualifications and Duties	174
„ II.—Training of Teachers	176
„ III.—Classification of Teachers, &c.	176
„ IV.—Salaries (Ordinary National Schools)	178
„ V.—Paid Monitors—their Salaries, &c.	179
„ VI.—Salaries, &c., to other than Ordinary National Schools:—	
A.—Evening Schools	179
B.—Schools connected with School Farms of the First Class, under exclusive control of the Board	180

PART IV.—TEACHERS—*continued*.
Section VI.—Salaries, &c.—*continued*.

	Page
C.—Schools connected with School Farms of the First Class, under Local Patrons	180
D.—Schools connected with Ordinary School Farms	180
E.—Industrial Schools	180
F.—Schools connected with Convents and Monasteries	180
G.—Model Schools:—	
(a.) Scale of Salaries to Head Masters and Mistresses of Model Schools	180
(b.) Scale of Salaries and Allowances to Assistant Masters and Mistresses of Model Schools	180
(c.) Allowances to Teachers of Model Schools for giving instruction in Singing, Drawing, and Physical Science	181
(d.) Salaries and Allowances to Monitors and Pupil-teachers in Model Schools	181
(e.) Gratuities to Pupil-teachers and Paid Monitors in Model Schools	181
H.—Gratuities to Literary Teachers of Workhouse National Schools	181
„ VII.—Gratuities, &c., to Teachers of Ordinary National Schools:	
A.—Premiums for order, neatness, and cleanliness	182
B.—Supplemental or Good Service Salaries	182
C.—Allowances for giving instruction in Vocal Music, Drawing, and Navigation	183
D.—Gratuities for instructing Paid Monitors	183
E.—Gratuities for extra instruction to unpaid Monitors	183
F.—Gratuities for preparing young persons for the office of Teacher	183
G.—Gratuities for preparing young persons for the office of Pupil Teacher in Model Schools	184
H.—Retiring Gratuities	184

PART V.
SUPPLIES OF BOOKS, SCHOOL REQUISITES, AND APPARATUS.

SECTION I.—Nature and Extent of Grants, and Conditions on which made	184
A.—Free Stock	184
B.—Requisites supplied at Reduced Prices	185
„ II.—Regulations to be observed by Managers in regard to Grants of Books, &c.	186

PART VI.
GENERAL INSTRUCTIONS TO MANAGERS AND CORRESPONDENTS 189

Appendix, No. 1.

RULES and REGULATIONS of the COMMISSIONERS of NATIONAL EDUCATION in IRELAND.

PART I.

GENERAL NATURE OF THE SYSTEM OF NATIONAL EDUCATION.

I.—*Its Object and Fundamental Principle.*

1. THE object of the system of National Education is to afford *combined* literary and moral, and *separate* religious instruction, to children of all persuasions, as far as possible, in the same school, upon the fundamental principle that no attempt shall be made to interfere with the peculiar religious tenets of any description of Christian pupils.

2. It is the earnest wish of Her Majesty's Government, and of the Commissioners, that the clergy and laity of the different religious denominations should co-operate in conducting National Schools.

3. The Commissioners by themselves, or their officers, are to be allowed to visit and examine the schools whenever they think fit. Those who visit on the part of the Commissioners are furnished with credentials under their seal.

4. The Commissioners will not change any fundamental Rule without the express permission of his Excellency the Lord Lieutenant.

5. The Commissioners will not withdraw, or essentially alter, any book that has been, or shall be hereafter, unanimously published or sanctioned by them, without a previous communication with the Lord Lieutenant.

II.—*Description of Schools to which the Commissioners grant Aid.*

1. The Schools to which the Commissioners grant aid are divided into two classes, viz.:— 1st. Vested Schools, of which there are two sorts, namely, first, those vested in the Commissioners; and, second, those vested in Trustees, for the purpose of being maintained as National Schools: 2ndly. Non-vested Schools, the property of private individuals. Both these classes of schools are under the control of local patrons or managers.

2. There are also Model Schools, of which the Commissioners are themselves the patrons, but which are conducted on the same fundamental principles as the ordinary National Schools.

3. The Commissioners encourage industrial instruction in National Schools in all suitable cases.

4. The Commissioners require that instruction shall be given in plain needlework in all female schools.

III.—*Use of School-houses.*

1. In Non-Vested Schools the Commissioners do not, in ordinary cases, exercise control over the use of the school-houses on Sundays, or before or after the school hours on the other days of the week; such use being left altogether to the local patrons or managers, of all religious persuasions, subject to the interference of the Board in cases leading to contention or abuse.

2. No National School-house shall be employed, at any time, even temporarily, as the *stated* place of Divine worship of any religious community, or for the celebration or administration of the Sacraments or Rites of any Church.

3. No aid will be granted to a school *held in a place of worship*, nor will the Commissioners sanction the *transfer* of an existing school, to a place of worship, even for a temporary period.

4. When a school-room is in any way connected with a place of worship, there must not be any *direct internal* communication between the school-room and such place of worship.

5. Vested school-houses must be used, *exclusively, for the education* of the pupils attending them, except on Sundays, when they may be employed for Sunday Schools, with the sanction of the patrons or managers, subject, in cases leading to contention or abuse, to the interference of the Commissioners.

6. No political meetings shall be held in National School-houses, whether Vested or Non-vested; nor shall any political business *whatsoever* be transacted therein.

7. When any school is received by the Commissioners into connexion with them, the inscription, "NATIONAL SCHOOL," shall be put up in plain and legible characters on the school-house, or on such other place as may render it conspicuous to the public. When a school-house is built partly by aid from the State, a stone is to be introduced into the wall having that inscription cut upon it. The Commissioners will not, when granting aid in

future,

future, sanction any inscription containing a title of a *denominational character*, or which may appear to them to indicate that the school is one belonging to any particular religious body. The Commissioners do not object to the terms, male, female, or infant; or the proper local designation taken from the city, town, parish, street, village, or townland, in which the school may be situated; or the name of the founder being included in the inscription.

8. No emblems or symbols of a *denominational* nature shall be exhibited in the school-room during the hours of united instruction; nor will the Commissioners in future grant aid to any school which exhibits on the exterior of the buildings any such emblems.

9. No emblems or symbols of a *political* nature shall at *any time* be exhibited in the school-room, or affixed to the *exterior* of the buildings; nor shall any placards whatsoever, except such as refer to the legitimate business of school management, be affixed thereto.

IV.—*Religious and Secular Instruction.*

1. Opportunities are to be afforded (as hereinafter provided for) to the children of all National Schools for receiving such religious instruction as their parents or guardians approve of.

2. Religious instruction must be so arranged that each school shall be open to children of all communions; that due regard be had to parental right and authority; that, accordingly, no child shall receive, or be present at, any religious instruction of which his parents or guardians disapprove; and that the time for giving it be so fixed that no child shall be thereby in effect excluded, directly or indirectly, from the other advantages which the school affords.

3. A public notification of the times for religious instruction must be inserted in large letters in the "Time Table" supplied by the Commissioners, who recommend that, as far as may be practicable, the general nature of such religious instruction be also stated therein.

4. The "Time Table" must be kept constantly hung up in a conspicuous place in the school-room.

5. When the religious instruction comes after the secular, the teacher must, immediately before the commencement of the former, announce distinctly to the pupils that the hour for religious instruction has arrived, and must at the same time put up and keep up, during the period allotted to such religious instruction, and within the view of all the pupils, a notification thereof, containing the words "Religious Instruction," printed in large characters, on a form to be supplied by the Commissioners. Similarly when the school commences with religious instruction, the teacher is to put up and keep up the same notification.

6. When the secular instruction precedes the religious instruction, in any National School, there shall be a sufficient interval between the announcement and the commencement of the religious instruction; and whether the religious or the secular instruction shall have priority in any National School, the books used for the instruction first in order shall be laid aside at its termination, in the press or other place appropriated for keeping the school books.

7. No secular instruction, whether literary or industrial, shall be carried on in the same apartment, during school hours,* simultaneously with religious instruction.

8. In schools towards the building of which the State has contributed, and which are VESTED in trustees, for the purposes of national education, or which are vested in the Commissioners in their corporate capacity, such pastors or other persons as shall be approved of by the parents or guardians of the children respectively, shall have access to them in *the school-room*, for the purpose of giving them religious instruction there, at times convenient for that purpose—that is, at times so appointed as not to interfere unduly with the other arrangements of the school.

9. In schools not vested, and which receive no other aid than salary and books, it is for the patrons and managers to determine whether any, and if any, what religious instruction shall be given *in the school-room*; but if they do not permit it to be given in the school-room, the children whose parents or guardians so desire, must be allowed to absent themselves from the school, at reasonable times, for the purpose of receiving such instruction elsewhere.

10. The reading of the Scriptures, either in the Protestant authorised, or Douay version, the teaching of catechisms, public prayer, and all other religious exercises, come within the rules as to religious instruction.

11. The patrons and managers of *all* National Schools have the right to permit the Holy Scriptures (either in the Authorised or Douay version) to be read, at the time or times set apart for religious instruction; and in *all vested schools* the parents or guardians of the children have the right to require the patrons and managers to afford opportunities for the reading of the Holy Scriptures in the school-room, under proper persons approved of by the parents or guardians for that purpose.

12. Religious

---

* The term "School-hours," is always to be understood to mean the entire time in each day, from the opening of the school to the closing of the same for the dismissal of the pupils.

12. Religious instruction, prayer, or other religious exercises, may take place at any time before and after the ordinary school business (during which all children, of whatever denomination they may be, are required to attend); but must not take place *at more than one intermediate* time between the commencement and the close of the ordinary school business. The Commissioners, however, will not sanction any arrangement for religious instruction, prayer, or other religious exercises *at an intermediate time*, in cases where it shall appear to them that such arrangement will interfere with the usefulness of the school, by preventing children of any religious denomination from availing themselves of its advantages, or by subjecting those in attendance to any practical inconvenience.

13. With the above exception, the secular school business must not be interrupted, or suspended by any spiritual exercise whatsoever.

Note.—The Commissioners earnestly recommend that religious instruction shall take place either immediately before the commencement, or immediately after the close, of the ordinary school business; and they further recommend that, whenever the patron or manager thinks fit to have religious instruction at an intermediate time, a separate apartment shall (when practicable) be provided for the reception of those children who, according to these Rules, should not be present thereat.

14. The registry kept in each school, according to the form furnished by the Commissioners, must show the religious denomination of each child on the school roll.

15. No pupil who is registered by its parents or guardians as a Protestant, is to be permitted to remain in attendance during the time of religious instruction in case the teacher giving such instruction is a Roman Catholic: and no pupil who is registered by its parents or guardians as a Roman Catholic is to be permitted to remain in attendance during the time of religious instruction in case the teacher giving such instruction is not a Roman Catholic. And further, no pupil is to be permitted to remain in attendance during the time of any religious instruction to which its parents or guardians object.

Provided, however, that in case any parent or guardian shall express his desire that his child should receive any particular religious instruction, and shall record such desire in a book to be provided in the school, when necessary for that purpose, this prohibition shall not apply to the time during which such religious instruction only is given.* The entry in the book shall be signed with the name or mark of the parent or guardian, and the book shall be submitted to the inspector as often as he visits the school.

The following is the form of the book :

Roll, No.   ,   School   ,   County
Name of Teacher who gives Religious Instruction,
Religious Denomination of ditto,

CERTIFICATE OF PARENT OR GUARDIAN.

[In case the parent or guardian should wish his child to receive religious instruction from a teacher who is of a different religious denomination from the child, or from a teacher who gives any religious instruction different from that which is in accordance with the creed of the child, the following certificate is to be made by such parent or guardian.]

Note.—As some doubts have arisen as to the interpretation of the rule, attention is requested to the following minute of the Board, dated 26th February 1867 :—

"The object of the Rule is more fully to carry out the general principle of the Board, that no child is to receive any religious instruction contrary to the wishes of its parent. Accordingly the Rule first provides for the case where the teacher is a Protestant and the child a Roman Catholic, or *vice versâ*. In this case the dissent of the parent is implied, and no religious instruction can be given to a child by a teacher of the different creed unless the parent expressly requests it. But where the teacher and the child are both Protestants, whether of the same or of a different denomination, the dissent of the parent will not be implied. In this case religious instruction may be given to the child unless the parent expressly forbids it. In each case, however, the assent or dissent, whether implied or expressed, may be modified by an entry, duly signed by the parent, in the Certificate Book of Religious Instruction. Cases may occur in which the conduct of the teacher, although not coming within the strict letter of the new Rule, is obviously contrary to the general spirit of the National system; as, for instance, if instruction should be given in the Catechism or Creed of a different persuasion from that of the child."

1(¹)   , being the (²)   of (³)   , who is registered by me as (⁴)   in the school register of the (⁵)   National School, hereby certify that it is my desire that the said (⁶)   shall receive instruction in (⁷)   , during the time set apart for religious instruction.

Signature of parent or guardian, (₈)
Witness, if signed by " mark,"
Dated   day of   18   .

* Such expression of desire may at any time be revoked by the parent or guardian, and shall thereupon become inoperative.
(¹) Insert the name of the Parent or Guardian who makes the Certificate.
(²) Insert the relationship of the Parent or Guardian, as "Father," "Mother," "Aunt," &c.
(³) Insert the name of the Pupil.
(⁴) Insert the registered religion of the Pupil.
(⁵) Insert the name of the National School.
(⁶) Insert the name of the Pupil again.
(⁷) Insert in full the nature of the Religious Instruction as, the Holy Scriptures in the Authorized Version; the Roman Catholic Catechism, the Protestant Catechism, &c., &c. This is to be written by the Parent or Guardian, but in case the Parent or Guardian cannot write, it may be written by the Teacher.
(⁸) The Parent or Guardian is here to inscribe his name. If the Parent or Guardian be unable to write his name, he is to sign by mark, but this mark must be witnessed by some respectable third party.

Appendix, No. 1.

CERTIFICATE OF TEACHER.

I hereby certify that before (¹)   signed the above certificate, I read aloud to (²)   the following rule of the Commissioners of National Education:—

"No pupil who is registered by its parents or guardians as a Protestant is to be permitted to remain in attendance during the time of religious instruction in case the teacher giving such instruction is a Roman Catholic; and no pupil who is registered by its parents or guardians as a Roman Catholic is to be permitted to remain in attendance during the time of religious instruction in case the teacher giving such instruction is not a Roman Catholic. And further, no pupil is to be permitted to remain in attendance during the time of any religious instruction to which its parents or guardians object.

"Provided, however, that in case any parent or guardian shall express his desire that his child should receive any particular religious instruction, and shall record such desire in a book to be provided in the school, when necessary for that purpose, this prohibition shall not apply to the time during which such religious instruction only is given." The entry in the book shall be signed with the name or mark of the parent or guardian, and the book shall be submitted to the inspector as often as he visits the school.

"* Such expression of desire may at any time be revoked by the parent or guardian, and shall thereupon become inoperative."—*Part I., Sec. IV., Par.* 15.

And I further certify that I believe when the said (³)   signed the above certificate (⁴)   had a full apprehension of the meaning and force of the rule, and also of the true intent and object of the certificate.

Signature of teacher

Dated   day of   18   .

CERTIFICATE OF INSPECTOR.

I hereby certify that I have examined the certificate of (⁵)   and also of the teacher (⁶)   above set forth, and that I am satisfied as to the genuineness of each.

Signature of Inspector

Dated   day of   18   .

16. A sufficient number of hours, to be approved of in each case by the Commissioners, is to be appropriated to the ordinary school business, during which all children of whatever denomination they may be, are required to attend.

17. In all National Schools (except those in which industrial instruction is the *chief* object) there must be literary instruction for at least *four* hours, upon five days in the week.

18. In industrial schools, that is, in schools where industrial instruction is the *chief* object, the Commissioners require that not less than *two* hours, daily, shall be devoted to literary instruction.

V.—*Use of Books and Tablets.*

1. The use of the books published by the Commissioners is not compulsory; but the titles of all other books which the patrons and managers of schools intend for the ordinary school business, are to be notified to the Commissioners; and none are to be used to which they object. The approval of any such books is to extend only to the particular edition which has been submitted to the Commissioners.

2. If any books, other than the Holy Scriptures, or the *standard* books of the church to which the children using them belong, be employed in communicating religious instruction, the title of each is to be made known to the Commissioners whenever they deem it necessary.

3. The Commissioners do not insist on the "Scripture Lessons" or book of "Sacred Poetry" being read in any of the National Schools, nor do they allow them to be read as part of the ordinary school business (during which all children, of whatever denomination they may be, are required to attend) in any school attended by children whose parents or guardians object to their being read by their children. In such cases the Commissioners prohibit the use of these books, except at times set apart for the purpose, either before or after such ordinary school business, and under the following conditions:—

First.—That no child, whose parent or guardian objects, shall be required, directly or indirectly, to be present at such reading.

Second.—That in order that any children, whose parents or guardians object, may be at liberty to absent themselves, or to withdraw, at the time set apart for the reading of the books above specified, public notification of the time set apart for such reading shall be inserted in large letters in the time-table of the school; that there shall be a sufficient interval between the conclusion of such ordinary school business and the commencement of such reading; and that the teacher shall, immediately before its commencement, announce distinctly to the pupils, that any child whose parent or guardian so desires may then retire.

Third,

(¹) Insert the name of the Parent or Guardian.
(²) Insert " him " or " her."
(³) Insert the name of the Parent or Guardian.
(⁴) Insert " he " or " she."
(⁵) Insert the name of the Parent or Guardian.
(⁶) Insert the name of the Teacher

Appendix, No. 1.

Third.—That in every such case there shall be, exclusive of the time set apart for such reading, sufficient time devoted each day to the ordinary school business, in order that those children who do not join in the reading of these books may enjoy ample means of literary instruction in the school-room.

4. When using the Scripture lessons, the teachers are prohibited, except at the time set apart for religious instruction, from putting to the children any other questions than those appended to the end of each lesson.

5. The Commissioners require that the principles of the following lesson, or of a lesson of a similar import (to be approved of by the Commissioners), shall be strictly inculcated, during the hours of united instruction, in all schools received into connection with the Board, and that a copy of the lesson itself be hung up in each school.

Christians should endeavour, as the Apostle Paul commands them, to live peaceably with all men (Rom. ch. xii., v. 18), even with those of a different religious persuasion.

Our Saviour, Christ, commanded his disciples to love one another. He taught them to love even their enemies, to bless those that cursed them, and to pray for those who persecuted them. He himself prayed for his murderers.

Many men hold erroneous doctrines, but we ought not to hate or persecute them. We ought to hold fast what we are convinced is the truth ; but not to treat harshly those who are in error. Jesus Christ did not intend his religion to be forced on men by violent means. He would not allow his disciples to fight for him.

If any persons treat us unkindly, we must not do the same to them ; for Christ and his apostles have taught us not to return evil for evil. If we would obey Christ, we must do to others, not as they do to us, but as we would wish them to do to us.

Quarrelling with our neighbours and abusing them, is not the way to convince them that we are in the right, and they in the wrong. It is more likely to convince them that we have not a Christian spirit. We ought, by behaving gently and kindly to every one, to show ourselves followers of Christ, who, when he was reviled, reviled not again (1 Pet. ch. II., v. 23).

6. The use of the tablet, furnished by the Commissioners, containing the Ten Commandments, is not compulsory.

7. The rules as to religious instruction do not apply, except in the way hereinbefore stated, to the Scripture lessons and the book of Sacred Poetry, or to the matter contained in the common school books, or in any other book, the use of which the Commissioners may at any time sanction for the purpose of united instruction.

VI.—*Management of National Schools.*

1. The local government of the National Schools is vested in the local patrons thereof.

2. The Commissioners recognise as the local patron the person who applies in the first instance to place the school in connection with the Board, unless it be otherwise specified in the application.

3. If a school be under local management of a school committee, such committee has all the rights of an individual patron.

4. The patron has the right of nominating any fit person to act as his representative in the local management of the school; such representative to be designated the "Local Manager." The patron may, at any time, resume the direct management of the school, or appoint another local manager. This rule applies equally whether the patronship be vested in one or more individuals.

5. When a school is vested in trustees, they have the right to nominate the local manager.

6. When a school is vested in the Commissioners, the name of the patron or patrons is inserted in the lease.

7. In the case of a vacancy in the patronship by death, the representative of a lay patron, or the successor of a clerical patron, is recognised by the Board (where no valid objection exists) as the person to succeed to the patronship of the school.

8. If a patron wishes to resign the office, he has the power of nominating his successor, subject to the approval of the Board.

9. In all cases, the Commissioners reserve to themselves the power of determining whether the patron, or the person nominated by him, either as his successor, or as local manager, can be recognised by them as a fit person to exercise the trust.

10. In all cases, whether the school be vested or non-vested, the patron, when nominating a local manager, ought to notify to the Commissioners whether or not the person so nominated is to exercise all the rights of patron during the period he acts as manager.

11. When a school is under the control of a committee, or of joint patrons, a "Local manager" should be appointed, to correspond with the office, sign documents, &c. &c.

12. The local patrons (or managers) of schools have the right of appointing the teachers, subject to the approval of the Board, as to character and general qualifications ; the local patrons (or managers) have also the power of removing the teachers of their own authority.

13. Patrons

13. Patrons and managers are permitted to close their respective schools for a reasonable time during the year, subject to the interference of the Commissioners in cases of abuse; such periods of closing should be limited to six weeks in the year, including the recognised vacations.

14. Managers of National Schools are requested to notify all changes of teachers to the office, and to the inspectors of the respective districts.

VII.—*Inspection by the Commissioners or their Officers.*

1. As the Commissioners do not take the control or regulation of any school, except their own model schools, directly into their own hands, but leave all schools aided by them under the authority of the local patrons or managers; the *inspectors* are not to give *direct orders*, as on the part of the Board, respecting any necessary regulations, but to point out such regulations to the local patrons or managers of the schools, that *they* may give the requisite orders.

2. The Commissioners require that every National School be inspected by the *Inspector of the District*, at least three times in each year.

3. The *District Inspector*, after each inspection, is to communicate with the local patron or manager, for the purpose of affording information concerning the general state of the school, and pointing out such violations of rule, or defects, if any, as he may have observed; and he is to make such suggestions as he may deem necessary.

4. Upon ordinary occasions, the inspector is not to give any intimation of his intended visit; but when the inspection is to be public, he is to make such previous arrangements with the local patrons or managers, as will facilitate the attendance of the parents of the children, and other persons interested in the welfare of the schools.

5. The inspector is to report to the Commissioners the result of each visit, and to use every means to obtain accurate information as to the proficiency of the pupils, and the discipline, management, and methods of instruction pursued in the school.

6. When applications for aid are referred to the district inspector, he is to have an interview with the applicant; and also to communicate personally, or by writing, with the clergymen of the different denominations, and with other parties in the neighbourhood, with the view of ascertaining their opinions on the application, and whether they have any, and what, objections thereto.

7. The inspector is also to supply the Commissioners with such local information as they may from time to time require from him, and to act as their agent in all matters in which they may employ him; but he is not invested with authority to decide upon any question affecting a National School, or the general business of the Commissioners, without their direction.

VIII.—*Admission of Visitors.*

1. The public, generally, must have free access to every National School (whether vested or non-vested) during the hours devoted to secular instruction, not to take part in the ordinary business, or to interrupt it, but, as visitors, to observe how it is conducted.

2. Visitors of all denominations are to be received courteously by all teachers of National Schools, and are to have free access to the school-rooms, and full liberty to examine the registers, daily report books, and class rolls; to observe what books are in the hands of the children, or upon the desks, what tablets are hung up on the walls, and what is the method of teaching; but they are not authorised to interrupt the business of the school, by asking questions of the children, examining classes, calling for papers or documents of any kind, except those specified, or in any other way diverting the attention of either teachers or scholars from their usual business.

3. Should any visitors wish for information which they cannot obtain by such an inspection, it is the duty of the teachers to refer them to the patron or manager of the school for such information.

4. As the religious instruction of the children given in the school-room is under the control of the clergyman or lay person communicating it with the approbation of their parents, the *Commissioners* can give no liberty to any visitor, whether clergyman or other person, to interfere therewith, or to be present thereat.

5. The Commissioners require that a copy of Part I, with selections from other parts, of these, their rules, on a form furnished by them, shall be suspended in every National Schoolroom.

PART II.

EXTENT OF AID, AND CONDITIONS UPON WHICH GRANTED.

I.—*Kinds of Aid.*

1. The Commissioners of National Education award aid under two general heads, viz.:—

    First—Towards building school-houses and providing suitable fittings and furniture. In such cases, the Commissioners also grant aid towards the payment of teachers, supply of books, &c., as hereafter explained.

    Secondly—Towards the support and maintenance of schools established without any assistance from the public funds for the erection of the buildings, or providing furniture.

2. The Commissioners desire it to be distinctly understood that they reserve to themselves in all cases, in vested as well as in non-vested schools, the right to withdraw any grant of salary or books, whenever they see fit.

II.—*Towards Building School-houses (Vested).*

1. Before any grant is made towards building a school-house, the Commissioners are to be satisfied that a necessity exists for such a school, that an eligible site has been procured, that a satisfactory lease of the site will be executed either to trustees for the purposes of National Education, or to the Commissioners in their corporate capacity; and that the applicants are prepared to raise, by local contribution, at least one third of the whole sum which the Commissioners deem necessary for the erection of the house, providing furniture, &c.

2. If the proposed site for a school be in a rural district, and be within three statute miles of a school-house erected with aid from the State, no grant will be made, except under special circumstances.

3. In a rural district, the site should contain one rood. In a town district, the site for a single school should be 100 feet in front, and 80 feet from front to rear; and for a double school, 100 feet square. It should be in a healthy situation, on a public road or street, and have a dry level surface, with a good foundation at a moderate depth, and be convenient to pure water.

4. Although the Commissioners do not refuse aid towards the erection of school-houses on ground connected with places of worship, yet they much prefer having them erected on ground which is not so connected, where it can be obtained; they therefore require that, before church, chapel, or meeting-house ground be selected as the site of a school-house, strict inquiry be made whether another convenient site can be obtained, and that the result shall be stated to them.

5. The school premises must be vested in the Commissioners, or in trustees, at a nominal rent, and for such term as, under the circumstances, the Commissioners may deem necessary.

6. The lease must be prepared in the office; the expense to be borne by the Commissioners of National Education.

7. The Commissioners will cause to be kept in repair the school-house and furniture, where the premises are vested in them in their corporate capacity.

8. When the school premises have been vested in trustees, for the purposes of National Education, it devolves on the trustees to keep the house, furniture, &c., in repair.

9. When grants are voted towards the building, &c. of a school-house, the conveyance must be duly executed *before the works are commenced.*

10. No grant can be approved until the district inspector shall have reported upon all the circumstances of the case; until the Board of Works shall have reported on the eligibility of the proposed site; and the law adviser of the Commissioners shall have given his opinion, from the information laid before him, that a satisfactory lease can be executed.

11. The Commissioners determine, from the information afforded them, what amount of school accommodation should be provided in the proposed building.

The following is the Scale of Grants for the Erection of School-houses, whether vested in Trustees or in the Commissioners.

Appendix, No. 1.

Class of School.	Number of Children to be accommodated.	Total Estimated Cost, including School Furniture and Out offices.	Board's Grant.	Description of School.
		£. s. d.	£. s. d.	
1	60	207 - -	188 - -	Single school-room.
2	75	235 - -	150 - -	- - ditto.
3	100	255 - -	170 - -	- - ditto.
4	120	306 - -	204 - -	- - ditto.
5	150	416 5 -	237 10 -	Two rooms on ground.
5 A	150	380 - -	240 - -	Two rooms, one over the other.
6	200	487 10 -	325 - -	Two rooms on ground.
6 A	200	435 - -	290 - -	Two rooms, one over the other.

Note.—In many poor localities, where buildings of a less expensive nature than those erected according to the above scale of grants may answer the necessary purposes, the Commissioners will be prepared to grant two-thirds of the expense of erection, provided—

(*a.*) That the general conditions already specified with regard to building grants be complied with.

(*b.*) That the erection of such *exceptional* class of building shall not cost more than 100 *l*.

(*c.*) That as regards the character and size of the building, the instructions issued by the Board of Works, from time to time, shall be complied with.

12. The cost of the house, &c., is determined by the number of children which it is intended to accommodate.

13. The Board of Works will furnish instructions as to the plan and specification, to which the parties receiving aid are bound strictly to adhere.

14. The Commissioners do not sanction grants for the ornamenting of school-houses, but merely for such expenditure as may be necessary for having the children accommodated in plain, substantial buildings. If buildings of another description be preferred, the whole of the extra expense must be provided by the applicants.

15. The Commissioners do not sanction grants towards the expense of erecting residences for the teachers.

16. The Commissioners do not sanction grants to purchase, alter, or furnish houses, for the purpose of being converted into school-houses.

III.—*Towards Support of Schools previously established* (*Non-Vested*).

1. The aid granted to schools previously established is limited to salary and books, and the benefits of inspection and training.

2. The Commissioners do not contribute towards repairs, fittings, or furniture; or to the rent of the school-house.

3. Before aid can be granted, the Commissioners must be satisfied that the case is deserving of assistance; that there is reason to expect that the school will be efficiently and permanently supported; that some local provision will be made in aid of the teacher's salary, in addition to the school fees; that the school-house is in good repair and provided with a sufficient quantity of suitable furniture; that a competent teacher has been appointed; and that the school is in operation.

4. Before the Commissioners consider any application for aid, they require from the inspector of the district a report upon all the circumstances of the case.

5. To entitle a school to a continuance of aid, the house and furniture must be kept in sufficient repair by means of local contributions; the school conducted in all respects in a satisfactory manner, and in accordance with the regulations of the Commissioners; and it must appear from the records of the school that there is a sufficient average daily attendance of pupils.

6. In mixed schools, *i.e.*, schools in which male and female children are taught in the same room, the teacher may be either male or female, as the circumstances of the school may require; but when a mixed school has been received into connexion by the Commissioners,

Appendix, No. 1.

missioners, under a male or a female teacher, the Commissioners will not sanction the appointment of a teacher of a different sex, unless previous application be made to them to sanction such change.

7. When a school has been taken into connection, as a school for males or for females solely, the Commissioners will not sanction the change from a male to a female school, or *vice versâ*, without their permission having been previously obtained.

PART III.

Different Classes of National Schools.

I.—*District and Minor Model Schools.*

1. District and Minor Model Schools are built and supported entirely out of the funds placed by Parliament at the disposal of the Commissioners, and are therefore under their exclusive control.

2. The chief objects of Model Schools are to promote united education; to exhibit the most improved methods of literary and scientific instruction to the surrounding schools, and to train young persons for the office of teacher.

3. In District and Minor Model Schools, the Commissioners appoint and dismiss of their own authority the teachers and other officers; regulate the course of instruction, and exercise all the rights of patrons. The Commissioners afford the necessary opportunities for giving religious instruction to the pupils, by such pastors or other persons as are approved of by their parents or guardians, and in separate apartments allotted to the purpose.

4. Some of the Model Schools have farms attached to them for the purpose of affording instruction in agriculture.

II.—*Ordinary Literary Schools.*

1. Such schools may be established either with aid from the State, or by local provision solely.

2. In vested schools the local expenditure need only be one-third of the expense, and the teachers' salaries are supplemented by the Commissioners.

3. In non-vested schools the State assistance is limited to salary and books and the benefits of inspection and training.

III.—*Agricultural Schools.*

1. To schools of this description farms are attached, for the purpose of illustrating and introducing the most approved systems of tillage and cropping, and general husbandry.

2. Agricultural schools of every class must have a literary department annexed to them, conducted on the principles of ordinary National Schools.

3. Agricultural Schools consist of two classes, those connected with school-farms of the first class, and those connected with ordinary school-farms.

4. School-farms are further subdivided into two classes, viz., those under the exclusive control of the Commissioners, and those under local patrons.

5. In all schools connected with school-farms of the first class, the Commissioners will grant salary to a teacher for the literary department *exclusively*, when the extent of the farm and other circumstances render such an appointment necessary.

A.—*School-Farms of the First Class under the exclusive Control of the Commissioners.**

1. The Commissioners defray the greater portion of the cost of erecting the necessary buildings; but they require the local parties to contribute in such proportion as may be deemed necessary, according to the circumstances of each case.

2. The Commissioners undertake the *entire* cost of the furniture, fittings, rent, taxes, maintenance, implements, stock, &c., &c.

3. A farm of sufficient extent must be conveyed to the Commissioners, at a moderate rent, and on a satisfactory lease.

4. The Commissioners exercise all the rights of patrons, as in the case of District and Minor Model Schools.

5. The Commissioners admit into these schools a limited number of free and also of paying resident agricultural pupils.

6. The Commissioners contribute a small weekly payment to the class of day pupils who work on the farm.

---

* The Commissioners have, for the present, ceased to take into connexion school-farms of the first class.

Appendix, No. 1.

B.—*School Farms of the First Class under Local Patrons.*
1. *Where the Premises are Vested.*

1. The Commissioners contribute a certain amount of assistance towards the erection of the buildings, in proportion to the amount of local contribution and the extent of the farm. The remaining portion of the cost of the buildings and furniture, and the whole cost of implements, stock, seed, &c., must be contributed by local parties.

2. The site of the buildings must be legally vested in the Commissioners, or in trustees, at a moderate rent, and on a satisfactory lease.

3. The only aid granted by the Commissioners towards the *maintenance* of such schools consists of salary to the master (who must be competent to conduct both the literary and agricultural departments); a sum towards the support of a limited number of resident agricultural pupils, and a weekly payment to the class of day pupils who work on the farm.

2. *Where the Premises are Non-vested.*

1 The entire cost of the necessary buildings, furniture, implements, stock, seed, &c., must be defrayed by local parties, and a farm of sufficient extent must be provided.

2. The Commissioners, besides salary to the master, contribute also towards the support of a limited number of resident agricultural pupils, and a weekly payment to the class of day pupils who work on the farm.

C.—*Ordinary Agricultural Schools.*

1. This class of schools consists of ordinary National Schools (either vested or non-vested), to which a small farm (from one to three acres), is annexed. The teacher must be competent to give instruction both in the theory and practice of agriculture, and must cultivate the land with the assistance of his pupils.

2. The only aid granted by the Commissioners is, an addition to the class salary of the teacher, and, in some special cases, a small weekly payment to an industrial class of pupils.

3. To entitle a school to such aid, the Commissioners require to be satisfied, from the reports of the agricultural inspectors, that the agricultural department is efficiently conducted.

D.—*School Gardens.*

The Commissioners award gratuities, on the recommendation of the agricultural inspectors, to the teachers of national schools, who exhibit the best specimens of garden culture, on ground attached to their respective schools, the ground to be cultivated by the pupils.

IV.—*Industrial Schools.*

1. In these schools, embroidery and other advanced kinds of needlework are taught. The Commissioners grant salaries to the teachers on the following conditions:—

First—That *all* the pupils of the industrial department shall receive literary instruction, for at least *two hours* daily.

Second—That no religious instruction or religious exercise shall take place during the time the pupils are engaged in industrial occupation.

Third—That a separate room be provided for industrial instruction.

Fourth—That, in addition to the literary teacher, there shall be a suitable person appointed to conduct the industrial department.

2. None but lay teachers are entitled to a salary from the Commissioners, for conducting an industrial department in connection with a *convent school.*

3. The amount of salary will depend upon the circumstances of each case.

V.—*Convent Schools.*

1. Convent schools receive aid under the conditions applicable to non-vested schools, and they are subject to the same rules and regulations.

2. The members of the community may discharge the office of literary teachers, either by themselves or with the aid of such other persons as they may see fit to employ; the salaries of such assistants to be defrayed by the community, except in the case of monitors.

3. The amount of salary awarded to convent schools is regulated by the average number of children in daily attendance, according to a scale laid down by the Commissioners.

4. The Commissioners will grant aid to *one school only* in connection with the same convent.

Appendix, No. 1.

VI.—*Workhouse Schools.*

1. Such schools are received into connection, and grants of books made to them, on condition that they shall be subject to inspection by the Commissioners, or their officers, and that all the rules of the Board applicable to non-vested schools be faithfully observed.

2. The Commissioners award gratuities to a certain number of the teachers of workhouse schools in each district, on the recommendation of the inspector.

VII.—*Schools attached to Prisons, Asylums, &c.*

Such schools are received into connection upon the same general principles as the workhouse schools, and grants of books are made to them. In special cases gratuities are awarded to the teachers.

VIII.—*Evening Schools.*

The Commissioners grant aid towards the support of evening schools, where the wants of the locality render such institutions desirable. The aid is limited to salary, books, and inspection.

PART IV.

TEACHERS.

I.—*Their Qualifications and Duties.*

1. National teachers should be persons of Christian sentiment, of calm temper, and discretion; they should be imbued with a spirit of peace, of obedience to the law, and of loyalty to their sovereign; they should not only possess the art of communicating knowledge, but be capable of moulding the mind of youth, and of giving to the power which education confers a useful direction. These are the qualities for which patrons of schools, when making choice of teachers, should anxiously look. They are those which the Commissioners are anxious to find, to encourage, and to reward.

2. No clergyman of any denomination, or member of any religious order, can be recognised as the teacher of a National School. This does not apply to the teachers of convent schools, nor to those of any monastery schools which have been at any time previously in connection with the Board.

3. Teachers of National Schools are not permitted to carry on, or engage in, any business or occupation that will impede or interfere with their usefulness as teachers. They are especially forbidden to keep public-houses, or houses for the sale of spirituous liquors.

4. Every teacher is required to have his daily report book lying upon his desk, that visitors may, if they choose, enter remarks in it. Such remarks as may be made, the teachers are by no means to alter or erase; and the inspector of the district is required to transmit to the Commissioners copies of such remarks as he may deem of sufficient importance to be made known to them.

5. Should the Commissioners consider any teacher in a vested school unfit for his office or otherwise objectionable, they will require that he be dismissed and another provided: in non-vested schools the grant of salary will be withheld until a suitable teacher be procured. Teachers are also liable to be fined, depressed, or suspended, at all times, when the Commissioners shall deem it necessary, on sufficient cause being shown.

6. Teachers whose schools may have declined in usefulness and efficiency, or who may have conducted themselves improperly, or who, from any other cause, may seem to merit punishment, may be fined, depressed, or deprived of salary.

7. *Newly appointed* teachers are not *entitled* to any salary from the Commissioners until examined and pronounced competent; and any teacher *newly appointed* to National Schools, who after examination by the inspectors, may be found wholly unqualified, must be removed.

8. If a teacher who has been dismissed from a National School for any cause, be appointed to another National School, the Commissioners reserve to themselves the right to determine whether the appointment can be sanctioned, or any salary paid to such teacher.

9. No teacher dismissed for incompetency is eligible for re-entry into the Board's service till after the expiration of at least six months from the date of such dismissal.

10. If a teacher who has been a considerable period out of the service of the Board shall again enter it, the Commissioners reserve to themselves the right to determine, in each case, whether such teacher shall retain the class he was in previous to quitting the service of the Board.

11. The Commissioners regard the attendance of any of the teachers at meetings held for *political purposes*, or their taking part in elections for Members of Parliament, or for Poor

Poor-law Guardians, &c., except by voting, as incompatible with the performance of their duties, and as a violation of rule which will render them liable to dismissal.

12. Teachers, to be eligible for entering the service of the Board, must, if males, have completed their seventeenth year; and, if females, their sixteenth.

13. No assistant teachers will be recognised whose qualifications are not at least equal to those required of probationers.

14. The same rule as to age applies to assistant as to principal teachers.

15. The Commissioners will not grant a salary to an assistant teacher in a boys' school in which there is not an average daily attendance of at least 60 pupils; but in the case of girls' schools, or mixed schools—that is, schools attended by both sexes—salary may be obtained for an assistant, when the attendance shall have maintained itself at an average of at least 50.

16. In mixed schools presided over by a master, it is desirable, where the attendance warrants it, that a female assistant should be selected.

17. The Commissioners will not grant salary to workmistresses in mixed schools, unless there be an average daily attendance of at least 45 pupils; and the Commissioners require that at least two hours each day be devoted to instruction in this branch.

18. If any workmistress, whose appointment has been sanctioned by the Commissioners, be employed during the remainder of the ordinary school-hours in giving literary instruction to the junior classes, it is competent for the district inspector, if he considers her qualified, to recommend that she be paid at the rate of salary awarded to "probationers."

19. In schools attended by female children only, under the care of a female teacher, such teacher must be competent not only to conduct the Literary Department, but also to give instruction in needlework; but if the average daily attendance amount to 45, application may be made for a grant of salary to a workmistress to take charge of the Industrial Department, which, however, must be superintended by the principal teacher, who will be held responsible for its efficient management.

20. The following practical rules are to be strictly observed by the teachers of national schools:—

I. To keep at least one copy of the *General Lesson* suspended conspicuously in the schoolroom, and to inculcate the principles contained in it on the minds of their pupils. This should be done at the time of combined ordinary instruction.

II. To exclude from the school, except at the hours set apart for religious instruction, all catechisms and books inculcating peculiar religious opinions.

III. To avoid fairs, markets, and meetings, but, above all, political meetings of every kind; to abstain from controversy; and to do nothing either in or out of school which might have a tendency to confine it to any one denomination of children.

IV. To keep the register, report book, and class rolls, accurately, neatly, and according to the precise forms prescribed by the Board; and to enter or mark in the two latter, before noon each day, the number of children in actual attendance.

V. To classify the children according to the national school books; to study these books themselves; to teach according to the improved method, as pointed out in their several prefaces; and to labour diligently to train up their pupils in each branch of knowledge to that degree of attainment or amount of proficiency pointed out for each class, respectively, in the *Programme of Instruction for National Schools*.

VI. To observe themselves, and to impress upon the minds of their pupils, the great rule of regularity and order—A TIME AND A PLACE FOR EVERY THING, AND EVERY THING IN ITS PROPER TIME AND PLACE.

VII. To promote, both by precept and example, *cleanliness, neatness,* and *decency*. To effect this, the teachers should set an example of cleanliness and neatness in their own persons, and in the state and general appearance of their schools. They should also satisfy themselves, by personal inspection every morning, that the children have had their hands and faces washed, their hair combed, and clothes cleaned and, when necessary, mended. The school apartments, too, should be swept and dusted every evening; and whitewashed at least once a year.

VIII. To pay the strictest attention to the morals and general conduct of their pupils, and to omit no opportunity of inculcating the principles of *truth* and *honesty*; the duties of respect to superiors, and obedience to all persons placed in authority over them.

IX. To evince a regard for the improvement and general welfare of their pupils; to treat them with kindness, combined with firmness; and to aim at governing them by their affections and reason, rather than by harshness and severity.

X. To cultivate kindly and affectionate feelings among their pupils; to discountenance quarrelling, cruelty to animals, and every approach to vice.

XI. To record in the report book of the school the weekly receipts of school fees, and the amount of all grants made by the Board, as well as the purposes for which they were made, whether in the way of premiums, salaries to teachers, or payments to monitors or workmistresses; also school requisites, whether free stock or purchased at the reduced prices.

XII. To take strict care of the *free stock* of requisites granted by the Board; and to endeavour to keep the school constantly supplied with the National School books and requisites, for sale to the children, at the reduced prices charged by the Commissioners; also to preserve, for the information of the inspectors, the invoices of free stock or purchased requisites, which will be enclosed with the grant.

Appendix, No. 1.

XIII. Should it be intended to close a school for a time not included in the recognised vacations, notice should be given some days previously to the Inspector; and when a teacher is summoned for training, and means to obey the summons, or intends resigning or removing, to another school, he should intimate his intention to the Inspector a month, at least, before his removal or resignation, in order that the latter may have an opportunity of visiting his school, and reporting upon the state of the premises, free stock, school accounts, &c., &c.

XIV. To attend to the ventilation of the school:—I. Immediately after entering the room in the morning; II. At the time of roll-call; III. About an hour before the school breaks up. The ventilation can best be effected by lowering, where practicable, the upper part of the windows, so as to admit a thorough air through the room.

21. In cases of illness, and upon medical certificates being submitted, the Commissioners allow to principal teachers, or assistants, one month's leave of absence from school duty in the year, for which time their salaries will be paid without deduction. If any more lengthened leave of absence be required, there must be competent substitutes appointed, such substitutes to be paid by the recognised teachers, at the rate of, at least, the salary allowed to probationers. In no case can leave be granted for more than six months.

II.—*Training of Teachers.*

1. The Commissioners have provided a normal establishment in Dublin, for training teachers and educating persons who are intended to undertake the charge of schools.

2. Teachers selected by the Commissioners for admission to the normal establishment must produce a certificate of good character; also a certificate from a member of the medical profession that they are in good health, and free from any cutaneous disease; and must be prepared to pass through an examination in the books published by the Commissioners. They are boarded and lodged at the establishments provided by the Commissioners; and arrangements are made for their receiving religious instruction from their respective pastors, who may attend at the normal establishment at convenient times appointed for the purpose. On Sundays they are required to attend their respective places of worship; and a vigilant superintendence is at all times exercised over their moral conduct. The teachers undergo examination at the close of the course, and they then receive a certificate according to their deserts. The teachers are, for a considerable time previous to their being summoned, required to prepare themselves for the course.

3. During the absence of the recognised teacher, a temporary teacher must be provided to take charge of the school, who is to be paid a portion of the salary falling due to the recognised teacher during such teacher's attendance at the normal establishment.

4. Assistant teachers of model schools, while in training, receive but half their accustomed share of the fees, and a deduction is made from their salaries at the rate of 20 $l.$ per annum in the case of males, and 18 $l.$ in the case of females: these deductions to serve as payment for their substitutes.

5. Should any teachers present themselves in a delicate state of health, or affected with any cutaneous disease, they will not be received or allowed any travelling expenses. No teacher can be admitted who has not had the small-pox, or been vaccinated.

6. The teachers trained in the normal institution are divided into three classes, namely:—

First—The general or ordinary class, composed of teachers (males or females) of national schools, who have been recommended by the district or head inspectors as eligible candidates for training.

Second—The special or extra training class, composed chiefly of teachers (males or females) who have been selected from the ordinary or general class, for additional training.

Third—The candidate or *extern* class, composed of a limited number of respectable and well-informed young persons, who wish to qualify themselves to act as teachers. The candidates admitted to this class are permitted to attend, without any charge, the model schools and the lectures of the professors, and at the end of the course they are examined and classed as teachers, according to their merits and qualifications. Permission is also given to teachers of schools not connected with the Board to attend the model schools as auditors or visitors, for any period that may suit their own convenience.

7. No teachers can be admitted to the general or ordinary class but those who have succeeded in obtaining classification after examination by a Board of Inspectors, or who may be specially recommended by the inspectors or professors.

III.—*Classification of Teachers, &c.*

1. All national teachers are either "classed teachers" or "probationers." The former are divided into three classes.

The class in which teachers are ranked depends (I.) upon their qualifications, as determined after examination by the professors, or by the inspectors; and (II.) on their proved capacity and efficiency as conductors of schools.

All teachers, on first entering the service of the Board, or who have not been classed, are termed probationers.

2. Besides

SELECT COMMITTEE ON CALLAN SCHOOLS.   177

2. Besides the principal and assistant teachers included under the foregoing heads, there Appendix, No. 1.
are junior literary and industrial assistant teachers, teachers of needlework, pupil teachers,
and paid monitors.

3. The Commissioners have determined upon a course of study for each class, in which
the teachers are to be examined, as one of the tests of their fitness for promotion.

4. Every national teacher will be furnished, on application to the district inspector, with
a copy of the programme of the course of study above referred to, in which is stated the
minimum of proficiency required for each class.

5. Teachers already classed are to be admitted to examination, with a view to promotion,
only on the recommendation of the district inspector, and no one on whose school a
decidedly unfavourable report has been made within the previous year is to be admitted.

6. (a.) Teachers will not be eligible for promotion, unless, in addition to satisfactory
answering in the course prescribed for the class to which they aspire, it appears from the
reports of the respective district inspectors, that the schools are properly organised and well
conducted; that adequate exertions have been made to keep up a sufficient average attendance; that their classes are taught according to the *Programme of Instruction for Schools*;
that while the junior pupils are carefully taught, a fair proportion of the pupils of the higher
classes, besides being proficient in the ordinary branches of reading, spelling, writing, and
arithmetic, are possessed of a respectable amount of knowledge in grammar and geography,
and able to write from dictation ordinary sentences with readiness and correctness. In
female schools it will be further requisite that instruction in plain needlework, including
sewing, knitting, and cutting-out, be given to all girls capable of receiving it, and that they
exhibit a due proficiency in this department.

(b.) It must also appear from the reports of the inspectors, that the school accounts have
been regularly and correctly kept; that the school premises have been preserved with
neatness and order; that cleanliness in person and habits has been enforced on the children
attending them, and that an adequate supply of *sale stock* of lesson books and other
necessary school requisites has been regularly kept.

(c.) It must also clearly appear that, JUDGED BY THE TOTAL RESULTS PRACTICALLY
REALISED IN THEIR SCHOOLS in the instruction and discipline of their pupils, they are
worthy of the higher class to which they aspire.

7. All teachers who have not been classed will be paid as probationers, until they be
classed at the first examination to which they shall have been summoned. Those who then
obtain classification will be paid from the commencement of their service under the Board,
according to the rate of salary attached to their class. This rule will not extend to those
teachers who, when summoned, shall fail, from any cause whatever, to present themselves
for examination.

8. All teachers who have been unsuccessful at their first examination, and who may be
retained on trial, will receive the salary of the class to which they may be promoted at any
subsequent examination, from the 1st of April of the year in which they offer themselves
for such subsequent examination.

9. Teachers who, after their first examination, have been retained on trial as probationers,
if not recommended for promotion by the head or district inspectors at the next ensuing
examination, cannot be continued in the service of the Board.

10. Classed teachers who may offer for reclassification will, if promoted, be paid according to their new grade from the 1st of April of the year in which they offer themselves for
examination.

11. The pupil teachers of district model schools, on taking charge of national schools
after the completion of their course of training, shall, if not already classed, rank as third
class teachers (provided they be deemed qualified for that class by the head inspector) until
they shall have been classed at the first examination held after their appointment, in the
district in which their schools are situated, when they will be paid, according to their classification, from the date of their appointment.

12. All teachers must remain *at least* one year in a lower *division* of any class, before they
are eligible for promotion to a higher division; and they must remain *at least* two years in
a lower *class* before they can be promoted to a higher class. These conditions, however,
being fulfilled, teachers of superior attainments and of eminent usefulness may be advanced
from any division of one class to any division of another, after their first classification, without being required to pass through the intermediate divisions.

13. This regulation does not apply to teachers who may be promoted on the recommendation of the Professors at the termination of their course of training.

14. Teachers who may have absented themselves from the examinations of previous
years, without satisfactory reason assigned, will be liable to be dismissed should they not
present themselves when again summoned.

0.93.   Z   15. All

Appendix, No. 1.

15. All teachers also who may be *specially* summoned, and who shall be absent without a sufficient reason, will be liable to be fined or depressed.

IV.—*Salaries (Ordinary National Schools).*

1. The Commissioners grant salaries to teachers of national schools at the following rates, subject to the foregoing and and annexed regulations:—

Principal Teachers.—		Males.	Females.
		£. s.	£. s.
First Class	1st Division	52	42
	2nd Division	44	36
	3rd Division	38	30
Second Class	1st Division	32	26
	2nd Division	28	24
Third Class	1st Division	24	20
	2nd Division	18	16
Probationers		16	14

(*a.*) As a general rule, a school, to be entitled to be taken into connection or to remain in connection, must exhibit an average daily attendance of at least 30 pupils.

(*b.*) Teachers cannot be admitted to the enjoyment of first class salary, nor allowed to continue in its enjoyment, unless their schools command an average daily attendance of 35 pupils.

(*c.*) Should schools of the ordinary class be retained in connection after the attendance shall have fallen below *thirty pupils*, as in certain circumstances they may be retained, their teachers will be paid according to the provisions of the modified scale given below.

(*d.*) But as regards the schools placed in connection with the Board *before* the close of October 1860, in every case where the attendance shall appear to be diminished by the admission of new schools, the Commissioners will not make any reduction of salary on the *first* occasion of such diminution taking place, but will defer making such reduction until a period of six months shall have elapsed from the termination of the quarter in which the attendance shall, on such *first* occasion, fall below the required minimum.

(*e.*) And in the case of schools taken into connection *since* October 1860, reduction of salary, proportioned to the decrease in attendance, will be made in the *next* quarter subsequent to that in which it first occurs, should the decrease re-appear.

Assistant Teachers.—	Males.	Females.
	£. s.	£. s.
Unclassed	15	14
If classed 2²	18	16
If classed 3¹, or higher,	24	20
Junior Literary and Industrial Assistants	—	14
Workmistresses	—	8

2. To entitle a school to the services of an assistant, the school, if for boys only, must have an average daily attendance of at least 60; but if for girls only, or if a mixed school, an average of 50 will suffice. While, however, the average daily attendance in such schools respectively remains under 65 and 55, no higher salary than that of III² can be awarded.

3. In mixed schools presided over by a master the assistant should be a female.

4. To entitle an assistant to the salary of III¹, the school, if for boys only, must have an average daily attendance of at least 65, or if mixed, or for girls only, an average daily attendance of 55.

5. In schools where the average attendance amounts to 110, salary of classification, up to 2¹, will be allowed to the first or senior assistant.

6. To entitle a girls' school, or a mixed school, presided over by a master, to the services of a workmistress, an average daily attendance of 45 pupils is required, of whom, in the case of mixed schools, 20 at least must be girls. The same rule applies to junior literary and industrial assistants in such schools.

Note.—In cases where schools enjoying the services of assistants (under which term are included monitors, workmistresses, and industrial instructors) fail to command the average attendance required for the amount of aid awarded for such services, managers must be prepared for the entire withdrawal or reduction of such aid in the second quarter in which the falling-off appears.

A like rule will be applied to evening schools.

7. The Commissioners in certain cases are prepared to act on the following modification of the above scale of salaries provided for principal teachers.

I. *Attendance*

I. *Attendance under 15 Pupils.*—Schools with an average daily attendance under 15 pupils, conducted on the principles and the system of the Board, will not be admitted to the enjoyment of salary, but may be allowed inspection, books, and apparatus, under existing regulations. The teachers will be eligible for training, and their service, from their connection with the Board, will count to their credit in respect to supplemental salaries, retiring allowances &c., should their schools afterwards become entitled to regular grants of salary, or should they be removed to others so entitled.

II. *Attendance 15 but under 20 Pupils.*—When the average daily attendance is 15, but under 20, in addition to inspection, books, &c., and training, the Commissioners will make an award of salary to the teacher, to the amount of two-thirds of a probationer's salary.

III. *Attendance 20 but under 25.*—When the average daily attendance is 20, but under 25, the full salary of a probationer, but no more, will be awarded to the teacher.

IV. *Attendance 25 but under 30.*—When the average daily attendance is 25, but under 30, salary as high as that of first division of third class, but no higher, will be awarded to the teacher, should his qualifications in other respects entitle him to such classification.

Note.—These modified grants the Commissioners are prepared to make where the means of religious instruction are not attainable by children of a particular denomination within a reasonable distance of their homes, in any existing National School; but they reserve to themselves the powers, in all cases, of preventing the unnecessary multiplication of Schools in any district, and will require as a condition of this modified aid that the managers of such schools shall be either clergymen or other persons of good position in society.

6. The Commissioners are anxious that a further income be secured to the teacher, either by local subscription or school fees, and they require that the payments made by the children shall not be diminished in consequence of any increase of salary which may be awarded to the teacher.

V.—*Paid Monitors—Their Salaries, &c.*

Junior Monitors.	£.	Senior Monitors.	£.
For the First Year	2	For the First Year	5
For the Second Year	3	For the Second Year	6
For the Third Year	4	For the Third Year	8
		For the Fourth Year	10

1. No school whose teacher does not rank at least in 3¹ Class, can get the benefit of the services of a junior monitor; nor can any school whose teacher ranks not at least in 2² Class, be allowed the services of a senior monitor.

2. The paid monitors are selected from among the best pupils in the National Schools of each district, and are appointed by the Commissioners upon the recommendation of the district inspectors.

3. No manager of a National School is obliged to employ a paid monitor, nor will such be appointed without his approval.

4. The appointment of a junior paid monitor cannot be held for a longer period than three years, nor that of a senior paid monitor for more than four years, at the expiration of which periods, respectively, the salary will be discontinued.

5. The salary may, however, be withdrawn at any time, should want of diligence, of efficiency, or of good conduct, on the part of the monitor, or any other circumstance, render such a course desirable.

6. The Commissioners select (on the recommendation of the inspectors) the schools in which the services of paid monitors may be employed.

7. When a vacancy in a monitorship occurs, whether before or after the expiration of a monitor's term of service, it does not necessarily follow that a successor shall be appointed in the same school.

8. The programme of the course of study for paid monitors can be obtained on application to the district inspector.

9. Paid monitors who have completed their course in a satisfactory manner are eligible, on examination by the inspectors, to offer as candidates for assistant teacherships, or for pupil teacherships in district model schools.

10. In the case of a few very large and highly efficient schools, the Commissioners are prepared to appoint young persons of great merit to act as first class monitors.

	£.
Salary for the First year	15
Ditto Second year	17

VI.—*Salaries, &c., to other than Ordinary National Schools.*

A.—*Evening Schools.*

The Commissioners grant salaries, generally amounting to 5 *l.* a year, to teachers of evening schools, for every 25 pupils in average attendance.

Appendix, No. 1.

B.—*Schools connected with School Farms of the First Class, under the exclusive Control of the Board.*

Teachers of this class of schools receive such amount of salary as the Commissioners may deem sufficient, according to the circumstances of each case.

C.—*Schools connected with School Farms of the First Class under Local Patrons.*

Masters of this class of schools, competent to conduct both the literary and agricultural departments, receive 10 *L* per annum in addition to the salary of the class in which they may be placed: but if their income from the Board, with this addition, should fall short of 30 *l.* per annum, the difference will be granted to them, so that in all cases such teachers shall have secured to them for their *combined* services a salary of 30 *L* a year at least.

D.—*Schools connected with Ordinary School Farms.*

Masters of such schools receive 5 *l.* per annum in addition to the salary of their class, provided they are competent to conduct both the literary and agricultural departments, and that the Commissioners shall have previously approved of agriculture being taught in the school.

E.—*Industrial Schools.*

In National Schools where embroidery and other advanced kinds of needlework are taught, the amount of salary granted for giving such instruction is regulated by the nature of the work, and the number of pupils engaged in it.

F.—*Schools connected with Convents and Monasteries.*

1. In schools of this description, salary is paid according to a per-centage on the average daily attendance:—

Average Attendance.		Salary. £.	Average Attendance.		Salary. £. s.
30 to 50		10	301 to 325		64 5
51 „ 75		15	326 „ 350		68 10
76 „ 100	Increase at 20 *L* per cent.	20	351 „ 375	Increase at 17 *L* per cent.	72 15
101 „ 125		25	376 „ 400		77 —
126 „ 150		30	401 „ 425		81 5
151 „ 175		35	426 „ 450		85 10
176 „ 200		40	451 „ 475		89 15
201 „ 225		45	476 „ 500		94 —
226 „ 250		50	501 „ 525		98 5
251 „ 275		55	526 „ 550		102 10
276 „ 300		60	551 „ 575		106 15
			576 „ 600		111 —

601 upwards, increase at 15 *L* per cent.

2. As the amount of salary to schools of this class will in all cases depend upon the average daily attendance of pupils, managers are to be prepared for augmentation or diminution accordingly, at the expiration of each quarter.

3. Schools of this class are entitled to the services of paid monitors.

4. For evening schools, an allowance is made at the rate of 10 *L* for every hundred pupils in average attendance.

G.—*Model Schools.*
(a.) *Scale of Salaries to Head Masters and Mistresses of Model Schools.*

1. The head master to receive 60 *L* per annum, and after the completion of three years' service to rise by 5 *L* per annum, until the salary amount to 100 *l.*, should he be reported faithful and efficient in the discharge of his duties.*

2. The head mistress to receive 55 *L*† per annum, and after three years' service to rise by 2 *l.* 10 *s.* per annum, on the same condition as in the case of males, until the salary amount to 75 *l.* a year.

3. Principals, both males and females, enjoy also one-half the school fees received in their respective departments.

(b.) *Scale of Salaries and Allowances to Assistant Masters and Mistresses in Model Schools.*

1. An assistant master to receive his class salary, a supplemental salary of 15 *L* per annum, and generally a certain proportion of the school fees.

---

* In case of head masters of model schools, residence is provided, or, in lieu thereof, in some cases, allowance for house rent.
† This includes 20 *l.* a year for lodging allowance.

2. An assistant mistress to receive her class salary, a supplemental salary of 12 *l.* per annum, and generally a certain proportion of the school fees.

3. The grant of such supplemental salaries to be contingent upon the report of the head and district inspectors.

(c.) *Allowances to Teachers of Model Schools who, possessing Certificates of Competency, shall give Instruction in Singing, Drawing, or Physical Science.*

1. The head master or mistress to be allowed 10 *l.* annually, but to be paid for teaching only *one* of these subjects.

2. The assistant master or mistress to be allowed for

	£.
Singing	8
Drawing	8
When both are taught	12
And an assistant master for teaching physical science	8

3. When the assistant teacher is engaged in teaching both physical science and *either* drawing or singing (for not more than *two* of these extra branches are to be taken by the same assistant), a sum of 12 *l.* annually to be granted to him.

4. If in the case of singing or drawing, the instructions of the teacher, principal, or assistant, are confined to but one department of the school, as the boys' or girls', but half the assigned rate of payment is allowed.

5. These allowances to be contingent upon the report of the head and district inspectors.

(d.) *Paid Monitors and Pupil Teachers in Model Schools.*

1. Monitors are allowed for the

	£.			£.
First Year	6	Third Year		10
Second Year	8	Fourth Year		12

2. In the case of pupil teachers resident in the house, an allowance at the rate of 20 *l.* a year is granted to the master for the board, &c., of each.

3. Extern pupil teachers are allowed at the rate of 20 *l.* a year each, in lieu of board, &c.

(e.) *Gratuities to Pupil Teachers and Paid Monitors in Model Schools.*

1. An annual gratuity not exceeding 30 *s.* may be awarded to pupil teachers (of *first* year) and paid monitors for good conduct, distinguished merit in their studies, and success in the instruction of the classes entrusted to their charge.

2. Pupil teachers who may be retained for training beyond their first year, will be allowed a gratuity of 30 *s.* a quarter, as reward for good conduct, &c.

3. These gratuities are granted on the recommendation of the head and district inspectors.

H.—*Gratuities to Literary Teachers of Workhouse Schools.*

1. The Commissioners of National Education (with the concurrence of the Poor Law Commissioners) award gratuities to a certain number (40 males and 40 females) of the teachers of the workhouse schools, in connexion with the National Board, who shall be recommended by the district inspectors.

The gratuities are divided into two classes:—

For Male Teachers	First Class	Twenty at the rate of 6 *l.* a year each.
	Second Class	Twenty " 4 *l.* "
For Female Teachers	First Class	Twenty " 5 *l.* "
	Second Class	Twenty " 3 *l.* "

2. The awards are made half yearly, for the periods ending 31st March, and 30th September.

3. It is to be understood that such gratuities are given in *addition* to the salaries paid to the teachers of workhouse schools under the provisions of the Poor Law Act.

4. No teacher is precluded from receiving the gratuity two or more half years in succession, if recommended by the district inspector as deserving of it; but a teacher having received a gratuity for one half year, is not thereby *entitled* to the payment of another for the succeeding half year.

5. If the local guardians know any just cause for withholding the gratuity from the teacher, they are to return the receipt unsigned, and communicate to the Commissioners of National Education the grounds for so doing.

6. The teachers of workhouse National Schools are also eligible to receive the gratuity for instructing pupils in vocal music.

Appendix, No. 1.

VII.—*Gratuities, &c., to Teachers of Ordinary National Schools.*

A.—*Premiums for Order, Neatness, and Cleanliness.*

1. The sum of 22*l.* 10*s.* will be allocated to each of the school districts, and divided into 13 premiums.

One of 4*l.* . . . . 4*l.*	Five of 1*l.* 10*s.* . . 7*l.* 10*s.*
Two of 3*l.* . . . . 6*l.*	Five of 1*l.* . . . 5*l.*

2. These premiums are awarded annually on the recommendation of the district inspector at the expiration of the year.

3. No teacher is eligible for this premium for more than two years in succession, or who shall be in receipt of good service salary.

4. These premiums will be awarded to teachers of all classes, provided the average attendance in each case shall not fall below that required for salary of teacher's class; but none will be deemed eligible to receive such premiums against whom there is any well-founded charge of neglect in the performance of their duties, of impropriety in their conduct, or whose schools are not conducted in all respects in a satisfactory manner.

5. If the patron or manager of a National School, knows any just cause for withholding the premium from the teacher, he is to return the receipt unsigned, and state his reasons for so doing.

B.—*Supplemental or Good Service Salaries.*

1. Supplemental or good service salaries are awarded to a certain number of teachers of National Schools, on the recommendation of the head and district inspectors, subject to the following conditions:—

   (*a.*) That the teacher ranks not lower than first division of third class.
   (*b.*) That the average attendance at his school amounts to 35 at least.
   (*c.*) That the teacher has given not less than eight years' service under the Board; period of service to be reckoned from the date from which salary as a classed teacher was first paid.

2. No teacher to be eligible for such supplemental salary who shall have been depressed or fined for misconduct or neglect of duty, or on whose school a decidedly unfavourable report shall have been made within the preceding three years, or who shall not have shown himself, throughout his whole career, to have been attentive and painstaking, and mindful of all the details of school keeping.

3. Any teacher to whom such good service salary shall have been awarded, but who shall subsequently cease to exhibit those qualities which first obtained for him this distinction, or whose school shall fall below an average daily attendance of 35 pupils, shall thereby forfeit such supplemental salary.

4. Teachers in receipt of good service salary who may become entitled to an increase, on the ground of a more lengthened term of service, or on account of promotion to a higher class, must be specially recommended by inspector for such increase.

5. In case of promotion from a lower to a higher class, teacher will not be entitled to the consequent increase of good service salary until he shall have been a year in his new class.

6. Payments to be made annually; and in no case without the united recommendation of the head and district inspectors.

	MALES.				FEMALES.		
Of Class		After Good Service of		Of Class		After Good Service of	
	8 Years.	12 Years.	17 Years.		8 Years.	12 Years.	17 Years.
	£ s. d.	£ s. d.	£ s. d.		£ s. d.	£ s. d.	£ s. d.
III²	3 — —	4 — —	6 — —	III¹	2 — —	3 — —	5 — —
II²	4 — —	5 — —	7 — —	II²	3 — —	4 — —	6 — —
II¹	5 — —	6 — —	8 — —	II¹	4 — —	5 — —	6 10 —
I²	6 — —	7 10 —	9 10 —	I²	4 10 —	5 10 —	7 10 —
I¹	7 — —	8 10 —	11 — —	I¹	5 — —	6 — —	9 — —
I¹	8 — —	11 — —	13 — —		7 — —	9 — —	11 — —

C.—*Allowances*

C.—*Allowances for teaching Vocal Music, Drawing, and Navigation.*

1. To every teacher, possessing a certificate of competency, who shall give instruction in vocal music in his school, a gratuity ranging from 3 *l.* to 5 *l.* a-year, according to the number under instruction and the success of the teacher's efforts.

2. To every teacher possessing a certificate of competency from the drawing-master in the Central Model School, or from the master of a school of art, who shall give instruction in drawing to a class with sufficient average attendance, an annual gratuity, varying from 3 *l.* to 10 *l.*, according to the number under instruction and the success of the teacher's efforts.

3. Gratuities for teaching singing and drawing are awarded to the conductors of Convent Schools, on the same conditions as in the case of ordinary schools, provided satisfactory proof is afforded of the competency of the teachers, and that the instruction is given during the hours of secular education.

4. To every teacher of a National School, possessing a certificate of competency from the masters of the Dublin, Belfast, Limerick, or Waterford Model Maritime Schools, who shall give evidence of having an average attendance of at least six pupils under instruction in navigation, an annual gratuity of 5 *l.* for an attendance of six pupils, and 10 *l.* for an attendance of 12 or more.

D.—*Gratuities for instructing Paid Monitors.**

		£.	s.	d.
Junior Monitors,	For each junior monitor, a gratuity of	1	—	—
Senior Monitors {	For each monitor of 1st year, a gratuity of	1	—	—
	Ditto - of 2nd year - ditto	1	10	—
	Ditto - of 3rd or 4th year, ditto	2	—	—
1st Class Monitors	Ditto - of 1st or 2nd year, ditto	2	—	—

E.—*Gratuities for Extra Instruction to Unpaid Monitors.**

1. A gratuity not exceeding *four pounds* may be awarded to teachers of organised schools, who shall give *extra* instruction to a staff of *unpaid* monitors appointed by the inspector or organiser.

(*a.*) Teachers must, to entitle them to such gratuities, keep a record of the time devoted by them to the monitors' instruction.

(*b.*) No gratuity can be awarded under this or the preceding head unless the answering of the monitors be satisfactory, and that such answering can be fairly referred, in great part at least, to the care bestowed by the teacher during the time of such special instruction.

F.—*Gratuities for preparing Young Persons for the Office of Teacher.**

1. For every pupil who, after having been appointed to a school shall pass respectably the *first* annual examination, held subsequently to such appointment, the master or mistress by whom such pupil shall have been trained will be entitled to a sum of not less than 2 *l.*, and not more than 3 *l.*, but in no year is the amount to exceed 15 *l.* to any one school or teacher as the reward of such services.

2. The conditions to be observed in regard to these gratuities are,—

(*a.*) That such pupil shall have attended in the school not less than two consecutive years immediately preceding his or her appointment as a teacher.

(*b.*) That the district inspector shall certify that the school in which such pupil shall have been trained is efficiently conducted in all other respects.

(*c.*) That the head inspector before whom such pupil shall have been examined shall certify that the teacher is entitled to the gratuity.

(*d.*) That not more than 12 months shall have elapsed between such pupil's first examination and the date of his leaving the school of his former instructor.

G.—*Gratuities*

---
* Teachers of Model Schools are excluded from obtaining this class of gratuities.

Appendix, No. 1.

G.—*Gratuities for preparing Young Persons for the Office of Pupil Teacher in Model Schools.**

1. A gratuity not exceeding 2 l. may be awarded to teachers from whose schools shall proceed eligible candidates for the office of pupil-teacher in the Model Schools.

2. The conditions to be observed in regard to these gratuities are,—

(a.) That such pupil shall have attended in the school not less than two consecutive years immediately preceding his appointment as pupil-teacher.

(b.) That the district inspector shall certify that the school in which such pupil shall have been trained is efficiently conducted in all respects.

(c.) That the head inspector before whom such pupil shall have been examined shall certify that the teacher is entitled to the gratuity.

Note.—In regard to the foregoing special gratuities, as in regard to the annual salaries of the teachers of National Schools, it is to be distinctly understood that the Commissioners reserve to themselves the right to determine, on cause shown, whether the payment is to be made in whole or in part, or is to be altogether withheld.

H.—*Retiring Gratuities.*

In particular cases the Commissioners have the privilege of granting gratuities of reasonable amount to deserving teachers of long standing in their service, when, from old age and infirmity, they are obliged to retire.

PART V.

Supplies of Books, School Requisites, and Apparatus.

I.—*Nature and Extent of Grants, and Conditions on which made.*

1. The Commissioners furnish gratuitously to each school a first stock of school requisites, in proportion to the attendance of children. These requisites are to be kept as a school stock, for which the master or mistress is held responsible, and are on no account to be sold or taken out of the school.

2. The funds of the Commissioners do not enable them to give a free stock sufficiently large for the entire wants of the school; and they therefore require that the local parties shall purchase a stock of books and other requisites, proportionate to the grant of free stock, for the use of the school, and for sale to the pupils. Any additional maps, stationery, slates, clocks, and other requisites, must also, as required from time to time, be purchased at reduced rates.

A.—*Free Stock.*

The value of the grant of free stock is regulated by the average daily attendance of pupils, as ascertained from the reports of the inspectors. The managers of schools have the privilege of selecting their grants of free stock from the following list, being at liberty to choose such of them as they most approve of, and to omit any to which they object:—

Slates, Large
Ditto, Small, ruled.
Slate Pencil Holders.
Ink Wells.
Patterson's Sheet of Illustrations to Zoology.
No. 1.
Ditto, Ditto, No. 2.
One Set Tablet Lessons, Arithmetic, 80 sheets; mounted on 30 Boards.
Ditto, ditto, Reading, Part 1, 35 sheets, mounted on 18 Boards.
One Set of Copy Lines, mounted.
Thirty-hour American Clock, in case.
Professor Sullivan's English Dictionary.
Fleming's Atlas (Outline Maps).
Dower's Atlas, 12 Maps, coloured
Kirkwood's Atlas, 12 Maps, coloured.
Dowers' Hints on Secular Instruction.
Young's Infant School Manual.

Larger Maps.

Map of the World.
" Ancient World.
" Europe.
" Asia.
" Africa.
" America.
" United States.

Map of Australia.
" British Isles.
" England.
" Scotland.
" Ireland.
" Palestine.

Johnston's School and Family Maps—size 23 by 27 inches, on rollers, varnished:—
Eastern Hemisphere. | America.
Western ditto. | Canaan and Palestine.
England. | Chart of the World.
Scotland. | Geographical Terms
Ireland. | United States and Canada.
Europe. | Chronological Chart of
Asia | Ancient History.
Africa.

These maps are of the same character as the large maps, but being smaller, may be more convenient to many schools.

Physical Map of the World.
Physical Map of Europe, with book.
Betts' Educational Maps—size, 23 by 20 inches, on rollers, varnished:—
England. | America.
Scotland. | Australia.
Ireland. | Palestine.
Europe | Eastern Hemisphere.
Asia. | Western ditto.
Africa

Interrogatory Maps, with Book of Exercises to each Map; to correspond with the Educational Series on roller, varnished:—
Europe. | England.
Asia | Scotland.
Africa. | Ireland.
America.
3-Inch

* Teachers of Model Schools are excluded from obtaining this class of gratuities.

SELECT COMMITTEE ON CALLAN SCHOOLS.

3-inch Semi-Globe, hinged.
View of Nature in all climates, mounted on roller.
View of Nature in ascending regions, mounted on roller.
The Human Species, 4 sheets, mounted on roller.
Machinery and Manufactures, mounted, viz.:—
   1. Condensing Steam Engine.
   2. High Pressure Engine.
   3. Locomotive Engine.
   4. Marine Engine—side Lever.
   5. Marine Engine—Oscillating.
   6. Marine Engine—Screw.
   7. Paper-making Machine.
   8. Printing Machine.
   9. Manufacture of Gas.
  10. Electric Telegraph.
  11. Fire Engine and Pumps.
  12. Malting and Brewing.
  13. Distilling.
  14. Principle of the Watch.
  15. Hydraulic Press.
  16. Manufacture of Cast Iron.
  17. Flour Mill.
  18. Suction and Force Pumps.
  19. The Barometer and its Uses.
  20. Threshing Machine.
  21. Gas Meter.
  22. Mechanism of a Clock.
  23. The Cotton Plant and its Cultivation.

Lardner's Illustrations of Mechanics, Natural Philosophy, &c., mounted on roller—
1. Mechanical Powers.
2. Machinery.
3. Watch and Clock work.
4. Elements of Machinery.
5. Motion and Force.
6. The Steam Engine.
7. Hydrostatics.
8. Hydraulics.
9. Pneumatics.

Graphic Illustrations of Animals, showing their uses in life, and after death, 21 prints, mounted.

Natural History, 150 prints, mounted.
Natural Phenomena, 30 prints, mounted.
Animals illustrated in their comparative sizes, on roller.
Tool Box, containing an assortment of most useful tools.
Centrifugal Machine.
Archimedean Screw; Working Model.
Black Boards:—42 by 30.
  Ditto   36 by 30.
  Ditto   30 by 24.
  Ditto   42 by 30, on Stand.
  Ditto   30 by 30, Ruled for Music.
Framed Black Boards:—42 by 30.
      Ditto   36 by 30.
      Ditto   24 by 18.
Easels:—Shut-up Easel, 7 feet.
  Ditto   Ditto   6 feet.
Framed Easel, 6 feet, double leg.
Lesson Post, suitable for Tablet Lessons.
Pointers, common, long.
  Ditto   short.
ARITHMETIC FRAMES:—
  Frame and Stand.
  Hand Frames, 17 by 10 inches.
    Ditto   15 by 13 „

The following requisites are included in the grant:—
District Inspector's Observation Book.
School Register.
Daily Report Book.
Roll Book.
General Lesson.
Commandments.
Time Table.
Commissioners' Rules.
Rules for Teachers.
Religious Instruction Tablet.
Religious Instruction Certificate Book.
Programmes of Instruction.

B.—*Requisites supplied at Reduced Prices.*

1. When books, &c., purchased from the Commissioners at the reduced prices are sold to the children attending a National School, it is directed that in no case shall any advance be made on these prices; and the district inspectors have instructions to inquire into and report upon any infraction of this rule.

2. The following is the list of books, school requisites, and apparatus supplied to schools at reduced prices:—

First Book of Lessons.
Second ditto
Third   ditto
Fourth ditto
Fifth Book (Boys').
Reading Book for Girls' School.
Biographical Sketches of British Poets.
Selections from the British Poets, Vol 1.
    Ditto   Ditto   Vol. 2
Introduction to the Art of Reading.
English Grammar.
Key to ditto.
First Book of Arithmetic.
Key to ditto.
Arithmetic in Theory and Practice.
Key to ditto.
Book-keeping.
Key to ditto.
Epitome of Geographical Knowledge.
Compendium of ditto.
Elements of Geometry.
Mensuration.
Appendix to ditto
Natural Philosophy, &c.:—
  Vol. 1 Mechanics, Hydrostatics
  Vol. 2. Electricity, Galvanism, &c.
  Vol. 3. Chemistry and Chemical Analysis.
Scripture Lessons (Old Testament), No. 1.
  Ditto   ditto   No. 2.
  Ditto (New Testament), No. 1.
  Ditto   ditto   No. 2.
Sacred Poetry.
Agricultural Class Book.
Farm Account Book.
Directions for Needlework.
  Ditto   with Specimens.

Tablet Lessons, Arithmetic, 60 sheets.
  Ditto   mounted on 30 Pasteboards.
  Ditto   Spelling and Reading Tablets, Part 1.
  Ditto   ditto   Part 2.
  Ditto   mounted on 17 boards, Part 1.
  Ditto   Ditto   Part 2.
Copy Lines.
  Ditto mounted.
Large Map of the World. | Map of Australia.
Map of Ancient World. | „ British Isles.
 „ Europe. | „ England.
 „ Asia. | „ Scotland.
 „ Africa. | „ Ireland.
 „ America. | „ Palestine.
 „ United States.
Thirty-hour American Clock, in case.
Eight-day Spring Clock, not striking the hours.
Copy Books, Large, } without head lines.
  Ditto   Small, }
  Ditto (Vere Foster's), with head-lines.
Quills.
Steel Pens (Nibs).
  Ditto   broad, medium, or fine points, No. 075 F, 075 M, 075 B.
  Ditto   broad, medium, or fine points, No. 0142 F, 0142 M, 0142 B.
Barrel Pen, N.
Holders for ditto.
Slates, Large.
Ditto, Small, ruled.
Slate Pencils.
Slate Pencil Holders.
Ink Stands.
Ink Powders.

Books not Published, but Sanctioned, by the Commissioners of National Education.

Professor Sullivan's English Dictionary.
  Ditto.   Spelling Book Superseded.
  Ditto.   English Grammar.
  Ditto.   Introduction to Geography and History.
  Ditto.   Geography Generalised.
  Ditto.   Literary Class Book.
Fleming's Atlas of Outline Maps, coloured.
Dower's Atlas, 12 Maps, coloured.
Kirkwood's Atlas, 12 Maps, coloured.
Dawes' Hints on Secular Instruction.
Easy Lessons on Reasoning.
Easy Lessons on Money Matters.
Young's Infant School Manual.
Household Work for Female Servants.
Patterson's First Steps to Zoology, Part 1.
  Ditto   Sheet of Illustrations to ditto, No. 1.
  Ditto. First Steps to Zoology, Part 2.
  Ditto. Sheet of Illustrations to ditto, No. 2.
  Ditto. Zoology for Schools, Part 1.
  Ditto.   ditto.   Part 2.
Dr. Thomson's Treatise on Arithmetic.
  Ditto. Key to ditto
  Ditto. Elements of Euclid, Part 1.
  Ditto.   ditto.   Part 2.
  Ditto. Introduction to Algebra.
Arithmetical Table Books.

Works for the Use of Agricultural Pupils.

Dr. Hodges' First Steps in Agricultural Chemistry.
  Ditto First Lessons in ditto.
Johnston's Catechism of ditto.
Murphy's Agricultural Instructor.
Campbell's Farmer's and Cottager's Guide.
Pringle on Green Cropping.
Stephen's Catechism of Practical Agriculture.

Wilhelm's Vocal Music, supplied only to Schools where the Teachers hold Certificates of competency to instruct in Singing.

Hullah's Manual.
  Ditto Songs for Schools, No. 1.
  Ditto   ditto,   No. 2.
  Ditto Set of Eight Large Sheets.
  Ditto Exercises, Book 1.
  Ditto   ditto, Book 2.
Slate, ruled for Music.
Tuning fork.

GLOBES :—
  12-inch, in Mahogany, low stand, Brass Meridian.
  12-inch, in Stained Wood, low stand, Iron Meridian.
  6-inch Semi-Globe, on Mahogany board.
  3-inch ditto   ditto.
  3-inch ditto   hinged.

MAPS :—

Johnston's School and Family Maps—size 28 by 27 inches, on rollers, varnished :—

Eastern Hemisphere.	America.
Western ditto.	Canaan and Palestine.
England.	Chart of the World.
Scotland.	Geographical Terms.
Ireland.	United States and Canada.
Europe.	Chronological Chart of Ancient History.
Asia.	
Africa.	

_{*} These maps are of the same character as the large maps usually supplied by the Commissioners, but being smaller may be more convenient to many schools.

Johnston's Physical Map of the World.
Johnston's Physical Map of Europe, with book.
Betts' Educational Map—size, 23 by 26 inches, on roller, varnished—

England.	America
Scotland.	Australia.
Ireland.	Palestine.
Europe.	Eastern Hemisphere
Asia.	Western Hemisphere.
Africa.	

Interrogatory Maps, with book of exercises to each map, to correspond with the Educational Series, on roller, varnished—

Europe.	England.
Asia.	Scotland.
Africa.	Ireland.
America.	

Geographical Slates—Each Slate has two Outline Maps permanently engraved on it, and accompanied with Key Maps—

England and the World.	United States and England.
Europe and Asia.	
Africa and America.	United States and the World.
Ireland and Scotland.	

Outline Maps—size, 17 by 15½ inches, printed on good paper, for Geographical Exercises—

England.	Africa.
Scotland.	North America.
Ireland.	South America.
France.	Eastern Hemisphere.
Europe.	Western Hemisphere.
Asia.	Palestine.

Key Maps—same size and sorts as preceding—coloured.

Physical Geography (Reynolds'), mounted—

1. Physical Features of the Land.	5. Distribution of Rain.
2. Volcanic System.	6. Distribution of the Winds.
3. Climates.	
4. Movements of the Waters.	

Griffith's Geological Map of Ireland, on roller.
School Atlas of Physical Geography, with Introduction, and 30 Maps, coloured, bound.
Atlas Illustrative of the Physical, Political, and Historical Geography of the British Empire, 10 Maps, coloured, bound.

DIAGRAMS :—Illustrations of National Philosophy (Johnston's), on roller, varnished, each accompanied by a book—

  No. 1. Properties of Bodies.
  No. 2. Mechanical Powers.
  No. 3. Hydrostatics.
  No. 4. Hydraulics.
  No. 5. Pneumology, No. 1.
  No. 6. Pneumology, No. 2.
  No. 7. Steam Engines.

Astronomy, 6 sheets (Reynolds'), mounted.
View of Nature in all climates, in wrapper.
View of Nature in all climates, mounted on a roller.
View of Nature in ascending regions, mounted on roller.
The Human Species, 4 sheets, mounted on roller.

Machinery and Manufactures, viz. :—

  1. Condensing Steam Engine.
  2. High Pressure Engine.
  3. Locomotive Engine.
  4. Marine Engine—side Lever.
  5. Marine Engine—Oscillating.
  6. Marine Engine—Screw.
  7. Paper-making Machine.
  8. Printing Machine.
  9. Manufacture of Gas.
  10. Electric Telegraph.
  11. Fire Engine and Pumps.
  12. Malting and Brewing.
  13. Distilling.
  14. Principle of the Watch.
  15. Hydraulic Press.
  16. Manufacture of Cast Iron.
  17. Flour Mill.
  18. Suction and Force Pumps.
  19. The Barometer and its Uses.
  20. Threshing Machine.
  21. Gas Meter.
  22. Mechanism of a Clock.
  23. The Cotton Plant and its Cultivation.

SELECT COMMITTEE ON CALLAN SCHOOLS. 187

Ludner's Illustrations of Mechanics, Natural Philosophy, &c., mounted on roller—
1. Mechanical Powers.
2. Machinery.
3. Watch and Clockwork.
4. Elements of Machinery.
5. Motion and Force.
6. The Steam Engine.
7. Hydrostatics.
8. Hydraulics.
9. Pneumatics.

Section of Screw Line of Battle-Ship, mounted.
Table of British Strata, mounted.
Natural Phenomena, 30 prints.
 Ditto ditto mounted.
Useful Plants, a set of 12 plates, coloured, in wrapper with Book.
 Ditto ditto mounted.
Natural History, 150 prints.
 Ditto ditto mounted.
Animals, illustrated in their comparative sizes, on roller.
Graphic Illustrations of Animals, showing their uses in life and after death, 21 prints, mounted.
The Animal Kingdom, 4 sheets, coloured, mounted.
Patterson's Zoological Diagrams, 10, mounted on rollers, varnished.
Set of Chemical Apparatus for performing experiments to illustrate Johnston's Agricultural Chemistry.
Tool Box, containing an assortment of most useful Tools.
Compound Portable Microscope.
Magnetic Ship's Compass, 10-inch.
Magnetic Compass, in brass case, 1½-inch.
 Ditto in mahogany case.
Thermometers:—Boxwood Thermometers.
Models, &c.:—Working Models of Mechanical Powers (Edwards).
Centrifugal Machine.
Archimedean Screw: Working Model.
Cards of Model Tools—Carpenter, Cabinetmaker, Bricklayer, Plumber, Painter and Glazier, Printer, Bookbinder, Goldbeater, Cooper, Farrier, Miner, Roadmaker and Pavior, Gardener, 12 sorts.
Geometrical Solids, set of, in box.
Conic Sections ditto.
Dissected Cone, in boxwood.
Dissected Cube, Octahedron.
 Ditto Tetrahedron.
 Ditto Dodecahedron.
 Ditto Pentagonal Dodecahedron.
Steel Goniograph, for illustrating Geometrical figures.
Tangible Arithmetic, consisting of 12 dozen cubes in box.

ILLUSTRATIONS OF THE USEFUL ARTS:—
 The Manufacture of a Needle described, with specimens of wire in its various stages up to the finished needle.
 The Manufacture of a Pin described, with specimens, showing the progress from the rough metal to the finished article.
 The Manufacture of Paper described, accompanied by 16 illustrative specimens.

EDUCATIONAL CABINETS:—
 Edwards' Educational Cabinet, consisting of Natural objects to illustrate Lessons on Common Things.
 M'Nab's Object-Lesson Cards, illustrative of the Vegetable Kingdom, with specimens.
 The Silkworm, exhibiting its various changes from the egg; in glazed case.

MATHEMATICAL DRAWING INSTRUMENTS:—
 Leather Pull-off Case of Patent Instruments, No. 0211, containing 5-inch steel-joint compass, pen-point, pencil-point, hand-pen, and 6-inch boxwood scale.
 Mahogany Case of ditto, No. 0212, containing 6-inch steel-joint compass, pen and pencil-points, divider, bow-pen, hand pen, pencil, box-scale, ebony parallel, and brass protractor.
Land Surveying Chains, English Measure.
 Ditto ditto Irish Measure.
Flat Rulers, Pear-Tree Wood, No. 3, 12-inch.
 Ditto ditto No. 3, 15 „
 Ditto ditto No. 4, 18 „
Round Ebony Rulers, 12-inch.
 Ditto ditto 18 „

Gunter's Scales, boxwood, 12-inch.
 Ditto ditto 24 „
Chain Scale, boxwood, 12-inch.
Plotting Scale, 12-inch.
Offset Scales.
Ebony Parallel Rulers, 15 inches.
T Squares, No. 1, 16-inch.
 Ditto No. 3, 26 „
 Ditto No. 4, 30 „
Black Boards:—42 by 30-inch.
 Ditto 36 by 30 „
 Ditto 30 by 24 „
 Ditto 42 by 30-inch, on Stand.
 Ditto 36 by 30-inch, Ruled for Music.
Framed Black Boards:—42 by 30 inch.
 Ditto ditto 36 by 30 „
 Ditto ditto 24 by 16 „
Easels.—Shut-up Easel, 7 feet.
 Ditto 6 feet.
Framed Easel, 6 feet, double leg.
Lesson Post, suitable for Tablet Lessons.
Black Canvas, stretched on Frames, 22 by 17 inches.
Drawing Boards, Clamped:—15 by 9½.
 Ditto Ditto 18 by 18½.
 Ditto Ditto 20 by 15½.

ARITHMETIC FRAMES:—
 Frame and Stand.
 Hand Frames, 15 by 13 inches.
Pointers, common, long.
 Ditto ditto short.
Sewing Needles:—Assorted sizes.
Packets of Needles.
Darning Needles:—Assorted sizes.
Crochet Needles:—Steel.
Knitting Pins.
Sewing Cotton:—Clarke's.
 Ditto Brook's.

THIMBLES:—
 Brass, common.
 Brass, steel top.

SCISSORS:—
 Cutting-out Scissors.
 Class Scissors, No. 90.
 Ditto No. 954.
 Penknives, No. 4,000.

WORKING MATERIALS:—
 Knitting Cotton, blue.
 Ditto white.
 Knitting Worsted, white.
 Ditto grey.
 Ditto black drab.
 Ditto black.
 Yellow Sample Canvas.
 White ditto.
 Yellow Stripe, ditto.
 White Muslin.

BLACK LEAD PENCILS, CHALK, &c.:—
 Black Lead Drawing Pencils, HB, B, BB, F.
 Common Drawing Pencils.
 India Rubber.
 White Chalk—French.
 Charcoal.
 Black Conté Crayons, Nos. 1, 2, 3.
 Drawing Pins.
 Porte Crayons, brass.

DRAWING PAPER:—
 Cartridge Paper.
 Ditto tinted.
 Medium Drawing Paper.
 Ditto ditto hand made.
 Royal ditto.
 Imperial ditto.

DRAWING MATERIALS:—
 Water Colours in boxes.
 School of Art Colour Box.
 Water Colours in boxes, best quarter cakes, slide lid.
 Ditto half cakes, slide lid.
 Indian Ink.
 Camel Hair Pencils, crow-quill.
 Ditto duck-quill.
 Ditto goose-quill.
 Cabinet Nests, 6 saucers.

DRAWING COPIES, &c.:—
Lineal Drawing Copies, mounted, in portfolio.
Easy Drawing Copies, ditto.
Hermes' Drawing Instructor, 64 Nos.:—
    Part 1 to 24—Landscapes.
    25 to 36—Flowers and Fruit.
    37 to 48—Heads.
    49 to 60—Arabesques.
    61 to 64—Horses.
School of Art Drawing Book.
Familiar Freehand Drawing Copies.

Green's First Studies in Landscape, 6 Nos.
Elementary Studies, by Julien and others.
Heads from the Antique, drawn by Smeeth, plain.
Ditto - ditto - tinted.

HARMONIUMS—with each Instrument an Instruction Book is supplied:—
    Harmonium (of 5 Octaves) with expression stop.
    Ditto - ditto - without stop.
    Ditto (of 4 Octaves).

II.—Regulations, &c., to be observed by Managers in regard to Grants of Books, &c.

1. All applications for books, school requisites, and apparatus, at reduced prices, must be addressed to the secretaries, and be accompanied by a money order for the amount, in favour of James Kelly, or William Homan Newell, Esq., and payable in Dublin on demand.

2. Half notes, cash, postage stamps, orders or cheques drawn on country banks, cannot be received in payment. If remitted, they will be returned at the risk of the sender.

3. When a post-office order or letter of credit is transmitted, and the amount is under 10 s., the cost of the remittance must be paid by the person applying for the same; but, if the sum exceeds 10 s., the cost of the remittance will be allowed, and requisites given for the *full amount* paid.

4. When the teacher of an ordinary national school advances, from his own resources, the amount of an order for requisites, and that such amount is not less than the sum of 1 *L* 5 s., an allowance of 20 per cent. will be made as commission on the order, if demanded.

5. When a national school has had a grant, either as free stock or at reduced prices, of a clock, or of any of the large maps, another will not be supplied until *three* years shall have elapsed, unless in special cases, the circumstances of which are to be stated, when the grant will be sanctioned, if the reasons assigned be deemed satisfactory.

6. Teachers are not permitted to include, in the application for requisites, *clocks* or *maps* for their own private use. Managers should, therefore, caution teachers that such irregularity, if reported, will subject them to a fine, or other serious mark of the Board's displeasure. *Books* for their own use may be purchased by the teachers at the reduced prices, but then they should be careful to indicate the fact to the manager, by writing the words "for teacher" after the name of the book in the list.

7. The patron or manager should not sign any application for books, requisites, or apparatus, without first ascertaining that they are actually wanted for the school on behalf of which the application is made. The inspectors are required to report to the Commissioners whenever it appears that an undue quantity of requisites, &c., has been ordered for a national school.

8. When there are separate roll numbers for male and female national schools the application should state for which of them the books, &c., are required, and, if for both, *two* forms should be used.

9. Parcels of books, &c., when so desired, will be forwarded, carriage free, to the depôt of the district in which the school for which they are required is situated, and the inspectors will inform the managers on what day they will be ready for delivery; or to the depôt of any other district if more convenient; but in the latter case, the inspector, who may not know the managers of any schools not in his district, cannot be expected to give notice.

10. Or the parcel will be forwarded to the railway station nearest to the manager's residence. In this case the manager must himself incur the risk of its safe delivery, and the expense of carriage.

11. Parcels are sent free to any place within the civic boundaries of Dublin.

12. When parcels are forwarded to the depôt of a district it is *not* the duty of the inspector to transmit the parcel to the manager's residence or to the school.

13. On the day appointed by the inspector for the delivery of parcels, the manager is required to send a messenger to the depôt with the order on the inspector (with which the manager will be furnished), and which order the inspector is required to transmit to this office as a proof of the delivery of the parcel.

14. If a parcel is to be sent by a carrier, he must call at the office in Dublin not sooner than two days after the manager's directions shall have been received, and must produce the manager's order to the storekeeper here, for its delivery, on the form supplied for the purpose.

15. The

15. The school apparatus must, on no account, be taken out of the school for which it has been procured, and must be used solely for school purposes. If it, or any portion of it, should be removed from the school, or any improper use be made of it, the Commissioners will adopt such measures as the nature of the case may demand.

16. The Commissioners do not supply books, requisites, or apparatus to the public, or to schools not connected with the Board of National Education.

17. The amount of each grant must be inserted in the daily report book of the school, and the invoice of the articles preserved for the examination of the school inspector, who will be required to report whether the articles in the school correspond with the invoice, and are in a good state of preservation.

PART VI.

GENERAL INSTRUCTIONS TO MANAGERS AND CORRESPONDENTS.

1. Persons desirous of obtaining assistance from the Commissioners of National Education will, upon intimating to the secretaries the nature of the aid required, be furnished with the Forms, upon which their application must be laid before the Commissioners: and all grants of salary will date from the *first of the month nearest to the return of* such application forms to the office.

2. Applicants for assistance are to understand that the Commissioners are not bound to grant the full amount of aid, as set forth in the foregoing regulations, in every case; nor can they grant any, unless the have sufficient funds for the purpose, which depends upon the amount placed at their disposal by Parliament.

3. The Commissioners desire it to be distinctly understood that they do not hold themselves bound to grant aid unless application shall have been made to them, in the first instance, on the proper form, and unless the application shall have been favourably, and finally decided upon by the Board. Applicants, therefore, should not incur any expense towards the payment of which they expect the Commissioners to contribute, until the decision of the Board shall have been communicated to them.

4. The managers of National Schools are particularly requested to attend to the following regulations respecting the payment of salaries or gratuities to teachers, as the Lords of Her Majesty's Treasury and the Commissioners for auditing the public accounts will not, in future, sanction any payments which are not in compliance with these Rules:—

Every receipt should be signed by the manager and by the teacher who is to receive the amount of salary or gratuity therein specified.

Whenever a manager or other person advances money to a teacher on account of the salary payable by the Commissioners of National Education, he should *take a receipt* for the same (stamped, if the amount be 2 l., or upwards), in order to have a proper voucher to produce to the office for repayment.

If a teacher die to whom any salary is due by the Commissioners at the time of his or her death which, with any other property he or she may have been possessed of, would amount to 20 l. or above, it will be paid only to the representatives or next of kin, on the exhibition, at the office, of letters of administration.

If the amount be over 5 l. and under 20 l. payment will be made without the production of letters of administration, to the alleged next of kin, on satisfactory proof that the just debts of the deceased have been paid, and on the party claiming payment giving a bond, on the form issued from the office, to free the Commissioners from any claim on the part of other next of kin or of creditors: if the amount be 5 l. or under, neither letters of administration nor bond will be required, provided the debts are certified to have been paid.

If a teacher leave a National School, and authorize the manager or some other person to receive the salary due from the Board, such authority must be given in writing, or the amount will not be paid.

5. All communications in reference to National Schools should be signed and made by the patron or manager. The Commissioners do not correspond with teachers of National Schools.

6. No attention can be paid to "anonymous" communications.

7. Correspondents are requested to attend to the following directions, viz.:—

To write at the head of any letter addressed to the office, the name and roll number of the school referred to, and the county in which it is situated.

To make communications on different subjects in separate letters.

To state in every case the writer's post town; and, in the case of persons whose

Appendix, No. 1.

names are not recorded as patrons or managers of schools, to give the name and style of address in full.

In replying to an official letter, to quote its number and date.

It is particularly requested that all letters may be written clearly, and on paper of foolscap size, or, at least, large size letter paper.

Letters or other communications addressed to the secretaries, on the business of the Board need not be prepaid.

8. All letters, or other communications, in any manner relating to the business of the Board, or to the National Schools, are to be addressed to the secretaries, and not to any other officer or person connected with the Board—such communications to be directed thus :—

> *The Secretaries,*
> *Education Office,*
>   *Marlborough Street,*
>   *Dublin.*

By order of the Commissioners of National Education,

James Kelly,
Wm. Homan Newell, } Secretaries.

Education Office, June, 1869.

Appendix, No. 2.

PAPER handed in by the Reverend *C. L. Morell*, in answer to Question 1206.

RESOLUTION of the BELFAST PRESBYTERY in the O'KEEFFE CASE, passed on Monday, 10th of February 1873.

Appendix, No. 2.

"The Presbytery having had under their consideration the last Resolution of the Board of Education Commissioners, confirming their Order for the removal of the Reverend Mr. O'Keeffe, Parish Priest, from the managership of the Callan National School, feel it their duty to express their deep regret at such decision of the Commissioners, inasmuch as nothing has been advanced against the Reverend Mr. O'Keeffe affecting his moral character, his efficiency in the discharge of his duty, or showing that the parents or guardians of the pupils attending his school desired his removal."

The above Resolution was moved by the Reverend H. Henderson, and seconded by the Reverend Hugh Hanna; the previous question was moved by the Reverend T. G. Killen, and seconded by the Reverend T. Macredy. On a division, the Amendment was lost, the only persons voting for it being the Mover and Seconder.

The Resolution was then carried amidst applause, the only persons opposing it being the Mover and Seconder of the Amendment.

Appendix, No. 3.

Appendix No. 3.

LETTER referred to at Question 318 in Mr. *Keenan's* Evidence.

Annaghlone Chapel House, Rathfriland,
5 March 1845.

Gentlemen,

The accusers of Mr. Grant, Rev. John Macken and Company, have pursued the same course to effect his ruin which they deem necessary to accomplish mine, that is not to let him see their faces, but to accuse boldly and refuse any oportunity of defence.

But if the testimony of the most respectable people and clergymen of different religious denominations given in open day can counterbalance the misstatements of malevolent traducers who dared not appear on the day of trial, the charges against Mr. Grant must be declared frivolous and vexatious. I was myself engaged in the cause of education for more than 20 years of my life as Principal of Dundalk Catholic Academy, and president of the Diocesan Seminary of Dromore at Newry, and I do confidently state that I never knew a single teacher better qualified to carry out the views of the Board in diffusing the different branches of knowledge which he professes to teach, than Mr. Grant; his talents as a teacher are high, and his moral conduct equal to his talents; and as to absence from his school, which is the specified charge against him, it is but fair to him that the Board should know that Mr. Grant, so far from showing a willingness to be absent from his post, did not avail himself of the usual indulgence of a week's recreation in July. Mr. Grant, since he got charge of his school, never gave one day's vacation in July. It is quite true, however, that he took a lively interest in the cause of his parish priest, and as an aggrieved parishioner joined in an appeal to the Catholic Primate for redress, and a hearing before sentence would be pronounced validly against me.

In doing this, he only exercised a strictly canonical right, which, so far from displeasing the majority of the parents of the children had their full sanction and approbation.

This is the head and front of his offending in the eye of his accusers, but to stand up for justice to the injured, and for common honesty and truth in a fair trial will be no crime, I am confident, in the eyes of the Commissioners of Education. I have good reason to know that many of those whose names Mr. Macken forwarded to the Board never signed the document accusing Mr. Grant, nor gave their consent to have their names attached to it.

I deem it right to inform the Board, that the whole question between Dr. Blake and me, can be brought to this point: Can a parish priest be condemned without a hearing and after a legitimate appeal has been put in, from a threatened sentence? I think the Most Rev. Dr. Murray will answer No; but, at all events, until the appeal is heard, I feel conscientiously bound to repel all aggression on my pastoral rights, such as is attempted by Mr. Macken, as soon as the Supreme Court decides, if it should decide against me, which I hold to be impossible, Dr. Blake shall get undisturbed possession. I trust the Commissioners will not allow Mr. Macken hereafter to interfere with my duties as manager, until the appeal is settled.

I have &c.
(signed) J. S. *Keenan.*

REPORT of Mr. *Robertson*, referred to at Question 263 in Mr. *Keenan's* Evidence.

Gentlemen, Superintendence Office, 3 April 1845.

In accordance with the Board's order of the 20th ultimo, as communicated to me in your letter of the 22nd, I proceeded to the Magheral National School, and on the 27th ultimo held an investigation in the schoolhouse on charges against the teacher, Michael Grant, of being irregular in his attendance, of being absent from the school on several occasions, and interfering in the dispute at present existing between the bishop of the diocese and the parish priest, the Rev. J. S. Keenan. Of the 10 witnesses brought forward by the accuser, the Rev. J. Macken (appointed administrator of the parish), only four had children of an age to attend the school, and of these four, the children of two are still pupils there; of the other two, one states that in consequence of this dispute he removed his children, except a boy who is in care of an uncle, and who still attends; the child of the other was turned away by Mr. Grant for alleged bad conduct, but as this occurred from nine to 12 months since, I do not consider it of any weight.

These persons were all of the class of peasants or small farmers, and their general statements

ments in evidence were to the effect that Mr. Grant was sometimes irregular in his hours of attendance, and was absent from the school on several days, namely, the 23rd and 27th July, the 3rd September, and the 13th November 1844, and the 16th and 23rd January 1845.

On the former point, the two, whose children are yet in the school, had no complaint to make; one of them said that his boy was not making much progress, but that it might be the child's fault; the other, whose demeanour impressed me very favourably, stated that he had seen Mr. Grant away from the school on one of the above days, and that he wished him to change his conduct regarding the "dispute." He also had some trifling complaint about one of his children being accused of tale-bearing, and not being admitted to the fire.

I should be inclined to lay more stress on the evidence of these two persons than on that of any of the others, who exhibited in general a very bitter and hostile spirit, particularly a person named James Lynden, a carpenter, on whose land the house is built, and who evinced a decided ill feeling both to the school and teacher.

Two of the witnesses made a "declaration" before a magistrate, that on a certain day Dr. Lyons met Mr. Grant going to the school at half-past 11 o'clock, whereas it appeared from the evidence of Dr. Lyons, that on the day in question, Grant was within two minutes' walk of the school, and the hour was a quarter after 10.

Mr. Grant procured a number of witnesses in his favour, and after a careful examination of all, I am of opinion that, though some trifling irregularities may have occurred, he has not been negligent or irregular in attending to his duties; and I cannot help expressing a decided conviction that, but for the part he has taken in the "dispute" alluded to, these charges would never have been heard of.

Mr. Grant acknowledges to have been absent on the days named, but I have the direct evidence of Dr. Keenan that it was with his sanction.

In each case the school was in charge of a substitute, except on one day, when the absence was occasioned by illness during the previous night.

He also acknowledges to have been engaged on the days in question in supporting Dr. Keenan's cause in the parish, being on one occasion on a deputation to some of the Roman Catholic clergy assembled in Banbridge, and on another "deputed to read an address" to the Most Rev. Dr. Crolly in favour of Dr. Keenan.

It appears also, from Dr. Keenan's evidence, that Mr. Grant attended and spoke at several meetings held in the chapel usually on Sundays, in support of him (Dr. Keenan); that these meetings were convened through the medium of printed placards, and in so far differed from the previous meetings of the parochial committee, at which Mr. Grant had been in the habit of acting as secretary. The proceedings and speeches at the late meetings were published in the newspaper.

On this point, I am of opinion that Mr. Grant has acted very indiscreetly in taking so warm and active a part in the differences at present agitating the parish, and that he has become more or less obnoxious to some of the opponents of Dr. Keenan; and though I could not discover by the evidence, or by an examination of the report book, that the school has suffered materially in consequence, I nevertheless conceive that steps should be taken to compel him to confine his attention exclusively to his school duties.

Among the numerous witnesses produced by Mr. Grant were members of the Established Church and Presbyterians, as well as Roman Catholics. Several were persons of respectability, and all bore the strongest testimony in his favour, both as to ability, general good conduct, and popularity with the majority of the parishioners.

During the investigation the house was surrounded by a considerable number, I should think several hundreds, all apparently decided, and some very violent supporters of Mr. Grant; as I was more than once obliged to interfere to prevent the hooting that occasionally assailed the witnesses against Grant on coming out. In this I was zealously assisted both by Dr. Keenan and Mr. Grant.

I should add, that among those whom I requested to withdraw before commencing the proceedings, was a newspaper reporter; I also declined the assistance of a magistrate, sent by the landlord, as I was informed, to receive evidence on oath.

I remain, &c.

The Secretaries, Education Office.   (signed)   *Thos. J. Robertson.*

Appendix, No. 4.

LETTER from Sir *Alexander Macdonnell* to *Mr. Cardwell.*

32, Upper Fitzwilliam-street, Dublin,
13 June 1873.

Dear Mr. Cardwell,

I UNDERSTAND that Judge Lawson has alleged that I, as Resident Commissioner, must on the occasion of Father Sheridan's removal from the managership of the Ratoath National School, have given to the Board some information as to the causes of his suspension, in addition to the simple fact stated on the papers in the case.

I beg to assure you and the Committee, that in reference to the Sheridan case, I had not a particle of information to present to the Board, beyond that contained in the documents.

I can truly add that to this day, I am ignorant of the cause of Mr. Sheridan's suspension; and that on the occasion of his removal from the managership of the school, as on all the previous similar occasions, I considered the simple announcement of the suspension as conclusive.

Believe me, &c.
The Right Hon. Edward Cardwell. (signed) *Alexander Macdonnell.*

REPORT

FROM THE

SELECT COMMITTEE

ON

CALLAN SCHOOLS;

TOGETHER WITH THE

PROCEEDINGS OF THE COMMITTEE,

MINUTES OF EVIDENCE,

AND

APPENDIX.

Ordered, by The House of Commons, to be Printed,
18 *June* 1873.

[*Price* 2 *s.* 2 *d.*]

255.

Under 20 *oz.*

INDEX

TO THE

REPORT

FROM THE

SELECT COMMITTEE

ON

CALLAN SCHOOLS.

Ordered, by The House of Commons, *to be Printed,*
18 *June* 1873.

the University of

[195]

INDEX.

[*N.B.*—In this Index the *Figures* following the Names of the Witnesses refer to the Questions in the Evidence; and those following *App.* to the Pages in the Appendix.]

―――

A.

ANNADUFF SCHOOL. See *O'Farrell, Rev. Mr. Sheridan, Rev. Mr.*

Appointment or Recognition of Managers (*National Schools*). See *Managers*, 1.

Attaghmore School (*Tyrone*). Dismissal by the Board, in 1837, of Mr. Robert Gay as manager of the Attaghmore National School, *Keenan* 36-38.

B.

Ballina School. Particulars in connection with the dismissal, in 1851, of the Rev. Mr. Malone, as manager of the Ballina National School, for having allowed the use of the schoolroom for a political dinner; subsequent recognition, as manager, of the Rev. Mr. Madden, who had been nominated by Mr. Malone, *Keenan* 41-63.

Ballinspittle School (*Cork*). Exercise of the power of dismissal by the Education Board in 1840, in the case of the Rev. Mr. M'Swiney, manager of the Ballinspittle National School (Cork), *Keenan* 38-41.

Official communication relative to the managership of this school in June 1840, showing that the Board of Education did not recognise *ex-officio* managers, *Newell* 1269-1272; *Mr. Justice Morris* 1329.

Belfast Presbytery. Condemnation of the action of the board in Mr. O'Keeffe's case by the Presbytery of Belfast, *Morell* 1204-1206.

Resolution of the Belfast Presbytery, passed on the 10th February 1873, expressing regret at the decision of the Education Commissioners in the case of Mr. O'Keeffe, *App.* 191.

Bequests, Board of. See *Charitable Bequests.*

Books (*National Schools*). Regulations adopted by the Board of National Education in 1832, as to the books to be used in the schools, and as to the control to be exercised in the matter by the Commissioners, and by the local ecclesiastical authority, *Keenan* 145; *App.* 184-189.

Breach of Rules. Instances of dismissal of managers for breach of rules, *Keenan* 36-63. 315-324—— Conduct of the Callan Schools in violation of the rules of the board, after the removal of Mr. O'Keeffe, so that it was necessary to strike them off the roll of National Schools, *ib.* 403, 404——Invariable practice of the board to give opportunity for explanation before removal for breach of rules, *ib.* 416-418.

C.

Callan Infant School. Distinct position of the infant school at Callan; impossibility of separating this school from the other Callan schools, as regards management, save with the consent of the school committee, *Keenan* 405-411——Opinion that the Callan Infant school, as well as the other schools in the case, was parochial in its character, *Mr. Justice Fitzgerald* 1463-1466.

Establishment of a work school for females by witness soon after his appointment as parish priest; this school was recognised from the first by the National Board, witness being

Report, 1873—*continued.*

Callan Infant School—continued.
being the manager, *O'Keeffe* 1531, 1532. 1541.——Conversion of the foregoing school into an infant school upon the death of the head master, *ib.* 1533. 1541——Argument that the Commissioners had no right or power to remove witness from his position as patron of the infant school, founded by himself, *ib.* 1539–1541——Establishment and ownership by witness of the infant school, which he can hand over to whom he likes, *ib.* 1611.

Callan Male and Female Schools. Nomination by the committee of the Callan male and female schools, called for by the board in accordance with their rules; subsequent appointment of Mr. O'Keeffe by the committee, dated 28th February 1863, *Keenan* 86–91.

Statement that the board has expressed no opinion as to the authenticity of the original nomination of Mr. O'Keeffe by the committee of the schools, *Keenan* 248–251——Nomination of Mr. O'Keeffe's predecessor in the parish (except the Rev Mr. Salmon) by the committee of the Callan male and female schools, as managers of those schools; form of nomination in Mr. O'Keeffe's case, *ib.* 391–393.

Consideration of the condition of the Callan schools under Mr. O'Keeffe, and of the inspector's report thereon in January 1873; willingness of witness to have discussed the question of dismissal on the score of mismanagement, *Mr. Justice Lawson*, 1109–1111. 1135–1141. 1161–1166.

When witness became parish priest of Callan, the Callan male and female schools were under a committee, or were so reported; doubt as to their being really under a committee, *O'Keeffe*, 1521. 1574–1579——The Education Board required first a recommendation by the committee in the case of the Callan male and female schools before the recognition of witness as manager, *ib.* 1513.——Form of recommendation drawn up (and signed) by witness, and signed by each member of the school committee whom he saw on the subject; entire inaccuracy of a statement by Mr. Patrick Cody that these signatures were forgeries, *ib.* 1524–1530.—— Right of the committee of the Callan male and female schools to continue witness as manager, or to remove him, there being no such right in the Education Board, *ib.* 1542.

Statement to the effect that the Callan male school was struck off the rolls of the board because French was taught too much, and the education was too high, *O'Keeffe* 1551–1555——Witness improved the school in many ways, and connected it with South Kensington, *ib.* 1553——Examination, showing that there were objections that the board rules were violated on the score of attendance, accounts, &c., *ib.* 1556–1570.——Charge by the inspector against the female teacher in this school of having falsified the accounts as to attendance; action brought against him in consequence, *ib.* 1571–1573.

See also the Headings generally throughout the Index.

Callan Union Workhouse. Illegality of the removal of witness from the office of chaplain of the Callan Union Workhouse, *O'Keeffe* 1627. See also *Poor Law Board.*

Charitable Bequests Quotation of certain rules of the Bequests Board of Ireland as having reference to the question of suspended clergymen, *Keenan* 144, 145——Question considered how far the rule of acting on the certificate of the ecclesiastical superior applies also to the allocation of funds under the Charitable Bequests Act, *Mr. Justice Lawson* 1048–1051——Clear distinction between cases under a Board of Bequests and the case of Mr. O'Keeffe, ex-officio appointment not applying in the latter case, *Mr. Justice Morris* 1328.

Clergy, The. Very general adhesion of the clergy of all denominations to the national system of education, more especially since the introduction of the non-vested system, *Henry* 694–697——Very limited co-operation of the clergy of the different denominations if the rule of the National Board had been different in cases of suspension by the ecclesiastical superiors, *ib.* 698——Great importance attached to the appointment of the local clergy, as managers of the schools, as likely to secure a good attendance, *Viscount Monck* 771, 772. 776–782——Doubt as to there being many cases of complaints from the public relative to clerical managers, or as to any such complaints having led to an inquiry by the board, *Kelly* 893–895——Explanation as to the large proportion of non-vested schools of which Roman Catholic clergymen or parish priests are patrons, *Mr. Justice Morris* 1336, 1337. 1340.

See also Ecclesiastical Dictation. Managers. Suspension and Dismissal.

Committees (Local). See *Callan Male and Female Schools. Managers. Patrons.*

Conscience Clause. Origin of the adoption of the practice of appointing a clerical manager of a single denomination as manager of a National School, statement hereon that there was a strong conscience clause, *Henry* 649–654.

Convent Schools. Explanation of the part taken by witness in reference to an alteration of the board's rules in the case of a convent school, *Mr. Justice Lawson* 1039.

Coolagh

Coolagh and Newtown Schools. Routine nomination of Mr. O'Keeffe at once made by the board, on the resignation of his predecessor, in the case of the Coolagh and Newtown Schools, as being now vested, *Keenan* 86-92——Conclusion as to Mr. O'Keeffe having become manager of the Coolagh and Newtown Schools as a matter of course on his becoming parish priest, *ib.* 389, 390.

Succession of witness, as parish priest, to the patronship of the Coolagh and Newtown Schools, the board having no right to deprive him of this position, *O'Keeffe* 1519-1523. 1543.

Explanation of the circumstances under which witness directed one of the teachers in the Coolagh National Schools to strike out witness's signature to a certain return, and to substitute the name of Mr. Martin, *O'Keeffe* 1591-1605.

See also Supervision and Dismissal.

Cullen, Cardinal. Entire inaccuracy of the assumption that the Education Board acted in deference to Cardinal Cullen in their removal of Mr. O'Keeffe, *Keenan* 100. 399, 400 —— Belief as to the entire absence of any communication of Cardinal Cullen with the board in Mr. O'Keeffe's case, or in any other case, *Mr. Justice Fitzgerald* 1440, 1441.

Circumstance of Cardinal Cullen not being the ecclesiastical superior entitled to suspend Mr. O'Keeffe, *Mr. Justice Lawson* 945——Denial by Mr. O'Keeffe that Cardinal Cullen had any right to suspend him, *ib.* 1037, 1038——Doubt as to Cardinal Cullen's order of suspension having been discussed at the board previously to the communication from the Bishop of Ossory, *Morell* 1210-1218——Invalidity of any suspension of witness by Cardinal Cullen, as having no jurisdiction over him, *O'Keeffe* 1627.

See also Legal Proceedings.

D.

Daly, Rev. Peter (the late). Case of the Rev. Peter Daly, of Galway; belief that, if suspended, his suspension was never brought before the Education Board, *Henry* 715-720 - Absence of any official intimation that the Rev. Mr. Daly was under suspension at a time when he was manager, *Kelly* 870-875. 896-900——Circumstance of the Rev. Peter Daly, of Galway, having continued school manager after his suspension until his death, no intimation of the suspension having been sent to the board, *Newell* 1278.

Comment upon the circumstance of the suspension of the Rev. Peter Daly not having led to his removal as manager, *Mr. Justice Lawson* 938——Continuance of the Rev. Peter Daly as manager of several schools until his death, although his suspension was perfectly well known to the board, *Mr. Justice Morris* 1297-1299——Case of the Rev. Peter Daly further adverted to; removal of his suspension before he died, *ib.* 1393-1396.

Derry, Bishop of. See *Strabane National School.*

| *Dismissal or Removal of Managers* | See *Ecclesiastical Dictation.* | *Lay Managers.* |
| *Managers,* 2. *Notice of Dismissal or Removal.* | *Precedents.* | *Suspension and Dismissal.* |

Documentary Evidence. Explanation as regards the correspondence moved for in Parliament in the O'Keeffe case, that it does not include the numerous letters prior to the 23rd April 1872, *Keenan* 880-884.

Witness produces certain papers and correspondence relative to the case of Mr. O'Keeffe, and submits explanations in connection therewith, *Newell* 905-918.

E.

Ecclesiastical Dictation. Entire inaccuracy of the statement that the commissioners were influenced by Cardinal Cullen and Bishop Moran adversely to Mr. O'Keeffe, *Keenan* 100. 399, 400——In no single instance has the board ever yielded to pressure or dictation on the part of the Roman Catholic clergy or of the Protestant clergy, *Right Hon. Sir A. Macdonnell* 576, 577.

Conclusion as to some of the commissioners having been actuated by the fear of giving offence to the Roman Catholic bishop and priests, and by the probable withdrawal of schools from connection with the board, *Mr. Justice Lawson* 969, 970. 975-979——Explanation that witness does not mean to imply that there was any actual threat or dictation on the part of the clergy, by which the board has been unduly influenced, though he considers that there have been instances of concession through fear of the withdrawal of schools, *ib.* 1127, 1128. 1172-1178——Instance of concession by the board in order to meet the views of the Roman Catholic Church, *Morell* 1208.

255.   C C 2   Positive

Report, 1873—continued.

Ecclesiastical Dictation—continued.

Positive denial of the imputation in Mr. Justice Lawson's letter that there was a reprehensible anxiety on the part of the board to yield, and be subservient, to ecclesiastical dictation, *Mr. Justice Fitzgerald* 1401.

See also *Cullen, Cardinal.   Suspension and Removal.*

Education Board. Summary of the mis-statements or charges brought against the commissioners as regards the removal of Mr. O'Keeffe, *Keenan* 96—— Firm conviction of the 12 commissioners who signed the memorial relative to those mis-statements, that they acted in accordance with the rules, and that the precedents for their action were complete, *ib.* 97-100——Desire of the majority of the board, who voted for removal, to act with entire impartiality in the matter, *ib.* 401, 402.

Different practice of the board at different periods as to taking down the names of members on divisions; record of the names since witness has been at the board, *Keenan* 436-440—— Explanation that the memorial before alluded to was never brought before the board; it was signed by 12 Commissioners, *ib.* 441-448.

Several mis-statements of facts in connection with the case of Mr. O'Keeffe, so that in addition to the papers before Parliament further explanations are proposed to be laid before the present Committee on the part of the Commissioners who signed the memorial on the subject, *Right Hon. M. Longfield* 555-560.

Reference to the increase in the proportion of the Roman Catholic Commissioners as a great improvement, *Right Hon. Sir A. Macdonnell* 576, 578.

Practice since the 17th June, 1853, of placing on record the names of those voting on each division upon any question before the board, *Keenan* 762-765——Practice of furnishing each of the Commissioners with an abstract of the previous board day's proceedings and a programme of papers to be submitted to the board at the next meeting; origin of this practice, *Kelly* 852-856.

Denial that there were any "grave mis-statements" in witness's letter relative to the action of the minority of the board in Mr. O'Keeffe's case, *Mr. Justice Lawson* 969—— Reference to witness's letter to the secretaries of the board, as not being a complete narrative of what took place in Mr. O'Keeffe's case, but as being rather a justification of the action of the minority of the board in the matter, *ib.* 996-999.

Witness is entirely responsible for the motion introduced at the board on the 9th April 1872 for the suspension of relations with Mr. O'Keeffe, *Mr. Justice Fitzgerald* 1394—— Justification of the memorial signed by witness and other Commissioners, as regards more especially the allusion therein to the "mis-statement" made with respect to the action of the majority of the board, *ib.* 1401.

Rules and regulations of the Commissioners of National Education in Ireland, *App.* 163-190.

See also *the Headings generally throughout the Index.*

Education (Callan Parish). Very injurious effect as regards education in Callan parish by reason of the continued exclusion of Mr. O'Keeffe from the management of the schools; reference hereon to an official letter of witness objecting to the course taken by the majority of the board, *Mr. Justice Lawson* 947. 956-964.

Comment upon the sending of an inspector to report on the schools, in consequence of a renewed application by Mr. O'Keeffe to be recognised as manager; refusal of recognition by the majority of the board, no matter how efficient the schools might be, *Mr. Justice Morris* 1385-1392.

Operation of four out of five of the Callan, &c. schools at the present time under the continued management of witness, *O'Keeffe* 1549, 1550.

See also *Possession of Schools.*

Ex-officio Managers. Right of the trustees, in the case of vested schools, to appoint whom they please as managers, whether laymen or clergymen; in these cases there can be no *ex-officio* clerical managers, *Keenan* 296, 297——Witness explains that parish priests have not strictly an *ex-officio* claim to the management, but only a general claim, *ib.* 315-324——Concurrence in the view that the parish priest does not as a matter of right become *ex-officio* manager of the local school; practice however of recognising the clergyman for the time being as manager where there is a parochial school, *ib.* 347-349. 380-384—— Partial extent to which there is *ex-officio* succession; that is, in its being usual to recognise the clerical successor, as manager, when nominated by the local authority, *ib.* 487-490.

Statement that in no case is a clergyman *ex-officio* patron, *Right Hon. M. Longfield* 520.

Concurrence

Report, 1873—continued.

Ex-officio Managers—continued.
 Concurrence in the view that managers of schools under the board have not any *ex-officio* right of appointment, *Right Hon. Sir A. Macdonnell* 574, 575; *Viscount Monck* 770. 773; *Newell* 1268. 1287, 1288——Conclusion that there is no such thing as an *ex-officio* manager of any school in connection with the board, *Mr. Justice Lawson* 925-927. 980-983. 1179-1183——Reference to a letter from the board in June 1840 as showing that *ex-officio* managers were not recognised, *Newell* 1269-1272——Conclusion that *ex-officio* managers were never recognised by the board, *Mr. Justice Morris* 1292-1295. 1329.
 Explanation that there are no *ex-officio* managers, though it is the rule to recognise as manager the parish priest when appointed, unless there be an objection urged against him, *Mr. Justice Fitzgerald* 1400. 1453-1482.
 See also Ballinspittle School.

F.

Fisher, Rev. Mr. Official correspondence in 1842 in the case of the Rev. Mr. Fisher of Market Hill School; order of the board, removing Mr. Fisher from the management in consequence of his suspension by his ecclesiastical superiors, *Keenan* 253-258. 481——Closing of Market Hill school for a time, after which it was re-opened under the auspices of Lord Gosford, who was recognised by the board as patron, *ib.* 259. 260.
 Explanations relative to the suspension of Mr. Fisher in 1842 from the ministry in Market Hill by the Armagh Presbytery, *Henry* 607-610——Letter from witness, as moderator of the Armagh Presbytery, to the National Board, dated 26th November 1842, suggesting Mr. Fisher's removal from the managership of the Market Hill Schools, *ib.* 610.
 Circumstance of Mr. Fisher not having been removed from the managership of Market Hill School till his ecclesiastical suspension had been confirmed by the General Assembly, *Henry* 610. 614-631. 674-676——Explanation as to Mr. Fisher's successor in the ministry not having succeeded to the management of the schools, according to the usual rule, *ib.* 611-613. 632-634.

Fitzgerald, The Right Honourable Mr. Justice (Analysis of his Evidence.)—Has been for some years a Commissioner of the Irish Education Board, 1367, 1368——Is entirely responsible for the motion introduced at the board on the 9th April 1872, for the suspension of relations with Mr. O'Keeffe 1399——It was proposed at the board that notice of the proceedings should be sent to Mr. O'Keeffe, but this was overruled, and the matter was, on the motion of witness, postponed for a fortnight, *ib.*——The case struck him as one of much importance, and inquiry was at once made at the board as to the question of precedent, 1399. 1421-1423.
 Correction of a statement by Mr. Justice Lawson, at the meeting of the board on the 23rd April 1872, to the effect that in the action then pending in the Court of Queen's Bench the very question of Mr. O'Keeffe's suspension was in issue, 1399, 1400——Conclusion as to the schools of which Mr. O'Keeffe was manager being parochial, and as to his managership having properly been discontinued when he was no longer parish priest; dissent hereon from Mr. Justice Lawson's views on the question of parochial schools, 1400. 1402-1404. 1432-1438——Statement that there are no *ex-officio* managers under the board, 1400——Recognition rather than appointment of managers by the board, *ib.*
 Careful consideration of the precedents at the board meeting of 23rd April, witness contending that these clearly laid down the principle of removal of a manager on receipt of a certificate of his ecclesiastical suspension, 1400. 1421-1426——Grounds for the conclusion that the board were perfectly justified in not making any inquiry into the validity of the suspension, and in not giving Mr. O'Keeffe any facility or opportunity for explanation before removal, 1400 *et seq.*——Discussion at the board on the 23rd April upon the question of an investigation, and not merely upon that of giving notice to Mr. O'Keeffe, without opportunity for explanation, 1400. 1514-1517.
 Justification of the memorial signed by witness and other commissioners, as regards more especially the allusion therein to the "mis-statements" made with respect to the action of the majority of the board 1401——Positive denial of the imputation in Mr. Justice Lawson's letter that there was a reprehensible anxiety on the part of the board to yield, and be subservient, to ecclesiastical dictation, *ib.*——Denial also of Mr. Justice Lawson's charge that the majority of the board were " prejudging a case which was actually in litigation," 1401. 1405. 1427-1431.
 Defence of the action of the majority of the board adverse to giving any notice to Mr. O'Keeffe before dismissal, 1406——Further reference to the precedents as justifying action upon the judgment of the ecclesiastical court, without inquiry into its foundation, 1407-1412. 1415, 1416. 1421-1426.

256.   C C 3   Obstacles

Report, 1873—continued.

Fitzgerald, The Right Hon. Mr. Justice. (Analysis of his Evidence)—continued

Obstacles and objections to any inquiry by the board into the foundation or validity of the suspension, 1412-1415. 1420——Exceptions taken to the view that as there was pending litigation the board should have stayed action till the whole matter was legally decided; great and injurious delay in such case, 1417-1419——Care taken by witness at the board discussions not to express any opinion upon the merits of the suspension; his sympathy at the time was with Father O'Keeffe, 1427-1431——Belief as to the entire absence of any communication of Cardinal Cullen with the board in Mr. O'Keeffe's case, or in any other case, 1440, 1441.

Full deference paid by the board generally to statements placed before them by Sir Alexander Macdonnell as resident commissioner, without however unduly accepting facts from him, 1442-1445——Explanation relative to some litigation with the board as to the payment of teachers' salaries in the Callan schools; denial that there was anything discreditable on the part of the board in their proceedings in the case of Woods, one of the teachers, 1446-1449——Apparent increase of public confidence in the board since the period of their action in the matter of the Callan schools, 1450-1452.

Further explanation that there are no *ex-officio* managers, though it is the rule to recognise as manager the parish priest when appointed, unless there be an objection urged against him, 1453-1462——Opinion that the Callan Infant School, as well as the other schools in the case, was parochial in its character, 1463-1465——Decision of the board merely that Mr. O'Keeffe, as being under ecclesiastical suspension, should cease to be their correspondent; nothing was decided judicially against him, nor did he lose anything through the board, 1466-1477.

Examination as to the course to be pursued by the board in the event of ecclesiastical suspension under different circumstances, and in the event of such suspension being set aside on appeal to the courts of law, 1478-1505.——Sufficient information before the board as to the legal proceedings in Mr. O'Keeffe's case to justify them in taking prompt action, without giving notice or opportunity for explanation, 1496-1513.

G.

Gibson, Mr. High legal position of Mr. Gibson (adviser of the General Assembly), one of the majority for the removal of Mr. O'Keeffe, *March* 1147-1150.

Glenvale School. See *Wilson, Rev. J. Kirk.*

Gort Schools. Extracts from the minutes of the board in 1872, and explanations thereon, relative to the dismissal of the Rev. T. Shannon from the management of the Gort National Schools for having permitted the use of the schools for a political banquet; eventual re-instatement of Mr. Shannon, he having apologised for violation of the board's rules, *Keenan* 64-68. 70——Statement that of the five schools in Gort parish two are non-vested, *ib.* 67, 68——Difficulty for a considerable period in the conduct of the Gort Schools, owing to the action of the trustees and others in supporting Dr. Keenan as manager after his suspension, *ib.* 137-140.

H.

Henry, The Rev. Pooley Shuldham, D.D. (Analysis of his Evidence.)—Has been a Commissioner of National Education in Ireland since 1838; was appointed as representative of the Presbyterian body, 580-583——Refers to a certain letter as showing the grounds upon which he concluded that the Commissioners were bound to recognise the ecclesiastical suspension of Mr. O'Keeffe, and to acknowledge Mr. Martin as his successor in the management of the Callan schools, 584, 585——Submits a section from a chapter of the Statutes of the Queen's Colleges, as containing general principles applicable to the case of Mr. O'Keeffe, 584.

Clear conviction of witness, when first he concurred in the suspension of Mr. O'Keeffe, that the precedents in the office would fully confirm the course taken as regards the Callan schools, 585. 721, 722——Formal notification of the ecclesiastical suspension of Mr. O'Keeffe to the board, 586——Statement to the effect that the Presbyterian Church would not in the first instance have joined or worked with the National Board, if the latter had decided not to accept the certificate of the Synod of Ulster, as stating the ground of deposition of a minister, 587-590. 689 693.

Strong objection, on the ground of discipline and religious instruction, to the continuance of a suspended clergyman as manager of any school, 591. 655-673. 725——Concurrence, formerly, of Archbishop Whately and Archbishop Murray in the view that a deposed clergyman ought in no case to be continued as manager of a school, 591-597

Information

Report, 1873—*continued.*

Henry, The Rev. Pooley Shuldham, D.D. (Analysis of his Evidence)—*continued.*

—— Information in connection with the deposition of Mr. Wilson, in 1850, by the Presbytery of Magherafelt and the General Assembly; doubt as to the nature of the certificate of suspension sent to the National Board, 598–604.

(*Mr. Keenan.*) Belief that in the foregoing case some certificate or document was laid before the board, besides the letter from Mr. Wilson's successor; the former cannot however be found, 605, 606.

(*Dr. Henry.*) Explanations relative to the suspension of Mr. Fisher in 1842 from the ministry in Market-hill by the Armagh Presbytery, 607–610——Letter from witness, as moderator of the Armagh Presbytery, to the National Board, dated 28th November 1842, suggesting Mr. Fisher's removal from the managership of the Market Hill Schools, 610—— Circumstance of Mr. Fisher not having been removed from the managership of Market Hill School till his ecclesiastical suspension had been confirmed by the General Assembly, 610. 614–631. 674–676——Explanation as to Mr. Fisher's successor in the ministry not having succeeded to the management of the schools, according to the usual rule, 611–613. 632–634.

Practical power of removal of managers of national schools by means of stopping the supplies, 635——Expediency of dismissal or removal of every clergyman, as manager, who is under ecclesiastical suspension, irrespectively of any legal decision, 635–643——Practice as to the dismissal of lay managers on the ground of bad character; no case has come before the board of a lay manager under excommunication, 644–648.

Origin of the adoption of the practice of appointing a clerical manager of a single denomination as manager of a national school; statement hereon that there was a strong conscience clause, 649–654——Circumstance of the board having removed Mr. Wilson, as school manager, although he had written to say he was not deposed from the ministry and intended to appeal to the civil tribunals against ecclesiastical jurisdiction, 677–686 —— Very imperfect remembrance of witness as to Dr. Keenan's case; belief that the board were unanimous as to removal, and that this took place after ecclesiastical suspension, 687, 688. 702–707.

Very general adhesion of the clergy of all denominations to the national system of education, more especially since the introduction of the non-vested system, 694–697—— Very limited co-operation of the clergy of the different denominations if the rule of the National Board had been different in cases of suspension by ecclesiastical superiors, 698 —— Concurrence of witness in all the decisions of the board in the case of Mr. O'Keeffe, 700, 701—— Action of the board in Mr. Wilson's case solely with reference to his suspension by the Presbytery, 708–713——Belief that in no instance has a suspended clergyman been continued in the management of a school, whose suspension has been notified to the Commissioners, 714. 721, 722—— Case of the Rev. Peter Daly adverted to; belief that, if suspended, his suspension was never brought before the board, 715–720.

Summary of witness's grounds for strongly approving of the rule of the Commissioners in falling in with the ecclesiastical jurisdiction as regards the nomination and suspension of clerical managers, 725–728 —— Explanation that, though concurring, as a rule, with the ecclesiastical nomination of any manager, the Commissioners do not relinquish their right of determining whether he is a fit person, 725–743.

I.

Inspectors (*National Board*). Circulars dated 6th March, and 27th July 1857, laying down regulations for the guidance of the inspectors where vacancies occur in the office of manager, *Keenan* 744. 747——Explanation that the circular of 27th July 1857, though it emanated from the office, was not submitted to the board nor issued under its authority; conclusion as to this circular being still in force, *ib.* 744–756. 759–762——There is no trace in the office of the origin of the circular, *ib.* 762.

Preparation in former years of a code of instructions for the inspectors; way in which newly appointed inspectors are informed as to the several circulars and instructions, *Keenan* 757, 758—— Duty of the inspectors to report any cases of suspension of clerical managers, *Kelly* 821.

Rules and regulations of the Commissioners as to the inspection of national schools, App. 169.

Investigation before Removal. See *Notice of Removal of Managers. Suspension and Dismissal (Clerical Managers).*

Report, 1873—continued.

K.

Keenan, Patrick Joseph, C.B. (Analysis of his Evidence.)—Official connection of witness with the Irish National Education Board, since May 1848; since December 1871 he has been resident Commissioner, 1-6——Rules of the board relative to the local management of the national schools, showing the distinction, in respect of the succession of managers, between vested and non-vested schools, 7-9. 14-18——Definition (by the rules) of the local patrons of the schools and of their right of nomination of representatives as local managers in their stead, 9——Power reserved by the Commissioners to determine whether the patron or the person nominated by him, either as his successor or as local manager, can be recognised by them as a fit person to exercise the trust, 9. 44-52.

Publication of the rules in question for the first time in 1855, though they had previously existed in the form of minutes of the board, 10-13——Division of vested schools into two classes, viz., those vested in the board in its corporate capacity, and those vested in trustees, 14——Division also of non-vested schools into two classes, viz., those under the control of committees and those under individual patrons, ib.——Reference had by the Commissioners not only to their code of rules, but to the precedents in the office in determining any cases of disputed succession of managers, 19-21. 34, 35.

Occurrence, within witness's knowledge, of only one case of disputed clerical succession in addition to those included in the Parliamentary Papers; this was the case of the Rev. Mr. Murray in 1845-48; 22, 23——Details relative to the foregoing case, and the correspondence in the matter; unanimous decision of the Commissioners that Mr. Murray, having ceased to be administrator of the parish of Kilfinan (Mayo), in which the Kinceen, Creeves, and other national schools, were situated, was not entitled to be restored to the management of the schools, and was properly succeeded in the management by his successor in the administration of the parish, 23-33. 36——Recognition of Mr. Lynch, a layman, as manager *pro tempore*, during the absence of Mr. Murray, and until the appointment of Mr. Jordan, 24-28. 208-211——Explanation as to the Rev. Mr. Murray's case not having been submitted to the board when the case of the Rev. Mr. O'Keeffe was under consideration, 34.

Dismissal by the board, in 1837, of Mr. Robert Gay, as manager of the Attaghmore (Tyrone) National School, 36-38——Further exercise of the power of dismissal, in 1840, in the case of the Rev. Mr. M'Swiney, manager of the Ballinspittle National School (Cork), 38-41——Conclusion as to dismissal being involved in the refusal of the Commissioners to hold any further correspondence with a manager, 38. 40. 44-48. 71-73.

Particulars in connection with the dismissal, in 1851, of the Rev. Mr. Malone, as manager of the Ballina National School, for having allowed the use of the school-room for a political dinner; subsequent recognition, as manager, of the Rev. Mr. Madden, who had been nominated by Mr. Malone, 41-63——Practice generally as to dismissal of managers, and the nomination or appointment of their successors, according to the different classes of schools, and whether vested or non-vested, 44-62——Careful consideration given by the board to all the circumstances involved in any case of disputed clerical succession, 63.

Extracts from the minutes of the board in 1872, and explanations thereon, relative to the dismissal of the Rev. T. Shannon from the management of the Gort National Schools, for having permitted the use of the schools for a political banquet; eventual re-instatement of Mr. Shannon, he having apologised for violation of the board's rules, 64-68. 70——Statement that of the five schools in Gort parish, two are non-vested, 67, 68.

Very rare instances, on the whole, of the exercise of the power of removal of managers, 69, 70——Conclusion that whether a manager is "removed" from connection with a vested school, or whether the board "decline to hold correspondence" with the manager of a non-vested school, it is equally a case of dismissal, 71-81——Instances in the cases of the Rev. Mr. O'Keeffe and the Rev. Dr. Keenan of managers having continued to keep the schools open after the board had refused to hold correspondence with them, 82-84.

Letter from the Rev. Edward Rowan, Mr. O'Keeffe's predecessor in the parish of Callan, dated 16th February 1863, submitting his resignation as manager of the Callan, Newtown, and Coolagh schools, 85, 86——Routine nomination of Mr. O'Keeffe at once made by the board in the case of the Coolagh and Newtown schools, as being non-vested, 86. 92——Nomination by the committee of the Callan schools called for by the board in accordance with their rules; subsequent appointment of Mr. O Keeffe by the committee, dated 28th February 1863, 86-91.

Statistics submitted showing the total number of managers, clerical and lay, under each denomination, and the total number of schools under each denomination, distinguishing between clerical management and lay management, 93.

Summary

Report, 1873—*continued.*

Keenan, *Patrick Joseph,* C.B. (Analysis of his Evidence)—*continued.*

Summary of the mis-statements or charges brought against the Commissioners as regards the removal of Mr. O'Keeffe, 96— -Firm conviction of the thirteen Commissioners who signed the memorial relative to these mis-statements, that they acted in accordance with the rules, and that the precedents for their action were complete, 97–100—— Entire inaccuracy of the statement that the Commissioners were influenced by Cardinal Cullen and Bishop Moran adversely to Mr. O'Keeffe, 100.

Proposal by witness to explain in detail to the Committee the different features of the several precedents, and to show how far they were parallel with the case of Mr. O'Keeffe, 101–104. 121—— Explanation in connection with a document sent officially to the board by Chief Baron Pigott, as well as with the origin of the memorial signed by the thirteen Commissioners, 105–120.

Information as to the way in which the suspension of the clerical manager was notified to the board in each of the four precedents and in the case of Mr. O'Keeffe, 122–124 ——Statement of the action of the board in each case, on receiving intimation of the suspension; invariable refusal to entertain any denial or legal appeal on the part of the person suspended, 125–133—— Twofold objections, on secular and on religious grounds, to the continuance of suspended clergymen as managers of schools, 126——Absence of any reference to the suspended clergyman before action was taken by the board, 127.

Explanation of the practice in each of the cases of precedent, as well as in Mr. O'Keeffe's case, as to the appointment of the successor of the suspended clergyman to the management of the schools in the parish, 134–136—— Desire of some members of the committee of the Ratoath schools to continue Mr. Sheridan as manager after his suspension; concurrence eventually as to the appointment of the Rev. Mr. Fulham, the new administrator of the parish, 134. 137.

Difficulty for a considerable time in the conduct of the Gort Schools, owing to the action of the trustees and others in supporting Dr. Keenan as manager, after his suspension, 137–140—— Resistance offered to the new manager of Callau schools on the part of Mr. O'Keeffe down to the present time, 140—— Special reference made by the board to Bishop Kilduff, in the case of Mr. O'Farrell, in order to elicit the fact of suspension before final action, 141. 170, 171—— Statement that the board attach no consideration to the fact, in some cases, that the suspended clergyman was the founder of the school, he having been the founder as clergyman of the parish or minister of the congregation, 142.

Quotation of certain rules of the Bequest Board of Ireland as having reference to the question of suspended clergymen, 144, 145—— Regulations adopted by the Board of National Education in 1832, as to the books to be used in the schools, and as to the control to be exercised in the matter by the Commissioners, and by the local ecclesiastical authority, 145.

Probable explanation of the omission of the board to apply to the trustees or committee of Magheral school before appointing Mr. Macken as successor to Dr. Keenan, 147–150. 201–207. 234–242—— Conclusion as to the appointment of Dr. Templeton, in lieu of Mr. Wilson, having been made by the board upon some document which has been mislaid or lost, 151–159—— Statement on the subject of a reference having been made to the committee of the Ratoath schools, after the suspension of Mr. Sheridan, and before the appointment of his successor; delay after the suspension before the board took action, 160–175—— Witness will obtain for the Committee all the correspondence in the foregoing case, 176–182.

Examination to the effect that the Commissioners do not directly nominate the managers, but "recognise" the nomination by the trustees, patrons, or committees; indifferent use by the board of the terms "recognition" and "appointment," 184–196. 201 —— Exceptional instance of dismissal of managers for neglect or want of attention to the management of the schools, 197–200—— Doubt as to there being any instances of laymen nominated by clerical managers as their successors, 208–213 ——Instance of a lay founder of a school having been recognised as manager, 212.

Recognition of the Rev. Mr. O'Farrell as manager during several years whilst he performed no ecclesiastical duties; the board were not aware of the latter circumstance, 214–216—— Recognition of the Bishop of Derry as manager of a parochial school in Strabane, after he had left the parish where he was rector; reason for the non-appointment at first of his successor in the parish, 217–220—— Case of a convent school near Dublin which is managed efficiently by the Rev. Canon Keogh, who has been removed from Dublin, 220.

Statement to the effect that the bishop, in the case of the Rev. J. Sheridan, requested that the latter might be recognised as manager of the Annaduff School, but did not actually nominate him for the post, 221–226—— Invariable rule of the Board to accept as manager the clerical successor to the outgoing clerical manager, if the former made application on the subject, 227–230—— Practice as to the management attaching to every succeeding

Report, 1873—*continued.*

Keenan, *Patrick Joseph,* C.B. (Analysis of his Evidence)—*continued.*

succeeding clergyman in the case of a school vested in the board in its corporate capacity where the name of the clergyman is inserted in the lease as the patron, 231–233.

View of the majority of the board, as regards Mr. O'Keeffe's case, that there was a vacancy in the management of Callan schools just as though Mr. O'Keeffe had died, 243–247——Statement that the board has expressed no opinion as to the authenticity of the original nomination of Mr. O'Keeffe by the committee of the schools, 248–251.

[Second Examination.]—Explanation on sundry portions of witness's former evidence relative to the case of Mr. O'Keeffe, and the cases of Mr. Wilson and Mr. Sheridan, 252.

Statement showing that in addition to the precedents (as in the Parliamentary Paper) of the dismissal of clerical managers, a further case has now been discovered, which occurred in 1842; 253——Official correspondence in the foregoing case, which was that of the Rev. Mr. Fisher of Market-hill School; order of the board removing Mr. Fisher from the management in consequence of his suspension by his ecclesiastical superiors, 253–258. 481——Closing of Market-hill School for a time, after which it was re-opened under the auspices of Lord Gosford, who was recognised by the board as patron, 259, 260.

Witness submits explanations in detail relative to the case of the Rev. Dr. Keenan, and the ultimate action of the board in ordering the removal of Dr. Keenan, and the appointment of the Rev. Mr. Macken, as school manager in his stead, 261–271. 296–301. 312–314. 339–345. 340–358.

Further information in connection with the case of Mr. Wilson; reference more especially to a letter from the Rev. Mr. Templeton, dated 25th May 1871, reporting the suspension of Mr. Wilson, 272–278. 482——Nomination of Mr. Templeton by the board as manager of Glenvale School, without any reference to the school committee, 275–277 ——Probable explanation of the statement by the board, in dismissing Mr. Wilson, that they would not recognise him as manager of "either the Glenvale or any other National school," 279–281.

Sundry letters produced, and explanations thereon, in further elucidation of the circumstances under which the Rev. Mr. O'Farrell was continued in the management of Lisduff School, and a considerable delay occurred before the appointment of the Rev. Mr. Sheridan thereto, who had succeeded Mr. O'Farrell in Annaduff parish, 282–287—— Peculiar character of Lisduff School, it being one of a very limited class of schools which are secured by bond, 282–285——There was never any imputation that Mr. O'Farrell was insane, 288.

Papers and correspondence in 1863–65 relative to the case of the Rev. Mr. Sheridan, manager of the Ratoath and Ashbourne Schools; full explanation therem of the circumstances under which much delay occurred before the appointment as manager of the Rev. Mr. Fulham, the successor of Mr. Sheridan, in the administration of the parishes in question, 288–293. 365–371——Oversight or omission on the part of the office, owing to which Mr. Sheridan, though suspended, remained in the management of the schools for a period of about two years, 288. 294, 295.

Right of the trustees, in the case of vested schools, to appoint whom they please as managers, whether laymen or clergymen; in these cases there can be no *ex-officio* clerical managers, 296, 297——Weight attached to the ecclesiastical suspension of any clergyman as unfitting him for school management, whether parish administrator or not, 302, 303. 325–338——Absence of any rule of the board embodying the proposition that no legal decision could reinstate a suspended clergyman as parish priest contrary to ecclesiastical jurisdiction, 304–306——Statement that the board has never officially interpreted the "competent authority" required for the removal of suspension, as in the case of Mr. O'Keeffe, 307–311——Reference had by the board to an ecclesiastical tribunal in alluding to a pending appeal instituted by Dr. Keenan against his suspension, 312–314 ——Instances of dismissal of managers for violation of rules, witness explaining that parish priests have not, strictly, an *ex-officio* claim to the management, but only a general claim, 315–324.

Further explanation that the dismissal of Mr. O'Keeffe from the Callan Schools was wholly and solely because he had been suspended ecclesiastically, 325–331——Direct effect of suspension upon the question of fitness, witness maintaining that in no case is a suspended clergyman a suitable person for manager of schools, 332–338——Practice of the board never to inquire into the cause of suspension, nor to apply for explanation to the person suspended, 334. 356–377. 401——Comparison between each case of removal, in consequence of suspension, as regards the question of promptitude of action on the part of the board when once the suspension was notified, 339–346. 350–375.

Statement with further reference to Dr. Keenan's case as relating in the first instance to the charges against Mr. Grant, the schoolmaster; short interval before Dr. Keenan's removal after his suspension was formally announced to the board, 339–345. 350–358——
Concurrence

Report, 1873—continued.

Keenan, Patrick Joseph, C.B. (Analysis of his Evidence)—*continued.*

Concurrence in the view that the parish priest does not, as a matter of right, become *ex-officio* manager of the local school; practice, however, of recognising the clergyman for the time being as manager, where there is a parochial school, 347-349. 380-388 —— Uniform course pursued in appointing the clerical successor of a suspended clergyman as manager in all cases of non-vested schools without committees, 378, 379 —— Circumstance of Mr. Wilson, though the founder of Glenvale School, having been removed in favour of his successor in the parish, 388. 454-456.

Conclusion as to Mr. O'Keeffe having become manager of the Coolagh and Newtown Schools, as a matter of course, on his becoming parish priest, 389, 390 —— Nomination of Mr. O'Keeffe's predecessors in the parish (except the Rev. Mr. Salmon) by the committee of the Callan male and female schools as managers of those schools; form of nomination in Mr. O'Keeffe's case, 391-393 —— Contention of Mr. O'Keeffe that he is still parish priest of Callan, 394, 395 —— Non-recognition by the board of any suspended clergyman as manager, even though still supported by the committee of the school, 396-398.

Entire inaccuracy of the assumption that the board acted in deference to Cardinal Cullen in their removal of Mr. O'Keeffe, 399, 400 —— Desire of the majority of the board who voted for removal to act with entire impartiality in the matter, 401, 402 —— Conduct of the Callan schools in violation of the rules of the board, after the removal of Mr. O'Keeffe, so that it was necessary to strike them off the roll of National Schools, 403, 404 —— Distinct position of the infant school at Callan; impossibility of separating this school from the other Callan schools, as regards management, save with the consent of the committee, 405-411.

Further reference to the case of Dr. Alexander, Bishop of Derry, and the Strabane National School, as showing that clerical succession was duly recognised in the management of the school, 412-415 —— Invariable practice of the board to give opportunity for explanation before removal for breach of rules, 416-418 —— Ministerial function exercised by the board in accepting as conclusive the certificate of the ecclesiastical superior as to suspension, 419-422. 491-497 —— Inquiry made however in the case of ecclesiastical nomination of a successor, 423-425.

Doubt as to complaint having been addressed to the board in Mr. O'Farrell's case that for several years he had not performed ecclesiastical duties, through being under suspension, 426-433 —— Different practice of the board at different periods as to taking down the names of members on divisions; record of the names since witness has been at the board, 436-440 —— Explanation that the memorial before alluded to was never brought before the board; it was signed by 13 Commissioners, 441-448.

Information as to the several cases of precedent in which there was a committee of the schools, 449-460 —— Denial that the action of the Poor Law Commissioners in Mr. O'Keeffe's case had any influence upon the National Board, 461-464 —— Admission that the question of the validity of Mr. O'Keeffe's suspension was introduced at the board, but this was not entertained by the majority, 465-473.

Inability of witness to state whether in any of the precedents the question of the validity of the suspension was raised at the board, 474-479 —— Doubt as to the ecclesiastical superiors by whom Presbyterian clergy are suspended, 480-482 —— Statement that in certain rules of the board the "appointment by the local patrons" is hardly correct, and that the word "nomination" should be substituted for "appointment," 483-486. 501-503.

Partial extent to which there is *ex-officio* succession; that is, in its being usual to recognise the clerical successor, as manager, when nominated by the local authority, 487-490 —— Provisional appointment of a manager by the board in cases where there is a delay before the local authority nominates, 498 —— Recognition of a layman, in lieu of the clerical successor, as manager, if the former be nominated by the local authority, 499, 500 —— Occurrence of only two instances of removal of managers since 1865; 504.

[Third Examination.]—Circular to the inspectors, dated 6th March 1857, issued by order of the board, with reference to the appointment of laymen as managers in cases of change of managers by death, transfer, &c., 744. 747 —— Further circular, dated 27th July 1857, laying down regulations for the guidance of the inspectors when vacancies occur in the office of manager, 744. 747 —— Explanation that the foregoing circular, though it emanated from the office, was not submitted to the board nor issued under its authority; conclusion as to this circular being still in force, 744-756. 759-762.

Preparation in former years of a code of instructions for the inspectors; way in which newly appointed inspectors are informed as to the several circulars and instructions, 757, 758 —— Practice since the 17th June 1863 of placing on record the names of those voting in each division upon any question before the board, 762-765.

255. D D 2 *Keenan,*

Report, 1873—continued.

Keenan, Rev. Dr. (Magheral School.) Decision by the board in Dr. Keenan's case, although they knew he had appealed against his suspension, *Keenan* 131. 133——Probable explanation of the omission of the Education Board to apply to the trustees or committee of Magheral school before appointing Mr. Macken as successor to Dr. Keenan, *ib.* 147–150. 201–207——Further reference to the case of Dr. Keenan, the board having decided the matter on receiving notice of his suspension from Bishop Blake, *ib.* 234–242.

Witness, who is now supplied with all the correspondence and documents in the case of the Rev. Dr. Keenan, submits an outline of the same, together with explanations on various points as to the ultimate action of the board in ordering the removal of Dr. Keenan, and the appointment of the Rev. Mr. Macken, as school manager in his stead, *Keenan* 261–271. 296–301. 312–314. 339–345. 350–358——Origination of the correspondence in Dr. Keenan's case with reference to the question of fitness of the teacher, Mr. Grant; charges brought against Mr. Grant by the Rev. Mr. Macken, and by Bishop Blake, so that the board, after inquiry, required his transfer to another school, *ib.* 261–288. 339–343——Recognition of Dr. Keenan by the board as manager of Magheral School, he having been probably nominated by the trustees in the first instance, *ib.* 298–301——Reference had by the Board to an ecclesiastical tribunal in alluding to a pending appeal instituted by Dr. Keenan against his suspension, *ib.* 312–314.

Statement with further reference to Dr. Keenan's case as relating, in the first instance, to the charges against Mr. Grant, the schoolmaster; short interval before Dr. Keenan's removal after his suspension was formally announced to the Board, *Keenan* 339–345. 350–358.

Probable cause of the neglect or the delay on the part of the secretaries in not promptly reporting the suspension of the manager of the Magheral School, *Right Hon. M. Longfield* 532–534——Very imperfect remembrance of witness as to Dr. Keenan's case; belief that the board were unanimous as to removal, and that this took place soon after ecclesiastical suspension, *Henry* 687, 688. 702–707.

Illegality of the appointment of Mr. Macken as successor to Dr. Keenan, there having been a Committee in the case, *Mr. Justice Lawson* 957——Difference between Mr. O'Keeffe's case and that of Dr. Keenan, *Morell* 1239–1243——Argument to the effect that the case of Dr. Keenan forms no precedent for the course pursued in Mr. O'Keeffe's case, *Mr. Justice Morris* 1307–1316.

Letter from the Rev. J. S. Keenan, dated 5th March 1845, protesting against certain charges made against Mr. Grant, as teacher, and also against the course pursued as regards his own suspension, *App.* 192.

Report of Mr. Robertson, inspector, showing the result of his investigation of the charges made against Mr. Grant, *App.* 192, 193.

Kelly, James. (Analysis of his Evidence.)—Official experience of witness as one of the Joint Secretaries of the Board of National Education since 1841; 793–798——Letter received by the secretaries from the Rev. Mr. Fulham, in January 1863, stating that he was administrator of Ratoath parish, in lieu of the Rev. Mr. Sheridan, who had been suspended, 799. 802——Reply to the foregoing by the Secretaries on the 19th February, referring Mr. Fulham to the Committee of the Ratoath Schools, as having the appointment of manager, the schools being non vested, 800–811——Explanation as to the omission on the part of the secretaries in not at once informing the board that Mr. Sheridan was suspended, the fact not having been notified till the 27th January 1865, 801. 812–819. 848–851——Statement on the subject of the inspectors not having informed the board as to the suspension of Mr. Sheridan, 820–828.

Doubt as to there having having been any cases of schoolmasters or lay managers dismissed on account of ecclesiastical censure, 829–831——Inability of witness to adduce any instances of removal of managers by the board, in addition to those recorded in the precedents, 832–841. 846, 847——Invariable inquiry by the board in the event of an inspector reporting that a schoolmaster was not fit for his post, 842–843——Long delay on the part of Mr. Fulham before renewing his application to the board relative to the managership of the schools in his parish, 848–851.

Practice of furnishing each of the Commissioners with an abstract of the previous board day's proceedings, and a programme of papers to be submitted to the board at the next meeting; origin of this practice, 852–856——Presence of witness on only one occasion when the case of Mr. O'Keeffe was under discussion at the board; the question of precedents was not then introduced, 857–861. 890, 891——Order, signed by the President Commissioner, and dated 18th February 1865, recognising Mr. Fulham as manager of the Ratoath Schools, 862, 863. 865, 866——Explanation as to the Rev. Mr. O'Farrell having continued manager of Lisduff School, after his ecclesiastical suspension and his removal from Annaduff School, 867, 868.

Witness does not recollect any case of a clergyman under suspension having been continued as manager, save the case of Mr. O'Farrell, 869——Absence of any official intimation that the Rev. Mr. Daly, of Galway, was under suspension at a time when he was manager,

Report, 1873—*continued.*

Kelly, James. (Analysis of his Evidence)—*continued.*
manager, 870–875. 896–900——Belief that there was a letter from Mr. O'Keeffe, in which he stated that he had been suspended for the fifth time, 876–879.

(*Mr. Keenan.*) Explanation as regards the correspondence moved for in Parliament in the O'Keeffe case, that it does not include the numerous letters prior to the 23rd April 1872, 880–884.

(*Mr. Kelly.*) First communication of Mr. O'Keeffe's suspension by letter from Mr. Harkin, the inspector, on the 29th November 1871; other letters in this case which were before the board in April 1872; 885–889——Doubt as to there being many cases of complaints from the public relative to clerical managers, or as to any such complaints having led to any inquiry by the Board, 893–895——Practice as regards reference to the ecclesiastical superior when a case of suspension is reported by an inspector, 901–903.

Keogh, Rev. Canon. Case of a convent school near Dublin, which is managed efficiently by the Rev. Canon Keogh, who has been removed from Dublin, *Keenan* 220.

L.

Lawson, The Right Honourable Mr. Justice. (Analysis of his Evidence.)—Experience of witness as Commissioner of National Education in Ireland since 1861; 920–923—— Absence of any rule of the board, providing that a clerical manager of a school should, upon suspension, be removed from the management, 924. 928. 933——Conclusion that there is no such thing as an *ex-officio* manager of any school in connection with the board, 925–927. 980–983. 1179–1183—— Dissent from the view that there any parochial schools connected with the board as distinct from national schools, 927. 1182, 1183——Opinion that in each case of suspension there should be full inquiry into all the circumstances before dismissal is resorted to, 928–930. 934, 935. 939.

Admission of suspension in the case of Mr. Sheridan, but not directly by himself; witness explains that he has no recollection of this case, or of being present at any decision of the board relative thereto, 931–933——Circumstance of Mr. Sheridan not having been removed as manager until long after his suspension was known to the office; inference that there was no absolute rule on the subject, 931. 937——Statement that suspension forms a *primâ facie* ground for inquiry, and in some cases, but not in all, should be conclusive as to removal from the management; circumstances under which removal should not be a consequence of suspension, 934–936. 972–974.

Probability of the suspensions formerly having been such as to call for removal, without proving there was any absolute rule on the subject, 936–938——Circumstance of the suspension of the Rev. Peter Daly not having led to his removal as manager, 938—— Intelligence before the board as to Mr. O'Keeffe's suspension for some months before they took any action in the matter, *ib.*——Explanation in detail of witness's views as to the several conditions to be complied with before an alleged suspension should be followed by dismissal from managership; conclusion that these conditions were wanting in the case of Mr. O'Keeffe, 939 *et seq.*

Circumstance of Cardinal Cullen not being the ecclesiastical superior entitled to suspend Mr. O'Keeffe, 945——Inadequacy of the offence, for which suspension took place, to justify Mr. O'Keeffe's removal from the schools, *ib.*——Argument that as an action was pending, in order to try the validity of the suspension, the board should have waited for the result of such action before proceeding to dismissal, as they thereby prejudged the question of the legality of the suspension, 946–955. 1037, 1038. 1043–1047. ——Very injurious effect as regards education in Callan parish, by reason of the continued exclusion of Mr. O'Keeffe from the management of the schools; reference hereon to an official letter of witness objecting to the course taken by the majority of the board, 947. 956–964——Continued possession of the schools by Mr. O'Keeffe after his suspension, 947. 968.

Absence of any real power in the board to appoint a successor to a manager, where the school is under a committee, 965–967——Illegality of the appointment of Mr. Macken as successor to Dr. Keenan, there having been a committee in the case, 967—— Denial that there were any "grave mis-statements," in witness's letter relative to the action of the minority of the board in Mr. O'Keeffe's case, 969——Conclusion as to some of the Commissioners having been actuated by the fear of giving offence to the Roman Catholic bishops and priests, and by the probable withdrawal of schools from connection with the board, 969, 970. 975–979.

Statement to the effect, that the board has no legal right to remove the manager of a non-vested school, though they have full power in the matter by stopping the supplies to the school, 984–985——Reference to witness's letter to the secretaries of the board, as not being a complete narrative of what took place in Mr. O'Keeffe's case, but as being rather a justification of the action of the minority of the board in the matter, 996–999 ——Examination

Report, 1873—*continued*.

Lawson, The Right Honourable Mr. Justice. (Analysis of his Evidence)—*continued.*

—— Examination to the effect, that a certain discussion at the board was upon the question of giving Mr. O'Keeffe notice of the proceedings, and not upon the question of giving him opportunity for explanation, 1000-1013.

Failure of duty on the part of the Commissioners if, when there has been a dispute as to the validity of ecclesiastical suspension, no notice has been given before removal by the board, 1014-1018——Examination upon the circumstance of witness not having stipulated for notice in the case of Mr. Sheridan before action was taken upon his suspension; distinction between this case and that of Mr. O'Keeffe, 1019-1036. 1040-1042. 1100, 1101. 1104, 1105. 1129, 1130. 1152-1154——Denial by Mr. O'Keeffe that Cardinal Cullen had any right to suspend him, 1037. 1038——Explanation of the part taken by witness in reference to an alteration of the Board's rules in the case of a convent school at Wexford, 1039.

Question considered how far the rule of acting on the certificate of the ecclesiastical superior applies also to the allocation of funds under the Charitable Bequests Act, 1048-1051——Examination upon a statement in witness's letter to the board, that it was involved in a litigation not very creditable to it with respect to the salary of Mr. Woods, one of the teachers of the Callan Schools, 1051*-1076 1184——Explanation as to a further statement in this letter that a proposal by witness for the payment of the teacher's salaries while the dispute about Mr. O'Keeffe was pending, was "defeated by an amendment, declaring that such payment would be a misapplication of the public funds;" reason for not setting forth this amendment in full in the letter, 1077-1091. 1184-1186.

Argument that so long as the Callan Schools were managed in accordance with the rules of the board, the ecclesiastical suspension of Mr. O'Keeffe for reasons not touching the question of his educational usefulness did not justify the summary action of the board in the matter, 1092-1108. 1130——Consideration of the condition of the Callan schools under Mr. O'Keeffe, and of the inspector's report thereon in January 1873; willingness of witness to have discussed the question of dismissal on the score of mismanagement, 1109-1111. 1135-1141. 1161-1166——Admission by witness, that he cannot quote any instance of the continued recognition of a clerical manager after his suspension was certified to the board, 1106-1108——Great weight attached by the board to the facts laid before it by the Resident Commissioner, Sir Alexander Macdonnell, in Mr. Sheridan's case, as well as in any other case, 1112-1126. 1169-1171.

Explanation that witness does not mean to imply that there was any actual threat or dictation on the part of the clergy, by which the board has been unduly influenced, though he considers that there have been instances of concession through fear of the withdrawal of schools, 1127, 1128. 1172-1178——Further statement, that as a judicial member of the Board, witness felt constrained not to prejudge Mr. O'Keeffe's case so long as there was a *bonâ fide* litigation pending as to the validity of the suspension, 1131-1134.

Question considered whether the Roman Catholic bishops might not, as patrons, by bringing the schools to the National Board in the first instance, have appointed the managers, and have had full power to remove them, irrespectively of the board, 1142-1151——Witness repeats, that whilst prepared to give all proper weight to decrees of suspension, he would not act upon mere suspension without further inquiry, 1152.1155-1160 ——Refusal of a court of justice to decide any question of trust in connection with the parish priest of Callan as manager of the schools, so long as it was in litigation whether he was parish priest, 1167, 1168.

[Second Examination].—Denial that witness was in error (as attempted to be shown by Mr. Justice Fitzgerald) in stating, that on the 23rd April the matter in issue between Mr. O'Keeffe and Cardinal Cullen was pointed out to the board, 1518——Exception taken also to certain comments by Mr. Justice Fitzgerald upon a statement by witness as to the board prejudging a case actually in litigation, *ib.*

Lay Managers. Statistics relative to the managers of national schools, distinguishing between clerical managers and lay managers, *Keenan* 96——Doubt as to there being any instances of laymen nominated by clerical managers as their successors, *ib.* 208-213—— Instance of a lay founder of a school having been recognised as manager, *ib.* 212—— Recognition by the board of a layman, in lieu of the clerical successor, as manager, if the former be nominated by the local authority, *ib.* 499, 500.

Reluctance of the board to dismiss lay managers for mere neglect of duty, *Right Hon. M. Longfield* 539, 540——Practice as to the dismissal of lay managers on the ground of bad character; no case has come before the board of a lay manager under excommunication, *Henry* 644-648.

Circular to the inspectors, dated 6th March 1857, issued by order of the board, with reference to the appointment of laymen as managers in cases of change of managers by death, transfer, &c., *Keenan* 744-747——Doubt as to there having been any cases of schoolmasters or lay managers dismissed on account of ecclesiastical censure, *Kelly* 829-831—— Reception of any school into connection with the National Board, whether it be brought by a lay or clerical patron, so long as the rules are observed, *Mr. Justice Morris* 1338.

Legal

Report, 1873—*continued*.

Legal Proceedings (O'Keeffe v. Cardinal Cullen). Argument that as an action was pending, in order to try the validity of the suspension, the board should have waited for the result of such action before proceeding to dismissal, as they thereby prejudged the question of the legality of the suspension, *Mr. Justice Lawson* 948-955. 1037, 1038. 1043-1047 —— Further statement that as a judicial member of the Board, witness felt constrained not to prejudge Mr. O'Keeffe's case so long as there was a *bonâ fide* litigation pending as to the validity of the suspension, *ib.* 1131-1134 —— Refusal of a court of justice to decide any question of trust in connection with the parish priest of Callan as manager of the schools, so long as it was in litigation whether he was parish priest, *ib.* 1167, 1168.

Inexpediency of the board acting at once upon any ecclesiastical suspension, the validity of which is disputed by the suspended person, *Morell* 1197, 1198. 1244 —— Information before the board (at the time of the removal of Mr. O'Keeffe), through Judge Morris, as to the pleadings in the case between Mr. O'Keeffe and Cardinal Cullen, *ib.* 1219.

Statement as to witness having produced at the board the pleadings in the suit of Mr. O'Keeffe against Cardinal Cullen, and having, as a judge, declined to prejudge the case, *Mr. Justice Morris* 1324-1326.

Correction of a statement by Mr. Justice Lawson at the meeting of the board on the 23rd April 1872, to the effect that in the action then pending in the Court of Queen's Bench the very question of Mr. O'Keeffe's suspension was in issue, *Mr. Justice Fitzgerald* 1399, 1400 —— Denial also of Mr. Justice Lawson's charge that the majority of the board were prejudging a case which was actually in litigation, *ib.* 1401. 1405. 1427-1431 —— Exceptions taken to the view that as there was pending litigation the board should have stayed action till the whole matter was legally decided; great and injurious delay in such case, *ib.* 1417-1419 —— Sufficient information before the board as to the legal proceedings in Mr. O'Keeffe's case to justify them in taking prompt action without giving notice or opportunity for explanation, *ib.* 1496-1513.

Denial that witness was in error (as attempted to be shown by Mr. Justice Fitzgerald), in stating that on the 23rd April, the matter in issue between Mr. O'Keeffe and Cardinal Cullen was pointed out to the board, *Mr. Justice Lawson* 1518 —— Exception taken also to certain comments by Mr. Justice Fitzgerald upon a statement by witness as to the board prejudging a case actually in litigation, *ib.*

Lisduff School. See *O'Farrell, Rev. Mr.*

Longfield, The Right Hon. Mountifort, LL.D. (Analysis of his Evidence.)—Experience of witness since 1853 as a member of the Irish Education Board, 505, 506 —— Uniform custom of the board not to recognise as manager of a national school any clergyman whose suspension has been notified, 507-511. 521, 522. 551 —— Explanation that the board has no jurisdiction over the patronage, save by declining to correspond with an improper patron or manager, 512. 522. 526 —— Revision of the rules as to management in 1853, in consequence of previous disputes at the board, 513, 514.

Withdrawal of the schoolmaster's salary by the board in the event of a suspended priest being maintained as patron, 515, 516 —— Equal treatment of the different kinds of school by the board, as regards the removal of patrons, 517-519 —— Statement that in no case is a clergyman *ex-officio* patron, 520 —— Practice to accept, without inquiry, nominated clergymen as managers unless some objection be raised, 523-525.

Conclusion, as regards removal or invalidity of suspension, that this can be effected only by the ecclesiastical superior, 527-531 —— Probable cause of the neglect or delay on the part of the secretaries in not promptly reporting the suspension of the manager of Magheral School, 532-534 —— Summary of the duties discharged by the manager of a school in connection with the board, 535-537.

Argument that a suspended clergyman or parish priest is not a proper person to be continued as manager, he having been, moreover, nominated in the first instance on the strength of his being parish priest, 538-552. 561-567 —— Acceptance by the board of the mere fact of suspension by the proper authority, 538. 541. 565-567 —— Reluctance of the board to dismiss lay managers for mere neglect of duty, 539, 540 —— Discord to be produced by not recognising the right of the bishop to suspend the parish priest, 541. 561-564.

Justification of the dismissal of Mr. O'Keeffe, without first going to him for an explanation as to his suspension, 553, 554 —— Several mis-statements of facts in connection with the case of Mr. O'Keeffe, so that in addition to the papers before Parliament, further explanations are proposed to be laid before the present Committee on the part of the commissioners who signed the memorial on the subject, 555-560 —— Approval of the recognition, as manager, of the successor to a suspended priest, although in exceptional instances discord might be produced, 561-564 —— Instances of the question of legality of suspension having been before the board, without influencing their action, 565.

M.

Macdonnell, The Right Honourable Sir Alexander. (Analysis of his Evidence.)—Was resident Commissioner of the Irish Education Board from 1839 till 1871; 571——Concurs generally in the evidence of Mr. Keenan and Judge Longfield, 572-575——Considers that no managers of schools under the board had an *ex-officio* right of appointment, 574, 575——In no single instance has the board ever yielded to pressure or dictation on the part of the Roman Catholic clergy, or of the Protestant clergy, 576, 577——Refers to the increase in the proportion of Roman Catholic Commissioners as a great improvement, 576. 578——Has a decided opinion that the course pursued in Mr. O'Keeffe's case was conformable to precedents, 579.

Great weight attached by the board to the facts laid before it by the resident Commissioner, Sir Alexander Macdonnell, in Mr. Sheridan's case, as well as in any other case, *Mr. Justice Lawson* 1112-1126. 1169-1171.

Full deference paid by the board generally to statements placed before them by Sir Alexander Macdonnell as resident Commissioner, without however unduly accepting facts from him, *Mr. Justice Fitzgerald,* 1442-1445.

Letter from Sir A. Macdonnell to the chairman of the Committee stating that he gave no information to the board in Mr. Sheridan's case, beyond what appeared in the papers laid before the board, *App.* 194.

Magheral School. See *Keenan, Rev. Dr.*

Malone, Rev. Mr. See *Ballina School.*

MANAGERS (NATIONAL SCHOOLS):

1. *As to the Appointment or Recognition of Managers.*
2. *As to Dismissal or Removal*
3. *Duties of Managers.*
4. *Statistics relative to Lay and Clerical Managers of different Denominations.*

1. *As to the Appointment or Recognition of Managers:*

Rules of the board relative to the local management of the National Schools, showing the distinction, in respect of the succession of managers, between vested and non-vested schools; explanations thereon, *Keenan* 7-9. 14-18. *App.* 168-169——Definition by the rules of the Education Board of the local patrons of National Schools, and of their right of nomination of representatives as local managers in their stead, *Keenan* 9——Power reserved by the Commissioners to determine whether the patron or the person nominated by him, either as his successor or as local manager, can be recognised by them as a fit person to exercise the trust, *ib.* 9. 44-52——Explanation of the practice generally as to dismissal of managers, and the nomination or appointment of their successors according to the different classes of schools, and whether vested or non-vested, *ib.* 44-62——Careful consideration given by the board to all the circumstances involved in any case of disputed clerical succession, *ib.* 63.

Examination to the effect that the Commissioners do not directly nominate the managers, but "recognise" the nomination by the trustees, patrons, or committees; indifferent use by the board of the terms "recognition" and "appointment," *Keenan* 184-196. 201——Invariable rule of the board to accept as manager the clerical successor to the outgoing clerical manager, if the former made application on the subject, *ib.* 227-230——Practice as to the management attaching to every succeeding clergyman in the case of a school vested in the board in its corporate capacity where the name of the clergymen is inserted in the lease as the patron, *ib.* 231-233.

Inquiry made by the board in the case of ecclesiastical nomination of a clerical successor as school manager, *Keenan* 423-425——Further statement that in certain rules of the board the term "appointment by the local patrons" is hardly correct, and that the word "nomination" should be substituted for "appointment," *ib.* 483-486. 501-503——Provisional appointment of a manager by the board in cases where there is a delay before the local authority nominates, *ib.* 498.

Practice of the board to accept, without inquiry, nominated clergymen as managers unless some objection be raised, *Right Hon. M. Longfield* 523-525.

Explanation that, though concurring, as a rule, with the ecclesiastical nomination of any manager, the Commissioners do not relinquish their right of determining whether he is a fit person, *Henry* 725-743.

Absolute right reserved to the board by their rules to determine whether a patron or his appointee is a fit person to exercise the trust of manager of a National School, *Viscount Monck* 769, 770——Conclusion that the recognition of a clergyman by his superiors

Report, 1873—continued.

MANAGERS (NATIONAL SCHOOLS)—continued.

1. *As to the Appointment or Recognition of Managers*—continued.
superiors as in charge of the parish is *primâ facie* evidence of his fitness for the office of manager of the local National Schools, *Viscount Monck* 772-774.

Absence of any real power in the board to appoint a successor to a manager, where the school is under a Committee, *Mr. Justice Lawson* 965-967——Recognition rather than appointment of managers by the board, *Mr. Justice Fitzgerald* 1400.

Rules and regulations of the Commissioners relative to the management of National Schools, and the nomination and recognition of local managers, *App.* 168, 169.

2. *As to Dismissal or Removal*:
Conclusion as to dismissal being involved in the refusal of the Commissioners to hold any further correspondence with a manager, *Keenan* 38. 40. 44. 48. 71-73——Very rare instances, on the whole, of the exercise of the power of removal of managers, *ib.* 69, 70 ——Conclusion that whether a manager is "removed" from connection with a vested school, or whether the board "decline to hold correspondence" with the manager of a non-vested school, it is equally a case of dismissal, *ib.* 71-81.——Instances in the cases of the Rev. Mr. O'Keeffe and the Rev. Dr. Keenan of managers having continued to keep the schools open after the board had refused to hold correspondence with them, *ib.* 82-84.

Exceptional instances of dismissal of managers for neglect or want of attention to the management of the schools, *Keenan* 197-200——Occurrence of only two instances of removal of managers since 1865, *ib.* 504.

Equal treatment of the different kinds of schools by the board, as regards the removal of patrons, *Right Hon. M. Longfield* 517-519——Explanation that the board does not remove the managers, but removes itself from connection with the schools, *Viscount Monck* 789-791——Inability of witness to adduce any instances of removal of managers by the board in addition to those recorded in the precedents, *Kelly* 802-841. 846, 847.

Question considered whether the Roman Catholic bishops might not, as patrons, by bringing the schools to the National Board in the first instance, have appointed the managers and have had full power to remove them irrespectively of the board, *Mr. Justice Lawson* 1142-1151.

Right of the board to judge of the fitness of a person to be patron or manager of a school on first appointment, but not to remove such patron or manager after having recognised him, *O'Keeffe* 1546-1548.

3. *Duties of Managers*:
Summary of the duties discharged by the manager of a school in connection with the board, *Right Hon. M. Longfield* 535-537.

General instructions of the Commissioners to managers and correspondents, *App.* 190, 191.

4. *Statistics relative to Lay and Clerical Managers of different Denominations*:
Statistics submitted showing the total number of managers, clerical and lay, under each denomination, and the total number of schools under each denomination, distinguishing between clerical management and lay management, *Keenan* 93.

See also the Headings generally throughout the Index.

Market Hill School. See *Fisher, Rev. Mr.*

Martin, Rev. Mr. Comment upon the assumption by the Rev. Mr. Martin to be recognised as manager of Callan schools in right of his appointment as administrator of the parish, *Mr. Justice Maurice* 1303. 1329-1333.

Monahan, Chief Justice. Circumstance of Chief Justice Monahan having voted for the giving of notice, though he has concurred in the removal of Mr. O'Keeffe, *Mr. Justice Morris* 1301. 1326.

Monck, The Right Honourable Viscount. (Analysis of his Evidence.)—Limited experience of witness as a Commissioner of National Education in Ireland, 766-768——Absolute right reserved to the Board by their rules to determine whether a patron or has appointed is a fit person to exercise the trust of manager of a national school, 769, 770——There is no *ex-officio* right to appointment, 770. 773——Great importance attached to the appointment of the local clergy as managers of the schools as likely to secure a good attendance, 771, 772. 776-782——Conclusion that the recognition of a clergyman by his superiors as in charge of the parish is *primâ facie* evidence of his fitness for the office of manager of the local national schools, 772-774.

Loss of influence in his parish by Mr. O'Keeffe subsequently to his suspension, 772 ——Consideration of the extent to which suspension may be looked upon as *primâ facie* evidence

Report, 1873—*continued.*

Monck, The Right Honourable Viscount. (Analysis of his Evidence)—*continued.*
evidence of unfitness, 773. 775. 783-789——Practice of the board whenever a clergyman has been suspended to appoint his successor as school manager, 789. 792——Explanation that the board does not remove the managers, but removes itself from connection with the schools, 789-791.

Morell, The Rev. Charles L. (Analysis of his Evidence.)—Has been a member of the Board of Education since May 1868; in the following June became Moderator of the General Assembly, 1187-1189——Submits ground for the conclusion that Mr. O'Keeffe should not have been removed as manager of Callan Schools without being afforded an opportunity for explanation as to his alleged suspension, 1190 *et seq.*——Considers that Mr. O'Keeffe's case differed from all the so-called precedents, 1192. 1210-1219. 1237-1243.

Opinion that, as a general rule, it is not desirable that a suspended clergyman should be manager of a school; but witness adduces several cases as exceptions to this rule, 1194-1196. 1255. 1256——Inexpediency of the Board acting at once upon any ecclesiastical suspension, the validity of which is disputed by the suspended person, 1197, 1198. 1244——Dissent from the evidence of Dr. Henry as to the views of the General Assembly, and the Presbyterian Church generally, upon the question of removal of suspended clergymen from the management of schools, 1199-1206. 1220-1226. 1245-1254——Condemnation of the action of the board in Mr. O'Keeffe's case by the Presbytery of Belfast, 1204-1206.

Concurrence in the evidence of Judge Lawson, in disapproval of the removal of Mr. O'Keeffe, 1207. 1209——Instance of concession by the board in order to meet the views of the Roman Catholic Church, 1208——Doubt as to Cardinal Cullen's order of suspension having been discussed at the board previously to the communication from the Bishop of Ossory, 1210-1218——Information before the board at the time of the removal of Mr. O'Keeffe through Judge Morris, as to the pleadings in the case between Mr. O'Keeffe and Cardinal Cullen, 1219——Respects in which the case of Mr. Wilson differed from that of Mr. O'Keeffe, 1227-1238——Difference also between the latter case and that of Dr. Keenan, 1239-1243.

High legal position of Mr. Gibson, adviser of the General Assembly, one of the majority for the removal of Mr. O'Keeffe, 1247-1250——Circumstance of Mr. Hall, witness's predecessor at the board, having concurred in the removal of suspended clergymen as managers, 1251-1254——Opinion that the whole circumstances of each case of suspension should be fully considered by the board, 1255.

Belief that there are no parochial schools under the board, 1257, 1258——Admission that witness is not aware of any instance of suspension, certified to the board, which has not been followed by dismissal, 1259-1262——Natural claim of Presbyterian ministers to succeed their predecessors in charge of schools, but not as a matter of right, 1263-1267.

Morris, The Right Hon. Mr. Justice. (Analysis of his Evidence.)—Experience of witness as a member of the National Board since 1868; also, as a member of the Commission which inquired into the primary education of Ireland, 1289-1291——Conclusion that *ex officio* managers were never recognised by the board, 1292-1295. 1329——Absence of any rule of the Board as to suspended priests and their removal as managers, 1296——Continuance of the Rev. Peter Daly as manager of several schools until his death, although his suspension was perfectly well-known to the board, 1297-1299.

Opinion that the suspension of a priest would, in an immense majority of cases, call for removal from the office of school manager, but that each case should be inquired into and dealt with on its own merits, 1300. 1302——Argument in support of the amendment moved by witness at the board on the 23rd April 1872, that notice should be given to Mr. O'Keeffe, with an opportunity of explanation, before the certificate of his suspension was acted upon, 1300-1302. 1324-1326——Defeat of the foregoing motion by a majority of one, 1301——Circumstance of Chief Justice Monahan having voted for the giving of notice, though he has concurred in the removal of Mr. O'Keeffe, 1301. 1326.

View of witness that if the schools under Mr. O'Keeffe were eminently successful, and if he were a fit and proper manager, the certificate of suspension should not be acted upon; explanation hereon as to witness not having moved for an inquiry by the board into the general merits of the management, 1302, 1353-1361——Comment upon the assumption by the Rev. Mr. Martin to be recognised as manager of Callan Schools in right of his appointment as administrator of the parish, 1303. 1329-1333——Division at the board on the 9th April upon a motion by witness that Mr. Martin's application should be notified to Mr. O'Keeffe; majority of one, by which the foregoing motion was lost, 1303.

Examination relative to the four precedents, so called, for the removal of clerical managers on the receipt of the certificate of ecclesiastical suspension: marked distinction between each of these cases and that of Mr. O'Keeffe, 1304-1324. 1341-1346——Refusal of witness at the board to look into any precedents if they went to establish the principle

Report, 1873—*continued.*

Morris, The Right Honourable Mr. Justice. (Analysis of his Evidence)—*continued.*
principle that a manager was to be dismissed unheard, 1304, 1312-1314.——Bad prospect of harmony by appointing a new manager whilst there is a manager *de facto* in possession, 1316.——Comment upon the inquiry addressed by the inspector to the board in Mr. Sheridan's case, whether a suspended clergyman should continue as manager of schools, 1322-1324. 1343-1346.

Statement as to witness having produced at the board the pleadings in the suit of Mr. O'Keeffe against Cardinal Cullen, and having, as a judge, declined to prejudge the case, 1324-1326.——Reference to a letter from Mr. O'Keeffe in January 1871, informing the board of his fifth suspension, 1325, 1326.——Amendment intended to be moved at the board by Mr. Waldron, to the effect, that Mr. O'Keeffe not having infringed the rules of the board, should not be arbitrarily removed, 1326, 1327.——Broad distinction between clerical appointments under the Poor Law Board and under the Education Board as regards the question of ecclesiastical suspension, 1328.——Clear distinction also between cases under a Board of Bequests and the case of Mr. O'Keeffe, *ex-officio* appointment not applying in the latter case, *ib.*

Absence of any powers in the board to appoint the manager of a school not vested in the Board, 1334.——Comment upon the inability of Mr. Marton to deprive Mr. O'Keeffe of the possession of the schools, 1335.——Explanation as to the large proportion of non-vested schools, of which Roman Catholic clergymen or parish priests are patrons, 1336, 1337. 1340.——Reception of any school into connection with the National Board, whether it be brought by a lay or clerical patron, so long as the rules are observed, 1338 ———Belief that there is no rule that would displace a patron of a non-vested school, if there were no vacancy by death or by resignation, 1339.——Special reference to Rule No. 7, as showing that the dismissal of Mr. O'Keeffe was not warranted, and was at variance with the rules, 1339.

Question considered as to the extent of the inquiry that might be necessary if Mr. O'Keeffe had been allowed opportunity for explanation, 1347-1352. 1364-1373.——Contention of the majority of the board that their duty was merely ministerial in view of the certificate of Mr. O'Keeffe's suspension, whilst the minority were anxious that the case should be treated on the general merits, 1353-1363.

Further statement that though suspension might almost invariably unfit a clerical manager in an educational point of view, an inquiry is necessary in order to prove that such effect is produced, 1364-1373.——Witness repeats that the "precedents" as to suspension and dismissal were not applicable to the case of Mr. Keogh, and contends also that no precedents can justify dismissal without notice and opportunity for explanation, 1374-1384 ——Distinction in the present case inasmuch as a civil suit was pending, 1383, 1384.

Comment upon the sending of an inspector to report on the schools in consequence of a renewed application by Mr. O'Keeffe to be recognised as a manager; refusal of recognition by the majority of the board, no matter how efficient the schools might be, 1385-1392.——Case of the Rev. Peter Daly further adverted to; removal of his suspension before he died, 1393-1396.

Murray, Rev. Mr. Occurrence, within witness's knowledge, of only one case of disputed clerical succession in addition to those included in the Parliamentary Papers: this was the case of Mr. Murray in 1845-1848; *Keenan* 22, 23.——Details relative to the foregoing case, and the correspondence in the matter; unanimous decision of the Commissioners that Mr. Murray, having ceased to be administrator in the parish of Kilfinan (Mayo), in which the Kinteen, Creeves, and other national schools were situated, was not entitled to be restored to the management of the schools, and was properly succeeded in the management by his successor in the administration of the parish, *ib.* 23-33. 36.

Recognition in the first instance of Mr. John Lynch as manager *pro tempore*, on the departure of Mr. Murray from the county in 1845; *Keenan* 24-28. 208-211.——Decision of the Commissioner that the Rev. Mr. Jordan, as Mr. Murray's successor in the parish, succeeded him in the management, *ib.* 24-27.——Communications subsequently from Mr. Murray, claiming to be restored to the management, such claim not having been admitted, *ib.* 30. 36.——Explanation as to Mr. Murray's case not having been submitted to the board when the case of the Rev. Mr. O'Keeffe was under consideration, *ib.* 34.

N.

Newell, William Homan, LL.D. (Analysis of his Evidence.)—Is one of the Joint Secretaries to the Board of National Education, Ireland, 904.——Produces certain papers and correspondence relative to the case of Mr. O'Keeffe, and submits explanations in connection therewith, 905-918.—In a letter dated 19th January 1871, Mr. O'Keeffe stated that he had been suspended for the fifth time, 914.——In a subsequent letter of 26th January 1871, Mr. O'Keeffe again refers to the fact of his having been suspended, 917.

[Second Examination.]—Non-recognition of *ex-officio* managers by the board, 1268. 1287, 1288.——Reference to a letter from the board in June 1840, as showing that

ex-officio

Report, 1873—continued.

Newell, William Homan, LL.D. (Analysis of his Evidence)—*continued.*

ex-officio managers were not recognized, 1269-1272——Statement on the part of the board in February 1840, that it had nothing to do with the selection of patrons, these being locally chosen by those persons who have established the schools, 1273-1275.

Circumstance of the Rev. Peter Daly, of Galway, having continued school manager during and after his suspension until his death, no intimation of the suspension having been sent to the Board, 1278——Explanation as regards the Ratoath case, that there was no ecclesiastical certificate of suspension, and that Mr. Sheridan continued manager until the suspension was reported by the inspector, after a long interval, 1279-1286——Clerical oversight, owing to which Mr. O'Farrell continued manager of a school in Lisduff for a considerable period after his suspension, 1280.

Newtown School. See *Coolagh and Newtown Schools.*

Non-vested Schools. Rules of the Board of Education (*App.* 168, 169), and explanations thereon relative to the succession or nomination of managers in the case of non-vested schools, *Keenan* 7-9. 14-18——Division of non-vested schools into two classes, viz., those under the control of Committees and those under individual patrons, *ib.* 14——Uniform course pursued in appointing the clerical successor of a suspended clergyman as manager in all cases of non-vested schools without Committees, *ib.* 378, 379.

Absence of any powers in the Board to appoint the manager of a school not vested in the board, *Mr. Justice Morris* 1334.

See also *Clergy. Managers. Suspension and Dismissal.*

Notice of Dismissal or Removal. Examination to the effect that a certain discussion at the board was upon the question of giving Mr. O'Keeffe notice of the proceedings, and not upon the question of giving him opportunity for explanation, *Mr. Justice Lawson* 1000-1013——Failure of duty on the part of the Commissioners if, when there has been a dispute as to the validity of ecclesiastical suspension, no notice has been given before removal by the board, *ib.* 1014-1018.

Argument in support of the amendment moved by witness on the 23rd April 1872, that notice should be given to Mr. O'Keeffe, with an opportunity of explanation, before the certificate of his suspension was acted upon, *Mr. Justice Morris* 1300-1302. 1324-1326——Defeat of the foregoing motion by a majority of one, *ib.* 1300-1302. 1324-1326——Division at the board on the 9th April, upon a motion by witness that Mr. Martin's application should be notified to Mr. O'Keeffe; majority of one by which the foregoing motion was lost, *ib.* 1303——Question considered as to the extent of the inquiry that might be necessary if Mr. O'Keeffe had been allowed opportunity for explanation, *ib.* 1347-1352. 1364-1373.

It was proposed at the board that notice of the proceedings should be sent to Mr. O'Keeffe, but this was overruled, and the matter was, on the motion of witness, postponed for a fortnight, *Mr. Justice Fitzgerald* 1394——Discussion at the board on the 23rd April upon the question of an investigation, and not merely upon that of giving notice to Mr. O'Keeffe, without opportunity for explanation, *ib.* 1400. 1514-1517——Defence of the action of the majority of the board adverse to giving any notice to Mr. O'Keeffe before dismissal, *ib.* 1406.

O.

O'Farrell, Rev. Mr. Special reference made by the board to Bishop Kilduff, in the case of Mr. O'Farrell, in order to elicit the fact of suspension before final action, *Keenan,* 141. 170-171——Recognition of the Rev. Mr. O'Farrell as manager during several years whilst he performed no ecclesiastical duties; the board were not aware of the latter circumstance, *ib.* 214-216.

Sundry letters produced, and explanations thereon, in further elucidation of the circumstances under which the Rev. Mr. O'Farrell was continued in the management of Lisduff School, and a considerable delay occurred before the appointment of the Rev. Mr. Sheridan thereto, who had succeeded Mr. O'Farrell in Annaduff parish, *Keenan* 282-287.

Peculiar character of Lisduff School, it being one of a very limited class of schools which are secured by bond, *Keenan* 282-285——There was never any imputation that Mr. O'Farrell was insane, *ib.* 288——Doubt as to complaint having been addressed to the board in Mr. O'Farrell's case that for several years he had not performed ecclesiastical duties, through being under suspension, *ib.* 426-433.

Explanation as to the Rev. Mr. O'Farrell having continued manager of Lisduff School, after his ecclesiastical suspension, and his removal from Annaduff School, *Kelly* 867, 868——Clerical oversight, owing to which Mr. O'Farrell continued manager of a school in Lisduff for a considerable period after his suspension, *Newell* 1280.

Notoriety

O'Farrell, Rev. Mr.—continued.

Notoriety of Mr. O'Farrell's suspension, whereas he continued manager of Lisduff School for a long period, *Mr. Justice Morris* 1321.

O'Keeffe, The Rev. Robert. (Analysis of his Evidence.)—In February 1863 witness was appointed parish priest of Callan, and as such took possession of the four National Schools which belonged to the parish, 1519–1522——Two of the schools were non-vested, and two were under a committee, or were so reported, 1521. 1575——Recognition of witness by the Board of Education as manager of the Coolagh and Newtown Schools, whilst the board required first a recommendation by the Committee in the case of the Callan Male and Female Schools, 1523——Form of recommendation drawn up (and signed) by witness, and signed by each member of the school committee whom he saw on the subject; entire inaccuracy of a statement by Mr. Patrick Cody that these signatures were forgeries, 1524–1530.

Establishment of a work-school for females by witness soon after his appointment as parish priest; this school was recognised from the first by the National Board, witness being the manager, 1531, 1532. 1541——Conversion of the foregoing school into an infant school, upon the death of the head teacher, 1533–1541——Intimation received by the witness from the board, on the 25th April 1872, that he was no longer recognised as manager of the schools under the Board, as having been suspended from the exercise of all clerical functions in the parish, 1534–1537——Denial by witness that he has ever been suspended; he is parish priest at the present time, 1538——Denial that the Commissioners were justified in removing witness if he had been validly suspended, 1539–1541.

Argument that the Commissioners had no right or power to remove witness from his position as patron of the infant school, founded by himself, 1540, 1541——Right of the Committee of the Callan Male and Female Schools to continue witness as manager, or to remove him, there being no such right in the Education Board, 1542——Succession of witness to the patronship of the Coolagh and Newtown Schools, the board having no right to deprive him of this position, 1543.

Error of the board in concluding that the five schools in question were equally in its possession as though they were vested schools, 1543——Material difference between witness's case and the precedents, so called, inasmuch as his suspension was completely null and void, and was never admitted by him, 1544——Action of the board in opposition to its own rules in all the cases quoted as precedents, 1545——Right of the board to judge of the fitness of a person to be patron or manager of a school, on first appointment, but not to remove such patron or manager after having recognised him, 1546–1548.

Operation of four out of five of the Callan, &c. Schools at the present time under the continued management of witness, 1549, 1550——Statement to the effect that the Callan Male School, re-organised by witness, was struck off the rolls of the board because French was taught too much and the education was too high, 1551–1555——Examination on the foregoing statement showing that there were objections that the board rules were violated, on the score of attendance, accounts, &c., 1556–1570——Charge by the inspector against the female teacher in this school of having falsified the accounts as to attendance, action brought against him in consequence, 1571–1573.

Right of witness as parish priest to the possession of the Callan Schools and of the Coolagh and Newtown Schools; doubt as to the former schools being really under a Committee, as concluded by the board, 1574–1579.

Statement as to witness having dismissed from one of the schools a teacher named Mary Ann Phelan for disowning his authority as parish priest, 1580–1590——Explanation of the circumstances under which witness directed one of the teachers in the Coolagh National School to strike out witness's signature to a certain return and to substitute the name of Mr. Martin, 1591–1605——Information on the subject of an application by witness to the Commissioners for payment of arrears of salary due to Mr. Woods, a teacher in the Callan Male School; positive denial of the imputation that witness wanted the money for himself, 1606–1610.

Examination in further support of the contention of witness that he has still a right to the possession of the four national schools in question, he being still parish priest of Callan, and not having transferred possession to any one else, 1611–1626——Establishment and ownership by witness of the infant school, which he can hand over to whom he likes, 1611——Succession of a new parish priest to the schools in the event of witness's death; necessity otherwise of his transferring possession during his lifetime, 1613–1624.

Illegality of the removal of witness from the office of chaplain of the Callan Union Workhouse, 1627——Invalidity of any suspension of witness by Cardinal Cullen, as having no jurisdiction over him, 1627——Denial that any sentence of suspension was conveyed to witness either by Cardinal Cullen or the Bishop of Ossory; reference herein to a certain registered letter addressed to witness which he declined to receive, 1627–1630.

Report, 1873—*continued*.

O'Keeffe, Rev. R. (Suspension and Dismissal). See the Headings generally throughout the Index.

P.

Parents. Weight attached to the opinion of the parents upon the question of a suspended clergyman being a proper person for school manager, more especially as regards religious instruction, *Morell* 1194–1196.

Parochial Schools. Dissent from the view that there are any parochial schools connected with the Education Board as distinct from national schools, *Mr. Justice Lawson* 927. 1182, 1183—— Belief that there are no parochial schools under the Board, *Morell* 1257, 1258.

Conclusion as to the schools of which Mr. O'Keeffe was manager being parochial, and as to his managership having been properly discontinued when he was no longer parish priest; dissent from Mr. Justice Lawson's views on the question of parochial school, *Mr. Justice Fitzgerald,* 1400. 1402–1404. 1432–1438.

Patrons (National Schools.) Reference to the rules of the National Board as defining the local patrons and their right of nomination of local managers, *Keenan* 9—— Explanation that the board has no jurisdiction over the patronage, save by declining to correspond with an improper patron or manager, *Right Hon. M. Longfield,* 512. 522. 526 —— Statement on the part of the board in February 1840, that it had nothing to do with the selection of patrons, these being locally chosen by those persons who have established the schools, *Newell* 1273–1275.

Rules and regulations of the Commissioners as to the recognition of patrons, and the nomination by them of local managers, *App.* 168.

See also *Clergy.   Managers.   Suspension and Dismissal.*

Phelan, Mary Ann. Statement as to witness having dismissed from one of the schools a teacher named Mary Ann Phelan, for disowning his authority as parish priest, *O'Keeffe* 1580–1590.

Pigott, The Right Hon. Baron. Explanation in connection with a document sent officially to the board by Chief Baron Pigott, as well as with the origin of the memorial signed by the thirteen Commissioners, in Mr. O'Keeffe's case, *Keenan* 105–120.

Poor Law Board. Denial that the action of the Poor Law Commissioners in Mr. O'Keeffe's case had any influence upon the National Board, *Keenan* 461–464—— Broad distinction between clerical appointments under the Poor Law Board and under the Education Board, as regards the question of ecclesiastical suspension, *Mr. Justice Morris* 1328.

See also *Callan Union Workhouse.*

Possession of Schools. Resistance offered to the new manager of Callan Schools on the part of Mr. O'Keeffe down to the present time, *Keenan* 140—— Continued possession of the schools by Mr. O'Keeffe after his ecclesiastical suspension, *Mr. Justice Lawson* 947. 968—— Bad prospect of harmony by appointing a new manager whilst there is a manager *de facto* in possession, *Mr. Justice Morris* 1316 —— Comment upon the inability of Mr. Martin to deprive Mr. O'Keeffe of the possession of the schools, *ib.* 1335.

In February 1863 witness was appointed parish priest of Callan, and as such took possession of the four national schools which belonged to the parish, *O'Keeffe* 1519–1528 —— Error of the Education Board in concluding that the schools in question were equally in its possession, as though they were vested schools, *ib.* 1543—— Right of witness as parish priest to the possession of the Callan schools, and of the Coolagh and Newtown schools; doubt as to the former schools being really under a committee, as concluded by the board, *ib.* 1574–1579.

Examination in further support of the contention of witness that he has still a right to the possession of the four national schools in question, he being still parish priest of Callan, and not having transferred possession to anyone else, *O'Keeffe* 1611–1626—— Succession of a new parish priest to the schools in the event of witness's death; necessity otherwise of his transferring possession during his lifetime, *ib.* 1613–1624.

PRECEDENTS (SUSPENSION AND DISMISSAL OF MANAGERS):

Reference had by the Commissioners not only to their code of rules, but to the precedents in the office in determining any cases of disputed succession of managers, *Keenan* 19–21. 34. 35—— Proposal by witness to explain in detail to the Committee the different features of the several precedents, and to show how far they run parallel with the case of Mr. O'Keeffe; evidence in detail hereon, *ib.* 101–104. 121 *et seq.*

Explanation of the practice in each of the cases of precedent, as well as in Mr. O'Keeffe's case, as to the appointment of the successor of the suspended clergyman to the management of the schools in the parish, *Keenan* 134–136.

Statement

Report, 1873—continued.

PRECEDENTS (SUSPENSION AND DISMISSAL OF MANAGERS)—continued.
Statement showing that in addition to the four precedents (as in the Parliamentary Paper) of the dismissal of clerical managers, a further case has now been discovered, which occurred in 1842; *Keenan* 253——Particulars of this case, which was that of the Rev. Mr. Fisher, of Market Hill School, *ib* 258-260. 481——Comparison between each case of removal, in consequence of suspension, as regards the question of promptitude of action on the part of the board, when once the suspension was noticed, *ib.* 339-346. 360-375——Information as to the several cases of precedent to which there was a committee of the schools, *ib.* 449-460.

Decided opinion that the course pursued in Mr. O'Keeffe's case was conformable to precedent, *Right Hon. Sir A. Macdonnell* 579——Clear conviction of witness, when first he concurred in the suspension of Mr. O'Keeffe, that the precedents in the office would fully confirm the course taken as regards the Callan schools, *Henry* 585. 721, 722——Presence of witness on only one occasion when the case of Mr. O'Keeffe was under discussion at the board; the question of precedents was not then introduced, *Kelly* 857-861. 890, 891.

Probability of the suspensions formerly having been such as to call for removal, without proving there was any absolute rule on the subject, *Mr. Justice Lawson* 936-938——Witness considers that Mr. O'Keeffe's case differed from all the so-called precedents, *Morell* 1192. 1210-1219. 1227-1243.

Examination relative to the four precedents, so-called, for the removal of clerical managers on the receipt of the certificate of ecclesiastical suspension; marked distinction between each of these cases and that of Mr. O'Keeffe, *Mr. Justice Morris* 1304-1324. 1341-1346——Refusal of witness at the Board to look into any precedents if they went to establish the principle that a manager was to be dismissed unheard, *ib.* 1304. 1312-1314.

Witness repeats that the "precedents" as to suspension and dismissal were not applicable to Mr. Keogh, and contends also that no precedents can justify dismissal without notice and opportunity for explanation, *Mr. Justice Morris* 1374-1384——Distinction in the present case, inasmuch as a civil suit was pending, *ib.* 1383, 1384.

The case of Mr. O'Keeffe struck witness as one of much importance, and inquiry was at once made at the board as to the precedents, *Mr. Justice Fitzgerald* 1309. 1421. 1422——Careful consideration of the precedents at the board meeting of 23rd April, witness contending that these clearly laid down the principles of removal of a manager on receipt of a certificate of his ecclesiastical suspension, *ib.* 1400. 1421-1426——Reference to the precedents as justifying action upon the judgment of the ecclesiastical Court, without inquiry into its foundation, *ib.* 1407-1412. 1415, 1416. 1421-1426——Action of the board in opposition to its own rules in all the cases quoted as precedents, *ib.* 1545.

Material difference between witness's case and the precedents, so-called, inasmuch as his suspension was completely null and void, and was never admitted by him, *O'Keeffe* 1544.

See also *Fisher, Rev. Mr.*   *Keenan, Rev. Dr.*   *Murray, Rev. Mr.*   *O'Farrell,*
    Rev. Mr.   *Rules.*   *Sheridan, Rev. Mr.*   *Wilson, Rev. J. Kirke.*

Presbyterian Clergy. Doubt as to the ecclesiastical superiors by whom Presbyterian clergy are suspended, *Keenan* 480-482——Statement to the effect that the Presbyterian Church would not in the first instance have joined or worked with the National Board if the latter had decided not to accept the certificate of the Synod of Ulster as stating the ground of deposition of a minister, *Henry* 587-590. 689-693——Concurrence of witness in all the decisions of the board in the case of Mr. O'Keeffe, *ib.* 700, 701.

Dissent from the evidence of Dr. Henry as to the views of the General Assembly and the Presbyterian Church generally upon the question of removal of suspended clergymen from the management of schools, *Morell* 1199-1206. 1220-1226. 1245-1251——Circumstance of Mr. Hall, witness's predecessor at the board, having concurred in the removal of suspended clergymen as managers, *ib.* 1251-1254——Natural claim of Presbyterian ministers to succeed their predecessors in charge of schools, but not as a matter of right, *ib.* 1263-1267.

See also *Belfast Presbytery.*   *Fisher, Rev. Mr.*   *Gibson, Mr.*   *Wilson, Rev. Mr.*

Public, The. Apparent increase of public confidence in the Education Board since the period of their action in the matter of the Callan schools, *Mr. Justice Fitzgerald* 1450-1452.

Q

Queen's Colleges. Witness submits a section from a chapter of the statutes of the Queen's Colleges as containing general principles applicable to the case of Mr. O'Keeffe, *Henry* 584.

Report, 1873—*continued.*

R.

Ratoath Schools. See *Sheridan, Rev. Mr.*

Roman Catholic Clergy. See also *Clergy. Cullen, Cardinal. Ecclesiastical Dictation. Managers. Suspension and Dismissal.*

Rowan, Rev. Edward. Letter from the Rev. Edward Rowan, Mr. O'Keeffe's predecessor in the parish of Callan, dated 16th February 1863, submitting his resignation as manager of the Callan, Newtown, and Coolagh Schools, *Keenan* 85, 86.

Rules (Management of Schools). Publication of the rules as to management, &c., for the first time in 1855, though they had previously existed in the form of minutes of the board, *Keenan* 10–13——Revision of the rules as to management in 1853, in consequence of previous disputes at the board, *Right Hon. M. Longfield* 513, 514.

Absence of any rule of the board providing that a clerical manager of a school should, upon suspension, be removed from the management, *Mr. Justice Lawson* 924. 928. 933 ——Argument that so long as the Callan Schools were managed in accordance with the rules of the board, the ecclesiastical suspension of Mr. O'Keeffe, for reasons not touching the question of his educational usefulness, did not justify the summary action of the board in the matter, *ib.* 1092–1108. 1130.

Non-existence of any rule of the board as to suspended priests and their removal as managers, *Mr. Justice Morris* 1296——Belief that there is no rule that would displace a patron of a non-vested school, if there were no vacancy by death or by resignation, *ib.* 1339——Special reference to Rule No. 7, as showing that the dismissal of Mr. O'Keeffe was not warranted, and was at variance with the rules, *ib.*

Copy of the rules and regulations of the Commissioners, *App.* 184–190.

See also *Breach of Rules. Managers. Precedents. Suspension and Dismissal.*

S.

Salaries of Teachers. Withdrawal of the schoolmaster's salary by the board in the event of a suspended priest being maintained as patron, *Right Hon. M. Longfield* 515, 516—— Practical power of removal of managers of National Schools by means of stopping the supplies, *Henry* 635.

Statement to the effect that the board has no legal right to remove the manager of a non-vested school, though they have full power in the matter by stopping the supplies to the school, *Mr. Justice Lawson* 984–995.

Explanation as to a statement in a certain letter from witness that a proposal by him for the payment of the teachers' salaries, while the dispute about Mr. O'Keeffe was pending, was "defeated by an amendment, declaring that such payment would be a misapplication of the public funds"; reason for not setting forth this amendment in full in the letter, *Mr. Justice Lawson* 1077–1091. 1184–1186.—See also *Woods, Mr.*

Shannon, Rev. T. See *Gort Schools.*

SHERIDAN REV. MR. (RATOATH AND ASHBOURNE SCHOOLS):

Desire of some members of the committee of the Ratoath Schools to continue Mr. Sheridan as manager after his suspension; concurrence eventually as to the appointment of the Rev. Mr. Fulham, the new administrator of the parish, *Keenan* 134. 137—— Statement on the subject of a reference having been made to the committee of the Ratoath schools, after the suspension of Mr. Sheridan, and before the appointment of his successor; delay after the suspension before the board took action, *ib.* 160–175 —— Explanation that the bishop, in the case of the Rev. J. Sheridan, requested that the latter might be recognised as manager of the Annaduff School, but did not actually nominate him for the post, *ib.* 221–226.

Papers and correspondence in 1863–65 relative to the case of the Rev. Mr. Sheridan, manager of the Ratoath and Ashbourne Schools; full explanation therein of the circumstances under which much delay occurred before the appointment, as manager, of the Rev. Mr. Fulham, the successor of Mr. Sheridan in administration of the parishes in question, *Keenan* 288–298. 365–371 —— Oversight or omission on the part of the office, owing to which Mr. Sheridan, though suspended, remained in the management of the schools for a period of about two years, *ib.* 288. 294, 295.

Letter received by the secretaries from the Rev. Mr. Fulham in January 1863, stating that he was administrator of Ratoath parish, in lieu of the Rev. Mr. Sheridan, who had been suspended, *Kelly* 799–802——Reply to the foregoing by the secretaries on the 19th February referring Mr. Fulham to the committee of the Ratoath Schools, as having the appointment of manager, the schools being non-vested, *ib.* 800–811——Explanation as

Report, 1873—continued.

SHERIDAN, REV. MR. (RATOATH AND ASHBOURNE SCHOOLS)—continued.
to the omission on the part of the secretaries in not at once informing the board that Mr. Sheridan was suspended, the fact not having been notified till the 27th January 1865; *Kelly* 801. 812-819. 848-851.

Statement on the subject of the inspector's not having informed the board as to the suspension of Mr. Sheridan, *Kelly* 820-828——Long delay on the part of Mr. Fulham before renewing his application to the board relative to the managership of the schools in his parish, *ib.* 848-851——Order, signed by the Resident Commissioner, and dated 18th February 1865, recognising Mr. Fulham as manager of the Ratoath Schools, *ib.* 865, 866.

Admission of suspension in the case of Mr. Sheridan, but not directly by himself; witness explains that he has no recollection of this case, or of being present at any decision of the Board relative thereto, *Mr. Justice Lawson* 931-933——Circumstance of Mr. Sheridan not having been removed as manager until long after his suspension was known to the office; inference that there was no absolute rule on the subject, *ib.* 933-937.

Examination upon the circumstance of witness not having stipulated for notice in the case of Mr. Sheridan before action was taken upon his suspension; distinction between this case and that of Mr. O'Keeffe, *Mr. Justice Lawson* 1019-1036. 1040-1042. 1100, 1101. 1104, 1105, 1129, 1130. 1152-1154——Witness repeats that he has no recollection of the case, or of having taken any part in the discussions of the board on the subject, *ib.* 1026. 1036. 1105. 1129. 1152-1154——Great weight attached by the board to the facts laid before it in this case by the resident Commissioner *ib.* 1112-1126. 1169-1171.

Explanation as regards the Ratoath case; that there was no ecclesiastical certificate of suspension, and that Mr. Sheridan continued as manager until the suspension was reported by the inspector, after a long interval, *Newell* 1279-1286.

Comment upon the inquiry addressed by the inspector to the board in Mr. Sheridan's case, whether a suspended clergyman should continue as manager of schools, *Mr. Justice Morris* 1322-1324. 1343-1346.

Letter from Sir Alexander Macdonnell to the Chairman of the Committee, dated 13th June 1873, explaining that he gave no information whatever to the board, in Mr. Sheridan's case, beyond that contained in the papers before the board, *App.* 194.

Strabane National School. Recognition of the Bishop of Derry as manager of a parochial school in Strabane, after he had left the parish where he was rector; reason for the non-appointment at first of his successor in the parish, *Keenan* 217-220.

Further reference to the case of Dr. Alexander, Bishop of Derry, and the Strabane National School was duly recognised in the management of the school, *Keenan* 412-415.

SUSPENSION AND DISMISSAL (CLERICAL MANAGERS):
    1. *As to the Case of Mr. O'Keeffe.*
    2. *As to Suspensions generally.*
    3. *Suggested Inquiry in each Case of Suspension, before Dismissal by the Board.*

    1. *As to the Case of Mr. O'Keeffe:*

Letter from Bishop Moran, dated 22nd March 1872, stating that Mr. O'Keeffe "had been suspended from the exercise of all spiritual authority in the Catholic Church, and from the office which he held of parish priest of Callan," *Keenan* 124——Opinion of the majority of the board that there was a vacancy in the management of Callan Schools through the suspension of Mr. O'Keeffe, just as though he had died, *ib.* 243-247——Explanation that the dismissal of Mr. O'Keeffe from the Callan Schools was wholly and solely because he had been suspended ecclesiastically, *ib.* 325-331——Contention of Mr. O'Keeffe that he is still parish priest of Callan, *ib.* 304, 395——Admission that the question of the validity of Mr. O'Keeffe's suspension was introduced at the Board, but this was not entertained by the majority, *ib.* 465-473.

Justification of the dismissal of Mr. O'Keeffe, without first going to him for an explanation as to his suspension, *Right Hon. M. Longfield* 553, 554.

Witness concurs generally in the evidence of Mr. Keenan and Judge Longfield, *Right Hon. Sir A. Macdonnell* 572-575.

Witness refers to a certain letter as showing the grounds upon which he concluded that the Commissioners were bound to recognise the ecclesiastical suspension of Mr. O'Keeffe, and to acknowledge Mr. Martin as his successor in the management of the Callan Schools, *Henry* 584, 595——Formal notification of the ecclesiastical suspension of Mr. O'Keeffe to the board, *ib.* 586——Loss of influence in his parish by Mr. O'Keeffe subsequently to his suspension, *Viscount Monck* 772.

Belief that there was a letter from Mr. O'Keeffe in which he stated that he had been suspended

Report, 1873—*continued.*

SUSPENSION AND DISMISSAL (CLERICAL MANAGERS)—continued.

1. *As to the Case of Mr. O'Keeffe*—continued.

suspended for the fifth time, *Kelly* 876-879——First communications of Mr. O'Keeffe's suspension by letter from Mr. Harkin, the inspector, on the 29th November 1871; other letters in this case which were before the board in April 1872, *ib.* 885-889.

In a letter dated 18th January 1871, Mr. O'Keeffe stated that he had been suspended for the fifth time, *Newell* 914——In a subsequent letter of 26th January 1871 Mr. O'Keeffe again refers to the fact of his having been suspended, *ib.* 917.

Intelligence before the board as to Mr. O'Keeffe's suspension for some months before they took any action in the matter, *Mr. Justice Lawson* 938.——Explanation in detail of witness's views as to the several conditions to be complied with before an alleged suspension should be followed by dismissal from managership; conclusion that these conditions were wanting in the case of Mr. O'Keeffe, *ib.* 939 *et seq*.——Inadequacy of the offence, for which suspension took place, to justify Mr. O'Keeffe's removal from the schools, *ib.* 945.

Grounds for the conclusion that Mr. O'Keeffe should not have been removed as manager of Callan Schools without being afforded an opportunity for explanation as to his alleged suspension, *Morell* 1190 *et seq*.——Concurrence in the evidence of Judge Lawson in disapproval of the removal of Mr. O'Keeffe, *ib.* 1207. 1209.

Reference to a letter from Mr. O'Keeffe in January 1871, informing the board of his fifth suspension, *Mr. Justice Morris* 1325, 1326——View of witness that if the schools under Mr. O'Keeffe were eminently successful, and if he were a fit and proper manager, the certificate of suspension should not be acted upon; explanation hereon as to witness not having moved for an inquiry by the board into the general merits of the management *ib.* 1302. 1353-1361——Contention of the majority of the board that their duty was merely ministerial in view of the certificate of Mr. O'Keeffe's suspension, whilst the minority were anxious that the case should be treated on the general merits, *ib.* 1353-1363.

Grounds for the conclusion that the board were perfectly justified in not making any inquiry into the validity of the suspension, and in not giving Mr. O'Keeffe any facility or opportunity for explanation before removal, *Mr. Justice Fitzgerald* 1400 *et seq*.——Obstacles and objections to any inquiry by the board into the foundation or validity of the suspension, *ib.* 1412-1415. 1420——Care taken by witness at the board discussions not to express any opinion upon the merits of the suspension; his sympathy at the time was with Father O'Keeffe, *ib.* 1427-1431.

Decision of the board merely that Mr. O'Keeffe, as being under ecclesiastical suspension, should cease to be their correspondent; nothing was decided judicially against him, nor did he lose anything through the board, *Mr. Justice Fitzgerald* 1466-1477.

Intimation received by witness from the board, on the 25th April 1872, that he was no longer recognised as manager of the schools, under the board, as having been suspended from the exercise of all clerical functions in the parish, *O'Keeffe* 1534-1537——Denial by witness that he has ever been suspended; he is parish priest of Callan at the present time, *ib.* 1538——Argument that the Commissioners had no power to remove witness, as manager, even if he had been validly suspended, *ib.* 1539-1541——Denial that any sentence of suspension was conveyed to witness either by Cardinal Cullen or the Bishop of Ossory; reference hereon to a certain registered letter addressed to witness which he declined to receive, *ib.* 1627-1630.

2. *As to Suspensions generally:*

Information as to the way in which the suspension of the clerical manager was notified to the board in each of the four precedents and in the case of Mr. O'Keeffe, *Keenan* 122-124——Statement of the action of the board in each case, on receiving intimation of the suspension; invariable refusal to entertain any denial or legal appeal on the part of the person suspended, *ib.* 125-133——Twofold objections, on secular and on religious grounds, to the continuance of suspended clergymen as managers of schools, *ib.* 126——Absence of any reference to the suspended clergyman before action was taken by the board, *ib.* 127.

Statement that the board attach no consideration to the fact, in some cases, that the suspended clergyman was the founder of the school, he having been the founder as clergyman of the parish or minister of the congregation, *Keenan* 142——Weight attached to the ecclesiastical suspension of any clergyman as unfitting him for school management, whether parish administrator or not, *ib.* 302, 303. 325-338——Absence of any rule of the board embodying the proposition that no legal decision could reinstate suspended clergymen as parish priests contrary to ecclesiastical jurisdiction, *ib.* 304-306.

Statement that the board has never officially interpreted the "competent authority" required for the removal of suspension, as in the case of Mr. O'Keeffe, *Keenan* 307-311——Direct effect of suspension upon the question of educational fitness, witness maintaining that in no case is a suspended clergyman a suitable person for manager of schools,

SUSPENSION.

Report, 1873—*continued*.

Suspension and Dismissal (Clerical Managers)—continued.
   2. *As to Suspensions generally*—continued.

schools, *Keenan* 332-338——Practice of the board never to inquire into the cause of suspension, nor to apply for explanation to the person suspended, *ib.* 334. 358. 377-401.
   Non-recognition by the board of any suspended clergyman as manager, even though still supported by the committee of the school, *Keenan* 396-398——Ministerial function exercised by the board in accepting as conclusive the certificate of the ecclesiastical superior as to suspension, *ib.* 419-422. 491-497——Inability of witness to state whether in any of the precedents the question of the validity of the suspension was raised at the board, *ib.* 474-479.
   Uniform custom of the board not to recognise as a manager of a national school any clergyman whose suspension has been notified, *Right Hon. M. Longfield* 507-511. 521, 522. 551——Conclusion, as regards removal or invalidity of suspension, that this can be effected only by the ecclesiastical superior, *ib.* 527-531——Argument that a suspended clergyman or parish priest is not a proper person to be continued as manager, he having been, moreover, nominated in the first instance, on the strength of his being parish priest, *ib.* 538-552. 561-567.
   Acceptance by the board of the mere fact of suspension by the proper authority, *Right Hon. M. Longfield* 538. 541. 565-567——Discord to be produced by not recognising the right of the bishop to suspend the parish priest, *ib.* 541. 561-564——Approval of the recognition, as manager, of the successor to a suspended priest, although in exceptional instances discord might be produced, *ib.* 561-564——Instances of the question of legality of suspension having been before the board, without influencing its action, *ib.* 565.
   Strong objection on the ground of discipline and religious instruction, to the continuance of a suspended clergyman as manager of any school, *Henry* 591. 655-673. 725; Expediency of dismissal or removal of every clergyman as manager who is under ecclesiastical suspension, irrespectively of any legal decision, *ib.* 635-643——Belief that in no instance has a suspended clergyman been continued in the management of a school, whose suspension has been notified to the Commissioners, *ib.* 714. 721, 722——Summary of witness's grounds for strongly approving of the rule of the Commissioners in falling in with the ecclesiastical jurisdiction as regards the nomination and suspension of clerical managers, *ib.* 715-728.
   Consideration of the extent to which suspension may be looked upon as *prima facie* evidence of educational unfitness, *Viscount Monck* 773. 775. 783-789——Practice of the Board whenever a clergyman has been suspended, to appoint his successor as school manager, *ib.* 789. 791.
   Witness does not recollect any case of a clergyman under suspension having been continued as manager (save the case of Mr. O'Farrell), *Kelly* 869——Practice as regards reference to the ecclesiastical superior when a case of suspension is reported by an inspector, *ib.* 901-903.
   Statement that suspension forms a *prima facie* ground for inquiry, and in some cases, but not in all, should be conclusive as to removal from the management; circumstances under which removal should not be a consequence of suspension, *Mr. Justice Lawson* 934-936. 972-974——Admission by witness that he cannot quote any instance of the continued recognition of a clerical manager after his suspension was certified to the board, *ib.* 1106-1108.
   Opinion that as a general rule it is not desirable that a suspended clergyman should be manager of a school, but witness adduces several cases as exceptions to this rule, *Morell* 1194-1196. 1255, 1256——Witness is not aware of any instance of suspension, certified to the board, which has not been followed by dismissal, *ib.* 1259-1262.
   Statement that though suspension might almost invariably unfit a clerical manager in an educational point of view, an inquiry is necessary in order to prove that such effect is produced, *Mr. Justice Morris* 1302. 1347-1361. 1364-1373.
   Examination as to the course to be pursued by the board in the event of ecclesiastical suspension under different circumstances, and in the event of such suspension being set aside on appeal to the courts of law, *Mr. Justice Fitzgerald* 1475-1505.

   3. *Suggested Inquiry in each Case of Suspension, before Dismissal by the Board*:
   Opinion that in each case of suspension there should be an inquiry into all the circumstances, before dismissal is resorted to, *Mr. Justice Lawson* 928-930. 934, 935. 939——Witness repeats that whilst prepared to give all proper weight to decrees of suspension, he would not act upon mere suspension without further inquiry, *ib.* 1155-1160——Witness considers that the whole circumstances of each case of suspension should be fully considered by the board, *Morell* 1255.
   Opinion that the suspension of a priest would in an immense majority of cases call for removal from the office of school manager, but that each case should be inquired into

Report, 1873—*continued.*

SUSPENSION AND DISMISSAL (*CLERICAL MANAGERS*)—continued.

 3. *Suggested Inquiry in each Case of Suspension, before Dismissal of the Board*—cont^{d.} and dealt with on its own merits, *Mr. Justice Morris* 1300, 1302, 1347-1361, 1364-1373.

  See also Callan Male and Female Schools. Coolagh and Newtown Schools. Cullen, Cardinal. Daly, Rev. Peter. Ecclesiastical Dictation. Fisher, Rev. Mr. Keenan, Rev. Dr. Legal Proceedings. Murray, Rev. Mr. O'Farrell, Rev. Mr. Possession of Schools. Precedents. Rules. Sheridan, Rev. Mr. Wilson, Rev. J. Kirke.

T.

Teachers. Invariable inquiry by the board in the event of an inspector reporting that a schoolmaster was not fit for his post, *Kelly* 842-845.

 Rules and regulations of the Commissioners on the subject of teachers, their qualifications, duties, salaries, &c., App. 174-184.

  See also Phelan, Mary Ann. Salaries. Woods, Mr.

Templeton, Rev. Mr. See *Wilson, Rev. Mr.*

V.

Vested Schools. Division of vested schools into two classes, viz., those vested in the board in its corporate capacity and those vested in trustees, *Keenan* 14.

  See also Clergy. Managers. Suspension and Dismissal.

W.

Waldron, Mr. Amendment intended to be moved at the board by Mr. Waldron to the effect that Mr. O'Keeffe not having infringed the rules of the board, should not be arbitrarily removed, *Mr. Justice Morris* 1326, 1327.

Whately Archbishop. Concurrence, formerly, of Archbishop Whately and Archbishop Murray in the view that a deposed clergyman ought in no case to be continued as manager of a school, *Henry* 593-597.

Wilson, Rev. G. Kirke (Glenvale School). Decision of the board in Mr. Wilson's case, though they knew he contemplated an action at law in order to remove his suspension, *Keenan* 131, 133——Conclusion as to the appointment of Dr. Templeton, in lieu of Mr. Wilson, having been made by the board upon some document which has been mislaid or lost, *ib.* 151-159.

 Further information in connection with the case of Mr. Wilson; reference more especially to a letter from the Rev. Mr. Templeton, dated 25th May 1871, reporting the suspension of Mr. Wilson, *Keenan* 272-278, 452——Nomination of Mr. Templeton by the board as manager of Glenvale School, without any reference to the School Committee, *ib.* 275-277——Probable explanation of the statement by the board, in dismissing Mr. Wilson, that they would not recognise him as manager of "either Glenvale or any other National School," *ib.* 279-281——Circumstance of Mr. Wilson, though the founder of Glenvale School, having been removed in favour of his successor in the parish, *ib.* 388, 454-456.

 Information in connection with the deposition of Mr. Wilson in 1850, by the Presbytery of Magherafelt and the General Assembly; doubt as to the nature of the certificate of suspension sent to the National Board, *Henry* 598-604——Belief that in the foregoing case some certificate or document was laid before the Board, besides the letter from Mr. Wilson's successor; the former cannot, however, be found, *Keenan* 605, 606——Circumstance of the board having removed Mr. Wilson, as school manager, although he had written to say he was not deposed from the ministry, and intended to appeal to the civil tribunals against ecclesiastical jurisdiction, *Henry* 677-686——Action of the board in Mr. Wilson's case, solely with reference to his suspension by the Presbytery, *ib.* 708-713.

 Respects in which the case of Mr. Wilson differed from that of Mr. O'Keeffe, *Morell* 1227-1238——Reference to Mr. Wilson's case as very different from that of Mr. O'Keeffe, *Mr. Justice Morris* 1317-1320.

Woods, Mr. Examination upon a statement in witness's letter to the board, that it was involved in a litigation not very creditable to it with respect to the salary of
                             Mr.

Report, 1873—continued.

Woods, Mr.—continued.

Mr. Woods, one of the teachers of the Callan schools, *Mr. Justice Lawson* 1051°-1076. 1184.

Explanation relative to some litigation with the Board as to the payment of teachers' salaries in the Callan Schools; denial that there was anything discreditable on the part of the board in their proceedings in the case of Mr. Woods, *Mr. Justice Fitzgerald* 1446-1449.

Information on the subject of an application by witness to the Commissioners for payment of arrears of salary due to Mr. Woods, a teacher in the Callan male school; positive denial of the imputation that witness wanted the money for himself, *O'Keeffe* 1606-1610.

www.ingramcontent.com/pod-product-compliance
Lightning Source LLC
Chambersburg PA
CBHW021816230426
43669CB00008B/774